STREET CULTURE IN CHENGDU

Street Culture in Chengdu

PUBLIC SPACE, URBAN COMMONERS,
AND LOCAL POLITICS, 1870–1930

Di Wang

STANFORD UNIVERSITY PRESS

STANFORD, CALIFORNIA

2003

Stanford University Press
Stanford, California

© 2003 by the Board of Trustees of the
Leland Stanford Junior University. All rights reserved.

Printed in the United States of America
on acid-free, archival-quality paper.

Library of Congress Cataloging-in-Publication Data
Wang, Di.
  Street culture in Chengdu : public space, urban commoners, and local
politics, 1870-1930 / Di Wang.
      p. cm.
  Includes bibliographical references and index.
  ISBN 0-8047-4778-4 (alk. paper)
    1. Popular culture—China—Chengdu. 2. Urbanization—China—Chengdu.
3. Chengdu (China)—Civilization. I. Title.
HM621.W36 2003
306'.0951'38—dc21

                                                          2003001557

Original Printing 2003

Last figure below indicates year of this printing:
12 11 10 09 08 07 06 05 04 03

Typeset by Classic Typography in 10/12.5 Sabon

For my parents and wife

Contents

Illustrations

Acknowledgments

This book would not have been completed without the many teachers, colleagues, friends, and family members who have given me generous help. I would like to express my most sincere gratitude to my adviser and friend William Rowe, who has followed this study along every step of the way and has given generously of his knowledge, time, and energy, as well as his encouragement, to help with my graduate study, my research papers, my publications, my dissertation, and the manuscript of this book. I owe special thanks to my friend Kristin Stapleton for her thorough reading of an early version of the manuscript and offering her valuable comments as well as sharing some very useful materials, including a handwritten copy of *Sichuan tongsheng jingcha zhangcheng* and microfilm of *Guomin gongbao* and *Tongsu ribao*. I am also indebted to my colleague and friend Terry Anderson for reading some chapters repeatedly and being my most demanding critic; he has taught me a great deal.

Suggestions, comments, and help of other kinds came from many people at various stages of this study, especially Mary Rankin, Perry Link, Edward Rhoads, Judy Wyman, Dale Baum, Arnold Krammer, Larry Yarak, Yang Nianqun, Grant Alger, David Gutelius, Elaine Parsons, and three anonymous readers of Stanford University Press. I am grateful to my colleagues and friends Ernest Young and Stephen Averill, who have been always supportive since 1991, when I began my new academic career at the University of Michigan and Michigan State University. To the latter, I owe the most, for leading me to enter Western scholarship during my early time in the United States and for giving thoughtful suggestions for almost all of my papers related to this study during these years. In my graduate study at Johns Hopkins, I have worked with Ronald Walters, Thomas Berger, and Yunxiang Yan, all of whom have expanded my scholarly horizons. Many thanks go to Ann Kellett for her assistance in copyediting, Jean Johnson for providing the photographs of Chengdu taken by her father more than ninety years ago, and Harriet-Jane Hoogendyk for permitting me to use three pictures collected by her father, Dr. David Graham, in the 1920s. I would also like to express my gratitude to Senior Editor Muriel Bell of Stanford University Press for her help, encouragement, and direction through all processes of publication of this book, to Senior Production Editor Anna Eberhard

Friedlander for guiding me through the production process, and to Sally Serafim for her expert and meticulous copyediting of the final manuscript.

Various institutions have helped this study. I owe thanks to the Milton S. Eisenhower Library of the Johns Hopkins University, the East Asian Division of the Library of Congress, Harvard-Yenching Library of Harvard University, Hoover East Asian Collection of Stanford University, Sterling C. Evans Library of Texas A&M University, First Historical Archives (Beijing), Sichuan Provincial Archives, Sichuan Provincial Library, Chengdu Municipal Archives, and Sichuan University Library. I am very grateful for the opportunity to thank the institutions that have financially supported this study. My graduate study was fully funded by doctoral fellowships from the Department of History at the Johns Hopkins University. The Institute of Global Studies in Power, Culture, and History at the Johns Hopkins University financed my research in Chengdu. The Harvard-Yenching Library at Harvard University offered me a travel grant to use its collections. The Sun Yat-sen Culture and Education Foundation in Taiwan awarded me a fellowship when I was finishing my dissertation. Texas A&M University provided three grants, including a College Faculty Research Enhancement Award, an International Research Travel Assistance Grant, and a Faculty Mini-Grant, to help me complete this book. Earlier versions of some material presented here have been published in the journals *Modern China* and *Journal of Urban History*. I am grateful to the editors and publishers for permission to reuse that material here.

I would like to offer my deepest gratitude to my wife, Wei Li, who has always been by my side with emotional and material support, and to my son, Ye Wang, who has always understood when I could not pay much attention to him due to my research and writing. They have gone through the whole long journey of this study with me and have provided a pleasurable environment for my writing and made my life more fun. Finally, my heartfelt thanks go to my parents and my elder brother, who have always provided their spiritual and material support.

                                                              D.W.

Abbreviations

For complete author names, titles, and publication data for the works cited here in short form, see Works Cited. The following abbreviations have been used in the captions and the notes:

CDRB	*Chengdu ribao*
CDTL	Fu Chongju, *Chengdu tonglan*
CSSN	*Chengdu shi shizheng nianjian*
CWZX	*Chengdu wenshi ziliao xuanji*
GMGB	*Guomin gongbao*
LMZ	*Longmenzhen*
SBTB	*Sichuan baolu tongzhihui baogao*
SCGB	*Sichuan guanbao*
SSSD	*Sichuan shengzhengfu shehuichu dang'an*
STJZ	*Sichuan tongsheng jingcha zhangcheng*
SWX	*Sichuan wenxian*
SWZX	*Sichuan wenshi ziliao xuanji*
SXGS	Wei Yingtao and Zhao Qin, eds., *Sichuan xinhai geming shilian*
TSHB	*Tongsu huabao*
TSRB	*Tongsu ribao*
WCMN	*West China Missionary News*

STREET CULTURE IN CHENGDU

1 Introduction

Chinese cities experienced a profound social transformation in the late nineteenth and early twentieth centuries, yet to date surprisingly little has been written about how these changes permanently altered public life. Scholars of that period in Chinese urban history have tended to focus on the coastal regions, neglecting inland cities. As an interior city, Chengdu maintained a much more traditional culture than port cities and was much more typical of Chinese urban life. Significant yet neglected, Chengdu is an ideal subject for a study of Chinese popular culture and everyday life. This examination of Chengdu street life attempts to provide a broader context for understanding Chinese urban history and cultural history and to answer some crucial unanswered questions: What function did public space serve in everyday urban life? What was the relationship between urban commoners and public space? Who were the major occupants of urban public space, and how was it used by ordinary residents? What role did the community and neighborhood play in public life? To what extent did state and local elites control the street and community? How was everyday life changed during the Reform Movement and Republican Revolution? How did popular culture and public space change during the transitional period? What was the nature of the relationship among commoners, local elites, and state power in public space? And how did popular culture and local politics interact?

In this book, I use the phrase "street culture" to signify the full range of cultural artifacts and activities that appeared on the street, from shop decorations and signs, folk performances, and celebrations to ways of earning a living. Street culture also includes the physical structures that lined the streets, such as stores, teahouses, and other public places. Street culture was an important part of popular culture, and street life was central to the daily lives of city dwellers, especially those in the lower classes. This study explores how Chengdu's urban commoners, social reformers, and state power brought about and reacted to changes in popular culture through their use of public space.

This book begins in the 1870s, when customary economic practices and lifestyles were beginning to change following the Taiping Rebellion, and concludes in the late 1920s, when Chengdu established a municipal government for the first time. On the national scene, this era included the Self-Strengthening Movement, the Reform Movement, the Republican Revolution of 1911, the warlord era, and reunification under the Nationalist Party (Guomindang) in 1927–28. As we will see, these national events were more or less reflected in the politics and popular culture of Chengdu. During this period, Western influences restructured the economies of Chinese cities and challenged their folk traditions, which resulted in greater politicization of urban society. While changes were most dramatic in the major Chinese port cities, inland cities also were affected. As Fernand Braudel pointed out, "A bend in a path or a street can take anyone back to the past. . . . Even in highly developed economies, the residual presence of the old material past makes itself felt. It is disappearing before our eyes, but slowly, and never in the same manner."[1] Through the study of street culture, I hope to open a new way of understanding Chinese urban society and culture during this transformation.

The main argument of this study is that life in public spaces—the site of the most visible cultural displays in Chengdu—was radically transformed in the early twentieth century, a transformation that resulted in the reconstruction of urban public space, re-creation of people's public roles, and redefinition of the relationship among ordinary people, local elites, and the state. This study reveals that commoners' everyday life typically was tightly connected to the streets, and that the people of Chengdu created and enjoyed a rich street culture. Urban residents, especially the poor, used the street as their shared space for everyday commercial, recreational, and ceremonial events. With the onset of social change, reformers who had been influenced by Western culture sought to regulate the use of public space, and commoners had to struggle to maintain their claim to the street. While during the 1911 Revolution commoners used the streets for political protest, they organized for self-protection when warlords and armed soldiers occupied public spaces in the 1910s and 1920s. Throughout this process, Chengdu's streets underwent significant physical and cultural changes while continuing to play a critical role in urban life.

Three major thematic points serve as the basis for the three parts of this book. First, in premodern Chengdu, the street was the major space for commoners' public activities, and ordinary residents enjoyed relatively greater freedom there for various activities related to their livelihood and recreation. The streets usually were more appealing than commoners' meager homes. Popular entertainers performed everywhere, reflecting China's rich folk traditions and the community's social networks. Festivals and ceremonies were the most powerful expression of local culture and prosperity; these usually involved street performances such as local operas, parades, and ceremonies. Such activities often provided a significant mode of inter-action between different social classes and groups. Furthermore, various voluntary organizations coordinated public ceremonial activities, from which poor and rich alike constructed images of local solidarity and social order.

Second, social reformers considered displays of traditional culture repre-sentative of the "old" order and therefore "backward." These reformers promoted many innovations, notably improving the streets and enhancing the city's image. Under the banner of Western-imitative "civilization" (wen-ming) and "enlightenment" (qimeng), reformers took advantage of the un-precedented opportunity to assert their hegemony. The early twentieth cen-tury thus became an important period of cultural transition in Chengdu; the cultural fabric became a tapestry that wove together the old and new, popular and elite. Popular culture absorbed new elements, such as public theaters, parks, exhibitions, and new teahouses, under the changing social structure, but the lower classes managed to cling to their street culture and their traditional way of life survived.

Finally, the reforms usually imposed greater restrictions on citizens, thereby affecting traditional forms of work and recreation. Implementing reforms often was achieved through coercion, which understandably gen-erated popular resentment as commoners struggled to retain their claim to the street. Therefore, everyday life in reform-era Chengdu could be said to reflect "the weapons of the weak against the reality of the established order."[2] During the revolutionary era, commoners first began to play a po-litical role on the street. When subsequent mass movements arose, urban elites became increasingly unable to restrict commoners' activities. The Rail-road Protection Movement, for example, became a large-scale, armed mass movement that the reformers never anticipated. After the collapse of the Qing dynasty (1644–1911), many reformers gradually began to recognize that they had unwittingly helped the revolutionaries foment the violent po-litical rebellion that they originally opposed. Early in the Republic, social unrest caused by political separatism and tyrannical warlords inspired commoners to again install leaders of their own. Although commoners still used the street as their everyday space, armed soldiers gradually became the dominant actors there, even transforming it into a battlefield.

During this period, commoners turned to leaders from the elite class to reorganize the community and ensure their livelihood, while the elites had to garner support from the masses to withstand the warlords' invasion of their social and economic arenas. Unlike their experience during the New Policies of the late Qing, Chengdu elites began to lose faith in government. They found that allegiance to powerful warlords and a strong urban ad-ministration did not bring them political and economic benefits, but rather weakened their own position in the community. Thus, Chengdu's commoners and elites cooperated once again to protect their mutual interests. They organized for self-protection, not only to defend their lives and economic security but also to preserve their cultural heritage.

Traveling Inland

Chengdu, the capital of Sichuan province and the center of the Sichuan basin, is a relatively isolated city surrounded by mountains in the upper Yangzi region.[3] Until the early twentieth century, traveling to the city from the eastern coast was extremely difficult; as Li Bai, the greatest poet of the Tang dynasty (618–907), complained, "Traveling to Sichuan is as hard as climbing to the sky." The Chengdu plain is home to some of the most spectacular views in the whole inland area, inspiring Westerners to call the province a "green and pleasant land." Western travelers and missionaries wrote that the plain was covered with numerous walled cities and busy market towns. Unlike North China, where farmers lived in villages for protection, on the Chengdu plain the country people were scattered. Their farmhouses and temples were surrounded with bamboo trees, prompting one missionary to write, "From hilltops the view over the plain is a panorama of groves interspersed with charming vistas of green or golden fields according to the season."[4] The English traveler Isabella Bird wrote in 1899 that Chengdu "has a superb climate, ranging from the temperate to the subtropical; a rich soil, much of which, under careful cultivation, yields three and even four crops annually of most things which can be grown." It also held vast natural resources, "forests of grand timber, the area of which has not even been estimated; rich mineral resources, and some of the most valuable and extensive coal-fields in the world."[5]

In the late nineteenth and early twentieth centuries, Chengdu had one of the largest populations among the country's inland cities. In 1910, its population was 335,000, with 68,000 households, and while some estimate that its size doubled by 1920, a more reasonable estimate was that by then it had about 350,000 inhabitants.[6] Westerners praised Chengdu's prosperity. Before her arrival there, Bird had heard from others that Chengdu was "among the finest cities . . . a second Peking." The Harvard professor Ernest Wilson even thought that Chengdu was "probably the finest city in the whole of China," built on "a totally different plan from that of Peking, or even Canton." A Japanese observer noted that the architecture of Chengdu revealed a "classical atmosphere" like that of Kyoto (Figures 1.1 and 1.2).[7]

Chengdu has a long history. During the Three Kingdoms period (220–80), it was the capital of the state of Shu. During the Tang dynasty, Chengdu

FIGURE I.I. Central Mansion Street (Zongfu jie), one of the most prosperous areas in Chengdu. The two-story "street houses" (*pumian*) shown in the picture were the city's typical style of housing. Usually the first floor was used as shops and the second as residences. From CSSN 1927.

was one of most prosperous cities in China, as a proverb proclaimed: "Yangzhou is number one and Chengdu second" (*Yangyi Yier*). Then came the transition from the late Ming to the early Qing, when Sichuan experienced more than a half century of war (1622–81), during which the economy was devastated and its cities, including Chengdu, were greatly damaged. Yet in the early Qing, especially during the Qianlong period (1736–95), the economy and culture were gradually restored.[8] It was during the post-Taiping era that the pace of development in Chengdu slowed compared to that of cities in central and coastal China. In their studies of Hankou and Zhejiang, William Rowe and Mary Rankin emphasize the social reconstruction during this period and note that native elites' participation in local public affairs resulted in the dramatic development of the public sphere. By contrast, Sichuan suffered little damage during the Taiping Rebellion and did not need much reconstruction immediately thereafter.[9]

Until the late Qing, the West had only a negligible influence on Chengdu. In fact, Isabella Bird wrote in 1899 that the city owed "absolutely nothing to European influence." During the 1920s, Ba Jin, in his well-known autobiographical novel *Family* (Jia), described Chengdu as a model of conservatism and despotism, while Shanghai, by contrast, represented modernism and freedom.[10] Such a belief, of course, reflected the radical thought espoused

FIGURE 1.2. Rising Happiness Street (Fuxing jie). In this commercial district we can see lanterns hanging under the eaves of shops and stalls and baskets on the sidewalks. From their clothing the people standing on the street appear to be merchants, students, coolies, and peasants. From CSSN 1927.

by some new and Western-influenced intellectuals who clearly embraced the trend eschewing Chinese culture; however, it did lend credence to the notion that Chengdu was relatively unchanged. The city maintained a much more traditional culture than did the cities of coastal, northern, and even central China, a distinction that makes Chengdu especially interesting and significant to the historian.

Sources

One major obstacle in the study of street culture is the difficulty of collecting and interpreting data. As we know, Chinese history was transmitted by members of the elite class; information on the everyday lives of commoners is virtually absent from standard historical accounts both locally and nationally. Overcoming this obstacle means sifting useful information from tremendous quantities of primary and secondary data sources. More challenging, however, is the interpretation of these data, almost all of which was generated by members of the elite class. In other words, the descriptions of commoners and their culture in this book originate from elites, although the primary subject is the commoner. How to handle written sources is a thorny issue in the study of popular culture. As Carlo Ginzburg noted, "the thoughts, the beliefs, and the aspirations of the peasants and artisans of the past reach us (if and when they do) almost always through distorting viewpoints and intermediaries." This has led some historians to raise the question, "Can the subaltern speak?"[11] I believe it can, although the answer is highly dependent on how such sources are used. In general, one must recognize the nature and limitations of using written accounts to study popular culture and the lower classes.

There are four conventional sources of data for developing a local history: official documents, mass media, investigations, and personal records. Different aspects of these sources also must be considered: who wrote them; who compiled them; and when, why, and under what circumstances they were written. Local gazetteers and archives can be considered official documents. The former were written and compiled by local government-appointed scholars. Three gazetteers of Chengdu were published in 1816, 1873, and 1934, respectively, including the *Revised Chengdu County Gazetteer* (Chongxiu Chengdu xianzhi) and two editions of the *Huayang County Gazetteer* (Huayang xianzhi).[12] In addition, the Archives of the Social Department of the Sichuan Provincial Government (Sichuan shengzhengfu shehuichu dang'an) in the Sichuan Provincial Archives is a valuable source of official documents. The second category of sources—the mass media—emerged in the late nineteenth and early twentieth centuries and grew quickly. Within ten years, Chengdu had more than twenty newspapers. Some lasted for quite a long time, for example the *Citizens' Daily* (Guomin gongbao), which continued until 1949. In addition, the monthly journal *West China Missionary News* reported news and published articles from a foreigner's point of view. The third category of source material is social investigation, one example of which in this case is the eight-volume *Investigation of Chengdu* (Chengdu tonglan). Compiled by Fu Chongju and based on his personal experiences, the work is a virtual encyclopedia of everyday life in late-Qing Chengdu.[13] Other examples are the city guidebooks, including *Guidebook of Chengdu* (Chengdu daoyou) and *New Chengdu* (Xin Chengdu), that some local scholars began writing in the 1930s.[14] Foreigners, including early twentieth-century Japanese, also contributed to this genre. These works, sometimes over a thousand pages in length, provide insight into the economy, community life, culture, people, and customs. They include *Investigation of West China* (Seishin jijo), *Investigation of Sichuan* (Shisen-shō soran), *Investigations of China's Provinces* (Shina shōbetsu zenshi), and *New Investigations of China's Provinces* (Shinshu shina shōbetsu zenshi).[15] The final useful source is personal records, which consist mainly of travel notes and memoirs. During the late nineteenth and twentieth centuries, foreign and local scholars and travelers wrote numerous diaries, notes, and memoirs, such as Isabella Bird's *The Yangtze Valley and Beyond*, Shu Xincheng's *Reflections on a Tour of Sichuan* (Shuyou xinying), and Yi Junzuo's "Seven Days in Chengdu" (Jincheng qiri ji). Since the 1960s, many materials on local history have been compiled in mainland China and in Taiwan, including *Collections of Literary and Historical Materials in Sichuan* (Sichuan wenshi ziliao xuanji) and *Documents on Sichuan* (Sichuan wenxian).

Using conventional sources to study popular culture and lower-class people entails some limitations. Gazetteers, for example, are one of the richest sources for local history and custom; however, they often espouse official opinion and orthodoxy and either contain very little about the lives of commoners or provide only distorted information. Thus, when drawing upon these materials, I try to distinguish between "culture *produced by* the popular classes" and "culture *imposed on* the popular classes," as suggested by Carlo Ginzburg.[16] This framework also can be useful when analyzing material from other sources. Local gazetteers and archives, for example, provide little direct information about street culture, but they hold valuable documents pertaining to government policy, social background, and political transformation. The value of source material largely depends on how it is interpreted. For instance, a regulation prohibiting gambling in public places reveals not only the government policy on this issue but also that people used street corners for this purpose. From the government policies found in archives, one can examine how and why the government formulated policy and explore the relationship between popular culture and the local political structure. Although archives have been regarded as the most reliable source, materials found there also are subject to interpretation. It is possible, for example, that the government exaggerated the extent of street gambling in order to control it.[17] Furthermore, some regulations found are in draft form and reflect official thoughts only at that particular time; some were completed but never promulgated; and some were issued but not implemented. Therefore, when dealing with such evidence, I attempt to distinguish between policies and regulations that had a social effect and those that did not.

The treatment of unofficial materials is also problematic. Local elites published an enormous amount in the early twentieth century, most of which dealt with social reforms or enlightenment. In the newspapers named above, columns such as "Provincial Capital City News" (*shengcheng xinwen*) or "Chengdu News" (*Chengdu xinwen*) provide vividly detailed accounts of commoners' everyday lives, but as filtered through the writer's elite bias. Beginning in the late Qing, new members of the elite class began to conduct investigations to benefit social reform and left excellent records about urban commoners, community life, and local culture. Huang Zhi, one of the writers of the prefaces of *Investigation of Chengdu*, noted that in the late Qing no counterpart works existed for Beijing, Shanghai, Canton, Nanjing, Suzhou, Wuchang, or Hankou, all of which were key nodes of transportation and prosperous commercial cities.[18] The value of Japanese investigations to historical research is clearly evident in Philip Huang's study of rural North China.[19] Although the investigations of the upper Yangzi region do not have the same quality and quantity as the Mantetsu materials, some of them still contain rich information. These investigations, however, were conducted for the purpose of Japanese expansion, and therefore could be highly selective and thus biased. Travel notes record direct observations of cultural phenomena that might otherwise have been lost forever and that are useful in uncovering a city's heritage. However, a traveler might have written about a topic simply because of its novelty, revealing only superficial knowledge or understanding. Most memoirs can be considered primary sources because the authors describe events they actually witnessed and participated in, but these, too, reveal the writer's passion, personality, and bias, even to the extent of containing misinformation. All sorts of writings about popular culture, in fact, invariably are infused with the prejudices of the elites. Therefore, when utilizing written sources, I try to distinguish actual street culture from what is merely *described* by elites or foreigners, to provide insight not only into authentic street culture but also into the attitudes toward it that were held by the elite class.

Because of the lack of conventional sources for historical research, scholars of Chinese popular culture have increasingly turned to literature—librettos from local operas, novels, and proverbs.[20] This study of Chengdu's street culture utilizes material from sources including folk literature, graphics, and even my own field investigations and interviews, all of which yield new perspectives. Although folk tales do not directly document historical events, they sometimes reveal a sense of the culture. As Michel de Certeau claimed, standard histories examine the "strategies of instituted powers," whereas "fabulous stories" offer audiences a basis for understanding their culture.[21] I have especially examined a form of folk literature known as bamboo-branch poetry (*zhuzhici*). Unlike other types of lyric poetry, bamboo-branch poetry was not meant to express the author's imagination, emotions, or philosophy. Rather, it was intended to objectively describe people and events and how local elites viewed urban public life and members of the lower classes.[22] I have examined local folklore, which can be regarded as a type of oral history, as well. Many accounts published in the local literary journal *Folk Tales* (Longmenzhen) were of actual events that provide a vivid picture of Chengdu's past. In addition, during the 1980s more than a thousand local scholars participated in a project to collect folk stories and songs, resulting in the huge *Treasury of Chengdu Folklore*

(Chengdu minjian wenxue jicheng).[23] The collection not only provides stories reflecting local history and culture but also reveals how and what ordinary people have passed on through the generations regarding their philosophy of life. Surprisingly, no historian in either China or the West has examined this cultural treasure.

Although Chengdu cannot claim great social literature comparable to that of Hugo and Balzac on Paris,[24] it does have Li Jieren's multivolume historical novel *The Great Wave* (Dabo) and Ba Jin's autobiographical novel *Family* (Jia). *The Great Wave*, a historical story about the Railroad Protection Movement in 1911 Chengdu, was published in 1937 and revised in the 1950s. *Family*, written in 1932, deals with intergenerational family conflict and its impact on political and social change during the 1920s. Li Jieren and Ba Jin, two great modern Chinese writers, were Chengdu natives who lived there in the early twentieth century and described the colorful social life of the era. Their descriptions of the architecture and residents of Chengdu, based on their own experiences, bring to life the customs and relationships found in all levels of society and in virtually all public places: temples, streets, shops, public squares, bridges, festivals, teahouses, and theaters.

The use of literature as a source of historical data also raises issues of interpretation. Although we have sufficient reason to believe that many literary works were based on historical facts, they, too, were shaped by the author's passions, ideologies, values, and imagination. This factor alone, however, should not prevent scholars from looking to literature to find the voice of heretofore voiceless Chengdu residents. Unlike the study of political events, for which validity depends on precision, the study of popular culture can benefit from vague descriptions, so long as they give voice to local cultural perceptions.

Graphics, including photographs and drawings, also reveal the uses of public space and the daily activities of people on the street. Since the late nineteenth century, missionaries, foreign travelers, and Chinese journalists have captured Chengdu life through photographs, which are found in various publications in China and the West.[25] Local artists also joined the effort to represent culture visually. Fu Chongju collected more than a hundred sketches of all occupations in the early twentieth century and published them in *Investigation of Chengdu* (Chengdu tonglan).[26] *Popular Pictorial* (Tongsu huabao), published during the late Qing and early Republic, included many drawings of "current affairs" (*shishi hua*), "satire" (*fengci hua*), and "awakening people" (*jingshi hua*) for the purpose of social reform. Local artist Yu Zidan also left many paintings of various street activities during the 1920s, which his friend William Sewell published with detailed descriptions. The drawings and photos provide very vivid and powerful resources for uncovering street culture, and they support descriptions from written sources. The viewer sees almost firsthand, without the need for text, the hustle and bustle of Chengdu street life: pedestrians, teahouse patrons, sidewalk barbers, and fashionable dressers.

A scholarly analysis of Chinese street culture is challenging because it requires close examination of culture and society from both historical and anthropological viewpoints. Chinese culture values highly the passage of history, both the community's and the family's, from generation to generation, and therefore I have been able to collect many narratives through interviews. While Chengdu has changed dramatically since 1949 under Mao's socialism and Deng Xiaoping's reform, I nevertheless was able to unearth a vivid historical legacy, especially through conversations with the elderly in teahouses or by visiting the small alleyways that remain from the old city. Also, while modern apartments separate living areas from public space, today's "street houses" in Chengdu still facilitate a close connection with public life. Chengdu inhabitants continue to spend much of their time on sidewalks talking with neighbors, doing daily chores, engaging in commerce, or playing mahjong, all which I captured during on-site research. Of course, I fully recognize the importance of refraining from imposing current social constructs and images onto past culture. Although some of my analyses are based on recent observation, I have attempted to brush the historical dust from my objectives and to connect my observations to written materials to capture Chengdu's street life as it existed a century or more ago and as it exists, although modified, today.

Past Scholarship and Terminology

Studies of Chengdu. China's vast geography has contributed to its rich and colorful regional culture. In his classic study of the relationship between marketing and local community, G. William Skinner emphasized the important role of geographical factors in Chinese economy, society, and culture. Skinner maintained that the local market minimized the exchange of goods with other marketing communities and thereby fostered cultural differentiation.[27] Skinner's model has inspired scholars to engage in regional studies, but urban historians have tended to concentrate on several major cities, such as Shanghai, Beijing, and Hankou, which reflected national standards regarding the economy, politics, and communication. Interior cities have been largely neglected, even though their unique folk traditions provide fascinating insights into Chinese culture and history.

Scholarly interest in Chengdu has increased since the early 1990s, and a few works on the city have been published in Chinese and English. Jeannette Faurot published *Ancient Chengdu*; Zhang Xuejun and Zhang Lihong produced a general history of Chengdu in Chinese; and Kristin Stapleton wrote a dissertation on the police force of the late Qing period. My own book on Sichuan history contains considerable information on Qing-era Chengdu, but it did not focus mainly on the city and was published only in Chinese. Since then, Stapleton and I respectively have published several articles about Chengdu's secret societies, urban administration, popular culture, and teahouses and public life.[28]

Kristin Stapleton's recent book *Civilizing Chengdu*, however, is the most comprehensive and profound study of Chengdu's urban history to date; it mainly "investigates the history of urban planning and administration" and reveals "the motives and actions" of the local officials and elite reformers who "implemented specific programs and of the people of the city to whom the new policies were applied." Stapleton's work examines elite activism, reform in the urban administration, and elite politics by focusing mainly on prominent figures such as police reformer Zhou Shanpei and warlord Yang Sen. She stresses that Chengdu had two waves of urban reform (one during the New Policies in the late Qing and the other in the 1920s) and carefully evaluates the dynamics and extent of the changes. Stapleton argues that between 1895 and 1937, "perhaps the greatest change was the acceptance of the idea of city administration itself."[29]

Like Stapleton, I also deal with reform issues, but my focus is on how reforms influenced everyday life, especially among the lower classes who constituted street life. While Stapleton emphasized organizations of elite reform and administration, my interest is how the new regulations were enforced in public spaces, and in particular on the streets. I explore how changes affected traditional neighborhood life and how Chengdu residents responded to the transformation of society from one having relatively high autonomy, little law enforcement, and a loosely affiliated cluster of neighborhoods to one controlled by a centralized urban bureaucracy. Furthermore, whereas Stapleton mainly focused on the two waves of urban reform in Chengdu, I see a constant transformation throughout the late Qing and early Republic, and my research suggests that major measures of social reform permeated the period from the New Policies to the establishment of the municipal government at the end of the 1920s.

The Street and Public Space.   The street, a shared public space, is one of the main focuses of this study, while I also often use the terms "neighborhood" and "community." These terms have slightly different meanings but have a very close, sometimes overlapping, connection. All of them, in my interpretation, have both spatial and conceptual denotations. First, they refer to certain areas where people live and are almost synonymous with the Chinese words *jie* (street), *lin* (neighborhood), and *she* (community). In Chinese dictionaries, *jie* is usually defined as "a wide road with houses at both sides," and is often considered the same as the term *"jiedao"* (street and road). From this other words are derived, including *jiefang* (neighbors), *jieshi* (downtown streets, or street and market), *jietou* (street corners), and *jietou xiangwei* (streets and lanes, or street corners and alleys), all of which appear throughout the materials cited in this study. In their historical context, these terms refer to far more than space or place, also indicating the relationships between people who live in the area, as well as between the people and the street. Whereas *jie* more often refers to a place physically, *lin* and *she* refer more to relationships found there, though they also have spatial connotations. The term *lin* is defined as "people and households who live nearby" and has developed into such terms as *linli*, which could indicate an area (neighborhood) or the people there (neighbors, which is synonymous with *linju*). The term *she* has two basic meanings: in ancient times, it was a place of worship of the patron deity (*tudi* or *tudi shen*), and today it means an organized body. Two important words derive from the first meaning of *she*: *shehui* (society) and *shequ* (community). Although some English dictionaries give the same definition of "persons as an organized body" for both "society" and "community," I believe it is more precise to use the modern Chinese term translated as "community" to indicate a spatial area that usually includes many streets and neighborhoods and also the people who live there. I prefer to use the term "community" to refer to "a body of people having common rights, privileges, or interests, or living in the same place under the same laws and regulations," as defined by *Webster's Dictionary*. In sum, from street to neighborhood to community, I believe a gradual transition has taken place in which the spatial sense of these terms has weakened and the notion of cultural identity strengthened.[30]

Public life in Chinese cities has long been neglected by urban historians, but it will be the major subject of this study, in which I seek to explore the relationship between commoners and public space and between street life and public life. Public space and public life, as strong expressions of local culture, have always played a central role in the life of Chinese cities, for they were the arenas in which urban residents participated in society and politics. In contrast, scholars of European and American history have long focused on public gathering places, such as coffeehouses, taverns, and saloons, as sites where strangers gathered and exchanged information and as locations for public life that lay outside the proximity of family and close friends.[31] Most of these urban histories, however, mainly examine indoor public spaces; this study will extend the analysis to shared outdoor spaces—the street, a city's most visible and highly utilized public space.

Western scholars have produced a number of studies that offer theoretical analyses of public space and everyday life. Michel de Certeau and

Agnes Heller have examined the "commonplace," "everyday contact," and "collisions of everyday life," while Richard Sennett has presented a broadly analytical study on the urban public world and public life. Scholars of Western history such as Susan Davis have recognized that the poor, in their "great gatherings," had a special affinity for activities on the street. In a society with well-defined social classes, city people, no matter what their social status, as Mary Ryan argues, "still enjoyed relatively free use of public space."[32] Thus, public space is the best location to observe social relations, the place where various people, especially the poor, conduct daily life.

The meanings of "public" and "public space" are varied. As Richard Sennett argues in his analysis of the early modern West, "The sense of who 'the public' were, and where one was when one was out 'in public,' became enlarged in the early 18th century in both Paris and London." When the word "public" was used in the later period, "it meant not only a region of social life located apart from the realm of family and close friends, but also that this public realm of acquaintances and strangers included a relatively wide diversity of people."[33] "Public" remains a developing term in the West. In Chinese history, William Rowe has examined the transition of the meaning of "public" and its relationship with the Chinese term *gong*. In this study, I use its original meaning of "open to general observation" or "accessible to all."[34] Similarly, "public space" refers to urban areas that were available for everyone, and "public life" means the way in which everyday life was enacted in such arenas. Perry Duis has classified three types of spaces in an urban area: some are formally public, such as streets, sidewalks, parks, and governmental property, and some are privately owned, such as business property and private houses. Spaces that lie between these two could be called "semipublic"; that is, those that are "privately owned but [allow] public access," such as stores, theaters, and barbershops.[35] In this study, "public space" includes those spaces in Duis's first category, especially streets and public squares, but also certain semipublic spaces, mainly those physically and socially connected to the street, such as shops, teahouses, and theaters.[36]

The street seems an obvious subject for researchers studying public space and everyday life, but few scholars have seriously focused on it. In 1943, William Whyte published *Street Corner Society*, a sociological study of gangsters in an American urban slum district. Since then, however, only a few works regarding the street have appeared. In 1983, Anthony McEligott investigated the "street politics" of the Nazis in Hamburg. Three years later, Christine Stansell surveyed the role of women, especially prostitutes, on the streets of New York. Susan Davis offered a study of "street theater" in Philadelphia, focusing on the relationship between public rituals and local power.[37] Authors have written much less regarding the street and public life in Chinese urban history. Among the exceptions are David Strand, who investigated rickshaw pullers of Republican Beijing, and Joseph Esherick and Jeffery Wasserstrom, who revealed how streets were used for "political theater" in modern China.[38] In contrast to those works, the focus of this study is on street culture and commoners' street life, which until now has been virtually absent.

Everyday Life and Popular Culture. This study explores ordinary people's everyday life in Chengdu, especially their cultural life on the street. Little study of everyday life in inland cities has been done; the few works published on the topic deal primarily with coastal cities, notably Shanghai. More than four decades ago, Jacques Gernet published *Daily Life in China on the Eve of the Mongol Invasion*, which focuses on Hangzhou and uncovered colorful urban life in the capital of Southern Song (1127–1229). Wen-hsin Yeh has studied middle-class professional employees in a Western-style institution by examining everyday life and workplace relationships in Shanghai, while Mau-Sang Mg observes daily life in 1940s Shanghai through a popular novel, Qin Shouou's *Qiuhaitang* (Begonia). Hanchao Lu recently contributed a profound study of everyday life in Shanghai. Lu argues that scholars have probably exaggerated the influence of modern and Western elements in Shanghai, noting that even though it was the most modern city in China, much of its tradition survived.[39] Unlike these studies, my focus is on the inland city of Chengdu, and although my study resembles Lu's in its stress on everyday life, my specific focus is on people's public life. Whereas Lu explores the prevalence of ancient customs beneath a veneer of modernity, my attention is on the changes and continuity of public life in Chengdu to reveal both traditional and modern aspects of everyday life. Moreover, while past scholarship generally assumes that inland China was influenced much less by the West and therefore changed less, little empirical support for this has been published. In this study, I use concrete evidence to determine what changed and what remained unchanged in public space, public life, and popular culture in a remote inland city.

Any study of street culture confronts the issue of how to distinguish popular culture from elite culture. Although historians are virtually unanimous in acknowledging a distinction between the two, the definition of each has long been the subject of scholarly debate.[40] Scholars of China suggest that popular culture embodies a broad meaning extending "from domestic architecture to millenarian cults, from irrigation techniques to shadow plays."[41] The popular culture discussed in this book is that created by and for commoners. In a premodern society, regional and local aspects of culture differed strikingly from place to place because there was relatively little cultural exchange. Therefore, popular culture was often linked with "folk culture." According to Antonio Gramsci, there are three categories of popular songs in folk culture: songs "composed by the people and for the people"; those "composed for the people but not by the people"; and those written "neither by the people nor for the people, but which the people adopt because they conform to their way of thinking and feeling." My main focus in this book is the first category, although, as Herbert Gans points out, "many popular culture creators are better educated than their audiences," and thus one sometimes must consider cultural artifacts that fall under Gramsci's second and third categories.[42]

Thus, I attempt to distinguish carefully between the concepts of elite culture and popular culture while recognizing their close but complex relationship. Some scholars who emphasize cultural unity in Chinese society suggest that each nation has a dominant culture, which can be accepted by all cultural groups notwithstanding disparities in education, ages, sex, and economic status. Bonnie McDougall wrote that elites and ordinary people were located at two ends of the same cultural continuum, transcending their differences in social status and economic condition. Richard Smith argued that "the most striking feature of premodern China seems to be its cultural unity" and noted that some styles of popular entertainment, from ball playing to mahjong, were promoted and enjoyed by both elites and commoners.[43] Other scholars, however, stress a separation of popular culture from elite culture. According to this approach, the effort of elites to control the thoughts and behaviors of the lower classes was less than successful, despite the dominance of orthodox culture in education and other institutions in the late imperial period. China's vast territory and the countless villages scattered in remote areas where state power hardly reached made it difficult for elites to achieve cultural hegemony. Perry Link and other scholars believed that popular culture "consists of ideas, beliefs, and practices that have origins at least partially independent of the state." William Rowe also emphasized that "the divorce between the Confucian high tradition and the most general popular religion (centered on placating ghosts and spirits) and popular literature (as transmitted, for example, by chanters and storytellers) must always be kept in mind when considering communal activism."[44] My view is that these elements of unity and separation in fact always coexisted in the relationship between elite culture and popular culture, and that the relationship in public life was much more complicated. Also, the relationship was malleable, depending on social, economic, and political factors. Indeed, popular culture clearly differed from and even often conflicted with elite culture, which is why local elites joined the state-sponsored campaign to reform and control the lower classes.

Commoners, Reformers, and Local Politics. The major focus of this study is the ordinary people; I try to reveal how the lower classes understood the street and formulated a cultural meaning from their experiences there. Studies of Chinese social history have heavily concentrated on the elites, especially those in the coastal areas.[45] We still know little about the everyday public life—typically the most visible aspect of Chinese urban society—of ordinary residents in remote inland cities. As Fernand Braudel pointed out, "Unfortunately, we know more about these great palace scenes than about the fish market, where the fish were brought live in tanks of water, or the game markets where a traveler saw one day a prodigious quantity of roe deer, pheasants and partridges. Here the unusual conceals the everyday."[46] This gap in our cultural understanding makes an examination of the everyday lives of the lower classes even more important.

The term "urban commoners" in this study refers to ordinary people, some of whom might be described by William Rowe as "men of the [same] street," "residents of a street sitting out in their doorways, chatting together while enjoying the cool evening breeze," or by Wen-hsin Yeh as "petty urbanities," or by Perry Link as urban dwellers who "live well below the standards of the wealthy class." In this study, my focus is on persons of lower social status, who could be "nobody," "anyone," "everyone," the "ordinary man," or even the "dangerous classes." These people worked and socialized on the street, creating what E. P. Thompson referred to as "plebeian culture."[47] The names of these people might not be remembered by history, but they occupied public space daily, creating street culture.

I use the term "social reformers" to represent commoners' counterparts at the opposite end of the socioeconomic scale—the self-consciously modernized and Westernized elites. This group included the "police reformers" described by Kristin Stapleton and Joseph Esherick's "urban reformist elite" who actively participated in social reforms.[48] Generally, elites inherited the tradition of social reform from previous generations that were concerned about people's livelihoods, and they used the traditional methods of relief, education, and domination to enact social reform. They differed from their predecessors, however, in that they were nearly universally interested in new and Western knowledge. Those who had traveled abroad sought to enhance the image of their hometown by comparing it with foreign cities.

Urban reformers fit into two basic categories. The first consisted of those who held sufficient political power to undertake urban reforms, such as Zhou Shanpei (1875–1958). Zhou, who visited Japan in 1902, became the director of the Bureau of Sichuan Police (1902–6) and head of the Department of Promoting Industry and Commerce (1907–11). He designed and conducted ambitious urban reforms in management, economy, and social life. The other category consisted of local intellectuals, merchants, and gentry who derived power not from official rank but from educational, commercial, and publishing activities, such as Fu Chongju (1875–1917). Fu was a local scholar, publisher, writer, and journalist. In the 1890s he worked for the *Sichuan Learning News* (Shuxue bao), and in the early 1900s he founded Publication Company (Tushu ju) and published the *Enlightening Popular News* (Qimeng tongsu bao). He also visited the International Fair in Japan in 1903.[49] Members of this group might have different interests and notions of reform. Most focused mainly on education and commerce, but Fu was more interested in social customs and folk traditions and thus served as Chengdu's chief social and cultural critic. During the early twentieth century, a large number of young men who graduated from schools in Japan or in Europe or from modern schools in China actively participated in urban reform.[50] Some of them entered government offices, while others became teachers, journalists or editors, heads of social organizations, or independent writers. They did not always share the same opinions or agendas for urban reform, but they efficiently employed their knowledge and social reputation to "modernize" the city and to influence urban commoners.

This study also examines the relationship between street culture and local politics in reform and Revolution-era Chengdu. Commoners and social reformers had a complicated relationship with street culture, and the mingling of these three forces influenced political movements.[51] In the early twentieth century, social reformers sought to "enlighten" commoners and to control public space because they believed that the social order had become dangerously unstable. The elites dramatically expanded their long-standing claims to leadership and instruction and tried to regulate commoners' public life while transforming the street into a new political arena that was available both to new urban social "forces of order" and to political protesters. Under these urban reforms, commoners' access to economic and cultural resources shrank, and everyday disruptions made their livelihoods increasingly difficult to sustain. Consequently, commoners organized popular movements and resistance. Under these new political influences, street culture underwent changes and gained new features.

This book has eight chapters, and the main body, chapters 2 through 7, is divided into three parts of two sections each. The parts largely reflect commoners' three major, and often overlapping, relationships (with public space, social reformers, and local politics) to show the transition of Chengdu's street culture from 1870 to 1930. While these three sections do not follow a strict chronological order, each does have a particular emphasis. Part I focuses on the time before the early-twentieth-century reform; Part II addresses this reform; and Part III largely deals with the revolutionary era and after. Of course, cultural change can occur very gradually and can appear continuous even if it occurs during radical political transformation. Thus, cultural phenomena that remained unchanged in the later periods still provide valuable evidence about the traditional relationship between commoners and public space. In other words, chronology is more important when addressing emerging social issues, but less so when discussing those cultural phenomena that remain relatively unchanged.

Part I examines the relationship between commoners and public space. Chapter 2 focuses on the different kinds of public space: commercial, everyday, and ceremonial. Here, I also deal with teahouses, which were important in daily life, as well as with neighborhood organizations and their influence. This chapter argues that residents enjoyed considerable autonomy in street life and that their economic and social activities were organized by themselves rather than by local officials. Chapter 3 shifts the focus to the people who inhabited these spaces. I examine a variety of public activities conducted by many social groups, especially the majority who comprised the lower classes. The key point of this section is that commoners, more than any other class, used public space for their livelihood and amusement, creating a street culture that strongly expressed folk tradition.

At the start of the twentieth century, the reform movement brought about tremendous changes in Chengdu's public spaces, street life, and culture. Part II explores these changes and the relationship between commoners and social reformers. Chapter 4 describes how new and Westernized elites, offended by lower-class public behavior, attempted to reshape the community by creating new public spaces and leisure activities, including fairs and parks, that further changed the city's landscape. The major argument in this chapter is that social reformers, under the movement of the New Policies supported by both the state and local elites in the early twentieth century, re-created the city's appearance and changed the way in which commoners interacted with the street. Chapter 5 studies the development and exercise of police controls, which, for the first time in the city's history, regulated all aspects of street life, from traffic and crowd management to hygiene and fire control. This chapter also examines how the police dealt with hoodlums, street vendors, and gamblers. Here, I present evidence confirming Chengdu's transformation from a largely autonomous city into a police-controlled one in which bureaucracies oversaw every aspect of urban life.

Part III focuses on the relationship between commoners and local politics. The reform movement not only politicized the use of public space, it also forced a closer interaction between residents and political leaders. Chapter 6 describes the struggles for use of the street among various social forces and ethnic groups. This chapter reveals how elites seized even greater power and control over commoners and how commoners responded. The main argument in this chapter is that public space was always rife with conflict, which basically occurred at four levels: between the state and local elites; the state and commoners; elites and commoners; and commoners themselves. Chapter 7 analyzes the transformation of the street brought about by the Revolution of 1911. Political instability changed street life and culture in the postrevolutionary era, when public space became a forum for protest and social turmoil. This chapter purports that the reformist and revolutionary movements brought the street and commoners into a political orbit, politicizing street culture and redefining the public roles of both elites and commoners. Finally, the conclusion in Chapter 8 weaves all the chapters into a broader view that values the transformation of street culture, public space, and urban commoners in this large inland Chinese city.

Part 1

COMMONERS AND PUBLIC SPACE

2 The Street

A city's most important public space is the street, which not only bears traffic but also provides an easily accessible site for social and economic activities. Before modern urban facilities were available in Chinese cities, the street served a variety of needs and was the most basic unit of a neighborhood or community. The street cultivated a sense of neighborliness among people that helped strengthen consciousness in the urban community. A city's streets reveal its past and represent its culture; travelers in China distinguished one city from another by observing the unique features of the street: city walls, city gates, street corners, shop decorations, peddlers' stalls, and public ceremonies. An examination of a city's streets contributes to a deeper understanding of its people and everyday life.

The lack of urban administration before the early twentieth century in China led to a local autonomy that made urban public space equally accessible to the members of all social classes. Commoners freely conducted all sorts of recreational and commercial activities on the street and in other shared spaces such as public squares, temple fronts, ends of bridges, and teahouses. The streets were controlled primarily through the neighborhood-organized *baojia* system. *Baojia* leaders were selected from local residents, but they were not formal officials in the city, though sometimes they represented the government to carry out "official" duties, such as security.[1] The Qing government had little direct involvement in control of the street. This pattern of management had a profound impact on urban everyday life; the activities organized by the residents of a street or neighborhood clearly reflected a degree of community cohesion and control.

What factors led to this relative lack of urban administration in Chengdu throughout the Qing period? The reasons vary, but relate primarily to the government structure at the time. As we know, the Qing dynasty's formal bureaucratic structure reached only to the county level, where severely understaffed yamen were unable to cope with the needs of the prefecture's huge, widely scattered population. Chengdu, for example, was managed by both Chengdu County and Huayang County, each of which had a heavily populated rural area.[2] Therefore, resources were available to handle only the most serious and urgent matters, such as taxation, crime, and security, in Chengdu proper.

There were two organs for local security in Chengdu: the Bureau of Bao-jia (Baojia ju), which regulated the *baojia* system, and the Battalion of the City Guards (Chengshou ying), which handled security. Because each organization reported to a different authority, "the boundary of their duties was unclear," and "inevitably they always shifted responsibility onto others."[3] Social boundaries were much more difficult to define and regulate than geographic ones, leaving vast regions without government oversight. Kristin Stapleton notes that until the late Qing, Chengdu was "a city of well-established customs, dominated by high provincial officials who had little interest in urban affairs."[4] Local elites sought to fill this power vacuum, but without official titles and authority, they could do little to regulate life on the streets.

Because the elites held no official titles or power, their role in the management of public space was quite limited, and street life remained virtually uncontrolled as a result. This scenario is quite different from the conventional notion that urban China was organized under a central bureaucracy that permitted no freedoms beyond those bestowed by the state. "What were Europe's differences and original features?" Fernand Braudel asked, answering that its "towns were marked by an unparalleled freedom" that allowed them to develop "autonomous worlds."[5] Yet when one digs deeper into Chinese urban society, to a city's streets and neighborhoods, one finds that issues of freedom and control were highly relative and that control was not as thorough as generally understood. Furthermore, whereas historians have done excellent work studying the relationship between social disorder and popular religion, there has been little scholarship regarding the relationship between social order and popular culture.[6] In other words, what did popular culture contribute to social stability and community solidarity? A study of a city's streets and neighborhoods reveals that urban dwellers enjoyed considerable autonomy because state power did not reach to that level until the early twentieth century and that they took advantage of this freedom to appropriate public space for their own needs.[7]

This chapter explores how urban dwellers used the street for a range of activities associated with commerce, everyday life, and ceremonies. It also examines the role of the teahouse, a major arena in everyday life that was virtually inseparable from street culture as a whole. Finally, it analyzes the role of voluntary organizations in the community and the relationship between these groups and social autonomy in urban society.[8]

The Setting: City Walls and Streets

A city's physical setting inevitably affects its culture and everyday life. A city's wall and gates, for example, separate townspeople from country dwellers and regulate their mobility. The city wall also provides the foundation for urban planning; all construction, especially that related to streets, had to conform to the existing design. The streets, in turn, defined neighborhoods and communities and the interplay among and between residents and their shared public spaces.

Nearly all major Chinese cities were fortified, and the city wall likely was premodern Chengdu's most important and prominent architectural feature.[9] The massive structure was about seven miles in circumference, with four defense towers and four gates (see Map 1). The wall was sixty-six feet wide at its base, thirty-five feet high, and forty feet across on top (Figure 2.1). The distance between the East and West City gates was 3.1 miles, and from the North Gate to the South, 2.4 miles.[10] In 1923, Oberlin College geographer George Hubbard observed:

This wall, like most city walls in China, is no trifling affair, but represents a prodigious amount of labor and contains an immense amount of materials. Beginning on the outside, one finds a stone wall four to eight feet thick at the base and about two feet thick at the top, thirty to forty feet high and set with columns, notches, and parapets all round. Through the columns are firing holes and peepholes. Forty feet or more inside this masonry is a second wall, not quite continuous, because allowed to fall down in places. This too is of stone and brick, but the brick here greatly predominate. The inner wall is about six feet shorter than the outer and is smooth on top. Between the walls, earth has been filled in until level with the inner wall, which really leans against the dirt. Over the top of the earth is a pavement of flat stones and large brick, covering all from wall to wall. Thus in cross-section, the wall is a great earth structure raised on the ground, retained on both sides and covered on top with stone and brick, the outer wall above the pavement on top being a series of parapets and slits with holes through which to use guns and watch the enemy.[11]

The wall was higher than most of the buildings inside, so it provided a view of "a sea of low roofs, well below the eye, [that] covers almost every foot of ground."[12] The wall played a dual role—protecting the city from external threats and controlling its inhabitants, at the same time serving as a site for recreation.

During the entire Qing dynasty, the four city gates were the only passageways by which Chengdu communicated with the outside world (see Map 1 and Figures 2.2 and 2.3). The East City Gate was called "Welcome Sunrise" (Yinghui); the South, "River Bridge" (Jiangqiao); the West, "Clear Distance" (Qingyuan); and the North, "Great Peace" (Da'an).[13] Geographer Sen-dou Chang has interpreted the symbolism of city gates and associated the four

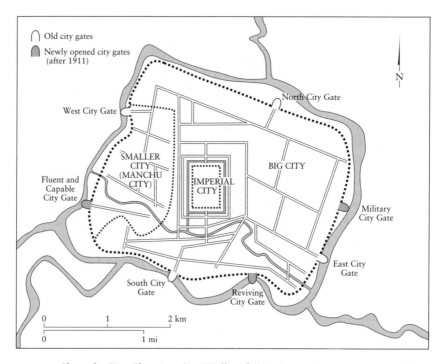

MAP I. Chengdu City, Showing City Wall and City Gates, 1870–1930

gates with the seasons: the south gate "symbolized warmth and life, and the north gate, cold and death. Civil pomp and ritual were associated with the south gate and its suburbs, whereas the north gate and the northern suburbs had military associations."[14] The gates were opened at sunrise and closed at night, and guards were present to question suspicious travelers.[15]

Whereas most Chinese cities had similar walls and gates, Chengdu's most distinguishing feature was its two smaller walled "cities"—the Smaller City (Shaocheng, also called "Manchu City") and the Imperial City (Huangcheng)—within the exterior wall (see Map 1). From a vantage point atop the Drum Tower (Gulou) in central Chengdu (see Figure 2.4), one could see "the broad Manchu City in the west, flags flying on the wall of the Imperial City in the south, crowded residents in the east, and magnificent barracks in the north." The Smaller City, located in the west of Chengdu, was home to the Manchus.[16] Isabella Bird described her first impressions of Chengdu upon entering through the west gate in the late nineteenth century: "The gates are very imposing, green glades lead into the Tartar quarter, a region of large, walled gardens, well wooded, and good-sized houses, frequently much decayed. In a street of shops several of the signs are written in Manchu." Banner garrisons were not uncommon in China; Mark Elliott wrote that by the mid-eighteenth century, Jiangnan cities alone had eighteen such garrisons. This phenomenon, however, was not as prevalent as some Western historians presume.[17]

The Imperial City was a historical relic of the Han dynasty (206 B.C.–A.D. 220) and was rebuilt during the Ming (1368–1644). Modeled after the Forbidden City in Beijing, it was so named because Chengdu had been the capital of several kingdoms, such as the State of Shu during the Three Kingdoms (220–65) and the State of Former Shu and State of Latter Shu during the Five Dynasties and Ten Kingdoms (907–60). The Imperial City was located in a central area east of the city and surrounded by the Imperial River (Yuhe). As a mid-nineteenth-century poem described, "Spring grass grows on the wall of the Imperial City. There are tens of thousand of houses [in Chengdu], but no one is as high as the wall of the Imperial City." In addition to houses, the Imperial City featured the Examination Hall (Gongyuan), where provincial civil service examinations were given. The wall of the Imperial City "sprouts grass and appears quite ancient." A large ornamental arch atop the main gate bore four large Chinese characters, "*Wei Guo Qiu Xian*" (searching for virtuous people for the country), in the Kangxi emperor's calligraphy.[18]

Besides the city wall and gates, bridges and temples were the most eye-catching structures. Rivers ran through and around Chengdu, making bridges

FIGURE 2.1. The Top of the City Wall. The city wall was the highest structure in Chengdu, and from it one could get an overview of the whole city and see that roofs nearly concealed the ground. The wide top of the city wall was often used by urban dwellers as a public gathering place. The tall building in the distance is the city gate tower. Note how close the residences are to the city wall. From Wallace 1907: 16.

FIGURE 2.2. The Fluent and Capable City Gate (Tonghui men). It was newly constructed in 1913. The men in uniform are postmen carrying mail through the gate. From Hosie 1914: 1.

both important traffic bearers and prominent city landmarks (see Map 1 and Figure 2.5). Bridge access points became regular gathering places for peddlers, merchants, seasonal workers, and folk performers. Some bridges boasted a long history. For example, outside the East City Gate stood a "red-sandstone bridge of nine arches, which is generally regarded as the bridge mentioned by Marco Polo."[19] The vacant areas under the bridge and along the riverbank bustled with activity as well. Chengdu also featured many temples, from Buddhist, Daoist, and Confucian to those dedicated to city gods and ancestral and local deities.[20] The temple fronts were popular spots for itinerant peddlers and folk performers, who attracted many customers and spectators. Each temple had its own celebrations and traditional "temple fairs," which were not only religious rituals but also public gatherings. All these activities were organized by local religious and civic groups and professional guilds, with little government interference.

The street was the most basic public shared space, but its appearance and functions varied. Chengdu had more than 400 streets and alleys by the

FIGURE 2.3. The South City Gate (Nanmen). Detail from the scroll painting *Old Chengdu* (Lao Chengdu) by Sun Bin, Zhang Youlin, Li Wanchun, Liu Shifu, Xiong Xiaoxiong, Pan Peide, and Xie Kexin (2000). Courtesy of the artists.

FIGURE 2.4. Drum Tower (Gulou). Detail from the scroll painting *Old Chengdu* (Lao Chengdu) by Sun Bin, Zhang Youlin, Li Wanchun, Liu Shifu, Xiong Xiaoxiong, Pan Peide, and Xie Kexin (2000). Courtesy of the artists.

MAP 2. Main Streets of Chengdu in the Early Twentieth Century

1. Smaller City (Manchu City)	16. Imperial River	31. East Great Street
2. Green Goat Temple	17. Examination Hall	32. Governor-General's Yamen
3. Two Deities Nunnery	18. Rear Gate Street	33. Liars' Square
4. Fluent and Capable City Gate	19. South River	34. New South City Gate
5. Golden Water River	20. South City Gate	35. Provincial Capital City
6. West City Gate	21. County City God Temple	36. Eastern Parade Ground
7. Western Parade Ground	22. Sun Yat-sen Park	37. Military City Gate
8. Smaller City Park	23. Festival Street	38. Newly Civilized Street
9. West Temple	24. Salt Market Corner	39. Birth Goddess Temple
10. Guanyin Temple	25. Education Circuit Intendant Street	40. Prefecture City God Temple
11. Fu River	26. Coolie Hospital	41. Pen and Copybook Market Street
12. Northern Parade Ground	27. Rising Happiness Street	42. East City Gate
13. North City Gate	28. Warm Spring Street	43. Imperial City
14. Wenshu Temple	29. Center for Promoting Commerce and Industry	
15. Five Baskets Hill	30. Joy Teahouse	

middle 1850s; 516 in the late Qing; and 734 in the Republican period.[21] They were laid out in grid form, with streets running north-south and east-west. Chengdu's narrow streets typically were cluttered with pedestrians, sedan chairs, and wheelbarrows, and were usually shaded by "awnings, mattings, shelters of boughs, big signs, and banners" (see Figures 2.6 and 2.7).

FIGURE 2.5. Nine Arches Bridge. This bridge was a busy traffic hub between the eastern suburbs and the city. Detail from the scroll painting *Old Chengdu* (Lao Chengdu) by Sun Bin, Zhang Youlin, Li Wanchun, Liu Shifu, Xiong Xiaoxiong, Pan Peide, and Xie Kexin (2000). Courtesy of the artists.

FIGURE 2.6. Rising Happiness Street (Fuxing jie) after Widening. This street was widened in the 1920s (see Figure 1.2, which shows it before reconstruction). From this picture we can see that the shops generally had cloth awnings, on which were written the names of the shops as their signs. From CSSN 1927.

FIGURE 2.7. A Shop, Shopkeeper, and Workers. The photograph was taken in Chengdu in 1906 or 1907 by Harrison S. Elliott, who served as the private secretary to the Methodist bishop. Courtesy of Jean Elliott Johnson.

The main streets in the commercial districts were kept clean and featured magnificent shops that were crowded with shoppers, while the small alleys were usually dirty, and no "decent people" went there. In the poorer residential areas, people lived in shabby rooms that were so small that daily activities such as meals, handicraft work, and hobbies had to be conducted outside. These backstreets were dirty, narrow, and crowded with stalls, peddlers, tables, and makeshift stands. Most of the streets were paved with flat stones and had covered sewers. Streets that were unpaved were lined with open ditches, and wheelbarrow traffic moved across a row of stones down the middle. Even the city's busiest commercial districts also featured residential sections with "children, chickens, and pigs playing in the streets." The entire milieu underscores the interplay of residents and the street; even the street names symbolized the unique culture found there (see Map 2).[22]

Commercial Space

Residents in ancient Chinese cities used the street for commercial as well as leisure activities. Thirteenth-century Hangzhou, for example, not only had intense commercial activity but also "boasted a multitude of restaurants, hotels, taverns and teahouses, and houses where there were singing-girls."[23] In the late Imperial period, these economic functions were strengthened in coastal and inland cities across China, and thus in Chengdu, which was the most prosperous city in West China.[24] Economic growth there brought about a rich commercial culture, both in designated commercial areas and on the street.

Street fairs were an especially important commercial activity, and people in ancient Chengdu participated in twelve per year (one per lunar month).[25] Although no evidence remains concerning their origin, street fairs can be traced back at least to the Yuan dynasty (1271–1368), and they are vividly described by Fei Zhu in *Record for Festivals* (Suihua jilipu). Qing Yu, a late-Qing folk poet, wrote twenty-four pieces of bamboo-branch poetry, two for each fair, describing these public celebrations. There was little break between fairs, reflecting the vitality of both commerce and culture. As one folk poem observed, "When the Lantern Festival has not ended, the Flower Fair is already underway."[26] The Flower Fair, held each spring at the Green Goat Temple, was the most popular, attracting crowds that were "as many as ants" (see Map 3). Pedestrians, horse carts, and sedan chairs passed in an endless stream along the Brocade River (Jinjiang), and several hundred shops sold a wide variety of exotic flowers, rare herbs, plants, and birds.

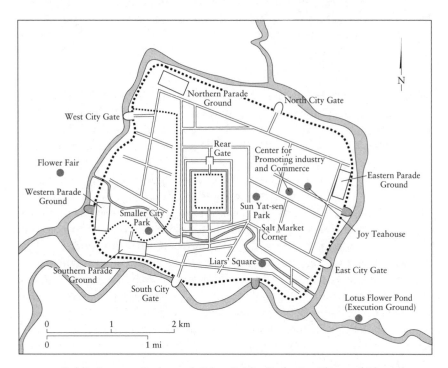

MAP 3. Public Squares, Parks, and Other Public Gathering Places of Chengdu, 1870–1930

FIGURE 2.8. A Farmers' Market on the Street. This photograph was taken by the author in October 2001 on Buddhist Monks Street (Heshang jie), a small alley behind the Great Benevolent Temple (Daci si). Chengdu residents today still use the street as their market. We can see that "bicycle stalls" that sell vegetables as well as a butcher are doing their business just in front of residential houses. The sign at the left says "Curing Ergot."

Women in particular enjoyed the Flower Fair. A folk poem describes how one woman rose at dawn on the opening day and urged her husband to buy more lotus flowers while she dressed and put on her makeup. The Flower Fair also was a market for other kinds of merchandise, which were "piled as high as a mountain."[27]

In addition to these special occasions, Chengdu residents adopted the streets as their regular markets (see Figure 2.8). Merchants and petty peddlers sold their goods on the street without restriction. Streets came to specialize in certain goods, becoming noted for selling salt, fish, pottery, cotton, vegetables, cattle, pigs, fruits, flowers, firewood, or other products. As a foreign traveler wrote, "different trades occupy their own particular quarter. Certain streets are devoted to carpentry in all its branches, boot-shops, shops devoted to horn-ware, skins and furs, embroideries, second-hand clothes shop, silk goods, foreign goods, and so forth."[28] This specialization is reflected in the street names still in use: Salt Market Corner (Yanshi kou), Jewelry Market Street (Zhushi jie), Geese Market Alley (Eshi xiang), Mule and Horse Market (Luomashi), and Cotton Street (Mianhua jie). Most vendors peddled their goods out of stalls, either "moving stalls," "sitting stalls," or "ground stalls."[29] As soon as night began to fall and traffic became lighter, some streets became locations for bustling "night markets"[30] (see Map 4). In the early twentieth century, these markets were found as far as Horse Riding Street (Zouma jie), Green Stone Bridge (Qingshi qiao), and East Imperial Street (Dongyu jie). As might be imagined, this activity influenced residents' nightlife; beginning in the early 1900s, shops that previously closed after sunset extended their hours of operation. This activity, however, attracted "unscrupulous merchants" who sold counterfeit goods and people who engaged in criminal mischief such as stealing, cutting the queues of unsuspecting men, and snatching hats.[31]

The streets became workshops as well as markets. At street corners and on sidewalks, artisans made products to be sold on the spot. Residential streets behind the busy commercial areas became places for production. Although "homes alone fill the streets and come to the front" along these small streets, in every home "something is manufactured for sale." Again, the names of some streets reflect the workshops found there, such as Summer Sock Street (Shuwa jie) and Red Cloth Street (Hongbu jie). On Red Cloth Street, for example, "the voice of reeling machines is like wind blowing and rain falling." A foreign visitor also noticed that silk-weaving was the "great industry" in Chengdu, with "hundreds of looms being in use."

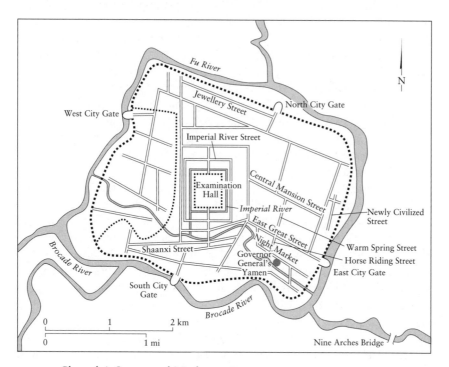

MAP 4. Chengdu's Streets and Markets, 1870–1930

Gauze Hat Street (Shamao jie) had both hat shops and workshops that sold what they produced.[32] In these workshops,

women wind cotton, yarn, thread, or silk; they embroider, weave, sew, make toys, incense sticks, flowers, or funeral money. Men make mats, tubs, buckets, baskets, or feather dusters, weave cloth, mats, or embroider scrolls or banners, shape iron, brass, or silver tools or trinkets, or work with the women on the projects they have in hand. Children down to six or eight years old often help at something—reeling yarn, sorting feathers, smoothing wood, mixing or grinding incense power, or any other little thing their unskilled hands can do. The products of these home activities are shouldered by some member of the family and peddled, or are taken out to a store on a more frequented street.[33]

Although Western goods entered Chinese markets in the late nineteenth century, local goods still dominated in Chengdu, and "most articles of Chinese manufacture are exposed at the shop fronts." Furthermore, the organizations that facilitated Chengdu commercial services, including "posts, banks, and systems of transferring money," were "all solely Chinese."[34]

Increased use of the street and public space resulted in the development of a consumer culture, as seen in the shop signs, store decorations, and displays. It also is found in the relationship between shop owners and customers, who worshiped the God of Wealth, in the performances of craftsmen, and even in the introduction of a language of commerce.[35] This burgeoning commercial culture never failed to impress visitors. At the end of the nineteenth century, a French tourist described Chengdu: "The streets are broad, with pedestrian paths like the big roads in Shanghai. All stores, such as those dealing in silk and satin, jewelry, local banks, china, and antiques, are decorated magnificently, presenting an unexpected vista. . . . Guangdong, Hankou, Chongqing, and Beijing cannot match it. Among the urban landscapes I have seen, that of Chengdu is the best."[36] At almost the same time, Isabella Bird wrote, "The city has wide, well-paved streets, crossing each other at right angles, and the handsome shops make far more display than is usual in China, the jewelers' shops specially, with their fine work in filigree silver, and even rich silk brocades are seen gleaming in the shadow in the handsome silk shops."[37] This commercial culture reflected religious practice as well as economic prosperity and social tradition; each shop had an altar to the God of Wealth, the object of worship by all shop employees each morning and evening. The shops also reflected local culture. Ernest Wilson noted that "to wander through the streets noting the varied industries carried on is a liberal education in Chinese ways of doing things." The shop signs, "lacquered and gilded, hang vertically downwards, and proclaim in their large artistic characters the titles of the shops and the wares on sale."[38]

The development of commerce created East Great Street, Chengdu's most prosperous area (see Figure 2.9). A Japanese tourist was full of praise for

FIGURE 2.9. East Great Street (Dongdajie). We can see a funeral procession on the street. Detail from scroll painting *Old Chengdu* (Lao Chengdu) by Sun Bin, Zhang Youlin, Li Wanchun, Liu Shifu, Xiong Xiaoxiong, Pan Peide, and Xie Kexin (2000). Courtesy of the artists.

the street, noting that "shops are big, wide, high, and splendid. The long and short shop signs and boards are shining. . . . The size of the shops is like those in Beijing but they are cleaner."[39] A Westerner described what he saw when he entered Chengdu from the East City Gate in 1892:

To walk up the Great East Street [East Great Street], with its shining lacquered counters, and its splendid display of merchandise, to behold the prosperity and apparent contentment of the people, to slowly realize that in this far western city there was a street incomparably more modern in its cleanliness, width, and general appearance than any street in any Chinese city that had been visited in the long journey up the Yangtze, gave rise to emotions not easily described.[40]

East Great Street still prospered a generation later. In the 1920s, a Japanese visitor described it in similar terms but added "modern factors." From the East City Gate, he first came upon the broad street, "the most prosperous street in Chengdu, as wide as over ten rooms," where uniformed men directed traffic, and traffic signs posted on trees said "pedestrians keep right."[41]

By all accounts, local officials had little control of fairs, markets, peddlers, and shops before the 1900s. When it was time for a fair, for example, vendors would congregate on the streets to attract customers, and these areas became the focal point for each fair. Because the streets were beyond official control and were shared by everyone, residents tried to exploit them as much as possible, resulting in an ongoing struggle between established merchants and street hawkers. Shop owners constantly tried to expand their limited space by adding signs, banners, stalls, and tables. Huge signs and banners—described as "big and strange"—were strung crosswise from one side of the street to the other, so densely that one covered another.[42] This scene became part of the city's landscape and commercial culture. Despite their encroachment, merchants maintained a tradition of mutual cooperation with their competitors on the street. As one observer pointed out, "Tens of thousands of merchants gather at the markets and all shops look splendid. As soon as the weather gets hot after spring, all shops contribute money to build awnings to shield themselves from the sunshine."[43] A photograph from the 1920s shows a length of awnings on which were written the names of shops (see Figure 2.6).

Everyday Space

Homes in Chengdu provided easy access to the street. Unlike early modern European cities such as Genoa, Paris, and Edinburgh, which grew "vertically" and where houses were built "with five, six, eight and even ten storeys,"[44] in Chengdu homes were typically Chinese in that they were one or two stories. The close proximity of Chengdu homes to the street facilitated the encroachment of the commercial into everyday life. Many residents lived in close proximity to, but not actually in, the "shop houses" or "street houses" that lined the commercial districts.[45] They did not have to travel far to buy items for everyday use; most daily goods were sold in stalls just off their doorsteps and sidewalks. "The sides of the Lane," one foreign sojourner described, "[had] small stalls in front of the closed shops, dimly lit by the smoky glow of rape-seed oil lamps. Oranges and peanuts in neat little piles, cigarettes in pairs and single cheroots were offered for sale, also purses and knick-knacks and bright metal frames, their tawdriness hidden in the gloom."[46]

City dwellers also turned to the street for everyday activities. Homes were built in close proximity to the street, and from this developed the close connection to street life.[47] Chengdu residents had three types of homes: walled compounds (*gongguan*), poor houses (*loushi*), and street houses (*pufu* or *pumian*). The walled compounds, usually found in the north and south of the city, were guarded by gatekeepers and typically were occupied by rich and big families, as described in Ba Jin's *Family* (*Jia*). They could also be rented to several families; such compounds were called "big, multi-household enclosures" (*dazayuan*). The homes of the poor were scattered throughout the city, but most were concentrated in the western part of downtown. Street houses were dwellings on either side of the street and were either used as domiciles or rented to shops, as was common in the eastern part of the city.[48]

People who lived in street houses conducted many of their daily activities at their doorways or on the sidewalk and street just outside (see Figure 2.10). When they wanted to meet their neighbors, people simply walked to the door and talked across the threshold. For any matter, whether routine or emergency, they could quickly solicit help from their neighbors. Borrowing

FIGURE 2.10. A Woman Spinning. Commoner women in Chengdu liked to do their work sitting in their doorways; there they could use daylight (it was usually quite dim inside their houses) as well as chat with neighbors. From Davidson and Mason 1905: 75.

or returning common household goods occurred routinely. If residents felt bored, they could simply go outdoors to have a conversation with their neighbors. However, privacy was nonexistent. Doors that faced the street were always kept open to allow sunlight and fresh air into the simple and crude rooms, as well as the glances of curious passersby. Residents did not feel bothered by the peddlers or itinerant artisans who came to the door to ask for business. Residents simply stepped outside to the street stalls, teahouses, neighborhood stores, and barbershops, which not only provided

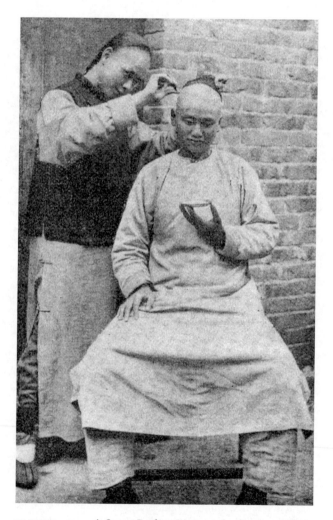

FIGURE 2.11. A Street Barber. Itinerant barbers provided their service on the sidewalks. From Davidson and Mason 1905: 89.

goods and services for everyday life but also served as centers for gossip and other communication. Barbershops, for example, offered "a unique opportunity for endless gossip," according to one foreign visitor. There were more than six hundred barbershops in late-Qing Chengdu (see Figure 2.11).[49]

Townspeople also liked to gather at markets, public squares, the ends of bridges, the front of temples, and street corners in search of amusement. There was no restriction of use for ordinary people, whether residents or outsiders.[50] As a folk poem described, residents were often "Going to the Peaceful and Fluent Bridge (Anshun qiao) to watch the decorated and colorful boats and visit the Wuhou Temple (Wuhou ci) for fortune-telling." Thus, even those who lacked access to formal entertainment could gather with friends and go to the "Three Arches Bridge (Sandong qiao) and watch the river flowing under the bridge." Activities such as cockfighting, cricket fighting, and various children's games often were held in public places. Cricket fighting was most popular during the eighth lunar month, when street peddlers sold rice-stem cages containing crickets and pumpkin flowers and children eagerly urged their parents to buy them. "People in various trades" gathered in the Liars' Square (Chehuang ba) near the New South City Gate (Xin nanmen) (see Map 3), which was very much like Sanbuguan ("three who-cares") in Tianjin and Tianqiao in Beijing.[51] Visitors and residents alike used public squares for various activities. The broad areas in front of temples often became public leisure centers, for instance, in front of the White Tower Temple (Baita si), Wuhou Temple, and Thunder Deity Temple (Leishen miao). Commoners liked attending parties and drinking and eating in teahouses, restaurants, and wine shops, where they could also enjoy performances by singers and dancers, especially during holidays.[52]

The local government did not even exert its power over the military-exercise squares—"parade grounds" (*jiaochang*)—located in the eastern, southern, western, and northern parts of Chengdu (see Map 3). Residents could use these spaces at any time except during troop drills. This nominal military presence does not seem to have bothered Chengdu residents much; the Japanese traveler Yamakawa Hayamizu found an interesting contrast on one street, where soldiers engaged in intensive archery and horsemanship drills on one side and civilians lived in leisure on the other. The Western Parade Ground was used by bannermen and the Eastern Parade Ground by Han soldiers. Residents would know the annual troop review was imminent when soldiers with bows, arrows, and powder-guns appeared in the streets. The garrison in the Manchu City always drew considerable attention and was depicted in several bamboo-branch poems. One describes the scene: "Barracks stand at the east of the city and willow trees are planted and surround the Eastern Parade Ground. Early in the morning, the desolate voice of the military bugle can be heard." Military drills took place regularly even during peacetime, and "a magnificent scene can be seen when cannons fire."

Once a year, the parade grounds were the site of the provincial military examination. The rest of the time they were the city dwellers' playgrounds, as seen in this folk poem describing the Eastern Parade Ground in the Qing period: "The annual troop review is no sooner over than kites are flown there. People enjoy the cool breeze in the summer, eating melons, and drinking tea, chatting during sunset at the front of the ground."[53]

The streets served as children's playgrounds as well. In spring, boys gathered at the Eastern Parade Ground to compete with their kites, which often depicted beautiful women or animals such as horses and goats. People considered it "a special treat to watch a fighting kite in action."[54] Children also had fun interacting with craftsmen, peddlers, and folk performers. Children flocked to shows with puppets or monkeys, and also loved to see peep shows, drawings of long-ago battles, pictures of foreign lands and illustrations from foreign magazines, or even pornographic pictures. These activities, of course, also attracted adults.[55] Children, however, were taught to avoid the foreigners ("overseas people") they occasionally encountered. In the late Qing, suspicious parents immediately took their children inside when foreigners entered a street. Visitors often saw children "with red crosses on green patches stitched on the back of their clothing, this precaution being taken in the belief that foreigners respect the cross too much to do any harm to children wearing the emblem." Clearly, this behavior reflected both Chengdu residents' fear of foreigners and also the antiforeign sentiment of the period. Prior to the 1911 Revolution, the governor-general of Sichuan sent a note to the British consul general expressing concern over the matter of children wearing the red crosses, and promised to institute measures to avert trouble.[56]

The Street Theater.   Chengdu streets often were used as a stage for theatrical performances, attracting large audiences for a low price. Some itinerant troupes did not even seek a real stage, preferring to perform in an open space surrounded by spectators. Local operas were the most popular entertainment. These were performed "along the streets" (*yanjie yanxi*) in the second lunar month, giving them the name "spring stage operas" (*chuntai xi*); they were also known as "spring operas" (*chunxi*) or "flower lanterns" (*huadeng*). Communities, neighborhoods, and guilds raised money and organized these activities. Anyone who wanted to find the operas just followed the sounds of gongs and drums and the throngs of spectators. As one poet described, "Ceremonies were held in Festival Street (Huifu), located north of Blue Cloud Nunnery (Qingyun an) and east of Drum Tower (Gulou), where nothing could draw commoners' attention but the songs and dances." People stood or sat along both sides of the streets watching these performances, although some thought that the men in the audience paid more attention to the women in the audience than to the unfolding drama. Many local operas were shown in front of temples, guilds, and native association halls that had permanent stages, called "ten-thousand-year stages" (*wann-ian tai*), where ceremonies were held throughout the year. Local residents called such performances "yard operas" (*baba xi*), because spectators stood or sat on their own stools or benches in the squares or courtyards to watch. Perhaps the claim that "a thousand operas could be seen within a year" was only a slight exaggeration. The spring operas attracted children as well as adults; in fact, one poet complained that children spent too much time watching operas rather than studying.[57]

The themes of local operas usually were romantic love, adventure, and the supernatural, as well as historical tales of great heroes and beauties. Local authorities rarely interrupted the performances. For instance, there was *Broken Silver Bottle* (Suiyinping), a love story about a general and his servant girl during the time Zhang Xianzhong, one of the most important leaders of the late-Ming rebellion, captured Chengdu. These local operas imbued their audiences with orthodox Confucian ideals of loyalty, filial piety, and chastity, influencing the attitudes of the lower classes to such a degree that, as Barbara Ward concluded, "the theater was the literal embodiment of Chinese culture and values" and "a superbly successful teacher." Although the government exerted more control over local operas in major cities than in rural areas, elites in Chengdu were unable to manipulate local operas that contained non-orthodox ideology.[58] As Johnson observed regarding the opera *Mulian* in Shanxi, the opera and its surrounding ritual in Chengdu became "the two most important institutions of non-elite community life in traditional China." Operas in Chengdu largely remained civil, although some, like *Mulian*, were thought to be "closely allied" with popular cults. *Mulian*, thought to "get rid of evils" and prevent "cases of murder," was performed in Chengdu in the second lunar month of every year, in front of the County City God Temple outside the North City Gate.[59]

While many kinds of regional operas were performed in Shanghai because of "the lack of a common urban cultural style,"[60] Sichuan opera dominated in Chengdu. Still, culture from other regions was not unknown in Chengdu; immigrants brought their local operas to the city. For example, when construction of a guildhall was complete or a guild holiday came, the guild would hire Buddhist monks to perform dedication rituals and hold performances of local operas. The Shaanxi Guild was known for its opera, in which "folk songs of Shaanxi are so attractive." The audience would sit on benches or stools to watch the performance, while "the sounds of exploding firecrackers and boisterous people would rise and fall." Each guild theater had its own protocol. The Shaanxi Guild, for example, valued punctuality. If a troupe did not begin its performance when the firecracker signaling show time went off, it would no longer be allowed to perform there.[61]

In addition to use of the street as a real stage for formal organized performances, the street also served as the setting for what some scholars call "street theater," activities associated with everyday life, recreation, and even political protest, reflecting a community's "social drama." This social drama displayed the relationship between urban commoners and public space and between them and street culture. To an external observer, the people on the street— and their expressions, language, gestures, styles of clothing—provided an endless real-life drama. Formal performances exploited the drama of the street by incorporating existing structures and audience members. As David Johnson's study of the opera *Mulian* demonstrates, the extension of operas into the streets or fields made the characters seem even more real to audiences.[62] The streets became a part of the setting, drawing audience members into the action.

The Socialized Space: Teahouses

Aside from the street, the teahouse was probably the most frequent gathering place in Chengdu. Drinking tea in teahouses had become a cherished social custom in nineteenth-century Chengdu, and little official power was exerted there before the 1900s.[63] As a local proverb said, "half of Chengdu people go to teahouses routinely." If a Chengdu native wrote about the city, the teahouses would nearly always be mentioned. Much of the well-known historical novel *The Great Wave* (Dabo) by Li Jieren took place in teahouses. Similarly, the remarkable native novelist Sha Ding wrote a famous short story, "In the Fragrant Chamber Teahouse" (*Zai Qixiangju chaguan li*), largely based on his own experience. The story was set in a small market town near Chengdu. He claimed, "there is no life if no teahouses, which has been proven accurate in a small market town of Sichuan."[64] Thus, the teahouse was a microcosm of Chengdu society, combining commercial and everyday space. Understanding the teahouse's expansive social, cultural, and political roles can aid greatly in understanding Chengdu society in general.

Many travelers believed that Chengdu surpassed all other cities in China in the number of teahouses. There were 454 teahouses in 1909–10 and more than 620 by 1931.[65] Teahouses were so important in Chengdu daily life that Japanese investigators even linked teahouses to the city's prosperity. When modern authors write about the "tea drinkers" (*chake*, literally "tea guests") of Chengdu, they note that its residents scorn the tea-drinking customs found elsewhere. Those in Chengdu consider themselves to be uniquely qualified to be called true tea drinkers, and Sichuan alone as a true "Kingdom of Tea" (*chaguo*). Certainly, as Sichuan was the birthplace of tea production and tea drinking, the Sichuanese are deservedly proud. Their teahouses, teahouse culture, and teahouse life are well known throughout China. A writer comparing the teahouses in Chengdu with those in North and South China found that "northerners are not as interested in tea as the

Sichuanese." Guangdong had teahouses, too, but "they are for the bourgeois and are not popularized like those of Sichuan." Shu Xincheng observed that in Nanjing people went to teahouses only in the morning, unlike Chengdu, whose natives spent the entire day there.[66]

The leisure business served all kinds of customers, whatever their economic status; leisure was an entitlement of the working class as well as high society.[67] The teahouses of Chengdu were in many ways similar to the coffeehouses, taverns, and saloons of the West. In the Hankou teahouses as described by William Rowe, "All of them offered a functional equivalent to the coffeehouses of Islamic and early modern European cities: one did not go to a teahouse to seek privacy, but deliberately to enjoy good talk."[68] Like the coffeehouses, taverns, and saloons of early modern European and American cities, teahouses in Chengdu functioned as far more than mere locations for leisure. If anything, the social and cultural roles of Chengdu teahouses seem even more complex than those of comparable institutions in the West. They served as places of public leisure, recreation, and entertainment, but also as work sites and arenas for local politics.

The Making of a Teahouse.   Chengdu, as a cultural and commercial hub, needed a convenient and comfortable public space for various activities, and the teahouse filled this niche.[69] The reasons for the large number of teahouses and teahouse-goers in Chengdu also related to its geographic location. The small paths across the Chengdu plain required human-powered transportation, and the wheelbarrow pullers, sedan-chair carriers, and other coolies needed places to rest. The quality of the drinking water itself probably also contributed to the growth of teahouses. High in alkali, the well water in Chengdu tasted bitter, so water carriers had to carry drinking water from the main river. Four Chinese characters, *"He Shui Xiang Cha"* (fragrant tea from river water), appeared on almost every teahouse sign because "nobody would patronize teahouses that used well water." It was difficult for the average family to get boiled drinking water, and, to conserve firewood, they would buy boiled or hot water from teahouses for two *wen* per kettle.[70] A traveler visiting Chengdu in 1935 found that many families did not set a fire during the day, preferring to frequent restaurants and teahouses. "It is a daily fact of life for every person in Chengdu that he goes to a teahouse after a meal in the restaurant." An elderly Chengdu resident in the Joy (Yuelai) Teahouse related why residents liked to have tea at a teahouse instead of staying at home: they preferred "newly boiled water," which was difficult for commoners to obtain. Teahouses also sold hot water and helped concoct medicinal herbs and stew meat at a small fee, all of which made daily life more convenient.[71]

To open a teahouse was, of course, a commercial activity aimed at earning a profit, and a unique way of opening one had been developed in Chengdu.

Generally, this endeavor did not require much capital, because the basics of tables, chairs, tea utensils, and a room did not cost much. In 1937, for example, 457 teahouses had a total capital of 58,400 *yuan*, averaging only about 120 *yuan* per teahouse.[72] Before opening for business, the keeper usually would rent out the toilet to a human-waste collector and a corner of the room to a barber; he would also receive deposits from a water-pipe man and a hot-towel man.[73] These prepayments would be enough to pay the deposit for rent and other start-up costs. A proprietor, it was said, could open a teahouse "without any capital if he had a good plan." The people who invested could conduct their business in the teahouse, but those who had not invested were usually not allowed to make a living there. A local newspaper reported that people frequently opened teahouses in this manner, but in at least one case a woman ran away after she collected the necessary start-up money. Keepers sometimes even asked newspaper sellers, shoe polishers, and petty peddlers to invest. One source, however, gave a different story: keepers usually did not interrupt vendors' comings and goings because they helped business. Peddlers sometimes would act on behalf of the teahouse if called upon, though they were under no obligation to do so.[74] These stories indicate that individual policies varied regarding the use of space. The process of opening a teahouse, and in particular the way of gathering capital, provides evidence of the entrepreneurship of Chengdu people, who would combine their capital for mutual benefit.

Some businesses, such as butcher shops and small restaurants, had a close economic relationship with teahouses, often as investors. In late-nineteenth- and early-twentieth-century Chengdu, ordinary families generally had meat only on special occasions. Those who were able to purchase meat often liked to drink a cup of tea before heading home. One can imagine the scene as the buyer savored his tea and relaxed a bit while contemplating a delicious meal to come. People also liked to drink a cup of tea after a meal or to eat something while drinking tea. For convenience, butchers and restaurants usually set up their booths, stalls, or tables immediately outside teahouses. Patrons could even ask their waiter to buy food for them.

The abundance of cheap labor also contributed to the low cost of running a teahouse. Teahouse waiters' salaries were based on the number of cups of tea sold each day, usually about seven or eight. Although it is clear from this that labor was very cheap during this time, teahouse waiters in fact received "soft" income. Money from selling "plain boiled water," or "water money" (*shuiqian*), belonged entirely to the waiter and often amounted to more than his regular wage. Stove keepers also could supplement their daily wages through "fire money" (*huoqian*), fees for services like stewing meat and concocting medicinal herbs. Less important workers were usually paid monthly, and the teahouse provided them meals.[75]

Compared to other businesses, a teahouse's profits remained quite stable. Business suffered relatively little when the economy was weak. In addition, the turnover on initial investment in teahouses was fast. As a folk poem claimed, "When night markets have slack business and customers ignore shops and stalls, nothing but teahouses enjoy prosperity, and all guests are attentive to story-telling." Proprietors would keep secret how much profit they earned, just as they did their formulas for blending teas.[76] To ensure profits, teahouses used a variety of strategies to attract more patrons, usually extending business hours and providing additional services. Most teahouses were open from five o'clock in the morning to ten o'clock at night, but some opened earlier and closed later. For example, the Prosperous and Peaceful (Taihehen) Teahouse on Cotton Street (Mianhua jie), located in the vegetable market, opened at three o'clock in the morning so that vegetable peddlers could stop by before going to the early market. A teahouse in the Hubei and Hunan Guild (Huguang guan) closed after midnight to accommodate restaurant workers on Warm Spring Road (Chunxi lu) and East Great Street. Teahouses paid more attention to early morning patrons and gave them more tea leaves because almost all of them were regular customers. Occasional teahouse visitors, seen as less discerning, got less. To make the teahouse attractive, the keeper made sure that his bronze kettles were carefully polished bright "like a mirror," and the tables and chairs were always kept neat and clean.[77]

Physical and Cultural Appearance of the Teahouse. Teahouse culture was reflected in their names and locations and the utensils used, as well as in their workers.[78] Sichuanese seldom called teahouses "*chaguan*" but used many other names, such as "*chashe*" (tea societies), "*chayuan*" (tea gardens), "*chating*" (tea halls), "*chalou*" (tea balconies), "*chating*" (tea pavilions), and "*chafang*" (tea rooms). However, the most common name for a Sichuan teahouse was "*chapu*" (tea shop). In fact, "Let's go to the *chapu*" is still heard today.[79] Teahouse owners chose names for their shops carefully; most of them evoked gracefulness or images from literature and nature, such as the Visiting Spring (Fangchun), Leisure and Carefree (Youxian), and Elegant Garden (Keyuan).

Teahouses were placed in locations convenient to customers. Ideally, owners located teahouses in easily accessible spots, such as on a major street or near a bridge; in a place with beautiful scenery, such as a park; or in a commercial or entertainment center, such as a temple fair. Street teahouses often sprang up in open spaces; almost none of them had a "gate," and the side facing the street often had neither wall nor window. When they opened in the morning, workers took the wooden wallboards down one by one, and when it closed, they put the boards back up. Waiters or patrons were free to move tables and chairs onto the sidewalks, where pedestrians and street activities provided entertainment and fodder for conversation. A bamboo-branch poem described the customers near the Flower Fair: "while sitting in the teahouse, they watched visitors of the Flower Fair coming and going through the street." The environment was crucial; teahouses in public gardens and temples enjoyed extraordinary patronage. A teahouse in the Guandi Temple was located by a pond filled with lotus flowers, with a beautiful view of trees and a red bridge. In a new teahouse on Confucian Temple (Wenmiao) Street, "flowers send forth a delicate fragrance in four seasons. At night, it attracts even more visitors, bustling with noise and excitement under bright 'goat-horn lanterns'" (yangjiao deng).[80]

Parks and public gardens in Chengdu usually had high concentrations of teahouses. The River View Tower (Wangjiang lou) became one of the most prominent structures in Chengdu; renowned for its structural beauty, it was the final site viewed by travelers departing the city via the river. Located under the tower was the famous Xue Tao well, named for an extraordinary female poet and courtesan of Chengdu from the Tang dynasty, which provided the city's best source of water. Fittingly, next to the well stood a teahouse. The Smaller City Park alone had four teahouses, all of which stood in the shade of the trees that provided natural beauty. In almost all the parks in Chengdu, the teahouse became the center. One observer even remarked that "the teahouse is crowded, but the playground is empty." The teahouse in the Central City Park occupied most of the north part of the park; the Zhiji Temple Park (Zhijisi gongyuan) seemed to be "one huge teahouse"; and the teahouses in the Smaller City Park occupied the largest space among many other facilities. Some teahouses outside of town also offered scenic views, thus attracting many townspeople.[81]

Most teahouses were located in prosperous commercial areas. The Center for Promoting Commerce and Industry (Quanye chang), established in the late Qing, was the first modern-style commercial center in Chengdu and was always crowded with shoppers and visitors to the famous Joy Teahouse. The Flower Fair had long been the biggest annual gathering of Chengdu's citizens. Every spring, the large open area between the Two Deities Nunnery (Erxian an) and the Green Goat Temple (Qingyang gong) became a huge market and exhibition ground. One source estimated that "there were more than 100 teahouses and wine shops and over 100,000 visitors per day."[82] These teahouses were temporary, dismantled after the fair ended.

People also used teahouses as entertainment centers, the best places for a diverse assortment of performers to make a living. Teahouses vied to host the better performers. Early theaters in Chengdu actually were founded in teahouses. In the beginning, a teahouse merely offered its location for a troupe's performance; later, it became a permanent theater. This differed from Shanghai, where, according to Bryna Goodman, commercial theaters arose out of theaters of native place associations. Because most teahouses faced the street, the sounds of gongs and drums from local operas inevitably drew the attention of pedestrians, some of whom simply watched for free outside. The Elegant Garden (Keyuan) is believed to have been the first theater in Chengdu, organized as a theater in 1906 after being known as the Reciting (Yongni) Teahouse. The Joy Teahouse, a new-style teahouse-cum-theater, was built shortly thereafter. After the Joy Teahouse, the Pleasure Spring (Yichun) and the First (Diyi) Teahouse came successively and faced one another, and when an opera troupe performed in one, the sound of gongs and drums could be heard in the other. This fits the Chinese proverb: "putting on a rival show" (*chang duitaixi*). A newspaper described this kind of rivalry as "a window to see how severe the competition among teahouses is."[83]

The tea settings and furniture used in Sichuan teahouses also symbolized the unique local culture. A tea setting consisted of "three pieces": teacup (*chawan*, literally "tea bowl" because it looks like a bowl), tea lid, and saucer (*chachuan*, literally "tea boat" because it looks like a boat). The saucer is used to prevent the cup from scalding the hands and to keep water from spilling; thus, tea in Sichuan teahouses is called "lid-cup tea" (*gaiwan cha*). The tables and chairs in Sichuan teahouses also strongly reflect local culture. "Originally, all tables were placed on the sidewalks with four stools each. No private rooms, no buildings, and no chairs, so no gentlemen went there." Later, smaller square wooden tables and bamboo chairs became popular. Most chairs had backs and armrests that matched the tables and made them more comfortable.[84]

Chengdu's teahouses emerged from the city's particular natural and social conditions and remained free from government interference before the early-twentieth-century reform. For a long time, they welcomed all sorts of people. Of course, teahouse proprietors originated these public gathering places, but it was the clientele—including laborers, petty vendors, and performers—who contributed most significantly to teahouse culture. Such a small public space created an extensive and complicated social stage, deeply imbued with local culture.

Ceremonial Space

Urban public space was an appropriate place for ritual ceremonies, usually street performances, that powerfully expressed local culture and attracted huge audiences. Any individual, social group, or organization could hold an activity in the street without getting permission from local authorities. Street performances that reflected social relations like dramas, parades, and ceremonies developed as significant ways to communicate between different social classes and groups, confirming Clifford Geertz's assertion that "a ritual is not just a pattern of meaning; it is also a form of social interaction." Such an activity required enormous amounts of money, labor, coordination, and communication. A community, as some scholars suggest, used ceremonies to develop constructs of local solidarity and social order. A ritual ceremony could also express a lineage's dominance over a local community or a symbiotic relationship between local society and national culture.[85] Some ritual ceremonies had multiple functions, while others served a specific purpose; some reflected religious truth, while others were merely entertainment; some had economic functions, while others prevented diseases; some related to natural conditions and the environment, while others celebrated folk customs. Public ceremonies were one of the most powerful tools for fostering identity among Chengdu people.

All ritual ceremonies were based on one of three cohorts: families or lineages, streets or neighborhoods, or communities. These categories, especially the last two, often overlapped. For example, a family-based ceremony could include neighbors, while a neighborhood ceremony could include many family-based rituals. In addition, these activities usually were open to strangers and poor people, even if organized by an upper-class family. Thus, beggars often could be found at a rich family's celebration, enjoying the food and shows, or receiving gifts and even money. Indeed, organizers used gongs and drums to attract as many participants as possible; the more participants, the more successful the event. These activities also left open the possibility of competition between families, streets, and communities to show off wealth, reputation, and organizational prowess.

Family- or Lineage-Based Ceremonies. Any family or clan could freely occupy the street or other public arena, and this became accepted social custom. Activities such as wedding processions, funerals, and even celebrations of a childbirth were common; families essentially transformed private ceremonies into public ones by performing them in public places. A typical funeral procession is described this way:

The first group carried various banners, followed by more than ten Buddhist monks who wore Buddhist robes and carried burning incense. After them, the members of the Filial Piety and Righteous Society (*Xiaoyi hui*) performed on gongs and drums. Clusters of people followed, wearing the costumes and makeup of characters from local operas. Duty Ghost (*zhiri gongcao*) wore a strange costume and the tail feathers of pheasants. Chicken-leg Deity (*jijiao shen*) had a ferocious appearance that resembled the statue in the City God Temple. The patron deity (*tudi shen*) and his wife walked along shoulder to shoulder. The patron deity wore a sackcloth gown that made him look both poor and scholarly and his wife resembled a country-woman, with little makeup and dark eyebrows. Following them were several men carrying a coffin, with two virgin boys and two virgin girls walking on each side. The boys wore formal clothes with large collars and the girls wore heavy and colorful makeup and held paper parasols.[86]

These activities were intended to summon ghosts, deities, and human beings, based on local operas and folk culture.[87] In Chengdu, any funeral would include Buddhist monks or Daoist priests, and the procession usually attracted large crowds of spectators.[88] The ritual of death is a good example of the issues from which individual households solicited the attention and participation of the larger community.

Other rituals were organized for families and the lineage at large. The Ghost Festival held on the fifteenth day of the seventh lunar month drew families from throughout Chengdu to temples for celebrations that lasted until midnight. Pure Brightness Day, however, was the most important festival commemorating the departed; residents held a ceremony before their ancestral altars or went to sweep graveyards. When Arthur Wolf studied the relationship of worshiping rituals between deities, ancestors, and ghosts, he pointed out that deity worship related to the community and centered on temples; ancestral worship related to lineage and focused on the shrine; and ghost worship related to both community and lineage. Therefore, a death ritual such as the funeral procession described above actually reflected a complex interaction of the three.[89]

Families also celebrated the Abstaining from Meat Festival (*chi jiuhuang-zhai*, literally "eating nine emperors' diet") on the ninth day of the ninth month, when all households, rich and poor, prayed and conducted ceremonies designed to avert disaster and attract happiness. Restaurants and itinerant kitchens pasted yellow paper couplets on stoves, pans, and bowls. During these nine days (or, in some cases, fourteen to twenty days) of abstaining from meat, households burned yellow candles to which they bowed. Many households pasted appropriate matched couplets on their doors. From a late Qing drawing, we can see such a couplet, which reads, "Nine heavens, nine emperors, nine days of abstaining from meat; ten numbers, ten gods, ten grains for making a circle."[90]

Celebration of the Chinese New Year, or Spring Festival, which could also be conducted at multiple levels (by family, neighborhood, and community), became the foremost occasion for the display of street culture.[91] Townspeople celebrated the Chinese New Year from the first to the fifteenth days of the first lunar month. As the holiday approached, the streets assumed a new appearance, and petty traders set up special stalls on sidewalks or market places, selling door-gods, ancestral hall bells, "joy cash" (*xiqian*), sticks of incense, and various other items used in worship.[92] Like festivals in the West, the Chinese New Year provided "the craftsmen with the opportunity to document the antiquity of their crafts and the usefulness of their labors." The decoration of houses and shops brought a holiday atmosphere to the city. Spring Festival couplets and "sacred edicts" (*shengyu*) were pasted on all doors (see Figure 2.12); "every door has been made like new, cleaned of old dust, and 'joy cash,' which are five red papers, is posted on the

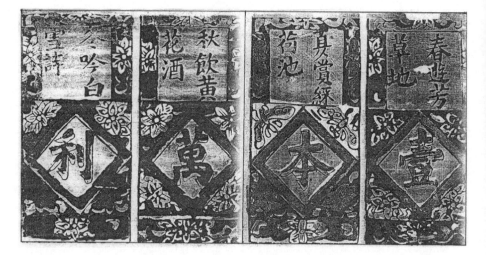

FIGURE 2.12. An Example of Mottoes. They were pasted on the doors at the Chinese New Year to express good wishes. From the right, the large characters read: "One piece of capital, ten thousand profits." The smaller characters above them are couplets, which read (from the right): "Touring on fragrant grassland in spring, enjoying the scenery by a lotus pond in summer, drinking chrysanthemum wine in autumn, reciting poetry on the white snow in winter." From Graham 1927: 154.

door." According to one account, the five "joy door cash" papers were torn down and burned before the gods to ensure the family's prosperity for the rest of the year. Even the doors of poor families reflected "the coming of a new spring."[93] People on the street were joyous; as one missionary observed:

In the streets all is smiles and swaying of wide sleeves, passersby every where stopping and saluting. Servants decked out in silk gowns and red tasseled caps hurry by with great card folders to present their masters' compliments, shopmen saunter along leading their pride, a son bangled and bedecked with tassels, lions and rows of golden Buddhas, while possibly most prominent of all, little girls in twos and threes and groups of many go past gaily in silks, pink powder, hair knotted to one side and quite evidently feeling fairy-like in their fluttering fringes.[94]

Commoners engaged in many outdoor activities during the Chinese New Year, when spring arrived on the banks of the Brocade River. Well-dressed men and women gathered on the streets to give customary Chinese New Year's greetings to each other. Firecrackers became associated with the holiday; as a folk poem remarked, "When firecrackers go off on street corners, it is the time when the old matched couplets on the doors need to be replaced with new ones." On the first day of the Chinese New Year, relatives and friends exchanged blessings by attaching their cards on the recipient's door, eventually covering it with many colorful greetings. After the fifteenth day of the first lunar month, residents went to the southern suburb to watch the ceremony of "Welcoming Happy God" (*ying xishen*). The Chinese New Year was a time of great joy for children, who "play games and strike drums and gongs" (see Figure 2.13). Folk performers enjoyed their best business on these days; "ballad singing (*qingchang*) competed with dulcimer performing, while vaudeville was performed everywhere. Townspeople could hear the 'lotus flower chanting' on the streets, and they especially favored the program, *Crying in Early Morning* (Ku wugeng), performed by Liao Er." After dark on the evening of the fifteenth, many participated in the tradition of stealing vegetables from neighbors' gardens and cooking them for supper.[95]

All family businesses closed on the last day of the year, and when they would reopen depended on the merchants' financial situation or on the "selection of lucky day." Some small shops opened on the first day of the first month, but many opened after the fifth, and some even after the fifteenth. When shops reopened, the God of Wealth was worshiped, firecrackers lit, and the signboards draped with red silk or calico. Some large shops took

FIGURE 2.13. Playing *Xianghuang*. The *xianghuang* was a popular toy for children in China until the 1960s. Today it can be seen only in acrobatic shows. The inscription reads, "*Xianghuang* are made of bamboo, which buzzes against a rope. Children eagerly buy them during the Chinese New Year. Beginning on the sixteenth day of the twelfth lunar month, toymakers from the surrounding areas rush into the city to sell such toys." From CDTL 3: 116.

down "one shutter a day" until the shop was "fully opened." Taking advantage of the situation, street vendors had their busiest days of the year, hawking clothing, food, fruits, nuts, candies, masks from local dramas, toys, and pictures. Folk artists and firecracker-makers took advantage of the opportunity to show off their wares and demonstrate their skills.[96] Thus, the Chinese New Year became an important expression of urban prosperity.

The celebration of festivals was always combined with religious ritual. As the Chinese New Year approached, on the twenty-fourth day of the twelfth lunar month, Chengdu people worshiped the Kitchen God (see Figure 2.14). They believed that the Kitchen God would go back to Heaven to kowtow to the Emperor of Heaven and return on the eve of the Chinese New Year, when people stayed up all night. People opened their doors early in the morning to "welcome the Happy God (*xishen*) coming from the East." All shops replaced their old images of Door Gods (*menshen*) with new ones (see Figure 2.15). Inside, shopkeepers swept away the dust to get rid of the past year's misfortunes. "Amongst the requisites, the door gods are the chief," wrote missionary J. Vale, "which were used by all classes of society." The door gods were made of paper, and their shape depended on "the taste or ability of the artist." During the festival, each household offered wine and a chicken at the altar and worshiped at the Patron Deity (*tudi shen*) after bowing before the God of Wealth (*caishen*). Throughout this ritual, "people speak only lucky words, and it is taboo to say any unlucky ones." In the morning of the first day of the new year, shopkeepers opened their doors to "welcome the God of Wealth" (*ying caishen*). These descriptions reflect the integral role of religious life in the celebration of traditional festivals in families.[97]

Street- and Neighborhood-Based Ceremonies. A "street" could be regarded as a physical unit, but the term "neighborhood" is more vague, probably including the people who live in the same vicinity as well as the streets there.[98] Some neighborhoods had their own style of ceremonies, which reflected the customs and cultural background of their residents, who often emigrated from the same native place. In Cattle Market Corner (Niushi kou), for instance, residents played "straw dragons" to prevent diseases. They paraded down the streets and visited the temple and households to worship at temple or family altars and recite fortuitous phrases. In return, the hosts were obligated to offer tea and tobacco. According to one observer, this was a unique way to exorcise diseases.[99]

Some street- and neighborhood-based events served family purposes. One example was the Birth Goddess Festival (*Niangniang hui*), held on the third day of the third lunar month. During the celebration, festival leaders threw small wooden dolls representing boys into the crowd. Those who caught the dolls took them to childless relatives, accompanied by musicians and firecrackers. This was called "sending one a little boy" (*song tongzi*).

FIGURE 2.14. An Example of the Kitchen God and Kitchen Goddess. These depictions were pasted up on the wall or door on the eve of the Chinese New Year. The couplet reads, on the right: "A commander among men"; and on the left, "the god who is the ears and eyes of heaven." From Graham 1927: 158.

The recipients would hold a feast and became "even more excited than if they had really got a baby," it was said. The role of those who participated in the ceremony was simply "sending it to a family, saying some lucky words, and enjoying a banquet." Another report describes the ceremony as local people carrying pumpkins and a colorful miniature pavilion while accompanied by gongs and drums. Sometimes, a similar activity would be held in winter. In one Chinese New Year celebration, a group made a snowman after an unusually heavy snow and carried it with a sign saying "sign of new birth" (*yuzhao huolin*), accompanied by gongs and drums, to a family in their neighborhood. It was called "sending one a snow boy."[100]

Some organized ceremonies were intended to help people overcome fears. Chengdu inhabitants often connected their fate with nature, and any

FIGURE 2.15. Two Examples of the Door God. The image on the left was drawn in the 1920s (Graham 1927: 159). On the right is a contemporary rendering purchased in Chengdu in 1997 by the author. It is nearly identical to that of the 1920s, reflecting the strong continuity of local popular culture.

unexplainable phenomenon could cause panic.[101] During a drought, for instance, a neighborhood might organize a ceremony to pray for rain. Residents of a particular street might erect altars to the dragon that was thought to control rain for that year and also set out a large jar of clean water that contained a willow branch. On occasion, children would dress a dog in men's clothing and carry it through the streets; this was accompanied by great excitement, because, as one proverb said, "if you laugh at a dog, rain will fall" (*xiao gou yao xiayu*).[102] In fact, praying for rain became a customary ceremony even when there was no drought. During summer, praying for rain called for a parade known as "holding a ceremony and praying for water" (*jianjiao qingshui*). This ritual required the mobilization of many people and resources. This is a detailed account:

On Central Mansion Street (Zongfu jie), the sound of gongs and drums was deafening and flags were flying. At the front, people carried several paperboards, with characters "*jianjiao qiufu*" (holding a ceremony for seeking happiness), followed by flag and canopy carriers and musicians. After them, a group of the North Sichuan Gongs and Drums (*Chuanbei luogu*) performed in an over a dozen-*zhang* long shed (one *zhang* = 10.9 feet). A group of costumed people whose faces were painted with five colors followed, dressed in red, unfurling long tongues and wearing white caps. They performed as various creatures, such as "smoking ghosts," "gambling ghosts," "dwarf ghosts," "horse faces," "ox faces," and so on. A more interesting view was that of a man, whose hands were tied in back, and who wore a sign on his back identifying him as a capital-criminal, playing a role in the *Story of Medicine and Tea* (Yaochaji), a traditional local play. A woman rode on a horseback and played Lady Xin Fourteen (Xin Shisi Niangniang), a role in the play *Sending the Bride to Runan Temple* (Runansi songqing guofu) from the famous novel of *Liaozhai* (Strange Stories Written in the Liao Studio). After that, two men played instruments and another two carried lion lanterns. Four small moving stages followed, each depicting a scene from a popular local play. The first was a scene from the *Designing Strategy in the Wine Balcony* (Jiulou sheji) in which a young man played the part of an old man, Yang Xiong, and the other played the young man, Wu Song. The second moving stage displayed a scene from the *Zhou Yuji Defeated in Daizhou* (Zhou Yuji shi Daizhou) of a helmeted warrior and his bodyguard. Then, two people enacted a scene from *Releasing Pei* (Fang Pei). Finally, a Buddhist monk enacted a scene from *Attacking Lung Fluke* (Gong laochong). After the last stage passed by, more than a dozen children in various garments rode by on stout horses. Some had noses painted white; some held red umbrellas; and some carried dragon lanterns. A man with rouge on his cheeks wore a female hairstyle and female clothing, waved a horsetail, jumped back and forth, and caused great laughter from onlookers. Then, a group of people carried "fire boards" (*huopai*), followed by "duty ghosts" (*zhiri gongcao*), who rode horses and were surrounded by burning incense. Behind them, sixteen men carried an open sedan chair, in which a man wearing a yellow helmet and a man wearing yellow armor carried golden whips, with a virgin boy standing at their left and a virgin girl standing at their right. The last group was the men who carried a huge palanquin containing a huge porcelain bottle, with more than ten Daoist priests carrying classic books.[103]

This ceremony visually represented a culture that ordinary people understood and shared. No religious boundaries existed; in fact, the ceremony freely incorporated both Buddhist and Daoist elements. Such ceremonies did not require adherence to a particular religious belief or routine. For example, the ceremony for rain on Along City Wall Street (Shuncheng jie) omitted some of the roles found in the Central Mansion Street ceremony described above but added some new ones such as hunchbacks, blind fortune-tellers, judges of hell, monkeys, and Zhong Kui, a professional ghost hunter found in folk culture.[104] Such ceremonies functioned not only as prayers for rain or religious rituals but also as a form of public entertainment, which always attracted many participants and enormous numbers of spectators.

Community and Social Autonomy

Whereas family- and neighborhood- (or street-) based ceremonies were limited to relatively smaller areas, community-based ceremonies filled a larger space and had more participants. Of course, the groups often overlapped, as previously discussed. The activities of families, neighborhoods (streets), and the community often could not be clearly distinguished, and the concepts of "neighborhood" and "community" were vague, although the former more closely related to physical space, while the latter mainly concerned social space and the people inhabiting it. The activities organized by the neighborhood or community strengthened social relationships among the inhabitants.

In Chinese communities, various voluntary organizations coordinated public ceremonial activities. According to Rubie Watson, ancestral halls in some Chinese cities and villages assumed an important role in the entire community's daily life, but in Chengdu the role of ancestral halls did not expand into the community. Whereas ancestor worship was regarded as the most important family ritual, the worship of gods was the most important ritual for the community. Worship of the gods ordinarily takes two forms: individual and community worship. In the former, people approach the gods as potentially powerful protectors, while in the latter all members of a community participate in a festival, usually annually, to celebrate the god's birthday and ask for protection as well. As a result, god worship becomes a collective activity for a community. According to numerous anthropological studies, worshipers usually presented offerings of an opera and food to the gods.[105] The community or lineage in charge provided opera performances or puppet shows to entertain the gods and residents, reflecting social harmony. In one town in Taiwan during the nineteenth century, for example, gates on the main street defined neighborhoods, and each year a different neighborhood took responsibility for the temple's annual festivals; every household along the street took part in the cult of the deity.[106]

The community in Chengdu, like other remote villages and small towns, was highly autonomous, organized by social groups or local elites rather than by officials. There, the street not only bore traffic, commercial space, and recreational space but also was the "glue" that created neighborhood cohesion. Elites led commoners in various aspects of community life that took place on the street, from holiday celebrations and public hygiene to charitable affairs and road repair. To a certain extent, the physical structure of Chengdu streets promoted this effort. Chengdu was divided into districts, each having an appointed head (lingyi). A "street clerk" (jieban) was in charge of civil affairs, and a patrolman (haicha) took responsibility for security in each subdistrict. Gates were installed at both ends of each street and were closed at night and guarded by a gatekeeper (zhafu) or night watchman hired by the street head.[107] People who lived on the same gated street had a "street bond," regarded each other as "jiefang linju" (close neighbors), and often had mutual-aid relationships. They became so close in everyday life that, as the saying went, "neighbors are dearer than distant relatives."[108]

Many ceremonies and celebrations stemmed from this sense of community, and from their organization and participation, one can better understand the relationship between inhabitants and communities. These events celebrated all sorts of occasions: folk traditions, public entertainments, seasonal holidays, and religious rituals. For example, the Climbing High to Escape Disease Festival (you baibing), held on the sixteenth day of the first lunar month, combined folk tradition and public entertainment in an effort to be protected from disease. Because there were no hills in Chengdu, people climbed the city wall, an event that attracted all kinds of peddlers, especially food vendors and traders of popular patent medicines, and even fortune-tellers. We do not know how the festival originated, but it apparently functioned to foster both socialization and physical exercise, while assuaging people's anxiety about illness.[109]

The Dragon-Boat Race Festival, on the fifth day of the fifth month, was another community celebration that became public entertainment on a large scale. The festival originated from a memorial of Qu Yuan, a great poet and politician of antiquity. During the festival, people hung herbs on their doors to exorcise disease and to entertain themselves. Boats decorated with fanciful dragonheads raced on the river. Young people participated in a contest to catch ducks. Residents also gathered on the Eastern Parade Ground to pelt each other with green plums. According to a missionary's memoir, on the fifth day of the fifth month in 1895, "it was estimated that sixty thousand people had gathered on the Great East Parade Ground [Eastern

Parade Ground] to witness the sport of throwing plums, a sort of sham battle," and women and children in bright colors covered the high slope of the City Wall.[110]

Some celebrations were national in scope, whereas others were known only in Chengdu, reflecting the relationship between local and national culture and the fact that cultural unity and uniqueness coexisted in the city. Some national festivals assumed local characteristics, too; examples are the Chinese New Year, the City God Parading the Street, and Pure Brightness Day. Furthermore, these festivals indicate how the community organized public life and the extent to which its actions were autonomous.

The Celebration of the Chinese New Year. Not only was the Chinese New Year the most important holiday for families, it was also a major community event. On the ninth day of the Chinese New Year, when residents worshiped the Civil God of Wealth (*wen caishen* or *xifu tianguan*), the headmen on each street organized a society and collected subscriptions from all the householders. They built high arches of "white lanterns" (*baiguo deng*), under which the god was worshiped and shadow plays performed; this became one way of beseeching happiness. The heads of the community arranged a banquet for residents and sponsored the performance of lion and dragon lanterns.[111]

During this festival, colorful Chinese New Year lanterns hung in the streets, public squares, and gardens, and as a result, the eve of the fifteenth day of the first lunar month became known as the "Lantern Festival" (*Yuanxiao jie*), even though it was still part of the new year's celebration. During the Lantern Festival, countless beautiful lanterns decorated the city, outlining Chengdu's magnificent landscape. A missionary described the streets at the time: "The city has gone holiday making. Streets are crowded day and night by orderly crowds" to watch the lanterns. "All the principal thoroughfares are roofed in with long strips of pink and red cotton, foreign or native." The festival lanterns became an expression of street culture. They were made of colored silk and paper in all sorts of shapes, such as flowers and figures of men, women, and animals. One was "a very pleasing figure of a deer, made of strings of beads laid over the usual bamboo framework." The lanterns were hung across the streets at intervals of about six or eight feet and also decorated doors and shop fronts. On the main streets there were "at longer intervals large stages set up across the middle of the street, upon which are displayed allegorical figures, set off with many pots of flowers, lamps, candles, and mirrors."[112]

The Lantern Festival attracted countless spectators. A bamboo-branch poem described the picture: "Beautiful and tiny lanterns are bright in the Lantern Festival, and the 'Brocade City' at night is permeated with prosperity. Little innocent and guileless boys and girls are urged to go out and watch firecrackers." A lantern fair was also held as a part of the Lantern Festival in the area of the Prefecture City God Temple and Civil Service Examination Alley (Kejia xiang), where "tens of thousands of candles are lit, accompanied by music. People are so attracted to the lanterns that nobody cares about the bright moon." Many men took this opportunity to watch well-dressed women pass by. As a poet noted, "countless beautiful women appear on the streets and their coquettish voices can be heard everywhere. When red [lanterns] mingle with green [women], we don't know whether the men watch lanterns or watch women."[113]

Traditional "playing dragon lanterns" (*longdeng* or *shaodeng*, literally "burning lanterns") was one of the most exciting public activities at the Lantern Festival (see Figure 2.16). These lanterns were made of long sheets of colored calico with a head and tail attached; the lion was supported and manipulated by two men and the dragon by more than ten. The performance and firecrackers attracted many spectators as the players moved from street to street, collecting money until midnight (see Figure 2.17). This activity often attracted "all residents of the city to come out to watch."[114] In addition to the public show, some rich families also paid for private performances. If the actors performed well, they would be given red sashes to

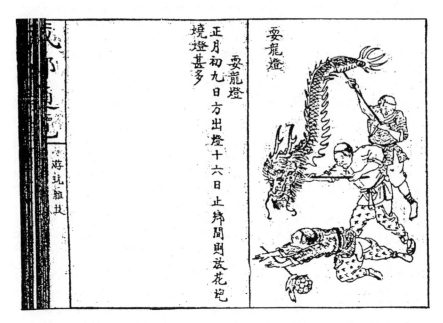

FIGURE 2.16. Playing Dragon Lanterns. The inscription says, "It begins on the ninth day of the first lunar month and ends on the sixteenth day; more people set off firecrackers and light lanterns in the countryside." From CDTL 3: 117.

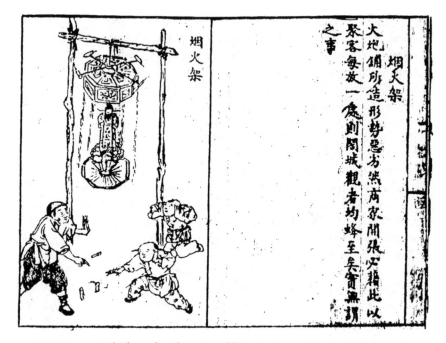

FIGURE 2.17. A Platform for Shooting off Firecrackers. The inscription reads, "Firecracker shops make the dangerous products, but whenever a new shop opens, it will set up firecrackers to draw more people's attention. Such an event is meaningless but often attracts spectators from all over the city." From CDTL 3: 114.

wear as a reward. Ba Jin, in his novel *Family* (Jia), described vividly how dragon-lantern players performed both in the street and in the courtyards of rich families:

To the pounding beat of the drums and cymbals, the dragon began to dance. From head to tail, the dragon consisted of nine sections, made of paper pasted over bamboo frames and painted to resemble scales. Each section contained a lit candle, and was manipulated by a dancer who held it aloft by a bamboo handle. Ahead of the dragon pranced a youth twirling a staff with a big ball of colored paper streamers at one end. The dragon bounded after the ball, rolling on the ground, or wagging its tail or shaking its head as if in great satisfaction, leaping and cavorting like a real dragon, while the beat of cymbals and drums seems to add to its awesomeness.[115]

Ba Jin also described how spectators deliberately tossed firecrackers onto the players' bare arms and shoulders, making them bear the pain of being burned while continuing to perform. Some elites regarded playing dragon lanterns as a "bad custom" because of its unpredictability. Ba Jin criticized the custom through the words of a leading character in his novel: "Do you really think enjoyment should be based on others' pain? Do you think just paying money entitles you to sear a man's flesh?"[116] Such an attitude toward the tradition should come as no surprise because it reflects the trend of intellectuals criticizing folk culture, which spread almost everywhere in elite writings.

The City God Parading the Street. "The City God Parading the Street" (*chenghuang chujia*), during which people carried the statue of the City God while marching down the streets, was a community celebration each spring in which all levels of society, from officials and local elites to ordinary residents and even beggars, participated (see Figure 2.18). One account described the ceremony: "When the city god is parading through streets, tens of thousands of people go out to watch." Simultaneously, a ceremony of "Giving Clothing to Ghosts" would be performed to allow

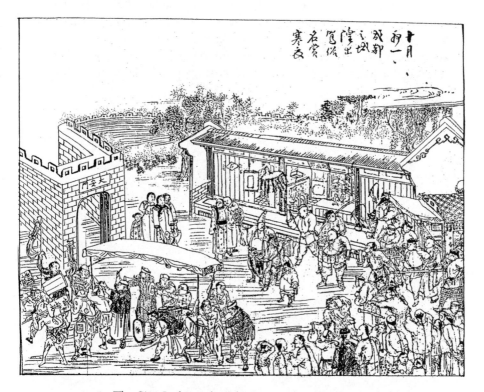

FIGURE 2.18. The City God Parading the Street. This drawing shows not only the spectacle of the ceremony itself but also what the shops, city wall, and city gate looked like. We can see beggars carrying cloth canopies in the parade. (See Chapter 6 for a discussion about beggars' roles in public and private ceremonies.) From TSHB 1909, no. 6.

"solitary ghosts" to "have a happy time." On the first day of the tenth
month, the City God would parade the streets again. The City God temples
(Chenghuang miao) provided large quantities of paper clothing, which were
paraded through the streets and then taken outside the city and burned at
the public burial ground.[117]

Max Weber noticed the importance of religious symbols in Chinese cities.
"As a rule," he found, "these cities had a corresponding religious symbol
standing for the associational cult of the burghers as such," and there was
usually "a city-god or city-saint specifically available to the burghers." Although city god temples, usually found in an administrative center, were
part of life in premodern Chinese cities, not every city worshiped the city
god. For example, Hankou, a major city in central China, had no city god
temple.[118] Chengdu, which combined three levels of administration (provincial, prefecture, and county), thus had three city god temples: the Provincial
Capital City God Temple on West Great Wall Street (Daqiang xijie); the
Prefecture City God Temple on Lower East Great Street (Xia dongdajie);
and the County City God Temple on Winnowing Fan Street (Boji jie) outside the North City Gate (see Map 5). These temples functioned as sites not

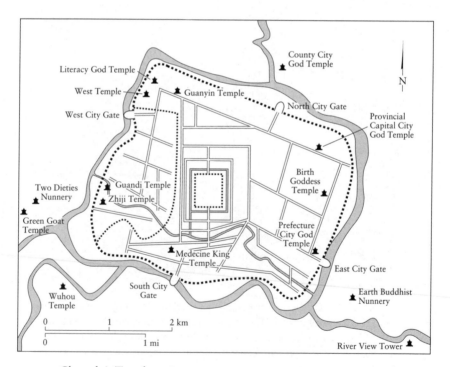

MAP 5. Chengdu's Temples, 1870–1930

only for religious rituals but also for social gatherings and business events. Fortune-tellers, food vendors, and traveling doctors made their livings there.

Urban dwellers regarded the City God as their protector, and local officials supported the cult. David Johnson argued that in small and remote cities, the City God cult experienced less control by officials; however, in the larger cities, where the population was more educated, the cult represented official ideas and became "an expression of ruling class ideology." In Chengdu, although the government and officials participated in the annual City God ceremony, the style of performance and parade more closely resembled the ceremonies of all other popular religions. This activity was organized by the "Association of the City God" (Chenghuang hui), a voluntary organization.[119] The ceremony of the City God functioned more as popular entertainment than as "an expression of ruling class ideology." More accurately, this phenomenon offers support for Johnson's other point: that various people understood city gods differently, depending on region, social group, and culture.

The Pure Brightness Day Festival. The celebration of Pure Brightness Day was probably the strongest indication of community solidarity in Chengdu. Anthropologists have studied the significance of the Pure Brightness Day Festival; according to Myron Cohen's study of North China, participation in this activity emphasized the domain of kinship associations. Rituals were performed in a communal setting, with each local lineage arranged as "Qingming associations" (*Qingming hui*), which combined individual lineages into a collective. In Chengdu, the patron deity association (*qingjiao hui* or *tudi hui*) had a similar function, to organize the worship ceremonies for its own neighborhood patron deity (*tudi*). Leaders were selected from among local residents. These associations were mostly Daoist and were called "thanksgiving societies" by Western missionaries, because they celebrated "a thanksgiving for peace to the neighborhood." The celebration organized by patron deity associations, according to C. K. Yang, provided "a collective symbol" for a local community.[120]

Each spring, before and after Pure Brightness Day, the association raised money from residents in the area and hired Daoist priests to perform ceremonies called *da qingjiao* to ward off the disasters of plague and fire. Although the headmen profited from the money collected, "the people's interest in them is partly owing to the pleasurable excitement of something happening on their street." This ceremony was held for seven days; the deafening clang of gongs and drums could be heard from morning to night. Generally, the residents of several streets shared an altar and associated costs. Residents of wealthy streets would set off fireworks, hire troupes to perform puppet shows or shadow plays on the street, and hold banquets that ostensibly aided in worshiping the patron deity but actually provided entertainment (see Figure 2.19). A bamboo-branch poem described vividly the excitement of such a celebration: "When shadow plays are performed at the front of the Happy and Moral Temple (Fude ci), explosions of firecrackers sound like thunder. The people laugh at the head of the patron deity association because he is drunk."[121]

The patron deity association not only functioned as a ceremonial leader of the community's spiritual life but also played an important role in everyday life. On Pure Brightness Day, the association organized residents for sewer and pond cleaning, which had to be done annually to prevent an overflow of sewage into the streets. While Chengdu's rivers provided convenient transportation routes and beautiful vistas, they also brought frequent floods. Man-made ponds and sluices adjusted drainage and rainfall but had to be frequently cleared of debris. However, after the local government assumed maintenance of the sewer system in the Republican era, the ponds gradually disappeared and sewers became barely functional, apparently as a result of population growth and general ignorance regarding floodwater management.[122]

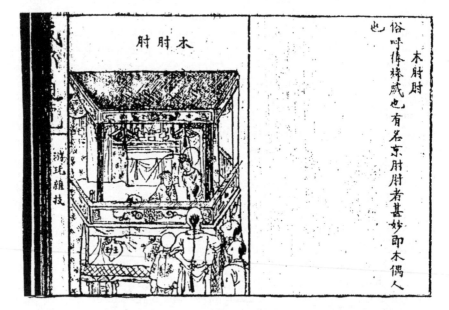

FIGURE 2.19. A Puppet Show (*Muzhouzhou*). The inscription says, "Locally it is also called 'stick opera' (*bangbang xi*) while some call it 'capital puppets' (*jinzhouzhou*). The opera is actually performed with wooden puppets, which are marvelous." CDTL 3: 115.

Although the influence of patron deity associations declined after the late Qing reforms and the Republican revolution, urban matters such as public hygiene and famine relief still remained primarily the responsibility of voluntary organizations. Charitable institutions such as the Benevolent Hall (Cihui tang) and Reliving the Poor Society (Jipin hui) were based on residence and functioned actively in matters of welfare, road repair, and street cleaning. Whereas the patron deity associations focused on their own streets or neighborhoods, charitable organizations served a larger area. Soup kitchens, which provided free meals to the poor during famines, became a major activity of these charitable organizations. Whenever a disaster occurred, the community still played a role. In the summer of 1914, for example, after flooding in the Smaller City left many households unable to prepare meals and many petty peddlers unable to make a living, charitable organizations went door to door to make an aid list, donated money, and distributed pancakes. When rice prices increased and rice shopkeepers took the opportunity to hoard and speculate, a charitable organization opened a new rice market in a public space in the Smaller City. When the main road from the South City Gate to the East City Gate fell into disrepair, muddy on rainy days and dusty on sunny ones, a local charitable society tried to raise money for its repair. During this period, street headmen still played a role in organizing community life. For example, the headman of Golden and Flourish Street (Jinhua jie) called a meeting of all residents to discuss road repair. The project included building wheelbarrow paths on both sides of the street. Although some opposed it because they thought that country residents had not contributed sufficiently to construction costs, supporters thought the shops would benefit from the increased convenience in transporting goods along the paths.[123]

In many late-Qing cities such as Shanghai, Hankou, and Chongqing, native place associations (*huiguan*) and guilds became the most prominent organizers of economic and social life. In Shanghai, native place associations were involved in community activities influencing everything from the economy to entertainment. In Hankou, "guild concerns and authority extended well beyond the governance of a guild's own membership and trade." In Chongqing, the heads of eight provincial native place associations (*basheng shoushi*) even played a semiadministrative role, overseeing taxation, local welfare, and other social affairs. Although Chengdu had many native place associations and guilds, it differed from these cities, where activities mostly focused on commercial affairs.[124] There, the organization of many social activities was left to the patron deity associations, which played a more important role in residents' everyday lives than did other social organizations.

3 *Street Life*

Ordinary citizens were the major occupants of Chengdu streets, which, because of the lack of official control, offered many opportunities for recreation, social discourse, and earning a living. Chengdu was inhabited by many kinds of people. As a missionary wrote in the late nineteenth century: "Monarchs, scholars, beggars, lords/Farmers, merchants, mighty hordes/A wondrous medley of mankind/Of rich, and poor, deaf, halt, and blind."[1] This diversity contributed to the city's lively street life and street culture. For men and women of the lower classes alike, the street was the primary place for work and leisure, because it was more accessible than any other public arena.[2] There commoners could make a living by various means. People who had poor living conditions and few facilities for recreation also tried to find cheap amusement in public places, such as on a street corner or in a shabby teahouse. Children in the underclass grew up on the street and were even called "street boys" (*jiewar* or *gaiwar* in the Chengdu dialect). Those at the bottom of the social ladder generally recognized that they would be unwelcome in the nicer, indoor spots. Even if they were not formally expelled, other patrons would snub and humiliate them. On the streets, whether grand roads or narrow lanes, they felt much less social discrimination.

Although commoners were the primary presence on the street, it is not the case that elites did not exploit it. Chengdu was home to many members of the "idle class"—retired officials, absentee landlords, degree holders, scholars, property owners, and rich merchants, who carefully tried to distance themselves from the lower classes. Members of the elite class appeared in public less, not because they had less opportunity but because they were limited by custom and social status. Indeed, they rarely appeared on the rough and dirty roads where the lower classes lived in simple and crude houses. It was socially unacceptable for members of the elite class to watch street performers or to mingle with those in the audience. Instead, elites frequented the splendid shops and elegant teahouses in the commercial districts. Similarly, wealthy families that could afford to hire performers for their private entertainment would not allow their children, especially girls, to venture into public except during the traditional public celebrations, when segregation by class and gender was less restrictive. The fact that Chengdu residents lived and worked in the same area brought people into constant close proximity and resulted in the formation of mutually dependent relationships.[3] In any neighborhood or on any street, all the people knew each other, and strangers were tolerated only with suspicion and intense scrutiny. As noted previously, gossip spread like wildfire and privacy was nonexistent, but such closeness provided a feeling of safety among residents.

Whereas the focus of the last chapter was on street as the space, this section deals with the people of the street and explores the nature of Chengdu "street life"—the everyday recreational, social, and professional activities of the lower classes that constituted "street culture." Commoners were the major occupants of public space, which served as market, work site, stage, shelter, and social center for the lower classes. Teahouse life was an extension of this public use of space. Even today, the teahouse is one of the best places in Chengdu to observe people's social connection and behavior. The relationship between people and their physical space also shifted as a person's social identity changed. A peddler, for example, might use a teahouse as a market for his wares during the day but as a place for socializing at night. Folk performers used the street as a stage, whereas those "living the vagrant life" used it as a place for temporary respite or shelter. For the same reason, the relationship between an individual and public space shifted accordingly, reflecting the complicated relationships between ordinary people and public places.

Peddlers: The Street as Market

Chengdu's hawkers, among the most visually striking people on the street, contributed significantly to the city's vitality.[4] According to J. Vale, "there seem to be endless ways of gaining a living by trading in a small way." He estimated that there were some 150 distinct trades on the streets of Chengdu that dealt with three categories of wares: foodstuffs, household necessities, and luxuries (see Figure 3.1).[5] Petty vendors had little capital and limited profits, but business yielded a quick return. They could adapt themselves to all seasons and purchase for resale whatever items were most in demand. The elderly and women who were unable to do heavy work could make a living by this means.

The way that peddlers advertised became a part of Chengdu's "voice." Missionaries thought that the peddlers' cries and calls were "as numerous and as unintelligible as those of the same class in the European or American city."[6] Each trade had its own special means of announcing its arrival. Gongs and bells were the most popular attention-getting devices, which, "when sounded or struck, in accordance with recognized rules and regulations,

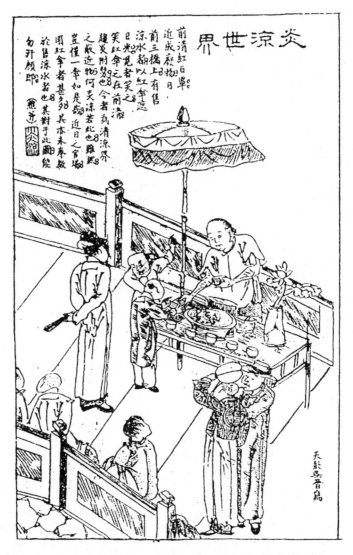

FIGURE 3.1. An Itinerant Water Seller at the End of a Bridge.
The title of this drawing is "Inconstancy of Human Relationship"
(*yanliang shijie*, literally "hot and cold world"). The inscription
says that the passersby are laughing about the water seller's red
sunshade umbrella, because in the Qing era such an umbrella
was used only by officials, but now it has been downgraded into
a utensil used by the lower classes. From TSHB 1912, no. 22.

[would] announce to the would-be purchasers the approach of the particular 'small trader' in the neighborhood." Some vendors carried small wooden boxes, crying out to attract buyers to their jade-ware, balls of string, cotton rope, mosquito-repellent incense, and other daily items over which women customers haggled. Distinctions could be found even for the same type of product: those who sold vegetable oil beat a wooden gong in the shape of a half moon; vendors of sesame oil beat a thin brass disk about the size of a small plate; and sellers of other kinds of oil shook two type of rattles. The bean-curd man struck a foot-long section of hollow bamboo; the seller of sweets, toys, and other articles, called "the children's friend," announced his arrival with a brass gong about three inches in diameter. Those who traded in embroidery and more expensive wares used a drum that was about six or seven inches in diameter, which they beat in a very dignified manner: "Commencing with one sharp stroke and then increasing the rapidity of the strokes till the drum resounds with the blows and purchasers can hear it several hundred yards away."[7]

Residents quickly learned to recognize the cries of the different peddlers and artisans. As a folk poem noted, "When a street peddler cries out at the front of the door with his bell jingling, the hostess and servant-girls run out and choose whatever they want to buy."[8] An elderly teahouse-goer recalled the cadence of the used-item trader's shout as follows, "Teeth, teeth, golden teeth; watches, watches, broken watches. Do you have pearls? Do you have agates? Do you have corals? Do you have teapots?"[9] From dawn to sunset, itinerant traders paraded up and down the streets, luring customers with their unique tunes. One can imagine the city awakening at dawn to the myriad voices from teahouses, street kitchens, wheelbarrows, and hawkers. At that hour, city dwellers most often heard cries of "Soft beans!" (*pa wandour*, cooked garden beans) and "Bean sprouts!" (*douyar*), which were common dishes.[10] After sunrise, vendors stepped onto their stage—the street—to add their own notes to the constant symphony of urban life.

Venders were an indispensable part of everyday life. Food peddlers, for example, put up their stalls almost everywhere—street corners; sidewalks; in front of temples, offices, and teahouses; public spaces; and so on. Chengdu is particularly known for its food, especially its numerous attractive, tasty, and aromatic "convenience foods" (or "small food"). In the late Qing, foreign visitors called the sellers of convenience food "street kitchens" or "itinerant restaurants." Street kitchens peddled their wares for long hours, usually from dawn to midnight. Their setup was simple: buckets hanging from a carrying pole served as bowls, pans, and stove. An open drawer contained a supply of bean curd, soy sauce, red peppers, ginger, spices, and pickles.[11] Some street kitchens provided a couple of tables and long benches, but most customers simply stood or squatted to eat.

Ordinary people, especially laborers, were the food peddlers' major customers. At key intersections, many food stalls served travelers and coolies, including sedan-chair carriers, wheelbarrow pushers and rickshaw pullers, and back carriers. Coolies who needed "something warm" before starting their long workday ate hearty ground rice balls that were about the size of a hen's egg with a little brown sugar in the center. As one missionary observed, "five of these served scalding hot for three or four cash form a good basis on which to walk six or seven miles before breakfast. The poorest coolie seldom starts out without partaking of this warming meal, especially in the autumn or winter." A foreign sojourner recalled that when a seller of fried snacks passed on the street, "it is almost compulsory to stop him and taste his wares." Local people enjoyed small fried flat cakes and twists of dough made from lightly fried common wheat flour. Another popular food among the working class was dumplings, kept hot in round steamers made of thin wood or shiny tin and eaten "on the way home after market, or if one needed a snack when the loads were heavy to carry." After dark and before going to bed, residents liked to step outside to buy a bowl of noodles, "piping hot, with good tasty soup, well flavored with the condiments of your choice."[12]

Peddlers who sold "daily items" for household use—and women bargaining with them—also were common. Flower vendors sold fresh flowers from baskets at teahouses and on the streets day and night. Peddlers who sold flowers, plants, jewels, and small foreign items were called "flower baskets" (huadanzi). Those who had stalls or carried baskets on the street, buying and selling used goods such as books, paper, and clothes, were called "used-item traders" (shouhuang, literally "collectors of waste items"). Itinerant booksellers hung their books "on a bamboo frame provided for the purpose and the book seller moves about from place to place, or enters tea shops or theatre-yards, in order to sell his books."[13]

Some peddled goods that could be found only in Chengdu or Sichuan. One type was the itinerant tobacconist (zhuang shuiyan, or water-pipe man), regarded by outsiders as having "an interesting occupation." Itinerant tobacconists usually conducted business in teahouses, opium dens, wine shops, theaters, and at fairs. They waited until a customer requested a brass water pipe and tobacco. If the pipe was not long enough, they prepared tubing to connect it. These techniques probably were developed to accommodate overcrowding in teahouses, allowing an itinerant tobacconist to provide his service to many patrons without having to move. The general price for five draws of the pipe was two cash, but some tobacconists allowed "the privilege of dividing these into two parts, that is, two today, and three whenever the itinerant meets his customer again."[14] This flexibility indicates how small venders adapted to meet the needs of patrons, even those who were very poor. Like the itinerant tobacconist, the "trader in hand and foot warmers" (*honglong*) emerged from the unique culture of Chengdu. The inhabitants of the Chengdu plain were known to "never light a fire except for cooking purposes," because fuel was expensive. During winter, these traders sold hand and foot warmers made of plaited bamboo in an earthenware dish that held charcoal or wood embers. The hand warmer, of course, was meant to be carried, but the basket was placed under one's long gown. When viewed from a distance "this gives the appearance of ladies wearing the 'bustle' of days gone by."[15] These items were so simple and cheap that even the very poor could afford them.

Small traders ensured their own success in a variety of ways. They worked very hard for long hours, walking from one street to another, summer and winter. They figured out how, when, and where to find clients, how to buy goods at low prices and sell them for profit, and how to make their products irresistible to attract customers. Missionary William Sewell described how peddlers took advantage of any situation to make money. After one major flood subsided, for example, "the itinerant sellers of noodles and bean curd arrived, clacking two pot spoons together to attract customers." Even a war could not deter the mobile vendors. As soon as the fighting stopped during the street battles of 1917, but before the regular shops reopened, hawkers risked their lives selling goods and food. Although most petty peddlers worked hard to earn "honest money," some tricked customers, sometimes by hiring imposters to pretend to be eager customers. Others, especially sellers of candles and food, used games of chance such as dice or a lottery to lure customers.[16]

The thousands of street vendors tremendously increased the city's commercial space and helped create and sustain Chengdu's vibrant street culture, along with the hundreds of small permanent shops that lined the streets. The street peddlers and their counterparts who worked as artisans and day laborers were the ones who most closely served the everyday needs of Chengdu residents. Without them, the city would have been much less animated.

Artisans and Laborers: The Street as Work Site

Like the petty peddlers, artisans were a major presence on the street and depended on their skills and strength for their livelihood. Those who could not afford to rent workspace carried their tools along the streets, on street corners, and in courtyards, crying out for customers. Thus, the street became their workshop. Street artisans provided considerable convenience for the residents of Chengdu; their services cost significantly less than their more established counterparts, and they could be found on any street or in their traditional gathering places during inclement weather. Repairers of cotton wadding most often gathered by the south and east gates, for instance, and those who fixed bamboo fans could be found in teahouses.[17]

In a traditional urban community, where the majority of residents were in the lower classes and material goods were expensive, the artisans who repaired these goods inevitably played an important role. They could repair almost any item: cotton wadding, bowls, vats, summer sleeping mats, fans, and umbrellas. Like petty peddlers, they used special devices to attract attention. For instance, the mender of old porcelain and the repairer of broken rice-pots carried a rattle made of five pieces of brass, which was called a "golden dial" (*jingui*); the sound produced by this rattle could be heard from a great distance. Fluffing the cotton of padded quilts that had become stiff from use was always done on the street or in a courtyard. When a riveter mended a broken bowl, he sat on a short stool, twirling his drill to make tiny holes into which he fitted rivets. So skillfully were the pieces put together that "except by looking underneath, it was difficult to see that the plates had ever been broken." By the time an umbrella maker set up his stall on the street, he had already assembled the material for the ribs; the bamboo pieces were all neatly shaped and tied together, and other slivers were glued firmly to the cover. With his brush, he painted the sturdy oiled paper cover red, blue, or green. Local folk artist Yu Zidan's paintings depict bricklayers, whitewashers, woodchoppers, tub makers, mat makers, blacksmiths, knife sharpeners, and tinsmiths. Working on the street and advertising their craft became a kind of "performance," attracting crowds of onlookers, especially children. Artisans formed a substantial part of the street landscape.[18]

Those who lacked a particular skill depended entirely on their physical strength to earn a living as laborers (see Figure 3.2). Because they were particularly vulnerable to setbacks caused by illness or injury, many of them lived in a state between free laborers and beggars. Each day they gathered at transportation hubs, such as harbors, sedan-chair stations, ends of bridges, and city gates, waiting to be hired. Back carriers transported loads as heavy as 220 pounds—some even 330 pounds—on their backs while leaning on bamboo canes. It is amazing the way that even the most cumbersome items, such as furniture, could be fitted together to make a single load for these workers, as can be seen in Yu Zidan's drawing. In hot weather, they kept one hand free to hold a bamboo fan. Shoulder carriers, who used a bamboo pole to carry heavy items, and were also called *laoda* (literally, "oldest brothers"), usually worked in the harbor area outside the East City

FIGURE 3.2. Construction Workers Taking a Break. From Davidson and Mason
1905: 231.

Gate, at the wood factory outside the North City Gate, and at the coal
stores at the four city gates.[19]

Chengdu citizens relied enormously on water carriers (see Figure 3.3). As
noted previously, drinking water had to be brought from the river outside
the city wall. Many poor men, especially outsiders, made a living carrying
water, balanced in two wooden baskets on a bamboo pole. Teahouses and
restaurants as well as households depended on this service. In late Qing, up
to a thousand laborers made a living carrying water from the river each day,
and more than 400 serviced Chengdu's 2,525 private wells.[20]

Water carriers kept alive a respected tradition. They moved quickly along
the street, stepping in rhythm with the springing pole they used for support. Elderly residents of Chengdu remember the water carriers fondly today. He Manzi, a well-known contemporary writer, recalls that river-water
carriers in the 1930s and 1940s wore no shoes, not to save money but
rather out of "professional ethics": barefoot, they could walk into the middle of the river to get the purest water.[21] For many, carrying water was not
only a livelihood but also a way to connect with the community by helping
elderly or injured customers with chores, for example. One resident wrote
of a water carrier he knew who took responsibility for several dozen families, totaling more than one hundred people, who lived in a large compound
on Revive China Street (Huaxing jie). Each time he brought a bucket of water, he drew one stroke of the five-stroke Chinese character *zheng* on the vat,
with each *zheng* representing five buckets of water. At the end of the month,

FIGURE 3.3. A Water Carrier. From Davidson and Mason
1905: 87.

each household's payment was collected based on the number of *zheng*.
The carrier and his customers trusted each other, and there was never confusion about payment.[22] This kind of trust was common in Chengdu, where
neighbors knew each other and interacted almost daily.

Entertainers: The Street as Stage

Before the emergence of professional theater in China, folk entertainers used streets, teahouses, or other public spaces as their stages, and
their colorful costumes and exotic behavior were often mentioned in the
memoirs of foreign visitors.[23] Folk entertainers enjoyed a great advantage

by working in public places. Unlike modern theaters that attract only the people who seek a performance, these performers were able to turn pedestrians into their audience. In this sense, we might say, street entertainers in premodern cities had a larger space for performing than do their contemporary counterparts. Rowe's description of Hankou tells of the activities of many "varieties of popular entertainers," such as street singers, female impersonators, actors, verse-chanters, storytellers, public lecturers, and clapper musicians.[24] Similar types of urban recreation appeared in cities in North, Central, and West China, while these regions retained their own strong folk culture. One could easily paint a similar picture for Chengdu, further indicating that Chinese culture contained both unified and diversified elements.

The elite classes shaped Chinese popular culture by infusing it with official ideologies. One such tool was sacred-edict preaching. Lectures on the Kangxi emperor's "sacred edicts" (*shengxun* or *shengyu*) in public spaces in cities and market towns were legally mandated, and they gradually became a form of popular entertainment. Since the early Qing, so-called preachers of the sacred edict (*jiang shengyu*) or preachers of morals were common on Chengdu streets. As some Western missionaries noticed, "common throughout the province, but especially prominent in Chengtu [Chengdu], is the frequent gathering of the people, in or near the public tea shops and 'kung kwans' [*gongguan*, resident compounds], to hear some teacher or scholar narrate stories illustrative of filial piety, or discourse on the Sacred Edict or similar books; this seems a usual evening occupation in both summer and winter." These preachers organized a society and usually preached from dawn to dusk daily in a public place. Wealthy families contributed from 300 to 400 cash to three or four silver taels to cover associated expenses.[25]

Sacred-edict preaching involved the interpretation of the "Sixteen Moral Maxims" and was always accompanied a ceremony that included the burning of incense, candles, and a sheet of yellow paper. Preachers often told stories from everyday life as part of their interpretation. For instance, in explaining the text regarding "mediating and settling disputes among local people," one preacher recounted how a minor dispute over ducks and geese escalated to litigation and, eventually, bankruptcy. In another example, a preacher told of an escaped convict who hid in his brother-in-law's home. The brother-in-law, a shopkeeper, was charged with harboring a criminal and sent to jail. This anecdote provided apt clarification of the sacred edict that advises: "Do not help fugitives to avoid being implicated."[26]

It has been said that in China storytelling as an occupation originated in the tradition of sacred-edict preaching. As one folk story described, in the early Qing, local officials sent preachers to teahouses in an effort to inform as many people as possible about the imperial edicts. The preachers usually began with a vivid story to draw the audience's attention before reading the sacred edicts. If someone fell asleep, the preachers beat the table with a wooden block; these came to be called "wake-up blocks" (*xingmu*). Gradually, preachers found that storytelling was a good way to make a living, and some became professional storytellers.[27] Storytelling has a long history in China, but we do not know when it became a profession. There is no other historical evidence to confirm this hypothesis, but it yields interesting insights into the relationship between popular entertainment and political change. It is also possible that early sacred-edict preachers conformed to a preexisting tradition of oral entertainment and storytelling. Nevertheless, from the similarity of styles of sacred-edict preaching and storytelling, we may also assume that each influenced the other and that practitioners might switch between the two.

In Chengdu, storytellers usually did their business in teahouses and other public places, such as at Liars' Square (Chehuang ba), in the public yards of temples, or in front of the town yamen. Teahouses also hired storytellers to "secure a crowd in the tea-shop in the evening." When shops prepared to close at night, the teahouses were often still full of customers listening to stories. As a foreign visitor recalled, "outside the full tea-shop, standing in the thin drizzle, people were listening enthralled to the story-teller reciting familiar tales." Highly skilled storytellers could attract audiences day after day, month after month, and even year after year. In similar fashion to the sacred-edict preachers, storytellers told their stories from a small rostrum. Audiences typically were critical, and a storyteller had to have a good memory and clever descriptive powers to succeed. The dress, mannerisms, and other details of each character had to be described precisely, and should the storyteller forget or confuse his own descriptions, his audience would soon disperse. In some cases, storytellers "passed the hat" to collect money after telling one chapter or episode; they usually collected twice per night. In other cases, the teahouse owner might pay by the night or give the story-teller a commission on each cup of tea sold, or audiences might be charged a single fee for tea and entertainment. Both methods, however, meant that only the customers who bought tea and sat inside the teahouse were charged. Many more gathered on the sidewalk, listening for free.[28]

The writers of folk literature liked to record tales by storytellers. One story about Zhong Xiaofan, a well-known storyteller in the late Qing and early Republic, was widespread:

Once, Zhong told the story of Meng Lijun in a teahouse.[29] He got to the point in the story where the emperor was on the verge of discovering that Meng Lijun was a woman pretending to be a man, after having tried to make her drunk to determine her gender by taking off her shoes while she slept. At this point in his story, when the audience yearned to learn what happened next, Zhong simply stopped the story. Day after day, the audience was held in storytelling limbo as Meng's shoes still remained on. Some soldiers who climbed over the wall of their military camp to the teahouse to listen were caught twice by their officer and beaten on their palms as a punishment, but they still took the risk to hear the rest of the story. By the tenth day, the soldiers could not bear the suspense any longer and warned Zhong "to take off Meng's shoes right away" or they would beat him.[30]

Undoubtedly, the storytellers' method of preaching, choice of language, and the environment they created all shaped local popular culture. Storytellers educated as well as entertained their audiences by passing on legends and historical accounts and also by unconsciously instilling Confucianism and other traditional values such as loyalty, filial piety, and chastity. Therefore, stories from *Romance of Three Kingdoms* (Sanguo yanyi) and tales of Yue Fei, a military hero of the Southern Song, were always crowd favorites.

Folk performances were held any place where they could attract an audience. In crowded teahouses, "folk performers present their shows one after another." Most of the forms, such as ballads, originated locally, but some came from elsewhere, notably "drum stories" from North China. Some forms of entertainment were nationally popular but were told with local color, using the dulcimer, "fish drum," and *huqin* (singing with a two-stringed instrument). *Huqin* was criticized as a "licentious folk song." A drawing of a *huqin* performance from the 1920s indicates that singers usually performed as a pair. The man wore the Chinese character "*shou*" (representing longevity) woven into black silk damask, which shone in the reflected light. While the man played the fiddle, the woman, seated on a chair of traditional design, played the castanets and the flat-drum. A similar entertainment was *yangqin*, which generally involved four to six entertainers singing while playing the dulcimer, drum, *huqin*, and *sanxian* (a three-stringed instrument). Unlike Sichuan opera, this music was peaceful and soft, and thus exceptionally pleasing to visitors from other provinces. Another form of folk performance was *zhuqin* (bamboo dulcimer), usually sung by a single performer, who played various roles, old and young, male and female. "Drum stories" (*dagu*) were quite popular in North China and could also be seen in late-Qing Chengdu. The New World Teahouse (Xin shijie) and Pure Stream Garden (Chunqi huayuan) became the most popular places for this kind of performance, which attracted large audiences at a cost of several *yuan* per patron.[31] Many folk entertainers performed regularly at a single teahouse, enabling audiences to find their favorite shows.[32]

Many folk entertainers, however, wandered the streets for their livelihood. Singers of "golden bamboo clappers" (*jinqianban*, literally "golden cash clappers") carried three slabs of bamboo, two in the left hand and one in the right, with which they beat time. An iron ring was attached to each piece of bamboo and made a jingling sound. These performers sang "from door to door in the forenoons, and in the afternoons take up a stand in the Liars' Square, and receive small donations from any who care to patronise them." "Story singing," performed by the blind, women, outsiders, and other commoners using various instruments, also was popular. Daoists provided a popular entertainment, called "beating the Daoist instrument" (*da daoqin*); these performances were a means of begging alms. They carried a long bamboo tube called a "fish drum" (*yugutong*) and two long bamboo clappers, like a pair of tongs, with which they beat out time. Some went from door to door singing, and others were hired to play in the larger houses in the evening. Often, a Daoist priest would get permission to perform the opening act at a teahouse. He would prostrate himself before the audience, and, if they were in a good mood, they would ask him to keep singing. Finally, a local leader, usually the head of a secret society, would say, "Please allow us to express our appreciation." The teahouse waiter would then collect money from patrons. If the head of the secret association favored the performance, he might invite the Daoist to stay longer, sometimes as long as six months or a full year. If the Daoist was talented at calligraphy or painting, he could earn even more money.[33]

Jugglers and monkey shows, which usually came from other towns, also performed on street corners, usually attracting lower-class audiences. Jugglers attracted audiences by beating gongs and drums and leading the crowd to an open space where there was room to perform. They frequently passed the hat during the performance, and everyone was expected to contribute. According to a missionary's observation, many of the acrobats were women and girls. The highlights of their performance included "walking the slack rope," "balancing the jar," and "climbing the cloud ladder." In "balancing the jar," three tables were piled to make a high stage, and an acrobat lay on her back on the topmost table while balancing a large wine jar with her feet. Other juggling feats included sword swallowing, stabbing oneself in the belly, making a wine cup disappear, hanging an egg in the air, producing wine and meats from thin air, breaking a fan and mending it again, and making gourds grow.[34]

Children favored monkey shows, crying "Monkey coming! Monkey coming!" as soon as they glimpsed the performers. "Wherever they were, a crowd soon gathered round." One of the most interesting shows involved "a monkey with a hat on." A children's song vividly described a family of itinerant performers: "Father leads a monkey and Mother leads a dog; go to the river bank for performing *liulianliu*."[35] Virtually all of the monkey players came from Henan province, where only one crop could be grown and residents were forced to make a living elsewhere for much of the year. They usually lived in temples, on sidewalks, and under bridges. A proverb mocked, "Sichuan folks are always led by Henan people" (*Sichuanren fu Henanren qian*), meaning that Sichuanese were fooled by the cunning of Henan people.[36]

Puppeteers most often performed at temple fairs, street or neighborhood ceremonies, and guild celebrations. Puppet shows, called "curtain opera" (*beidan xi*) by natives and "street puppets" by foreigners, became very popular (see Figure 3.4). In Sichuan, puppeteers were called a "basket troupe" (*dandan ban*) because they carried their belongings in baskets on poles. Generally, a troupe consisted of eight people—four to operate the puppets and four to play the musical instruments. The names of the shows corresponded to the months of the Chinese calendar, such as the "Pure Brightness Day ceremony opera" (*qingjiao xi*) and the "Guanyin opera."[37] The principal program in their repertory was a show about a tiger that killed a widow's only son. After the tiger was caught, the magistrate ordered it to look after the widow for the rest of her days as punishment. The tiger provided her with food and money and, after she died, mourned at her grave. This story is another example of how the profound Chinese moral tradition permeated popular

FIGURE 3.4. Watching a Puppet Show. Such a scene could often be seen at a temple fair or on a street corner. From Davidson and Mason 1905: 85.

entertainment enjoyed by even the lowest levels of society; in this case, the moral is that "children should look after their parents in their old age."[38]

Living the Vagrant's Life

Chengdu also was home to another, much more complicated, group of performers—the *jianghu* (or *pao jianghu*), literally "river and lake runners," who told fortunes, performed magic, sold Chinese medicine, and performed acrobatic stunts (see Figure 3.5). In premodern Chengdu, lower-class society was customarily divided into the so-called "seventy-two occupations," with "sixteen sorts of itinerants" (*shiliu men*). The second category consisted of actors who worked on the Chengdu streets and other public places, who were called *pao jianghu* by local people and "startlers" or "itinerants" by foreigners.[39] These people were also often mixed with the "people in various trades." Most of them were from other areas and customarily congregated in Liars' Square (Chehuang ba) near the New South City Gate, an area similar to Tianqiao in Beijing. Though some were local residents, they, too, were classified as people who "lived a vagrant life" because of their occupation. These itinerants were the subjects of endless speculation and a large number of folk stories.[40]

From various accounts, we learn that *jianghu* did not have a good reputation and were accused of deceit, often with good reason.[41] Their primary ruses, according to J. Vale, included magic, the "guarantee degree" method, and the "underhanded" method. In the underhanded method, for example, the *jianghu* would write several rows of large characters on a piece of yellow paper, which he pasted in a conspicuous public place. If someone stopped to read the message, he stepped forward to describe his magical powers in areas such as "exorcising demons" and "calling for rain and wind." If the potential client appeared to be a student, the trickster would tell him that he could cause him to get a degree, father a son, or become wealthy. One magician who usually worked in Liars' Square hung up a price list and a sign claiming that he could do thirty-six "big tricks" and seventy-two "small tricks," such as changing leather belts into snakes, shoes into rabbits, and leaves into fish. The most popular trick was to make a bill or a coin bear "baby money." The magician would lead interested patrons to a quiet teahouse and, after receiving payment, would explain how to offer a sacrifice to a bill or coin by using chicken blood for forty-nine days, or something similar.[42] Audiences would quickly surround magicians wherever or whenever they appeared. Most people, of course, were just interested in being entertained, although some occasionally would shell out their money, to the further amusement of the crowd.

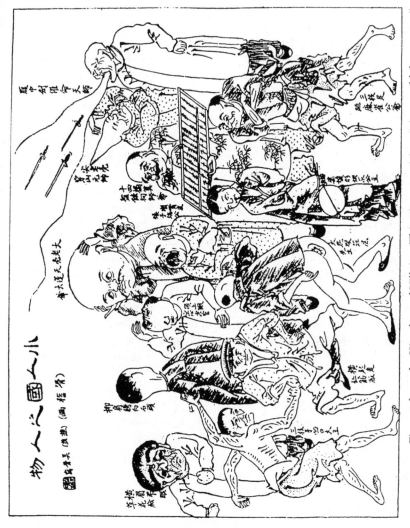

FIGURE 3.5. Figures from the Kingdom of Villains. This picture satirizes "river and lake runners" (*pao jianghu*). Depicted in the front row, from the left, are "King with Three Hands," "Man Who Walks Like a Crab," "Mr. Big Anus," "Opium Princess," and "Duke Three Legs." In the second row, from the left, are "Fierce-Browed Face," "Man with No Shoulders," "Big-Headed Man," "Short Witch Doctor," "Greedy Private Adviser," "Marshal Pinhead," and "Sinister Master." From TSHB 1912, no. 17.

Whereas the *jianghu* who set up stalls openly played tricks, some, locally called "water line" (*shuixian*), would wander the streets looking for opportunities to make money. In one case, a tailor noticed a cloth seller passing by and called him in to his shop. As the tailor inspected the wares, a customer entered and said that he would like to buy the cloth to have a coat made. The tailor told the customer the amount of cloth needed and gave the customer permission to take the cloth across the street to show to somebody. Both the tailor and cloth merchant assumed that the customer lived there, but when he failed to return after two hours they investigated and found him long gone. The cloth seller accused the tailor of being part of the swindle, but in fact the tailor did not know the man.[43] Some vagabonds accomplished their trickery through more aggressive methods using one or two assistants; for example, the "wind itinerant" usually had a woman helper, and in many cases a husband and wife worked together. In one case, a man bought a length of silk, then went with his female partner back to the shop to exchange it. The shopkeeper refused, claiming the cloth was in good condition when it was sold. During the ensuing dispute, the man secretly took a piece of broken china from his pocket and scratched his face until it bled, and then accused the shopkeeper of injuring him. In this case, the shopkeeper had to pay a settlement to the couple.[44] Such stories, found in written documents as well as oral tradition, illustrate the bad reputation of *jianghu* but might also indicate the bias that the elite class held against the lower classes. Because the *jianghu* included many swindlers, contemporary Chinese often use the term "*jianghu pianzi*" (itinerant swindlers). The *jianghu* cleverly exploited the resources of the street in making a living, demonstrating the mutual dependence and conflict that characterized their relationship with Chengdu residents.

Not all *jianghu* resorted to trickery. In fact, many doctors of Chinese traditional medicine, called *jianghu yisheng* (itinerant doctors), fell in this category. In Chengdu, doctors were classified into those who "put stalls in the streets," "run in the streets," "sit in sedans," or "official doctors." Members of the first two categories often served the poor, sometimes even offering free diagnosis. Many sellers of Chinese medicine also gave advice on common ailments. Chengdu's strength in the national medicine market pushed many people into earning a living through medicine.[45] Some medicine traders were called "sellers of dog-skin plasters" (*mai goupi gaoyao*), after the little black patches put on sores or boils. These sellers boasted continuously about the effectiveness of this treatment, and even today Chinese often call any form of exaggerating or boasting "selling dog-skin plasters." Many residents, however, trusted witch doctors to cure ailments, and procedures performed on the streets attracted large crowds. The most common methods used by witch doctors included "watching gods" (*guanxian*), "drawing eggs" (*huadan*), and "visiting hell" (*zouyin*).[46] When a witch doctor practiced his ritual, he would shout incantations before a row of lit candles, a bowl of water, and long sticks of incense, waving a sheaf of burning paper in one hand and rattling a circular wand in the other. Observing witch doctors' performances was always interesting; their exotic clothing, tools, gestures, and language piqued spectators' curiosity.

Fortune-tellers were another fascinating group of *jianghu*, and could be found on almost every street and teahouse. Fortune-tellers, who attempted to make a connection between present and future, and between people and nature, played an important role in street life and street culture in Chengdu. Most were men but some were woman, called "divining women" (*guapo*), and many were blind. Although fortune-tellers usually set up their stalls on street corners and sidewalks or gathered in the space between the inner and outer city gates, many also wandered the streets in search of customers. Popular methods of divination included playing cards, drawing pictures, or writing a Chinese character to predict fortune or misfortune. Some fortune-tellers helped people choose auspicious dates for events such as making a stove, starting construction of a house, and holding a wedding or funeral.

Geomancers (*yinyang xiansheng*) specialized in "checking a grave and opening a way for the dead" by using compasses to choose the best location for a tomb. They catered to many believers, both elites and commoners.[47] Local writers and artists frequently depicted them in literature and drawings, reflecting their visibility in public space. Two bamboo-branch poems written by different authors described the fortune-teller Fu Haishan of the early nineteenth century. One reported that Fu Haishan was among the best-known fortune-tellers in Chengdu; the other described him as a sophisticated person with rich social experience who taught people morality and how to deal with problems. Such admiration was rare, as elites usually criticized fortune-tellers in their writings. Yu Zidan drew a picture of a fortune-teller in the 1920s, with a description by Sewell. In it, a man who looks like a remnant of the scholar-gentry wears an old Chinese long gown, holding a book in one hand. A small altar has been set up by his side, which has burning sticks of incense and two brass or pewter candlesticks, each shaped like the classical Chinese character *shou*, representing "longevity." There is a central tablet behind these, on which is written *shengyu* (sacred edicts). To the right of the tablet are listed the moral principles of filial piety, obedience, loyalty, and trust (*xiao ti zhong xin*), and to the left, the principles of propriety, righteousness, honesty, and sense of shame (*li yi lian chi*).[48] Sewell states that fortune-telling, although found in popular culture, promoted orthodox ideology, providing a good example of the interaction between elite culture and popular culture.

Divination has a long history in China and reveals a great deal about its society, culture, religion, philosophy, and cosmology. As Richard Smith wrote, "divination touched every sector of Chinese society, from emperor to peasant." Whereas history informs one of the past and ritual the present, divination is thought to inform one of the future. Actually, "it reflects different social perspectives, different ways of world-making." Diviners were a sort of "cultural liaison" between nature and humans, and fulfilled the basic human need to find meaning in seemingly arbitrary natural phenomena and thus bridged popular culture and elite culture. As divination came under increasing attack from both reformist movements and state authorities, and as scientific knowledge advanced in the early twentieth century, however, divination gradually declined.[49]

The documentation that does exist was written by the elite and focuses on the moral shortcomings of the *jianghu*, neglecting their unique lifestyle and contributions to Chengdu popular culture. In this section, we have examined several groups of itinerants who have been little reviewed by historians. A notable exception is Philip Kuhn, whose book *Soulstealers* is about itinerant Buddhist monks and Daoist priests during the Qianlong period. His study explored the attitudes of the government and society toward this group and their interactions with local people. Kuhn, however, focused mainly on issues of conflict during the "sorcery scare" era and therefore offers little insight into others who lived the "vagrant life." In fact, this group formed much more complex and interdependent relationships with other groups, becoming an integral part of Chengdu street culture.

True Believers: The Street as Altar

Although street life often centered on making a living, it also offered spiritual outlets that often were associated with general entertainment. Chengdu residents commonly placed altars or tablets for worship in their doorways or on the sidewalks or streets. Parades in honor of Buddhist, Daoist, or folk deities were common, and temple fairs celebrating a deity's "birthday" regularly attracted thousands of participants. People attended religious rituals for various reasons; Buddhists, for example, believed that these activities helped them accumulate "benevolence" that could improve their fortune in this life or the next. Many people participated for reasons other than religious devotion; in fact, the entertainment value often eclipsed the spiritual.

In ancient times, disease was a constant threat, and ceremonies created to seek divine protection became an important part of folk tradition. For example, the Medicine King Festival (*Yaowang hui*) celebrated the birthday of the Medicine King god, on the twenty-eighth day of the fourth lunar month. On that day, all Chinese medicine stores and clinics would have horizontal inscribed boards made and sent to the Medicine King Temple on

Shaanxi Street (see Maps 4 and 5). All worshipers, male or female, rich or poor, old or young, walked there instead of traveling in a sedan chair. As they walked, many of them kowtowed at regular intervals—sometimes with every step—to express their faith. This practice was called "kowtowing to fragrant incense" (baixiang) or "kowtowing to altars" (baitai). Chengdu residents followed numerous practices for healing disease, including paying ten wen to touch the two bronze goats at the Green Goat Temple. Headache patients were instructed to stroke the head of the goat.[50]

Gradually, people added a variety of ghosts and deities thought to aid health to their rituals. When a plague broke out, for example, they would make a propitiatory offering (da wenjiao) to the God of Pestilence (wenzu) or construct an altar on the street for the Commissioner of the Gods (jie ling-guan). Such ceremonies could also be found in other areas. Both Paul Katz and Carol Benedict have described how the Chinese responded to plagues. In many places, local residents created images of epidemic demons, plague gods, and Marshal Plague (Wen Yuanshuai), a practice that became an important part of popular belief and religious cults. In Chengdu, as in the coastal regions, these festivals "featured a powerful symbolism, expressing both a strong sense of guilt and a deep-rooted fear of marginal or external forces."[51] Such a "disease culture" was deeply rooted in everyday life. Through the centuries, wen in the Chengdu dialect came to mean not only "illness" but also "evil" or "misfortune." Today, however, wenshen remains part of Chengdu dialect but is used to describe people who misbehave or do something wrong.

Guanyin (Avalokitesvara), the Goddess of Mercy, was one of the most important Buddhist deities in Chengdu, especially among women. Placards claiming that Guanyin could prevent disaster were frequently pasted along the street or on the doors of homes. Women went to the Guanyin Temple to burn incense sticks three times in a year—the nineteenth day of the first, sixth, and ninth lunar months (see Map 5 and Figure 3.6). Men went there, too, although not for spiritual purposes but to watch women. Buddhists nuns, according to some critics, used the opportunity to collect money. Of those who came to the temple to burn incense, many stayed and contributed 100 wen and a peck of rice in exchange for a vegetarian meal.[52]

Buddhist monks and Daoist priests did not always live in temples. Many actually wandered the streets collecting alms or "deliberately speaking mysteriously to attract people," which involved standing in the doorway of a household and predicting bad fortune for the family. When the residents asked how to avoid the impending disaster, the monk or priest would request money and rice before supplying any details. These itinerant monks usually had a letter of identification that indicated an affiliation with a temple. Since the early Qing, wandering clergy were generally regarded as unstable

FIGURE 3.6. Women at the Guanyin Temple. From TSHB 1909, no. 6.

elements; elites accused them of making people believe in "superstition" and of "seducing the women of good families." Even the possibility of attack by the government during the Qing period, such as those described by Philip Kuhn, did not deter the thousands of wandering monks and priests, whether legitimate or simply beggars playing the part.[53]

Many secular aspects of life in Chengdu also underscored the desire for peace, pleasure, and protection from harm. The activity of "respecting printed paper" is a good example. The Chinese traditionally regarded literacy as a sacred gift, and consequently "the written character was held in the greatest reverence." Any paper containing Chinese characters, whether printed or handwritten, therefore, could not be discarded as garbage, and it was regarded as a "work of merit" to collect such paper. People who desired to "amass merit" collected paper door to door. Most were old, poor, and uneducated, but they worshiped Chinese characters even though they could not decipher them. Sometimes very poor people combined this effort with begging, carrying a large basket and a pair of long tongs to strip old posters from the walls. Some also distributed wastepaper baskets to residents, on which were written the words "Respect printed paper" (*jingxi zizhi*) or "Respect printed paper and you will obtain happiness; respect printed paper and you will prolong your life" (*xizi defu, xizi yannian*). Small canvas bags were tacked onto the street gates, so that passersby could dispose of stray pieces of written-on paper. The paper was then burned in the "character treasury" (*ziku*) or the cash paper center (*qianlu*) found in some temples. A society for the collection of written paper (*xizi hui*) was organized, with headquarters in the Character Respecting Hall (*xizi gong*).[54]

"Respecting printed paper," practiced both in premodern times and in the Republican period, became a national as well as a local custom. In addition, it was a popular cult that affirmed orthodox ideology. Many records, especially from the Qing, show that the practice spread to North China and the coastal areas. In the 1920s, an article in a Chengdu newspaper accused those who used printed paper as toilet paper of "despising the written language of their motherland," arguing that "to treasure written language is not superstitious." The custom remained even into the 1930s, as indicated in an article by Lu Xun, one of China's most important modern writers. Fei Xiaotong, a pioneer of Chinese anthropology, recalled that his grandmother always told him to treat printed paper with respect. Although printed paper was an object of worship, it was still used in daily life. Decorative wrapping paper was common, for example, indicating the utilitarian nature of Chinese folk tradition. Ironically, though most of the illiterate poor respected printed paper, some educated elites opposed this custom. According to Fu Chongju, the collectors had "an especially disgusting habit," which "everybody hates": tearing announcements and advertisements off walls. Fu believed that this activity harmed commerce and should be restricted.[55] That some elites adopted this attitude is not surprising, considering the radical ideas of the Westernized elites during the New Cultural Movement. Lu Xun, for example, regarded all Chinese characters as purveyors of a "backward" tradition.

Women in Public

Historians have done little work on ordinary women in urban China to date; a few outstanding books on Qing women have been published since the 1990s, such as Dorothy Ko's *Teachers of the Inner Chambers* and Susan Mann's *Precious Records*. These works, however, mainly focused on the elite women of the seventeenth and eighteenth centuries in the lower Yangzi region, their lives behind closed doors, and their writings. These studies of premodern Chinese women have stressed that elite women shared "many assumptions about Confucian virtue" with men but that only a tiny portion of the female population could be considered "highly educated."[56] How did the vast majority of women in the late empire live? We know little about them, but what we do know provides an interesting counterpoint to the afore-mentioned studies. The general assumption is that Chinese women were re-stricted to the sphere of home and family and that their dealings in public—especially where men were present—were dictated by social custom and traditional morality. Although scholars have seldom attempted to study women according to region or social class, there is evidence to indicate that in premodern Chengdu, women, especially in the lower classes, actually en-joyed considerable freedom in public. Indeed, women played a crucial role in Chengdu street life, even though it appears to have been traditionally the domain of males. The restrictions on women in public, at least in Chengdu, were not as severe as has been usually presumed.

The majority of women in Chengdu belonged to the lower classes that lived in shabby rooms along the streets and had direct and constant contact with peddlers, water carriers, neighbors, and others. Furthermore, many of them had contact with the public as they sat in their doorways to take ad-vantage of the sunlight and companionship while they did handicrafts such as weaving, matchbox making, and knotting. Watching the crowds or con-versing with neighbors broke the tedium of their chores. In addition, they often went out to buy food or other necessities, an indication that they probably felt comfortable outside the home and that men would not have been surprised by their presence there. This clearly is radically different from the situation of women in the elite class, whose presence on the street would be viewed with shock and curiosity. Upper-class women always traveled by sedan chair when they went out, as described in novels and poems.[57]

The appearance of Chengdu women in public impressed foreign visitors, too. Isabella Bird wrote that on Chengdu streets in the late nineteenth cen-tury, "it was refreshing to see the tall, healthy-looking women with 'big feet,' long outer garments, and roses in their hair, as in Manchuria, stand-ing at their doorways talking to their friends, both male and female, with something of the ease and freedom of Englishwomen."[58] The women she saw were probably Manchus, who did not bind their feet, but Manchu cus-toms undoubtedly influenced the public activities of Han women, although this influence should not be overstated. Before the 1911 Revolution, a wall separated the Manchu and Han people. Han women, particularly the elite, looked down on Manchu women and their public behavior. These distinc-tions mattered less to lower-class women, whose daily struggle to survive took precedence over traditional notions of "women's virtues."

Celebrations and ceremonies gave women a great opportunity to enjoy public activities; even women from elite families joined in public celebrations. Women participated in almost all temple ceremonies and festivals, with roles that often were more enthusiastic and important than those for men. On these occasions, women from all social classes could mingle, although the wealthy women usually drew more attention. Women dressed up carefully to show off their beauty at festivals, and Chengdu's sophisticated silk production facilities gave them access to the most fashionable and highest quality silk clothing. Early in the morning of the first day of the Chinese New Year, many women would "try to be the first ones to burn incense sticks in the temple." Pure Brightness Day, when families visited the gravesites of ancestors and loved ones, became an opportunity for city dwellers to take a trip outside town. As a local writer noted, "It is a bright day for cleaning graves, and women's sedan chairs follow one after another. Moving through the streets and over the city wall, they arrive in the field where yellow flowers are blooming." Feng Yuxiang, a *juren* degree holder of the Guangxu period (1875–1908), wrote ten poems on the Temple of the Medicine King, which indicate that women were major visitors to this temple. One poem described that on a clear day, when flowers and grass were fresh after a rain, many women went to the temple; "through the gauze curtain, people can see their beautiful silhouettes and shining jewelry." While making their wishes, "they do not like others to overhear because they do not want them to know what they are praying for." Many women went to the Birth Goddess Temple (Guangsheng miao), located behind the Great Benevolent Temple (Daci si), to pray for sons. At the Green Goat Temple, "the true female believers touch the green bronze goat and pray to the god quietly. They kowtow sincerely and do not care about others laughing." In the "Climbing High to Escape Disease Festival" (*you baibing*) of the sixteenth day of the first lunar month, Chengdu women strolled along the entire city wall. As an early-nineteenth-century folk poem described, "They carefully hold up their long dresses while trying to tie their hair. Don't say their feet are too small to walk—they can climb the city wall without help." A century later, the same activity was mentioned in another folk poem: "women with unbound 'big feet' walked so fast that women with bound 'golden lotus' feet felt ashamed," suggesting that "three-inch golden lotus" feet may have begun to fall out of favor among women.[59]

Furthermore, at festival time, the boundaries of gender as well as of social class were loosened. In traditional Chinese society, women were not supposed to consort with strange men in public, but this rule did not apply to religious activities and festival celebrations. For example, during the second lunar month, "men and women carry umbrellas and walk along streets. Whenever they reach a temple, they enter it to burn sticks of incense and kowtow at altars." In spring, when bamboo arches were built on the streets, "women and men held the ceremony in the Temple of the Medicine King by burning incense sticks." During the "Climbing High to Escape Disease Festival," a local writer teased, "men and women made eyes at each other on the streets."[60] Although this comment reflected the author's displeasure with such public behavior, it confirmed Isabella Bird's observation mentioned above. In fact, any activity in which women participated attracted more men, many of whom sought any legitimate opportunity to feast their eyes on crowds of well-dressed women.

Women's appearance and gestures revealed their family backgrounds. When some young women sat in a sedan chair, "the curtain must be put down to avoid the gaze by pedestrians," while other women "do not like to sit in sedan chairs, but instead like to walk." About the latter one observer remarked, "their hair is carefully combed in the new style with flowers in it, and their small feet are so attractive. They do not care about gossip." These accounts indicate a dichotomy between conservative and shy women who clung to orthodox traditions and those who were freer from social convention. Generally, the former came from elite families and the latter from the lower classes. Wu Haoshan wrote several bamboo-branch poems describing these class distinctions: some women "wear pearl jewelry all over their heads and silk garments over their whole bodies," and some sit in new glass sedan chairs "because they have married rich men." The poems also provide insight into fashions of the time: "Women pursue new hairstyle trends and they make their lips up and draw their brows a bit. They wear green clothing with colorful and embroidered edges." Some poems described their gestures: the women move slowly as they chat with girlfriends and stroll along the street "because they are afraid of soiling their shoes with mud."[61]

Some accounts focused on working women. Fu Chongju criticized the small vendors known as "old flower women" (huapozi) for "using the excuse of selling flowers, jewelry, and jade ware to seduce the women of good families."[62] In Chengdu, midwifery was a prosperous business. Midwives hung wooden boards under the eaves of their houses to announce their services, and if they delivered boys, they would receive "red bags" in which money was wrapped. A female shop owner was also described: "Her house is located by the bank of the Brocade River, and the sign of her wine shop hangs from the top of the tree. She is so beautiful that you would be drunk even if you might not drink wine." Although folk poets at times criticized women, the poets' basic tone was pleasant and appreciative of their beauty, quite unlike the social reformers in the early twentieth century, who were strongly hostile toward women's appearance.[63]

Many descriptions of Chengdu women in this section were based on bamboo-branch poems written by local literati. The surviving poems contain very few such detailed sketches about men's roles in festivals and cele-

brations. The reason obviously is that women in public drew the most social attention. Of course, men spent more leisure time on the street than did
women, but why were the elites more interested in women's public amusements than men's? Probably, as is commonly understood, men on the street
were associated with working, whereas women there often signified amusement or relaxation.[64] The evidence shows that Chengdu women, like men,
had become an inseparable part of street life and contributed greatly to
street culture.

The Idle and the Busy: Teahouse Life

As discussed previously, the street, an expansive space that accommodated all sorts of people, was a major arena for public life. By compari-
son, the teahouse, a much smaller public space, also attracted people of all
trades. The teahouse undoubtedly served primarily as a place for leisure
and social discourse, yet it also assumed almost all of the roles of the street,
from marketplace to stage. Furthermore, the teahouse provided a more
comfortable environment that was unaffected by bad weather and conducive to hosting activities such as hobby clubs, business transactions, and
even quasi-civil courts.

In a doggerel verse about his tour of Chengdu in the 1930s, Huang Yanpei,
a preeminent educator in Republican China, wrote: "One idle person wan-
ders the street, counting paving stones; two idle persons go to a teahouse
to spend the whole day." This concise verse presents a vivid picture of the
lifestyle of determined leisure that was once common in Chengdu. Similarly, Shu Xincheng, another famous educator, who visited Chengdu in the
1920s, said his strongest impression of the city was how highly residents
valued leisure time. He expressed surprise at the huge number of teahouse-
goers and how long they stayed there each day: "Every teahouse is crowded
from sunrise to sunset; there is often no room to sit." Still another Chinese
visitor noted that in Chengdu, "to eat a meal takes no time at all, but to
drink tea in a teahouse takes at least three to four hours." Foreign travelers
also noticed this widespread culture of leisure. According to George Hubbard,
some people had "little else to do on the street but wander and chat."[65]
This was the landscape of early-twentieth-century Chengdu; the hectic pace
usually associated with urban life was hardly evident.

It is understandable that visitors had such reactions. The pursuit of leisure permeated everything and was actively promoted. As a matched couplet
posted by a tea and wine shop advised, "Work hard for reputation and
work hard for profit, but find leisure time to drink a cup of tea; work hard
for thinking and think hard for working, but seek happiness to sip a little

wine." A song sung by gambling-stall keepers on the sidewalks expressed a similar sentiment: "Don't hurry and don't be busy. What busy man has a good fate?" Local people joked that their hometown was a city of the "Three Plenties": plenty of idle people, plenty of teahouses, and plenty of lavatories.[66]

Who patronized the teahouses of Chengdu? A guidebook from 1938 and a travel note from 1943 list two categories: the "idle class" (*youxian jieji*) and the "busy class" (*youmang jieji*).[67] The idle class in Chengdu, as commonly understood, was the leisure class: local scholars, absentee landlords, retired officials, and other elites. The busy class included those who had to work for a living. The busy class in a teahouse could be classified into three groups. First were those who used the teahouse as a theater, such as local opera performers and storytellers. Second were those who used the teahouse as a place to transact business, such as merchants, fortune-tellers, doctors, and artisans. Third were those who used the teahouse as a market, such as peddlers of food and sundries and day laborers.[68] We must recognize, however, that here the terms "idle" and "busy" are used very loosely, and not as strict definitions of social class. Although the term "idle class" was often used to describe those who could support themselves without having to earn a living, it was never formally defined as an independent class, and its members could come from various economic backgrounds. In Chinese cities, both a rich person and a poor person who had nothing to do were generally considered "idlers." Nonetheless, these two terms properly represented the two groups that gathered in the teahouse. All of them, regardless of background or social class, shared a common public space.

Gathering for Free Talk and Common Hobbies. Teahouses were the preferred places to meet friends, do business, sell goods, perform, have a chat, take a break, or just kill time. Unlike workers in the industrial cities of the West, who had to work at least an eight-hour day, in Chengdu people did not have stable working hours, and their time was quite flexible. They could simply stay in teahouses when they were not working, day or night. In the early twentieth century, Westerners compared the "restaurants and tea-drinking saloons open to the street" in Chengdu to "the place of the public houses in England" and remarked that such places were "a great deal less harmful" when used for "social chat." These teahouses had a definite neighborhood character. As a foreign teacher who lived on Wheelbarrow Lane during the early Republican period put it, the teahouse in his neighborhood served as "the Lane's social centre." Like the saloon in American cities, the teahouse in Chengdu also provided the lower classes "alternative spaces to spend that leisure time away from crowded homes." Nevertheless, we can also say that the teahouse offered a bustling and lively place for elites to gather away from their private and spacious walled compounds. Teahouses became so attractive that some office clerks even frequented them during working hours, only to be punished when caught by their bosses.[69]

The teahouse represented a place of freedom for males. If a man felt hot, he could strip to the waist. If he needed a haircut, a barber could be summoned to cut his hair at his seat, even if the clippings fell into the teacups of other patrons. He could also take off his shoes and have his nails clipped by a pedicurist.[70] If he was alone, he could eavesdrop on other conversations or join in if he preferred. He could stay as long as he liked. If he had an errand to run, he could simply move his cup to the middle of the table to signal the waiter to "hold it" until he returned.[71]

Unlike American cities, where many forms of leisure activities were available,[72] in Chengdu going to the teahouse was almost the only choice, especially given that street life was not active after nightfall. A teahouse could become a gathering place for those with common interests, much like a social "club." The Archery Society (shede hui), for instance, had a teahouse in the Smaller City Park for those who practiced archery. The teahouse on Sun Yat-sen Street (Zhongshan jie) was near the pigeon market, so it became a "pigeon club." The Broadway (Bailao hui) Teahouse was at the bird market and became a "bird club." Some devoted bird lovers visited every morning, hanging their birdcages under the eaves or on trees and enjoying the birds' singing as they drank their tea. Of course, the feeding and training of birds was a favorite topic of discussion. Some teahouses, such as the Pleasure Wind (Huifeng) Teahouse in Sun Yat-sen Park, became regular markets for the bird trade. Local opera aficionados were another major group that frequented teahouses. They gathered there to practice local operas with simple instruments and wearing no costumes or makeup. This was called "sitting around and beating drums" (da weigu) or "sitting opera" (bandeng xi). A picture in Investigation of Chengdu depicts this activity.[73]

The most attractive thing about the teahouse for many customers, however, was the free flow of conversation. Teahouses in Chengdu, like those in nineteenth-century Hankou, were the sites of "non-class-restrictive discussions of current news and events." In a teahouse, people could talk about anything; there was even a teahouse in West City Gate simply called "Free Talk Pavilion" (Geshuo ge). According to the guidebook New Chengdu (Xin Chengdu), teahouse-goers would "tell ancient and modern stories, comment on society, play chess, gamble, criticize public figures, investigate private matters, and gossip about the secrets of the boudoir."[74] We know little about the actual content of teahouse talk, but fortunately journalists recorded what they heard in public, including in teahouses, in a regular column in the Citizens' Daily (Guomin gongbao). From this column we learn that teahouse-goers complained about the decline of social morality, discussed new government policies, and remarked on various trends in society.[75] Frequently, patrons found humor in the life of the teahouse, as seen in this tale of a man who liked to boast:

A man liked pretending to be rich and would become angry if no one noticed his apparent wealth. One day, while drinking tea in a teahouse, the patrons complained about their hard life, having only porridge with pickled vegetables to eat every day. He said, "That's your own fault because you don't manage to get along well. I can have cooked rice with meat every day." Others did not believe him, so he jutted out his lips, shining with oil, as if he had just eaten meat. Later, his son rushed in the teahouse and yelled anxiously: "Dad, your piece of meat was stolen by the cat." He pretended carelessness and asked his son, with a conspiring wink, "Which one, the three *jin* piece or the five *jin* piece?" His son failed to take the hint and answered, "We don't have three or five *jin* pieces of meat, only the small piece of meat that you use to polish your lips every day." The man was so angry that he slapped his son, causing him to cry out: "It was the cat that stole the meat, not me." This caused everybody to laugh at the man.[76]

This anecdote can be thought of as a live "social drama," with teahouse-goers playing the role of "public man as an actor."[77] Just as Balzac's works are a rich source for scholars who study the public life of nineteenth-century Paris, as Richard Sennett points out, the local literature of Chengdu can also tell us much about the nature of street life.

Public talk was usually described as "gossiping" or "spreading rumors." This was always regarded by new elites as an "unhealthy" aspect of the teahouse. Some contemporary studies, however, have suggested that gossiping is a "form of sociable interaction" and "a way of speaking." Gossip, therefore, is "seen as simply one of the many inevitable performances of everyday life." James Scott has gone so far as to define gossip as a "form of resistance" and as a "kind of democratic 'voice.'" For good or ill, regulating gossip in Chengdu teahouses was almost impossible. The poor probably gossiped not merely for curiosity or for fun but, according to Scott, to allow "the expression of opinion, of contempt, of disapproval while minimizing the risks of identification and reprisal."[78] The objects of commoners' gossip were usually local notables or the wealthy. Gossip about their life of luxury and splendid weddings provided a means for commoners to complain about society's inequities; rumors about adultery proved that the rich were "immoral"; and unfortunate incidents befalling the rich gave commoners a sense of satisfaction.

The Teahouse as Market and Office.   Behind its leisurely facade, the teahouse served society in multiple ways. The teahouse could be called a "free market," because people such as craftsmen, servants, and free laborers gathered there to hawk their labor, skills, and goods. Vendors shouted back and forth between tables, while patrons remained undisturbed. Petty peddlers were very active in teahouses; "as soon as a customer enters a teahouse and calls for a cup of tea, he is surrounded by a crowd of food-peddlers asking him to buy cigarettes, fried seeds, and peanuts." Patrons could even buy cigarettes individually instead of by the pack if they chose. Some vendors sold everyday items such as brushes, fans, straw sandals, and straw caps.[79]

Peddlers often used their special skills, which strongly reflected the local folk culture, to amuse patrons. For instance, the melon seed peddlers, who engaged in "one of the few trades that do not change with the change in seasons," pursued their trade on the streets and in teahouses, opium dens, and other places. A missionary also was impressed by the skill of these peddlers: "It is quite an art . . . to crack these seeds between the teeth and extract the very meager seed." Fried-seed peddlers sold seeds by the plate while also playing games of chance with customers. There were two ways to participate in this gambling: one was to guess the number of seeds and the other was to "pick the right number." In the first game, the buyer took a number of seeds in his hand (usually around a dozen) and let the peddler guess. If the peddler was wrong, the seeds were put aside. This would continue until the peddler got the correct answer. The other game required the peddler to pick the correct number of seeds (arranged by both sides) in a handful. If the peddler picked the wrong number, the seeds would be put aside and the peddler would pick another handful until he got the right number. A highly skilled seed peddler could get the right number the first time. A visitor in the 1930s noted that one girl sold her seeds quickly because she could seize in a handful the exact number of seeds requested by the customer.[80] From this, we can deduce that peddlers in teahouses were not only selling their products but also providing entertainment.

A teahouse was also a labor market, where many free laborers and peasants sought work. Generally, laborers who practiced the same trade gathered at the same teahouses so that employers knew where to look for the help they needed. For example, back carriers usually gathered in the teahouses in Frying Pan Alley (Luoguo xiang) and Grinding Stone Street (Mozi jie). "It is very convenient. Whenever you call, they can come with you." When a foreign teacher needed to hire a servant, her Chinese friend told her to go to the "tea-shop inside the South Gate of the city where, every morning, women gather who wished to hire themselves out."[81] Thus, during the 1920s, women as well as men used the teahouse as a sort of employment broker.

The teahouse gathered "people of all walks of life." Many artisans worked in the teahouses repairing household items for patrons. An old photo of a Chengdu teahouse in *Canadian School in West China* shows several people, old and young, male and female, sitting around a low tea table and chatting. At the side of the table, a man in shabby clothing sits on a small, low stool attentively working on something with his hands. It is obvious that he is not there to sip tea or to join the conversation. Although we cannot be certain, most likely he is repairing shoes. Fortune-tellers also met at their regular teahouses for business. Pedicurists and barbers provided their services in the teahouses despite hygiene regulations. Some beggars even sold so-called "cool wind"—fanning a patron for money. This was actually more a form of begging than a service; a beggar would fan a patron, and if the patron appreciated it, and was in a good mood, he would give some change to the beggar. The most interesting people were the ear pickers, who had over ten different kinds of ear-picking tools to meticulously pick, grip, scrape, or rinse ears. Their customers did not necessarily want their ears to be cleaned but instead sought the kind of sensation produced by the process.[82]

Chengdu people also used teahouses as reception rooms for meeting friends. Because most common people lived in very small quarters, they felt more comfortable socializing in a teahouse.[83] They could often find their friends in the teahouse without advance planning. An elderly editor recalled that during the 1930s and 1940s there was a special teahouse for intellectuals, where he met his writers to assign and receive articles, thereby saving both postage and time. Many residents made decisions about their daily lives in teahouses. Sewell's memoir told a story of how, when one of his friends was in trouble, they discussed the solution in a teahouse. Some occupations, social organizations, and students used teahouses as meeting places. The Sleeping Stream (Zhenliu) Teahouse became a gathering place for students, extremely crowded on weekends and holidays. While intellectuals favored the Cultural (Wenhua) Teahouse, teachers gathered at the Crane Singing (Heming) Teahouse. Even rickshaw pullers, secondhand goods traders, and latrine cleaners had their own teahouses.[84]

Many business deals were sealed in teahouses, and merchants had their customary teahouses for talking business while drinking tea. Traditionally, the Oil and Grain Guild met in the Peace and Joy Temple Teahouse (Anlesi chashe); the Yarn and Cloth Guild gathered in the Leisure Teahouse (Xianju chashe); and the secret societies who smuggled opium and weapons gathered in the Tasty Teahouse (Pinxiang chashe). A teahouse at the rice market near the South City Gate served as a gathering place for rice-shop keepers and peasants who came to Chengdu to sell their wares. So many business conversations were held in a teahouse daily that one man asked for compensation, claiming that a fight there had ruined his business negotiations.[85] Han Suyin has written about such business talk in her autobiography: "The call: 'I buy tea', uttered so frequently in the teahouses . . . prefaced amicable talk of business, respect to an elder, demand for a favour, or any of those transactions of land or merchandise which are normally done in a teahouse or a restaurant because the home is no place for such mundane matters."[86]

Western travelers, too, noticed the function of commerce at the teahouse, noting that a teahouse was not only a place for public chat but "a large proportion of the business is also done there." In 1920s Chengdu, Hubbard saw "merchants hurry to meet prospective buyers or sellers at their shops or in a tea room. And the peddler is always there, hawking his wares with an intonation, whistle, gong or clapper, everywhere characteristic of his trade." The use of teahouses as places of business was not unique to Chengdu, but nowhere else did teahouses serve so many functions in the lives of ordinary citizens.[87]

"Drinking Settlement Tea." Teahouses not only filled cultural and economic functions but also often played a role in maintaining social stability. An unwritten rule gradually took shape in Chengdu: when conflict arose, people would seek mediators in teahouses instead of going to court. Philip Huang has analyzed the three stages of civil lawsuits in Qing China, finding that many disputes were settled before they reached the magistrates. In fact, even more disputes were usually solved before going to court because of the social mediation offered at teahouses. This activity in Chengdu was called "arguing one's case in a teahouse" (*chaguan jiangli*), or "drinking settlement tea" (*chi jiangcha*). From this role, we might call the teahouse a "quasi-civil court." Generally the two parties concerned would invite a prestigious public figure to a teahouse to hear their case. That is why "there is seldom any real fighting" in Chengdu, according to one observer, though this might be overstated.[88] Of course, disputes solved in the teahouse were usually civil conflicts over issues of daily life and business, things like verbal abuse, debts, property disputes, and even violent fights if no death was involved; otherwise, the matter would be addressed in the yamen.

Because this activity occurred regularly, some men, usually the leaders of powerful local secret societies, became professional teahouse mediators. In his short novel *In the Fragrant Chamber Teahouse* (Zai Qixiangju chaguan li), Sha Ding described someone who was invited to handle "drinking settlement tea" in the teahouse as a mediator: "Master Xin is a *xiucai* [degree] holder of the last civil service examination in the Qing, and had been a commander of a local militia and a leader of the Sworn Brotherhood Society for ten years. He retired eight years ago, and has seldom involved himself in local affairs since then, but his opinion is still as influential as when he was the commander."[89]

Some details about "drinking settlement tea" have been recorded. One account by a foreigner reveals that when quarrels arose, "after the principals have emptied themselves of all the abuse they can deliver, they are hurried off to a tea-shop or perhaps invite each other to go, and there the grievances are gone into before a crowd of people who sip tea while listening, and in the end, the one who is in the wrong must pay the score."[90] From various sources, we know that mediations occurred almost daily. In his famous historical novel *Before the Storm* (Baofeng yuxian), Li Jieren offered a satirical description of how people reached a settlement in the teahouse:

The common format for settling disputes was that each party had a cup of tea and explained his case in front of the mediator. The two parties usually tried to gather as many supporters as possible to show they had powerful backing. Generally, if the two parties did not have equivalent power, it was easy to handle the case. After hearing the dispute, the mediator would criticize the weak side and judge it wrong. The wrong side usually did not need to apologize to the other and only paid the entire cost of the tea, sometimes for two tables of tea and sometimes for a dozen.[91]

If both sides were found at fault, however, both were obligated to share the cost of tea. Therefore, there is a proverb in Chengdu: "A [tea] table has four legs, and you can go [without paying] if you are not wrong." Settling disputes sometimes led to violence. Furniture or other items could be damaged, or a fight sometimes could lead to injury or even death. Street officers (*jiechai*) and the neighborhood headman (*baozheng*) would deal with the situation. The people involved in the fighting would compensate the teahouse for its loss. "It was a good time for the teahouse, which might take out all broken tables, chairs, and cups, some of which might be broken a long time ago, for compensation." For this reason, Li noted sarcastically, most teahouses welcomed dispute settlements.[92]

That residents preferred the verdicts of mediators to those of local government not only suggests that the people did not trust their "muddled officials" but also might reflect the expansion of the power of nonofficial forces in Chengdu. Several scholars of Chinese history, such as Mary Rankin and William Rowe, have emphasized the dramatic development of elite activism—disaster relief, granaries, charity, civil construction, and other managerial activities—after the mid-nineteenth century and its profound impact on society. Still, they do not include the teahouse in their analysis. Whereas Rankin, Rowe, and David Strand have adapted the concept of "public sphere" to analyze social transformation, Philip Huang has suggested that a "third realm" of the justice system lay between the state and society and performed as a semi-institutionalized sphere.[93] I suggest, however, that elites' participation in the activity of "drinking settlement tea" indicates another aspect of elite activism that shows how elites handled conflicts among individuals and between individuals and society. It is also a window into how the community of Chengdu tried to maintain social stability and how civil order existed outside the official justice system.

Of course, such mediating activities could be found elsewhere in pre-modern and modern China and had become an important part of social self-control. As discussed previously, the absence of government authority in many areas left a large power vacuum that attracted local elites, whose activities became a foundation for community stability. The reason that teahouse settlement became popular was that most people preferred to conduct mediation in a public place, where it would appear to be as "equal" as possible under the watchful eye of the public. Otherwise, public opinion might go against the reputation of the mediator. This is how the term "drinking settlement tea" became a synonym for mediation. In addition, violence was much less likely to occur there when mediation was not successful. What social mediation represents here extends far beyond the activity itself; it reveals that in Chinese society, a nonofficial force always existed and played a crucial role in everyday life, even though it grew weaker after the early twentieth century.

Part **11**

COMMONERS AND SOCIAL REFORMERS

4 Reshaping the Street and Public Life

In the early twentieth century, all of China experienced an enormous social and cultural transformation. In Chengdu, many new phenomena could be seen on the street, although probably less dramatically than in the major coastal cities. The arrival of foreign goods and missionaries and the spread of Western cultural models inevitably influenced street culture. Urban commoners' customary interaction with public space and the resulting street culture underwent dramatic changes in the late Qing. Social reformers who were dissatisfied with the uses of urban space and commoners' public behavior sought to restructure public space and "re-educate" commoners. Part II focuses on the relationship between commoners and social reformers, and this chapter explores the early-twentieth-century movement supported by both the state and local elites in which social reformers sought to reshape public space, change the city's appearance, and alter the street life of ordinary residents. These reforms resulted from the rise of a local and national reform movement, dissatisfaction among elites regarding the public behavior of commoners, and Western influences on the economy and culture, including an increasingly consumer-oriented culture.

Urban reform in Chengdu was primarily driven by two forces: the national reform movement, which emerged at the end of the nineteenth century and was led for the most part by nongovernmental elite reformers, and the "New Policies," which were adopted in the early twentieth century and promoted by the Qing central government.[1] The movement also reflected the influence of reformers who sought to make Chinese cities more like those they had visited in Japan and the West. In early-twentieth-century Chengdu, the New Policies ushered in great economic, political, and educational changes. In the economy, the policies resulted in the creation of many new factories, workshops, and other organizations such as joint-stock companies, chambers of commerce, and various occupational associations. In politics, the constitutional change established a provincial assembly and a city council and took steps toward judicial reform, making local elites more directly involved in local politics. The most significant reforms occurred in education.

With the abandonment of the civil service examinations in 1905, modern public schools gradually replaced traditional private academies. Those who held degrees from the former civil service examination system as well as traditional students entered the new schools. Many even went abroad to study. Meanwhile, new elites published unprecedented numbers of newspapers, journals, and books.[2]

All these changes affected the everyday lives of commoners in Chengdu. Introduction of new goods not only developed people's material life but also fostered their curiosity about the rest of the world. As a result, this relatively isolated city became home to new schools, book publishers, and newspapers within a fairly short period, further strengthening the movement to reform public space and street culture. Reformers had successfully put forth the notion that many aspects of the city, from its physical landmarks to the minds of its residents, were in need of change.

The leaders of the reform movement viewed ordinary people as passive objects to be controlled and regulated, and social reformers as the driving force. If the traditional pattern of public space and street life emerged naturally from the economic and cultural milieu, the new pattern was driven solely by politics. The elite class used the reform movement as a tool with which to shape the behavior of the masses. The reformers' main agenda was the transformation of Chengdu into the model of their choosing, without concern for the welfare of ordinary citizens; any resulting benefit to commoners was purely peripheral.

There is no doubt that the early twentieth century was a "reformist era" in Chengdu, but how did social reformers understand the term "reform"? What were their standards or models? An article in *Popular Daily*, titled "On Reform" (*Shuo weixin*), answered at least part of the question. According to the article, the word "*xin*" (new) was the complete opposite of "*jiu*" (old). In the real world, the author claimed, anything based in the past represented the "old" and anything in the present, the "new." Therefore, all established traditions and customs were old, and thus unreliable and in need of reform, and the resulting changes signified the "new." Some social reformers considered all types of traditions backward simply because they were old. The word *wenming* (civilization; civilized) became popular during the late Qing, but it referred to "civilized" Western ideas and practices, many of which the reformers introduced to Chengdu.[3] This perception indicates the elites' sense of urgency. Others involved in the movement, however, believed the ideal social behavior for commoners could be found in a combination of traditional Chinese morality and Western virtues. Reformers judged commoners' "uncivilized" public behavior against both the new Western standard and traditional Chinese values such as loyalty, benevolence, filial piety, and trust. Whereas previously the elites had based their claim to cultural superiority on Confucian orthodoxy, in the late Qing, as new Western ideologies emerged, elites as social reformers found a new urgency to assert their legitimacy.

Commoners' Public Behavior in the Eyes of Elites

The documents left by elites that describe and criticize commoners' public activities provide good sources for an examination of their attitude toward the masses and popular culture. Elite criticism of ordinary people and popular culture can be traced to the premodern period, long before the reform movement. The elite writers denounced virtually every aspect of ordinary people's lives, from what they wore to how they acted. In their view, commoners were indecent, stupid, vain, and dishonest, with "nothing to do but play cards and then get drunk."[4] Elites also targeted what they called "bad street boys": longhaired hoodlums who played with dogs, carried daggers, and consorted with prostitutes after drinking and gambling. Since local toughs typically congregated in certain areas, such as the bank of the Imperial River (Yuhe), one of them advised, "don't go to the bank of the Imperial River, where good people could be affected by bad habits." However, they reserved their harshest criticism for so-called "superstition," including religious ritual. For example, on the fifth day of the first lunar month, people sought to repel "poverty ghosts" (qionggui) by gathering pebbles that represented golden ingots. Elites mocked that "the poverty ghosts might not hide in their homes; instead they might drive the 'God of Wealth' out of the gates."[5]

This criticism reached new heights in the early twentieth century, when elites began to compare their own people to "civilized" Westerners. By every measure, ordinary citizens fell short of this new ideal: old men gathered in teahouses only to gossip; young men hid by the city wall to watch prostitutes; and women were obsessed with fortune-tellers and witch doctors. The elites approached even minor issues with the same seriousness. In the column "Review of Current Affairs" in Citizens' Daily (Guomin gongbao), a short essay entitled "Detestable" (kehen) castigated those who broke branches off trees. The author extended his argument to ridiculous lengths, claiming that foreigners posted signs reading "Chinese and Dogs Not Admitted" at their amusement parks in Shanghai not in an effort to discriminate against and humiliate Chinese but to break them of the habit of cutting down tree limbs. The article also touched on the notion of "civilization" and pointed out that such behavior was no different from that of animals. As is widely known, the sign "Chinese and Dogs Not Admitted" was regarded by Chinese nationalists as the prime example of how Westerners shamed Chinese, and it was often mentioned to promote anti-imperialism.[6] In this case, however, the article argued from the Western perspective, revealing the urgency with which reform was viewed.[7]

Reformers believed that popular entertainment was largely responsible for commoners' "wicked" public behavior. In their eyes, all actors and actresses were "unbearably vulgar" and "deliberately behave in an ugly manner," and some folk performances were "unhealthy." Comic dialogue performed on the street, which routinely attracted audiences of more than one hundred, featured "dirty" and "licentious" language. *Liulianliu*, however, was regarded as the "lowest entertainment." In it, a performer, carrying a bamboo stick on which were attached a few copper coins, would sing, tapping the stick on his body for accompaniment. *Liulianliu* performers used vulgar slang that elites criticized as "intolerable to the ear." The favorite *liulianliu* song, "Young Widow Going to Her Husband's Grave" (*xiao guafu shangfen*), was considered by elites to be "ugly."[8]

Like their predecessors, many elites of this era criticized so-called "superstitions"—such as idolatry, fear of bad omens, and belief in the powers of witch doctors—and used every available opportunity to sneer at practitioners. For instance, after a woman caused a fire when burning incense to Guanyin at her home, the local newspaper report took a satirical tone: "She kowtowed to Guanyin, but the God of Fire showed up." In Chengdu, it was considered unlucky to accidentally pour vegetable oil on the street, and the person responsible had to buy "paper money"(*zhiqian*), put it on the oil, and burn it, while chanting to rid himself of the curse.[9] This was called "burning the street" (*shaojie*). Once, more than a dozen people watched this ritual as the fire spread across half the street and blocked traffic, according to a newspaper report. The reporter commented, with apparent exasperation: "It is hard to understand why so many people surrounded the fire and watched it on such a hot summer day." They mocked Chengdu people for being "so foolish and superstitious as to concern themselves too much with the door god when the Chinese New Year is approaching."[10] Similarly, *Popular Daily* published an article criticizing the cult of the God of Wealth. The twenty-second day of the seventh lunar month was designated for worshiping the God of Wealth, when firecrackers were set off in the streets and alleys and residents kept busy burning incense. Such ceremony caused reformers to lament:

It's ridiculous that all shopkeepers and residents regard worshiping the God of Wealth as the most important activity on that day. Can they not see that people are increasingly poor year after year? Do they not worship the God of Wealth? . . . According to these believers, anyone who does not worship the God of Wealth will become a beggar. Yet, why have people who do not worship the God of Wealth already become rich? Why are foreigners who do not worship the God of Wealth still rich? Why do the merchants in other countries have more money than Chinese merchants do? That is the pity: stupid people reject the truth and instead trust lies. In fact, not only does this worship not make you richer, it also makes you poorer, because you have to buy firecrackers, sacrifices, candles, and so on. This could cost twenty to thirty taels of silver for a well-to-do family and two or three days' wages for a poor family. . . . If you were to put this cost into your business, you could be rich in the future. Why do Chinese merchants become poorer and poorer year after year? Why are the people still not awake? There is simply no such a thing as sitting at home, worshiping the God of Wealth, while money drops from the sky.[11]

Such a notion also reflected the belief among the elite that success resulted from hard work, not from the worship of gods. The elites did not understand the importance of spirituality in the lives of commoners, who could hardly aspire to material abundance in the present life.

Witch doctors became a favorite target of social reformers. Witch doctors, as noted in Chapter 2, persuaded people that their "supernatural power" could save them from being pursued by "ghosts." Many in Chengdu believed in witchcraft and relied on witch doctors to heal the sick. During these healing rituals, it was reported, "ghosts' screams and deities' cries could be heard in the neighborhood at midnight. They perform their rituals accompanied by striking drums and gongs, and nobody cares that the patients are severely shaken." Witch doctors hung charms under the roofs to ward off prowling spirits. Unfortunately, witch doctors "do not have enough power to control ghosts and they charge too much." As a result, some critics pointed out that "witch doctors are supporters of ghosts" because they "kill people without using knives." A local newspaper printed a story about a witch doctor who complained of being tricked by ghosts after falling into a pond one night on his way home from his practice. The reporter called him "water witch doctor" (*shui duangong*) and asked: "Since the witch doctor claimed to have the ability to control ghosts, why was he himself fooled by ghosts? Now we can understand the true nature of the witch doctor's magic."[12] The practice of consulting witch doctors remained popular through the 1920s, as we see in Ba Jin's autobiography, *Family* (Jia), when the protagonist's grandfather is frightened to death by a witch doctor:

One night, shortly after dark, all doors were shut tight. The compound was converted into a weird and ancient temple. A thin-faced witch doctor with flowing locks arrived. Dressed in peculiar vestments, uttering shrill cries, he scattered burning resin, exactly like an actor impersonating a devil upon the stage. He ran about the courtyard making all sorts of frightful noises and gestures. Entering the patient's apartment, he leaped and yelled and flung things to the floor, even throwing burning resin beneath the bed. The loud groans of the old man—induced by the clamor and terror—in no way deterred the witch doctor. His performance gained in frenzy. He made such wild menacing thrusts that the old man cried out in alarm. The room was filled with thick black smoke and the glare and smell of sputtering resin.[13]

Although Ba Jin described the scene realistically, his language also reveals his prejudice against such practices. This prejudice existed across China; as Prasenjit Duara put it, "Modernizing reformers in the state and among the elite saw the realm of popular religion and culture as a principal obstacle to the establishment of a 'disenchanted' world of reason and plenty." The reformer Fu Chongju supported a policy of turning local temples into schools—precisely the policy adopted by the state in rural North China—saying, "this is absolutely the right way." He also favored imposing a tax on Buddhist and Daoist clergy. Like Fu, other reformers—particularly members of the Provincial Assembly—forbade works they deemed "bizarre" and "superstitious," including Chinese classics such as *Investiture of the Gods* (Fengshen yanyi), *Journey to West* (Xiyou ji), and all books dealing with monsters, divination, Buddhism, and Daoism.[14] Thus, in the late Qing, a latent radical movement to attack popular culture and popular religion was already under way, led by "modernized" social reformers.

Reformers espoused throughout their writings the notion that Chinese tradition was backward while foreign culture was always progressive. The *Popular Daily*, for example, proclaimed that Japanese and Westerners commonly bought and read newspapers in all kinds of places, including at railway stations, aboard ships, in barbershops, on rickshaws, and in restaurants. In 1908, according to this report, some new-style teahouses, such as Concerning (Huaiyuan) Teahouse and Spring (Yichun) Teahouse, began to offer newspapers to their patrons, and some restaurants followed suit. The new elites deemed this to be "a way to civilization." When a family in Chengdu violated custom by performing a double wedding ceremony, a local newspaper praised this decision as "absolutely civilized" and "not only breaking old customs, but also saving money." On the other hand, traditional weddings were mocked by the new elites. They claimed, for example, that using the *laba* (a brass-wind instrument) was a "decrepit formation," whereas they praised Western-style marching bands as a "joyful and civilized choice."[15]

Countering this trend, however, some elites refused to blindly pay homage to the West. They criticized people who wore foreign dress; for example, a drawing published in the *Popular Pictorial* (Tongsu huabao) depicts an old man who is taunted as "half Chinese, half Western" because of his style of dress (see Figure 4.1). The author of an item in the *Popular Daily*, entitled "A False Foreigner Falling into a Real Ditch," ridicules a man dressed in foreign-style clothes who had fallen into a ditch and torn his clothing. Displaying no sympathy, the reporter made fun of the "false foreigner's misfortune."[16] In the late Qing, "worshiping the West" was popular. A story in *Popular Daily* scorned those who did so, however, telling of one man who brought back many exotic items from his foreign travels. When his relatives visited him, they found his appearance greatly

（社會百怪之八）

中西人

一身洋裝滿口華語
遍身洋貨不遺下體
又非討吃狗混挾起
好像悶頭豬嘴吽起
又不阿屎把煙咬起
全錢外輸國貨不喜
祇恨父母非洋種子
不中不西人而無恥
社會改良個個笑你

FIGURE 4.1. A Half-Chinese, Half-Western Man (One Hundred Queer-Looking People of Society, No. 8). The poem reads: "Western-style clothes on your whole body, but you speak Chinese. You are not a beggar, but why do you carry a dog-beating stick? You spend your money only on imported goods because you do not like Chinese ones. . . . You hate his parents, who did not give you a foreign face. You are shameless, neither Western nor Chinese. In a time of social reform, everybody laughs at you." From TSHB 1912, no. 24.

changed—he had dispensed with the traditional pigtail and instead sported a mustache to go with his foreign clothes. They asked him what he had learned during his trip. As he showed them each item from his suitcase, he extolled its quality, saying, "You see, these foreign goods are better than anything manufactured by the Chinese." Finally,

he picked up a rattan pillow and said: "You see how elegant this rattan pillow is! It is light as well as cool [if used during the summer], and was probably made by machine. Our Chinese could never have done such a fine work." An old man could not help remarking: "You inherited this pillow from your father and took it with you when you left home. It seems to me that you mistakenly think it of foreign origin." The traveler felt very embarrassed and explained that "since it had traveled in the West, it looks much better than before." Everyone who heard him could not help laughing.[17]

From this "pillow story," we can ascertain the negative attitude toward the young man who blindly admired the West; this attitude was common. If we consider this story along with the descriptions of Chengdu in the novels of Ba Jin and Li Jieren, which reveal deep generational conflict, we can surmise that whereas younger people embraced Western ideas and material culture, older residents were more likely to keep the old traditions. Between the extremes of the new and the old, some people might find a middle ground and be able to keep a balance between Western and Chinese culture; they promoted the Western ideas that they believed were useful for reform, but still advanced Chinese traditional values. For them, these two cultures were not necessarily contradictory.

Apparently, elites had held a basically hostile attitude toward popular culture for a long time. Whereas the earlier elites did not, at least from available evidence, conduct any concrete measures for change, new elites in the early twentieth century launched an aggressive campaign to re-create the city's image and reshape its public space. Most of the social reformers inherited the moral tradition of Confucian orthodoxy, but felt that Western ideas were not contradictory to their established Chinese values and indeed adopted a very practical attitude toward ideologies of China and the West. What reformers did during the reform period proved that they still held strong traditional values even as they accepted some Western ideas. In other words, they appropriated what they thought would be useful from ideological resources, whether from their own or a foreign culture.

Creation of a New Public Leisure

Social reformers in Chengdu believed fairs to be useful vehicles to promote cultural change, science and technology, and commerce and industry; they also attempted to appropriate temple fairs for their own purposes. In 1904, the Bureau for Promoting Manufacturing (Quangong ju) opened a display hall "following Japan's model." The next year, the Chengdu Chamber of Commerce (Chengdu zong shanghui) promoted local festivals as places where goods could be displayed and sold. The Bureau of Commercial Affairs and the Chamber of Commerce collected hundreds of traditional and Western-style goods to exhibit at the latter's headquarters. After this, new public spaces were added quickly. In 1909, the Center for Promoting Commerce and Industry (Quanye chang), which housed more than 150 shops selling high-quality merchandise and featured an exhibition for foreign and local products, was constructed (see Figure 4.2). Reformers regarded the Center as an important step in Chengdu's "commercial modernization." The Center represented the new commercial space and culture of late Qing Chengdu. In 1910, it was renamed the Commercial Center (Shangye chang), and in 1918, following a fire, it was expanded to more than three hundred shops.[18]

This was the first facility in Chengdu, and in all of Sichuan, that concentrated many shops under one roof. Also, never before had foreign and domestic goods been displayed together, an act that transformed the landscape and public space of the city. This new facility not only attracted more shoppers but also offered some new economic ideas. The social reformers used the Center to convince commoners of the notion that "new is good"; people learned about the outside world and about a new way of doing business from the Center. The Center, in fact, represented Chengdu's emerging new commercial culture. It was the first commercial establishment in the city to require price tags on all merchandise, obviating cheating by shopkeepers. Consequently, the Center attracted shoppers from across Sichuan, and business blossomed. This success also influenced shops in other major commercial areas such as Horse Riding Street, East Great Street, and Main Office Street; gradually, most of the businesses in Chengdu adopted the same practices.[19]

The Center not only functioned as a shopping mall but also became a site for public recreation. Children, for example, used it as a playground. According to editorials in a local newspaper, children were a nuisance, jumping on the floor, climbing fences, running back and forth, and being generally boisterous. When two children failed to heed a warning to behave, policemen forced them to kneel on the floor to "enforce the rules." When the number of visitors at the Center became overwhelming, it was decided that women would not be allowed to visit at night and that large groups would be prohibited on the second floor. A reporter from *Popular Daily* counted 33,756 men and 11,340 women visitors to the Center in one day, and more than 5,000 men and women during the evening hours on the first day of the first lunar month. As a schoolboy, Guo Moruo, one of modern China's preeminent scholars and politicians, wrote several bamboo-branch poems about the Center in his homework journal. One of them noted that

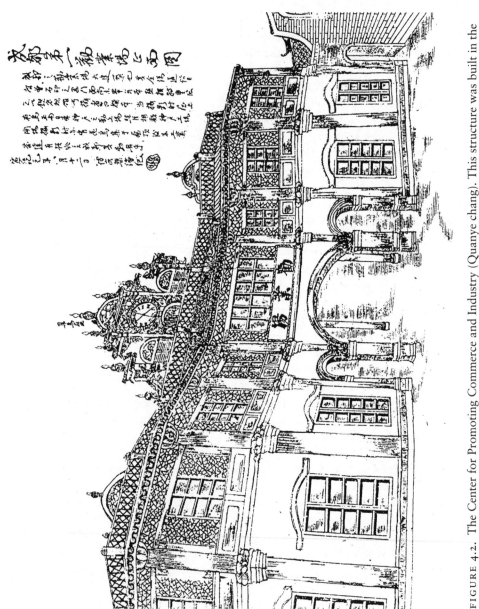

FIGURE 4.2. The Center for Promoting Commerce and Industry (Quanye chang). This structure was built in the late Qing and is obviously Western in style. If we regard the clock at the top of the roof as a "clock tower," it was constructed earlier than the one in Shaanxi Street. From TSHB 1909, no. 3.

"women with beautiful hairstyles gather and walk in the Center for Promoting Commerce and Industry. No wonder even bees light on their heads because their hair is like flowers blooming."[20]

Reformers perceived many problems with the old-style shops: merchants developed many "bad habits," such as not treating customers courteously. When a customer entered a shop, the shopkeeper did not always rise to greet him. Shopkeepers treated peasant customers with outright contempt or ignored them. They often refused to answer customers' questions or check their inventory for a requested item. If a customer tried to haggle over the price of an item, the shopkeeper might become angry and even verbally abusive. Some even argued that the only thing shopkeepers desired was to have customers leave as quickly as possible.[21] In 1909, the Department of Promoting Commerce and Industry in Sichuan, led by reformer Zhou Shanpei, issued a public notice to promote the new commercial culture and thus enhance local commerce. It included several suggestions for improving customer service, including greeting all customers with a warm welcome, thoroughly checking for additional items in inventory, and referring customers to other stores where an item might be available. Shopkeepers were advised never to refuse outright a customer's initial price offering, but rather to negotiate politely. They were also asked to be more patient and even to offer tobacco and tea. After such favorable treatment, it was believed that the customer might consider it ungracious not to buy something or at least return in the future. If a shopkeeper abused his customers or acted unprofessionally, the department warned, there was no doubt that the business would founder. The Department of Promoting Commerce and Industry required all shops to display this notice on their doors and to follow its guidelines. "The shop owner tells the shopkeeper, the shopkeeper tells the master, and the master tells the apprentices. All shops should take these guidelines very seriously. If any master fails to conform, he should be replaced by a new one; if any apprentice fails to conform, he should be beaten on his palms."[22] The physical punishment of shop apprentices was customary and was still supported by the "Westernized" elites.

Reformers also succeeded in changing the name of the traditional Flower Fair to the Festival for Promoting Industry (see Figure 4.3). As noted in Chapter 2, the Flower Fair served as the largest public gathering in Chengdu. The Bureau of Commercial Affairs changed the traditional Flower Fair at the Green Goat Temple into the Festival for Promoting Industry (*quangong hui*), where goods from throughout Sichuan were sold. The first festival, held in the spring of 1906, displayed more than 3,400 varieties of goods from shops, factories, and workshops and provided lodging, rest areas, and entertainment. Later, a zoo opened in the fair and exhibited many "rare and freak animals," such as a single-legged dove and an opium-addicted monkey. Prior to

1911, this festival was held six times in Chengdu.[23] It actually increased support of urban reform; visitors could not fail to be impressed by the new festival. Every spring, the fair became one of Chengdu's most popular destinations. As spring approached, the city showed signs of renewed strength and vitality and engaged in outdoor activities.[24] The fair was also the occasion for construction of the city's first "highway," which provided access to horse carts for the convenience of city dwellers. At the Flower Fair, a popular means of local transportation, "cock carts" (*jigong che*), which balanced on a single wheel, were used. The carts were ridiculed in one bamboo-branch poem: "Although both boats and horse carts are ready to take people to the Flower Fair, they hire cheaper cock carts to save money."[25]

After the Qing collapsed, the fair reclaimed its old name, but as the Flower Fair it remained the largest public gathering in Chengdu every spring. Many accounts described how people dressed, how the commercial sheds were built, how beautiful girls and women attracted attention, and how much fun people had there. Customarily, the Flower Fair ended late in the second lunar month. Because of its increased popularity, it was extended much longer, even until the middle of the third lunar month. Overcrowding caused many problems, such as an increase in disorderly conduct

FIGURE 4.3. The Flower Fair. Detail from the scroll painting *Old Chengdu* (Lao Chengdu) by Sun Bin, Zhang Youlin, Li Wanchun, Liu Shifu, Xiong Xiaoxiong, Pan Peide, and Xie Kexin (2000). Courtesy of the artists.

and lost children; the local newspapers even urged parents not to bring their children at all. Beginning in 1919, the Flower Fair hosted an annual martial arts championship, which attracted even more people. In the 1920s, when the festival to promote provincial industry reopened after many years, it featured horse racing as well as exhibits.[26]

The establishment of a public park represented another milestone in the late-Qing reform movement in Chengdu. The Smaller City Park (Shaocheng gongyuan) opened in the early twentieth century on land that formerly was an archery range and a place for the bannermen of the Smaller City to practice horsemanship (see Map 3).[27] With the bannermen's decline, their practice grounds had gradually been converted to rice fields and vegetable gardens. In the late Qing, the practice grounds became a fashionable place for Chengdu residents to spend their leisure time, with new pavilions, teahouses, stores, and a theater, as well as gardens and a park, located there. Development continued on the Smaller City Park after the 1911 Revolution. In 1913, the departments of Education, Economy, and Internal Affairs joined together to build an exhibition hall and a library there. Electric lights were also installed, so that the park could remain open after dark, although women were not allowed to stay in the evening. In 1914, an exhibition hall, a zoo, a small canal, and a pond were added, and the landscaping was improved. The park was funded by the government, and admission was free for students. This angered some, who thought that admission should be free for all Chengdu residents, and led to frequent disputes between residents and park gatekeepers.[28]

In addition to transforming public space, social reformers also devoted energy to mental enlightenment, primarily through promoting local operas, the most popular public entertainment. How did reformers regard the relationship between local operas and society? They knew that the theater could influence, or even establish, popular taste and believed that to reform local opera was one of the best ways to reform social customs, declaring it "as good as newspapers published in the local dialect." An article in *Popular Daily* tried to explain why people spent time and money at the opera. First, the opera helped relieve frustration. If an ill or troubled person stayed at home all day, the reporter surmised, he might dwell on his condition and feel worse. But if he spent a little money to join his friends to watch a play, he would think of other things and feel better. Second, watching local opera could be mentally stimulating. A scholar or student who felt mentally blocked could rejuvenate his thought processes at the opera. Third, it could foster morality. Although the plots might often seem ridiculous or historically incorrect, they could touch people's hearts and instruct them on the difference between good and bad. The article concluded that the reformed operas could promote a new social climate.[29]

As Tanaka Issei has pointed out, both the elites and the authorities feared that the old plays would have a negative effect on people's minds and behavior. A reform would be needed. In 1903, the Chengdu police tried to censor local operas and to "purify" theaters by requiring that "theatrical troupes submit their scripts to the bureau and not perform any songs or dialogues harmful to public morality." With the official support of the Chengdu Chamber of Commerce, the Opera Reform Association (Xiqu gailiang hui) was established for writing and rehearsing new plays that would "educate misguided or errant people." Young women from good families, virgins, and widows were the objects of particular concern; if they watched "licentious operas" (yinxi), the effect, reformers declared, would be "unthinkable." Therefore, reformers advised, the families of "educated persons, who understand moral value, share a sense of honor and shame and a concern for reputations," should not allow their women to attend the theater. "Violent operas" (xiongxi), they argued, encouraged "uneducated young men" to learn to fight and taught evil ways to knife-wielding hoodlums. According to Fu Chongju, "licentious operas" were those in which male and female characters embraced, or actresses bared parts of their bodies, and the like, while "violent operas" featured fights with real weapons and simulated bloody wounds and burning people alive. Some of the more common inappropriate scenes were "hands grabbing pants," "licentious noises," "movements in curtained beds," "unbuttoned clothing," "hand holding," and "kissing." These criticisms strongly reflected traditional Confucian ethics, values, and ideology. "Rape and adultery cases," elites believed, "will decrease after licentious operas are prohibited, and homicide cases will decrease as well after violent operas are prohibited."[30]

Under the growing trend of urban reform, new local operas, as well as other forms of entertainment, emerged in Chengdu. New material was created by making changes in the content and language of existing plays or writing new plays based on historical stories or current affairs. In general, these new local operas expressed a clear political orientation that encouraged "new thought." Reformers established the first new-style theater, the Joy Theater (Yuelai juchang) in Joy Teahouse, and installed a new troupe that specialized in "reformed local operas." This new form of theater provided a focus for cooperation among new local intellectuals, and it came to figure prominently in the transformation of local politics.[31]

Although these new operas were supported wholeheartedly by the elites, the performers who made them possible were not. Even their most minor request was treated with undue gravity. For instance, policemen at the Flower Fair reported problems when actors, who normally came into the fair through the entrance reserved for males, requested permission to use the entrance for females. The official response clearly reflected the social image of actors at the time: "Although these actors are different from ordinary men, they are still men. Therefore, it is not appropriate that the actors be allowed to enter from the female entrance. Let them make a detour and enter the fair from the west gate." Others remarked on the low moral character of the performers: "although performers are men, they behave like prostitutes who care nothing about morality. This is precisely why people scorn them." This example and the police regulations regarding actors show the very strong prejudice social reformers held against actors; they did not even consider actors normal people who should enjoy the same rights as others. The reformers also believed it was the performers who made reform of the opera more difficult. Thus, "to promote new operas," they emphasized, they "must reform performers' character first."[32]

The introduction of other forms of entertainment was as important as reforming local operas. The motion picture, which had appeared in China as early as 1904, probably was Chengdu's first "modern" entertainment, we see from an advertisement for the "American moving electric opera" (*Meiguo huodong dianxi*) in the *Chengdu Daily* (Chengdu ribao). In *Investigation of Chengdu*, the text accompanying a picture of an "electric light opera" (*dianguang xi*) says that Fu Chongju brought a movie projector from Japan to show moving pictures in public (see Figure 4.4). Motion pictures amazed many, particularly when the new teahouse-theaters Enlightened Garden (Qizhi yuan) and Elegant Garden presented foreign films. The programs in a 1909 advertisement included monster stories, London scenery, navy training, battles of the Russo-Japanese War, and Western magic. The reformers believed that foreign films were particularly effective in promoting the qualities of heroism, loyalty, and trust, because they were generally realistic and emotionally moving.[33]

Influenced by this new trend, teahouses as well started to incorporate new styles and fashions. In 1906, the first new-style public theater of Chengdu, the Elegant Garden (Keyuan, formerly the Reciting [Yongni] Teahouse), was opened on North Festival Street (Huifu beijie). At first, women and men were segregated, but after several incidents of mischief, women were prohibited altogether. In the early Republic, some new teahouses experimented with new styles of entertainment. For example, the Invigorated Pavilion (Taoran ting) Teahouse, which opened in 1912, had a "bowling room," where it offered "civilized games from the West for healthy leisure," as well as newspapers and food. The Joy Teahouse, always a pioneer, became the first to introduce modern stage dramas in the early 1920s.[34] These new facilities usually attracted more customers, and thus profits. Profit, not social reform, undoubtedly was the basic motivation behind these innovations.

Public leisure activities in Chengdu became increasingly sophisticated as reformers sought to change the customs of the lower classes through new

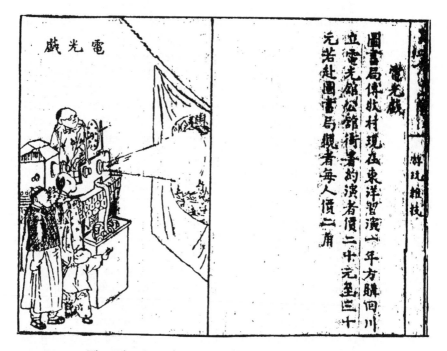

FIGURE 4.4. The "Electric Light Opera" (*dian'guang xi*). The inscription says: "Fu Qiaocun [Fu Chongju] of the Publication Company (Tushu ju) practiced operating a film projector in Japan for one year and recently brought one back. He has opened a show room. Families living in walled compounds and street organizations pay 20 to 30 *yuan* for special events, and individuals pay 20 cents per ticket at the Publication Company location." From CDTL 3: 114.

forms of entertainment, music, and sports. From a picture drawn in 1909, we can see many city residents watching a huge hot-air balloon hover over the Eastern Parade Ground (see Figure 4.5). In 1915, Chengdu residents saw their first air show. When they heard the sound from the sky, they climbed up on rooftops to watch. The plane dropped colorful confetti, and "everyone applauded and was excited." The first foreign performance troupes came to Chengdu at this time as well. More than a thousand people watched a Japanese "magic art troupe" perform various "electric arts" (*dianshu*) and "camouflage arts" in Guandi Temple, for example. Modern schools brought Western-style public performances and sports, and to a certain extent the student population became an important new avenue for introducing leisure activities to Chengdu public life. For example, the new Workhouse for the Education and Rearing of Children (Youhai jiaoyang gongchang) organized a marching band. After a few months of practice, when it was ready for "marching performing" and "sitting performing,"

FIGURE 4.5. Watching a Balloon Fly over the Eastern Parade Ground. From TSHB 1909, no. 3.

the workhouse made the band available for hire to promote "reformed and civilized rites." On the street, city dwellers could often see students "marching along, great and small in single or double files led by flags, horns and drums heading for some open space to drill." In 1906, the first interscholastic sports were held in the Northern Parade Ground, where "a great oval arena has been mapped out." A military band and more than forty schools took part in the competition. During the late 1920s, Chengdu incorporated new sports, such as soccer. A "Society for Dance Instruction" (Tiaowu buxi she) was set up to teach ballroom dancing, although men and women were taught separately. There were even public performances of Beethoven's works. Unable to compete, some traditional styles of recreation, such as puppet shows and shadow plays, gradually lost their audiences.[35]

These descriptions of the new cultural life, though incomplete, provide a clear sense of what kinds of changes took place during this period. Public leisure had been altered on a large scale, from the reform of local operas to new theaters, new teahouses, motion pictures, hot-air balloons, air shows, marching bands, ballroom dancing, and symphony orchestras—with changes in every aspect of content and form. Most profound of all, popular entertainment absorbed new elements from the West, and for the first time the inhabitants of this inland city had the opportunity to enjoy non-Chinese entertainment. Such a cultural change reflected the transformations occurring throughout society, including changes in material life.

Changes in Material Life

Any social change had its reflection in public life. The increased importation of foreign goods was the most prominent change in material life. As early as the middle of the nineteenth century, Western goods started arriving in Chengdu, but by the early twentieth century they were popular, as clearly demonstrated by the prevalence of advertisements in local newspapers.[36] Foreign goods, mainly coming from France, Britain, and Japan by way of the Yangzi River, became popular. These imports included clothing, shoes, clocks, glassware, metal products, wine, tobacco, fruit, medicine, food, porcelain, paper, stationery, and similar items. "These goods were of good quality, cheap, and exquisite, [to] meet Chinese taste." This influx began to challenge the traditional family-based handicraft workshops to a certain extent.[37] A store in the Center for Promoting Industry and Commerce sold telescopes, gold and silver clocks, and Western drums. Another store there demonstrated a record player, which impressed local people by its "clear and beautiful sound"; they exclaimed that listening to it was "like sitting in the theater" (see Figure 4.6). Some of the new stores began to sell firearms made in both China and foreign countries, while bow-and-arrow shops on Provincial Military Commander Street (Tidu jie) went out of business. After the 1920s, Western products had grabbed quite a large share of Chengdu's market, leading some shoppers to comment that at the Flower Fair, "more foreign goods are displayed than local ones." The way many commoners earned a living had been changing gradually since the late nineteenth century, when the flow of foreign goods into this city increased. As an article in *Popular Daily* (Tongsu ribao) noted, however, ordinary people who earned only a few dozen *yuan* annually could survive because of cheap local products. But after trade was established with the outside world in the late Qing, this changed. Foreign trade caused prices for local goods to skyrocket, so that making a living as an artisan or other common laborer became increasingly difficult.[38]

In early-twentieth-century Chengdu, changes in material culture became especially noticeable. In succession, three new means of transportation—the rickshaw, bicycle, and automobile—appeared in the late Qing and early Republic. The rickshaw was transplanted from Japan. In 1906, the Bureau of Commercial Affairs (Shangwu ju) appointed Fu Chongju to promote locally made rickshaws, to be used only at the Flower Fair, and soon there were more than a hundred of these rickshaws with uniformed pullers. Almost simultaneously, the people of Chengdu began to ride foreign-made bicycles,

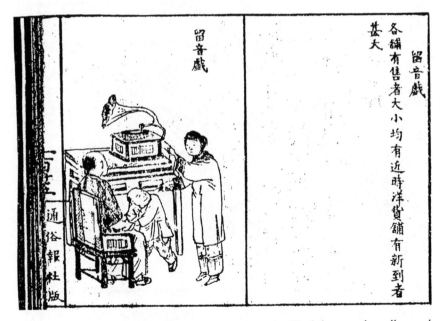

FIGURE 4.6. A Record Player. The inscription reads: "Both large and small record players are sold at all kinds of shops. The new imports in the foreign goods shops are even bigger." From CDTL 3: 115.

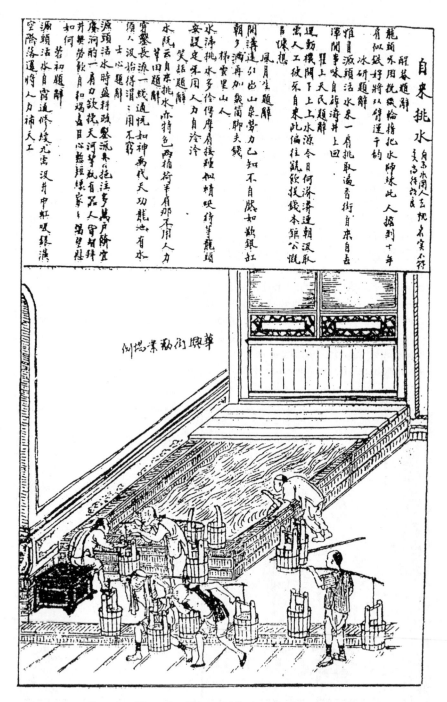

FIGURE 4.7. Carrying "Running Water." The inscription reads: "Running water still needs to be carried by men, and it is the name that falls short of the reality." This picture depicts water carriers carrying water, as well as their baskets and carrying poles. From TSHB 1909, no. 5.

which indeed were called "foreign horses" (*yangma*) in Sichuan until the 1960s. A few were manufactured locally, but they were so heavy they required "four people to carry one up over the threshold." Automobiles appeared in Chengdu in the 1920s. When a U.S.-made truck was used as public transportation for the first time, many curious people went to see the so-called "foreign house walking" (*yangfangzi zoulu*), or the "colorful sedan-chair farting" (*huajiao dapi*); to those who had never seen an automobile, the exhaust sounded like farting. Still others were frightened by the new vehicles, calling them "city tigers" (*shihu*). The arrival of the truck elicited many rumors; it was thought to be a monster capable of killing people, and its "fart" to be a lethal poison that could wipe out the population. Most of the rumors originated from rickshaw shop owners and pullers, who sought to withstand this new competitor. A few dozen rickshaw pullers marched to the harbor to protest the truck's arrival. Even though automobiles did not replace rickshaws, they created a formidable struggle for right-of-way on the street. Accidents, usually involving an automobile knocking down a rickshaw driver, were frequent. People's fear of automobiles was by no means irrational, given their dangers. The introduction of this new mode of transportation did, however, bring about street improvements, for they required better and wider roads.[39]

The city's infrastructure was improved in other ways during this period, notably with the introduction of running water, electricity, and the telephone. The Center for Promoting Commerce and Industry was the first establishment to have running water. The earliest "running water" in Chengdu, however, was that transported by waterwheels from the river to water pools in the city, where water carriers collected it for distribution. This prompted some to dub the system "carried running water" (*rentiao zilaishui*) (see Figure 4.7). Nonetheless, this service provided a great convenience. A picture in *Popular Pictorial* shows the early running-water device and how the water carriers transported their load. The inscription above the picture reads: "Running water still needs to be carried by men, which means that this term falls short of reality. Therefore the designation should be changed." When Western-style running water appeared in Chengdu, many carriers lost their jobs. Although the residents sympathized with the carriers, running water was too great a convenience to do without. One poignant story describes a water carrier's failed attempt to resist this new technology, and from it we can see the unfortunate fate of many commoners following modernization in Chengdu.[40]

At almost the same time, the city started generating electricity, which reshaped urban life, especially nightlife. At first, a generator provided electricity only for the shops, teahouses, and public bathhouses in the Center for Promoting Commerce and Industry. Following the installation of electric lights, the Center attracted more visitors than ever, many of whom went especially to witness the moment the lights were turned on. Every evening, teahouses in the area brimmed with patrons awaiting the coming darkness, and their cheers "resounded like rolls of thunder" when the lights flashed on. Soon, new teahouses opened, prompting a construction boom that one newspaper reporter called a "frantic trend." In 1909, the Enlightening Electric Light Company (Qiming diandeng gongsi) began providing electricity throughout the major commercial areas.[41] This made it possible for shops to remain open past nightfall, which attracted many shoppers and nonshoppers alike.[42] At first, most people lived without electric lights in their homes because they were more expensive than traditional oil lamps. However, when the company offered discounts of 30 to 50 percent, it was successful in attracting customers. Electric lights enabled shops to remain open past nightfall and also encouraged residents to leave their homes to spend time in brightly lit public places.

Increased material wealth also brought about a greater emphasis on fashion, resulting in what Richard Sennett called a "new image of the body." According to *Investigation of Chengdu* (Chengdu tonglan), women's fashions changed annually, even though the city was relatively isolated. Fu Chongju wrote that "the styles in the local dramas influence woman's clothing." Students favored "foreign-style" leather shoes, and many stores displayed colorful shoes for the natural (i.e., unbound) female foot. Young people also began to wear glasses to "pretend to be students" or to "follow foreign fashions." With the development of modern schools, student uniforms became a common sight. A missionary observed, "Everywhere on the streets one meets students of the various schools in almost as various uniforms but with the invariable peaked caps, top boots, and foreign type trowsers [trousers] and jackets, the latter usually resplendent with brass buttons, gold braid, silver throat characters and a dragon on the left slieve [sleeve] the special symbol of each school." The early-Republican *Popular Pictorial* (Tongsu huabao) displayed different styles of caps and clothing; there were twenty-four styles of caps alone (see Figure 4.8). We can also find pictures of men's and women's fashions, including gowns, pants, skirts, caps, and shoes.[43] All these give us some idea of the "image of the body" in early-twentieth-century Chengdu.

Innovations in material life resulted from both economic transformations and reformers' efforts. Improvements such as new modes of transportation, running water, and electricity not only provided greater convenience but also transformed lifestyles. This was an era when traditional ideologies and material goods coexisted with Western ones. People's daily lives had undergone little change, but they were beginning to accept some new things and were demonstrating a willingness to incorporate new material goods—if not new ideas—into their lives. Social reformers launched their

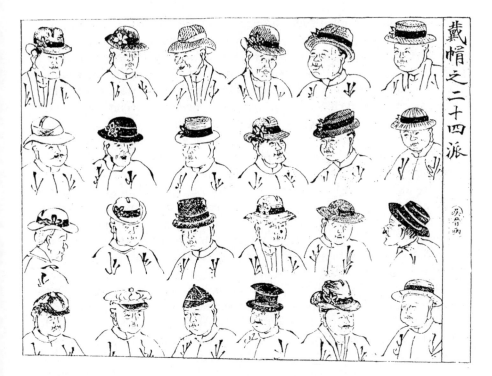

FIGURE 4.8. Twenty-four Styles of Wearing Hats. From TSHB 1912, no. 40.

reformist movement at the level of material and cultural life with encouraging results. The acceptance of new things gradually seeped into cultural life, beginning with new fashions and forms of entertainment and advancing to new ideas (to be discussed in Chapter 7). We cannot state that all of these changes took place because of the reformers' efforts; some were the inevitable results of social and economic development. But there is no question that social reformers played a positive role in introducing new material culture into the everyday lives of Chengdu citizens.

Reshaping Public Space

Along with the development of material life and the expansion of commerce, the physical landscape of Chengdu changed in the early twentieth century as well. New commercial centers, theaters, parks, roads, and other facilities sprang up as the old city walls, city gates, temples, and other structures were dismantled. Therefore, reshaping public space was a dual process of construction and destruction, which brought a new appearance to the city while destroying part of its heritage.

The influx of foreign goods brought some new sights to the city, including the first clock tower in Chengdu, which was built in 1909 on the roof of the Center for Promoting Commerce and Industry. It is clearly depicted in a drawing published in *Popular Pictorial* (see Figure 4.2). The missionary hospital in Shaanxi built a more prominent clock tower in 1916. This became the "social clock" of Chengdu; everyone with "a concept of time" reportedly regarded this clock as the "standard time."[44] The Chinese concept of time was changing. Previously, only the most rudimentary measurements of time sufficed: roosters crowing in the morning, the position of the sun during the day, and the night watchmen's beating of drums or bamboo boards at night. A woman on the street, for example, might say, "since the sun is at the top of the tree, I should go home to cook lunch." The introduction of other technological advances also increased the average person's interest in precision regarding time. Schools began operating on specific schedules, and government offices, stores, and factories also adopted regular hours of operation.

Under urban reform, some traditional public spaces were gradually put to other uses; the County City God Temple on Winnowing Fan Street (Boji jie), for example, became a theater. Reformers regarded temples as a "ready source" of funds, and temples were taxed to pay for new programs. The population of Chengdu gradually increased, further spurring the development of commerce. New shops opened from Small South Gate (Xiao nanmen) to Small North Gate (Xiao beimen), as well as on Ancestor Temple Street (Citang jie). During the 1910s and early 1920s, the streets in the Smaller City were widened and straightened. Furthermore, because the Manchus were increasingly interested in trade and many Han people moved into the area, the formerly desolate Smaller City had become a prosperous place just two or three years after the 1911 Revolution.[45]

Throughout the reformist and revolutionary movements in the late Qing and early Republic, the city wall and the Imperial City experienced dramatic destruction. With the increase in Chengdu's population, the four city gates could no longer bear the traffic, and residents began to complain of the inconvenience of the city wall. Some elites even condemned the city wall as an obstacle to urban development, arguing, "There are no walls in the cities of most Western countries. Tianjin became prosperous only after the city wall was dismantled, and the best part of Shanghai was that the city did not have a city wall. All these cases demonstrate that a wall inhibits the future of commerce." People constantly suggested opening new city gates; some proposed that Chengdu needed at least eight gates, and others recommended dismantling the entire wall. Beginning with the opening of the Fluent and Capable City Gate (Tonghui men) in 1913, located near the Western Parade Ground to connect the Green Goat Temple and the Smaller City

Park (see Figure 2.2), other sections of the city wall were perforated to allow ingress and egress. The Military City Gate (Wuchengmen) near the
Eastern Parade Ground was opened in 1915, and the Reviving City Gate
(Fuxing men), located between Upper Lotus Pond Street (Shang lianchi)
and Lower Lotus Pond (Xia lianchi), was built in 1939.[46] The opening of
new city gates eventually made some districts more prosperous, including
the area of the Fluent and Capable City Gate, which became the main
route from the town to the Flower Fair. After this area became overcrowded, local authorities expanded commerce into the surrounding streets
by adding commercial centers and a market.[47] Thus, opening more city
gates resulted in an expansion of urban space, and the areas outside the
wall increased their connections to the urban economy and daily life.

Brick thieves dealt another blow to the integrity of the city wall. The
wall contained many bricks from the Han and Ming dynasties that featured decorative bas relief carvings. All kinds of people, from city residents
to soldiers to warlords, legally or illegally removed the ancient bricks for
use in building houses, repairing streets, and shoring up sewers. The city's
powerful leaders especially coveted the bricks as decorations for their magnificent compounds. Simultaneously, the new city authority dismantled the
wall of the Smaller City, uniting the "big city" and the "smaller city." After
the street war of 1917 (which will be discussed in Chapter 7), a more radical plan was suggested: the destruction of the Imperial City so that it could
not be used for military purposes, with the bricks and wood to be used to
provide relief for homeless victims of the wars.[48]

The few who sought to preserve the Imperial City as a historical site had
little influence with the prevailing antitraditional sentiment. The Imperial
City eventually escaped destruction, not because local authorities tried to
preserve it but because in 1917 provincial authorities had offices there. The
next year these offices were moved to make room for new schools, just in
time for the order to be issued in 1919 to halt the dismantling of the Imperial City and to declare it a historical site. The structure survived until
the Cultural Revolution of the 1960s and 1970s, when it was torn down.[49]
The fate of the city wall reflected the destiny of the city's traditional
lifestyle, social customs, and street culture. Both elites and commoners let
these cultural artifacts disappear before their very eyes.

The local government also tried to improve the streets. In the early 1920s,
Governor Yang Sen, a warlord, carried out a large-scale road construction
project. Conditions in some areas were indeed improved. For example, Wheelbarrow Lane, according to teacher William Sewell, who lived there, became
"a real road," with paving stones to cover the sewers. A new hard surface of
mud and lime replaced the old ruts. Wheelbarrows with narrow iron-shod
wheels, however, were forbidden. Warm Spring Road (Chunxi lu) was also

built during this period. Running between Central Mansion Street and Horse Riding Street, it has since become one of Chengdu's most prosperous commercial areas, after Great East Street and the Commercial Center.[50] The improvements in the streets of Chengdu set the standard for other towns in Sichuan. A British diplomat described what he saw in 1930: "A striking feature of present-day Szechwan is the surprisingly modern and up-to-date appearance of many of the large towns." Chengdu and other cities in Sichuan had undergone "a wholesale reconstruction within the past few years, and are now conspicuous for their wide streets, rows of clean and uniform houses and shops, and good sanitation."[51] From this perspective, we can see one achievement of urban reform. Street reconstruction was the most visible change to the city's appearance. But if wider streets improved traffic flow, the resulting demolition of some traditional space for the lower classes and increased regulations provoked resentment.

The social reformers' successful engagement in local public affairs enlarged the scope of their influence. They now decided that they needed more public space for their mission. They had two major strategies for achieving this goal: to shape urban space according to their own design and to consolidate their leadership. Beginning in the early twentieth century, these reformist elites orchestrated profound urban reforms with state support. As in modern Western cities, where social reform and control often center on the politics and class struggles of urban public life, so, too, in early-twentieth-century Chengdu "the reform of popular values and customs inevitably became intimately bound up with" issues of "public order."[52] The people targeted by the social reformers were usually at the bottom levels of the urban class structure, people whose existence reflected the gap between rich and poor, educated and uneducated, and residents and outsiders. When the elites tried to achieve their mission, they exploited blatant cultural discrimination and class prejudice. In fact, the elites' criticism of commoners' public behavior revealed a power struggle over control of the street as much as or more than it did their desire to "civilize" commoners.

5 Street Control

The most important change in early-twentieth-century urban Chengdu society was the establishment of an organized police force. The police force, established in 1902, was the first specialized municipal administrative unit in Chengdu. Previously, all Chengdu households had been organized into a *baojia* system, which provided local control and security but had no role in setting policy for urban management and administration. Similarly, local patron-deity associations assumed some responsibilities in the community but never acted in any official capacity. Because of the absence of a municipal government during the first two decades of the twentieth century, the police played a triple role, taking responsibility for local security, for urban administration, and for social reform. The police force dismissed all of the old "street clerks" and patrolmen and appointed 50 district heads (*juzheng*) and 383 street heads (*jiezheng*).[1] About nine hundred men between the age of twenty and forty who were free from disease and were not opium smokers were recruited; these earliest policemen were acknowledged to be of strong moral character.[2]

Urban elites had always sought opportunities to shape the values and habits of the lower classes. In this period, both local elites and officials tried to strengthen their influence on street life, and the establishment of the police force provided a powerful means to impose their reformist ideas. Thus, social reformers enthusiastically supported and even initiated police reforms. Many innovations were transplanted directly from Japan, as Fu Chongju's *Investigation of Chengdu* (Chengdu tonglan) demonstrated. As in early modern Europe, where the elite class and political authorities sought to transform society via the institution of the police, in late-Qing Chengdu the police also functioned from the very beginning in a role of social reform through regulation of street activities.[3] Social reformers hoped to promote "civilization" by teaching the lower classes public behavior that was appropriate for these more progressive and attractive new public spaces.

As soon as Chengdu's police force was organized, it carried out measures of street control. The commoners' public appearance and behavior—everything from what they wore to what they saw and said—remained a constant concern for the elites and police. On the street, police could investigate and even arrest anyone for a variety of vague offenses, including "bizarre speech," "unusual behavior," "weird clothing," or "evil and licentious talk." Singing purportedly "licentious" folk songs and gathering in public to "disturb the peace" by shouting were forbidden. For the first time, regulations governed traffic, prostitution, gambling, and hygiene, as well as the behavior of specific groups of people, such as monks and nuns, second-hand item traders, and witch doctors.[4] These new street rules provide the first evidence that the city was beginning to institutionalize the tenets of modern municipal management.

The police tried to take over many responsibilities formerly controlled by such community organizations as patron-deity associations, charitable organizations, and guilds. During the period of the New Policies, elites and local officials often cooperated to promote reform projects, and therefore it is difficult to distinguish elite initiatives from the state's, although their agendas were often quite different. The police were a major force of local reform and represented the power of the state, but they were led by new elites whose policies reflected class-based ideas more than they did state-sponsored ones. Whereas the elite reform was largely promoted by the state and the New Policies were supported enthusiastically by local elites in the late Qing, the widening rift between the two became increasingly visible during the early Republic. This issue is discussed in greater detail in Chapter 7.

This chapter examines how the police dealt with issues such as traffic, public order, begging, using opium, gambling, hooliganism, hygiene, fire-fighting, and prostitution. Kristin Stapleton offers a general survey on the relevant policies and leadership in the late Qing in her recent book.[5] My discussion here details the implementation of new regulations and looks at how the reforms reached people on the streets. Furthermore, my discussion extends beyond the Qing until the late 1920s, to demonstrate that street reforms were enforced into the early Republican era. Despite the transformation from an imperial to a Republican system, the measures of street control remained largely the same.[6] This chapter will also explore little-touched issues relating to street hoodlums, urban popular cults, and teahouses, to reveal what real changes took place in ordinary people's public life under the reform movement.

Regulating the Street

Controlling public space meant increasing restrictions on the street, which created enormous inconvenience for ordinary people, especially those who made their livings there.[7] For example, Chengdu began to control traffic for the first time. Sedan chairs and horses were the major means of urban transportation, and as their numbers increased, accidents and injuries to pedestrians became increasingly common. To bring order to the chaos, the police issued a "Regulation on Sedan Chairs, Horse Carts, and Pedestrians," requiring all sedan-chair carriers and horse-cart drivers to follow traffic signals and punishing violators. In addition, the police required sedan chairs and horse carts to have lit lanterns at night and horse carts to have bells. Rickshaws, which appeared in the late Qing, were frequently involved in accidents. To regulate this growing business, the police demanded that rickshaws run on the right side of the road, enforced speed limits, and prohibited stops in restricted areas. Violators would be fined fifty *wen* or receive physical punishment according to the severity of the violation. The police also issued licenses—a white wooden board with red numbers—to each puller, without which a rickshaw could not operate legally. In extreme cases, the police confiscated the licenses of recalcitrant pullers. Wheelbarrows were also restricted; residents of "neat and improved streets" who did not want wheelbarrows going through their neighborhoods could ask the police to install a sign prohibiting them. The new traffic regulations also forbade people to ignite firecrackers when a horse was passing. If a frightened horse galloped away, the "street people" (*jiezhong*) were instructed to shut the gate at the end of the street; the rider was required to pay for all damage. In addition, children under six were not allowed to play in the street. Residents were not allowed to put their belongings on sidewalks and were required to dismantle any sheds or other structures that blocked traffic.[8]

The police also regulated commercial use of the street. Under a new rule, no peddler stalls were allowed at intersections and no stalls along the streets could extend beyond the eaves of the buildings. Temporary markets, such as the vegetable stands at the four city gates, generally had to close before ten in the morning, and stall owners were required take turns cleaning their areas. The police also instituted detailed regulations regarding hygiene in marketplaces, such as banning the sale of animal meat that was not fresh, and would confiscate the goods when peddlers were found to be in violation of the rules.[9] The police banned gatherings of peddlers and stallkeepers at hubs such as the North City Gate Bridge due to traffic concerns. They even tried to control prices; when the price of rice soared, for example, policemen supervised sales at each rice store.[10]

The police watched some street businesses closely, such as the secondhand trade (*shouhuang*), which was thought to deal often in stolen goods. This trade had supported more than seven hundred households in late-Qing Chengdu. Under the new regulations, those who engaged in the secondhand business had to have a "shop guarantor" (*pubao*) plus two other households to form a "circle of guarantors" (*lianhuan bao*). These traders labored under some particularly stringent rules: no one was allowed inside the shops when they were opening in the morning and closing in the evening, and purchases could be made only outside. They were not allowed to buy weapons, stolen goods, or official property or purchase anything from sellers wearing soldiers' uniforms. They had to record sellers' names and addresses and keep purchases for at least five days before reselling them. They were required to assist in police investigations of theft and had to turn in to the police anyone suspected of selling stolen property. Any such trader who planned to move had to receive permission from the police in advance. People who did not live in Chengdu were forbidden to engage in the business. Finally, a permit was required to be hung on the front of each shop, stall, and basket; those who operated without a license were punished.[11]

The police also sought to regulate the street labor market. Although literally meaning "sellers of human beings," *renfan* were actually employment brokers. A minority were indeed guilty of selling people, however, and their activities were restricted by the police. The police issued a regulation requiring all employment brokers to move to West Imperial River Street (Xiyuhe jie) and Imperial City Street (Huangcheng bianjie) in order to live and work under police supervision. Those who did not comply were not allowed to continue in the profession. In the early Republican era, Rear Gate Street (Houzi men) along the West Imperial River (Xiyuhe) became the largest labor market (see Map 3) and even offered employment for women as wet nurses and servants. The police regulated all aspects of this business as well, requiring brokers to register and put wooden label boards on their gates to indicate licensure. Once an employer hired a laborer, the broker was required to list his or her wages and address. Brokers who served as marriage matchmakers were required to investigate their clients' backgrounds. No broker was allowed to procure servant girls or nurses for brothels. Finally, brokers assumed all responsibility for employees who stole from their employers.[12]

Many social reformers felt that how the streets looked was an important indicator of the city's well-being. This might explain why so much social reform was aimed at improving the streets' appearance through improved hygiene. In traditional Chengdu, public hygiene was poor, particularly in lower-class neighborhoods. A French traveler complained in the late nineteenth century that "if you made a mistake and entered a blind alley, you had to cross refuse dumps, where it was slippery and smelly." In some streets, Fu Chongju wrote in *Investigation of Chengdu*, "water accumulates and bad smells assail one's nose." On rainy days "dirty water and excrement flow everywhere," while on sunny days "the air is full of dust." Missionaries observed that it was difficult for women to walk down Chengdu streets because of the latter's poor condition. There were "ill-smelling crocks" on every street corner; people threw trash on the street, and "great ugly pigs, fowl and rats were the scavengers."[13]

The police regulated street hygiene, cleaning up refuse and dead animals, prohibiting pig slaughtering in the town, removing urine pits along paths, and improving public latrines and sewers. Furthermore, social reformers suggested other measures for keeping the city clean, such as requiring ox-cart drivers and street sweepers to clean up ox droppings and relocating smelly leather tanneries to the outskirts of town. They also suggested protecting people's health by prohibiting water carriers from carrying polluted water from the Imperial River. Chengdu residents had had a tradition of keeping domestic animals such as pigs, goats, chickens, and ducks, and many of them lived in the street. To improve sanitation, the police banned all domestic animals from public thoroughfares.[14]

The police started to hire street sweepers in the late Qing. According to missionary Vale, they wore a distinctive uniform with the three characters "*Qing Dao Fu*" on the back and front, representing a wheelbarrow, a wicker basket, and a broom. All households were to take their garbage out before the sweepers started collecting garbage and sweeping streets at seven o'clock; the refuse they collected was transported to an assigned dumping ground.[15] Nevertheless, before the 1920s street sweepers were not common, and residents still customarily swept the areas in front of their houses themselves. Often "each man or woman before his own door with a small hand broom of brush gathers the trash together, as he pleases, until someone who wants street sweepings comes and removes the pile." Local authorities encouraged city dwellers to take responsibility for the cleanliness of public spaces. A 1928 hygiene regulation required that "no trash and dirty water are to be dumped on the street"; that "while sweeping a house overlooking the street, water is to be sprinkled first to avoid flying dust"; and that "no dirty clothes are to be hung over sidewalks."[16]

The public toilet seems always to be a prominent issue in urban hygiene. The police ordered all lavatories to be modified to follow official designs in 1903.[17] Previously, some streets did not have lavatories; pedestrians urinated in "manure pits" at the side of the street. Under the new regulations, these pits were to be filled in, and anyone who urinated in the street was to be punished by a fine of fifty *wen*, or a day's work if the offender could not pay the fine. Because most Chengdu people didn't know about sanitation, urinating in the street often occurred, causing clashes between violators and policemen. One news story told of "a rude and uneducated man" who not only refused to stop urinating in the street when he was caught one night, but insulted the policeman. When the policeman attempted to take the scofflaw to the police station, he punched the officer, ran home, and locked himself inside. The next day he was arrested and charged with violating sanitation regulations and assaulting a policeman. Until the early Republic, however, the issue of the public lavatory was still unresolved because of residents' ignorance of sanitation. In 1914, the police ordered district policemen and owners of toilets to improve hygiene. The police made a special effort to enforce the prohibition on urinating in the street; offenders were to be put in jail for a day or pay a fine of at least one *yuan*. Despite the new public toilets and new rules, however, some people continued the old practice. One local newspaper reported such a story: a residential compound on a quiet street was frequently used as a site for urinating. The owner pasted a notice on the wall that said, "*wanglairendeng bude zaici xiaobian*" (no passerby is allowed to urinate here). One day he saw a man urinating there and asked, "Didn't you see the notice?" The man answered, "Yes, I urinated here because I saw your notice. Doesn't your notice say '*wanglairen, dengbude, zaici xiaobiao*' (passersby who cannot hold it can urinate here)?"[18] If the notice had been punctuated differently, the man would have been right, but obviously he was deliberately misinterpreting and challenging the public notice.

The police also forced the removal of unburied bodies, which had customarily been saved in temples. Chengdu was a city of immigrants, most of whom arrived in Chengdu after the Zhang Xianzhong Rebellion in the late Ming and the reconstruction of the city in the early Qing; when they died, their bodies would be sent back to their hometowns for burial, as was the custom.[19] Until arrangements could be completed, however, the deceased were temporarily stored in caskets in the temples outside town. For a variety of reasons, many caskets ended up being kept at the temple for years, even decades, and some were actually abandoned. In 1909, the police reported that in the temples outside the East and North City Gates alone there were 327 coffins, some of which had been there for over thirty years. The authorities then issued a public notice requiring relatives of the deceased to bury the caskets within three months. Obviously, this custom could not be changed easily or quickly. From various documents, we find that this burial practice still existed in the 1930s and 1940s.[20]

Whereas cleaning the streets and other public places gave the city a better appearance, installing streetlights altered the landscape and nightlife of the city, as well as expanded its public space. Unlit streets were filled with danger after nightfall. As one criminologist said, "a light is as good as a policeman." He even went so far as to suggest that he "would rather have plenty of electric lights and clean streets than all the law and order societies in existence."[21] Early streetlights in Chengdu were oil lanterns, lit by night watchmen hired by the police; as a foreigner described, "oil lamps are set up on low posts at short intervals, and are lit every night." All households had to pay a "lighting oil tax." After the 1911 Revolution, the management of streetlights was transferred from the police to the local "neighborhood militia" (*tuanfang*). According to complaints received by the police, the oil lamps used during this period were very dim and poorly maintained.

Although the early streetlights had many problems, they made possible outdoor activities at night and also brought a new look to the city. Furthermore, streetlights were sometimes used for other purposes as well; for instance, sedan-chair carriers would count them as they passed to determine fares.[22]

All these changes were related to physical conditions of the streets and reflected the police's efforts to improve the city's appearance. Some of these measures, such as traffic control and market management, had never been enforced before, while some previously were the responsibility of voluntary organizations. In either case, efficiency dramatically increased after the police took over, and the city's improved appearance created considerable support for the reform movement. The social reformers' agenda, however, extended even into the behavior and appearance of individuals. Their main targets were the "law offenders" and the poor.

Hoodlums, Gamblers, and Policemen

The police defined public order as one of its major duties, "controlling bad people and prohibiting bad things." Anyone who disrupted the public peace by "playing the bully" would be warned and possibly arrested. After policemen began to patrol the streets, admirers noted that "well-dressed policemen are now stationed at frequent intervals through the city. Each is armed with a light stick, and all seem well disciplined. Without doubt the cause of law and order is advancing" (see Figure 5.1).[23] The appearance of policemen in public indeed was a threat to local toughs. The police paid special attention to so-called hoodlums and gamblers.

Hooligans liked to gather on the street, typically in groups of three or five or even more.[24] Women were the hooligans' primary targets on the street, especially those from ordinary families who sat in their doorways sewing or doing other daily housework.[25] Groups of rowdy young men also often lurked at public events, such as the Flower Fair, where they would congregate at entrances or exits and comment or otherwise try to take advantage of women as they entered and exited. According to a new regulation, police were to follow and investigate those who looked like "rogues" (wulai), did not behave, were frivolous, lured "young boys from good families," or congregated in groups in theaters, teahouses, or wine shops. Anyone who wore "bandit dress"—in green, red, and black—would be ordered to take it off.[26] Local newspapers often reported how the police dealt with the "hoodlums." In one case, when two young women visited the Center for Promoting Commerce and Industry, some "frivolous young men" commented on their appearance from head to toe and slandered them as prostitutes. The police caught the culprits and hauled them to the police station. Another case involved a man who made a pass at a shop-keeper's wife and was subsequently detained and punished. To avoid harassment, the police ordered separate entrances at the Flower Fair for men and women, but they caught some men who "pretend to be women" trying to enter through the women's entrance.[27]

FIGURE 5.1. Police Beating a Wrongdoer with a Stick as Punishment. From TSHB 1912, no. 16.

Some local toughs had organized into gangs, which the police tried very hard to break up. These people acted collectively, bullying and extorting from ordinary households, shops, and other small business. One group of "wandering riffraff" frequently rushed into brothels "with fierce and arrogant faces" to extort money. Their brazen actions caused furious attacks from the police.[28] In the early Republic, some "profligate sons of the rich" organized into a "Society of Evil Deities" (Duoshen hui) and gathered in theaters and restaurants, deliberately drawing public attention by "not behaving themselves." Because they often caused trouble on the street, the police posted a public notice that prohibited their activities and ordered their parents to restrict their sons. According to the new rule, the profligate sons of the rich were not allowed to wander on the street. If they violated the rule, their parents would be punished along with them.[29]

The police punished these "misbehaving" men severely, usually through public humiliation. For instance, some men often threw fruit and rocks at women traveling in sedan chairs or otherwise abused them. The hooligans caught were subjected to the public humiliation of wearing a yoke publicly for a whole day, "losing face before a thousand people." The police furthermore erected a stone pillar outside the main gate of the Two Deities Nunnery (Erxian an), on which was inscribed "the public place for locking up hooligans." Hooligans were often paraded through the street as a punishment, although this form of punishment was usually reserved for those who committed capital offenses.[30]

Some so-called "cases of taking liberties with women," however, were obviously exaggerated by the conservative social environment. For instance, when a girl went to a shop and a sedan-chair carrier followed her and tried "to talk and make jokes with her," she called the police, and policemen took him to the police station for punishment. Another case occurred when one well-dressed man carrying a camera saw several beautiful girls drinking tea by a lotus pond; pretending to take pictures of the scenery, he actually focused on the girls. He was caught by the police, convicted as a hooligan, and whipped.[31] In another case, a young man, regarded as a "hooligan," was beaten with a truncheon two thousand times and locked to the stone pillar in front the Two Deities Nunnery as nearly a thousand people watched. What had he done to merit such severe punishment? When a woman walked over a ditch, he said to her: "your feet are so small; let me hold your hand."[32] Such behavior seems merely frivolous today, but in the 1910s it was a serious crime.

Suppressing Gambling. Apprehending rowdy youths on the street proved much easier than regulating opium use and gambling. Opium smoking and gambling became major targets of the police after each was criminalized (Figures 5.2 and 5.3). The anti-opium campaign was relatively successful;

opium use ended almost entirely by 1911.[33] Gambling, unlike opium smoking, most often occurred in public places and was virtually indistinguishable from many other leisure activities, particularly mahjong.

In late-Qing Chengdu, various games of chance, such as "bird fighting," playing cards, and mahjong, were popular and took place on street corners, under bridges, and in teahouses, residential houses, and brothels (see

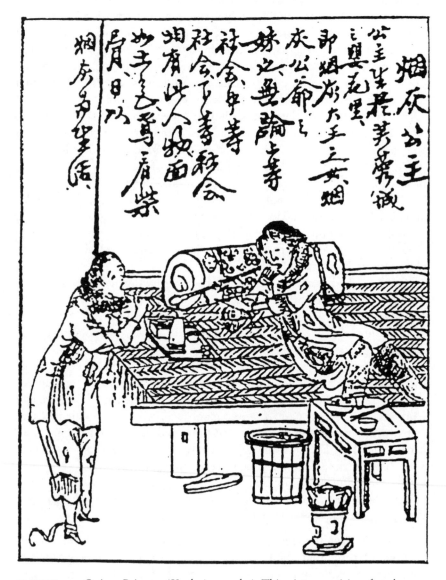

FIGURE 5.2. Opium Princess (*Yanhui gongzhu*). This picture satirizes female opium addicts. From TSHB 1909, no. 6.

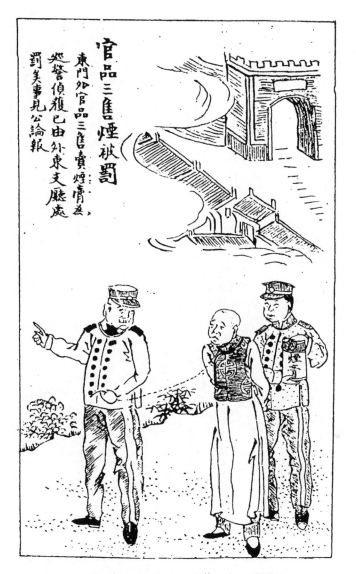

官品三隹煙被罰

東門外官品三隹賣煙膏茲，茲警偵獲已由外東支廳處，罰美事見公論報

FIGURE 5.3. Catching an Opium Seller. From TSHB 1912, no. 11.

Figure 5.4). Because some gamblers set up traps to take money from the in-experienced, reformers worried that gambling destroyed families and contributed to social disorder (see Figure 5.5). In the early twentieth century, reformers appealed to the police to send the "dangerous gamblers" to prison, and the police enacted regulations to forbid gambling, including the traditional pastime of mahjong.[34] Social reformers supported this policy by writing many articles on the depraved aspects of mahjong. *Popular Daily,*

打龍

某街於十三夜人聲
鼎沸乃某宅打牌
有雀角之爭因座
中人誤打一龍以致
莊家吃虧某君少年
得意氣火甚大遂起
街哭後經路人解勸
其事始寂

（時事畫）

FIGURE 5.4. Fighting over Mahjong. According to the inscription, several people got into a fight after betting on mahjong at
a street residence. They calmed down after pedestrians helped
mediate the dispute. From TSHB 1912, no. 3.

for instance, published a "Song of Ten Bad Things About Mahjong," written
in rhyme, with each line containing four characters so that it could be easily
understood and remembered. The song described how mahjong could destroy health, morality, and family, and what serious consequences could result for anyone—officials, gentry, students, teachers, merchants, soldiers, and

young women alike—who gambled. The new elites even declared that eliminating gambling was a prerequisite to establishing a "civilized society." They attempted to promote the "healthier activities" found in Europe and America and exhorted citizens to "play ball, exercise, paddle boats, and ride horses," all of which were "good for social reform." *Popular Daily* published

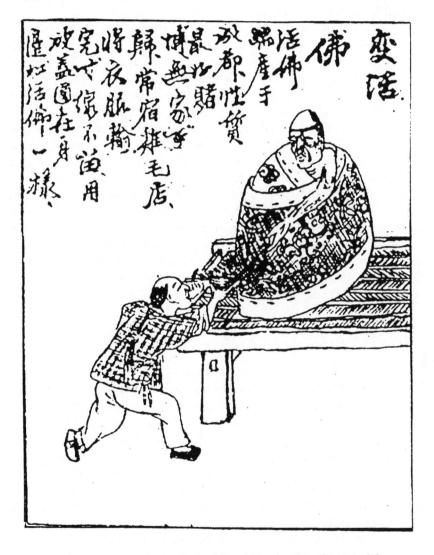

FIGURE 5.5. Becoming a "Living Buddha" (*bian huofo*). The gist of the inscription to this satirical drawing is that a gambler who loses everything, even his clothing, has to stay in a "chicken-feather inn" wrapped up in a cotton quilt like a living Buddha. From TSHB 1909, no. 6.

another essay under the title "Lecture on Forbidding Gambling," which described in plain language the evils of gambling. The article explained that "hardened gamblers" cheated and seduced others to gamble, and warned people not to go to "gambling dens," where, it cautioned, there was no such a thing as "a sure bet." A person who lost money gambling, it was explained, would sell his clothes, furniture, land, and even his house, hurting not only himself but also his entire family.[35]

The police took this issue very seriously, searching houses and streets to arrest gamblers; collecting as much information as possible on gaming establishments, their purveyors, and participants; and making quick arrests of violators, who received fines and physical punishment. The police even prohibited hawkers of candy, cake, and peanuts from using lotteries and bets to entice children to buy their products, even though the practice had previously been considered socially acceptable. As a result of these severe measures, gambling was brought under control although never completely eradicated. In the spring of 1910, the police attempted to cut off gambling at the root by banning, within three days, both the manufacture and sale of mahjong equipment. All mahjong equipment in storage was to be destroyed, and anyone who made such products would be severely punished.[36] From banning gambling to prohibiting mahjong, this policy reflected not only reformers' resentment against gambling but also a denial of the most popular leisure activity in Chengdu. Far from bringing an end to gambling, the police's actions simply angered Chengdu residents, and illegal gambling flourished after a slight downturn.[37]

Taking the Poor Off the Street

How to deal with the poor was always one of the major issues of urban reform. Traditionally, local elites regarded charitable activities as one of their responsibilities. The long history of Chinese local welfare institutions became, of course, a basis for the modernized charitable projects at the end of the Qing era. From 1903 to 1906, the police established various institutions for the poor, which were similar to the social institutions for the poor in America, such as the seventeenth- and eighteenth-century public almshouses and the nineteenth-century houses of refuge and asylums. These institutions, also like their American counterparts, "did help many people lead happy and productive lives," though their function was limited. The 300-bed Coolie Hospital (Kuli bingyuan) was set up for poor laborers who became ill. Additionally, the Hospital for the Aged, Handicapped, and Ill (Laoruo feiji yuan) accepted more than a hundred patients. The police notified all sedan-chair shops, coolie guilds, and "chicken-feather inns" (jimao *dian*) that any homeless people or coolies who were ill should be sent to the hospital, where they could get help for their ailments as well as for opium addiction. Most of the programs established in the late Qing survived after the 1911 Revolution, but some were transferred from police control to the public sector.[38]

Taking "unemployed wandering people" and beggars off the street was another major goal of street reform. A missionary in Chengdu described as "revolutionary" the changes that took place after a new regulation required police to arrest anyone who wandered the street. The homeless were sent to workhouses and abandoned children to orphanages. Those who merely looked like beggars, but could prove employment and make their own living, were allowed to continue. Policemen on patrol were ordered to arrest any "ferocious beggars" who persisted in begging in doorways. The police converted old temples and soup kitchens into workhouses where beggars were forced to do supervised labor. A workhouse was built in 1905 specifically to recruit the poor and vagrants "to teach them both working skills and morality," reflecting the view of social reformers that the poor were morally inferior. The House for Training and Education (Qianshan suo), built the same year, promised rehabilitation to petty criminals through labor. The next year, the police established other two workhouses for beggars (*qigai gongchang*) near the East and South City Gates (see Figures 5.6 and 5.7). The police herded more than 1,500 panhandlers into the workhouses within six months. The Workhouse for Rearing and Educating Children (Youhai jiaoyang gongchang), built at almost the same time, could house 1,000 homeless children. Children under six were cared for by nurses, and those between six and fourteen were taught reading, counting, and basic working skills. At age fourteen, the children left the workhouse to make a living on their own. Within a year, the workhouse hosted more than 500 wandering and mendicant children.[39]

Little today is known about the inside of workhouses, but missionary J. Vale's reports in *West China Missionary News* provide some details about working conditions, wages, and the living situations of inmates. As soon as beggars were sent to a workhouse, they were given a number, and their hair was shaved "the width of two fingers on either side of the head," as a mark to distinguish them if they ran away. According to another source, however, their hair was cut into the "shape of a shoe." Their clothes were taken, and they wore uniforms made from old military uniforms. The sleeves of the uniforms only reached to the elbows, and the legs to the knees. This style was designed for convenience in work as well as to prevent their being stolen and sold. Some workhouse inmates did outdoor tasks, while others worked indoors. The inmates who worked indoors were taught to make straw sandals and weave cloth. Outdoor work was divided into "public" and "private." Public work was usually done on the streets and included carpentry and masonry; inmates learned how to repair houses, build walls, dig drains, or fill in roads. Thus, they were able to work on government projects when needed. Private work involved all kinds of physical labor for private families or in shops. Families that needed help with events such as funerals or weddings found workers at the workhouses; this became a tradition in Chengdu. Before the reform, however, households could hire beggars directly from the street to carry banners and flags for such ceremonies, but under the new rule, they could be hired only from the workhouses. Twice a day, each inmate received a basin of rice gruel and a saucer of salted vegetables. Those employed in outdoor work were given an additional bowl of boiled rice. The supervisor called the roll at dawn and dusk. Each man was to shave and take a bath every ten days.[40]

Beggars provided a steady supply of cheap labor for the police. Inmates hired by private individuals were paid only 70 percent of what they would have been paid as regular workers; when they labored on public works, they were paid even less, only 40 percent of the regular wage. Adults worked fourteen hours a day. One of each ten working inmates was appointed a foreman to oversee the others. Each workhouse kept its workers' time sheets, which recorded all wages earned in outdoor labor and all articles produced through indoor work each day. At the end of the third month after he entered the workhouse, the amount of wages each workman had earned and the value of articles made would be totaled. After a deduction for food and

FIGURE 5.6. Some Reformed Beggars. The photograph was taken by Harrison S. Elliott in Chengdu in 1906 or 1907. Courtesy of Jean Elliott Johnson.

FIGURE 5.7. A Chengdu Reformatory for Beggars. This photograph was taken by Harrison S. Elliott in Chengdu in 1906 or 1907. Courtesy of Jean Elliott Johnson.

materials, the balance would be handed to the worker, who was allowed to leave the workhouse to seek a living. Anyone who did not try to find a job after his release might be arrested again. To identify former inmates, the police kept their photographs on file.[41]

Taking the poor off the street became important work for the police reformers; they believed that achieving this goal would result in at least three advantages. First, it would stabilize public peace. Elites always regarded poor people as the cause of trouble such as robberies and thefts, so controlling the poor would improve security. Second, since the presence of shabbily dressed vagrants interfered with the new image of the city that the elite class sought to cultivate, taking them off the street would improve that image. Finally, social reformers claimed that putting these people to work in workhouses was done in their own best interest and would both provide them with shelter and teach them skills for future employment. The majority of lower-class people in Chengdu did not appreciate the changes, however, and tried to cling to their traditional way of life, as we will see in the next chapter. It could be said that whereas in the past beggars had nothing but their freedom, during the period of the reform they lost even this.[42]

Policing Everyday Life

Before the emergence of the police, everyday life in the city was largely unregulated. The *baojia* system and voluntary organizations were concerned only with issues of security, charity, and community ceremonies. But, beginning in the early twentieth century, the police became involved in almost every aspect of everyday life, from public gatherings to religious activities, increasing their span of control while also providing a public service.

In the late Qing, the police began regulating all public gatherings. The elites had often criticized Chengdu people for their extraordinary curiosity, "gathering and watching immediately whenever a small matter occurred." A foreign visitor also noticed that any unusual happenings on the streets would attract "a large and inquisitive crowd." It was said that such public gatherings frequently caused disputes. Under the new regulations, anyone who wanted to set up a stall for performing in public had to obtain advance permission. The police were responsible for maintaining order at these events, and hawkers, young women, and children were forbidden to attend, in order to prevent any disruptions. Policemen also stood along the parade routes for popular religious ceremonies to help expedite traffic, prevent disputes, protect young women and children, and control those who took these opportunities to "call mass gatherings, fight, and steal."[43]

The policies controlling public space were consistently enforced and became increasingly restrictive. During the "winter defense" (dongfang) in 1916, for instance, policemen were ordered to watch strangers carefully, especially in certain areas such as the Imperial City.[44] The local government restricted the traditional Flower Fair because of alleged overcrowding and the difficulty of distinguishing between "good people" and "bad ones." Only the selling of agricultural tools, plants, and flowers was allowed; sales of all other wares were banned. Furthermore, teahouses, wine shops, and food peddlers were forbidden to build sheds at the fair. In 1917, the police issued regulations prohibiting gambling, urination on the fairgrounds and roads, gossiping (this referred only to women), fortune-telling, hooliganism, abuse and fighting, and prostitution. Those who violated the rules were fined.[45]

In addition, the police made an effort to control children who gathered in groups on the street or in other public places to "make trouble." Children often amused themselves on the city wall, but some made mischief by throwing pieces of brick, breaking branches of trees, and hitting pedestrians. Some boys who threw bricks and rocks from the wall and broke the tiles of roofs were caught and their parents forced to repair the damaged roofs under the street head's supervision. Reformers suggested that parents should pay closer attention to their children who liked to play games on the street, because some of them caused injury.[46] Many children had gone to teahouses and wine shops in the evening, but the police banned them from such places, issuing a public notice warning parents to discipline their children and keep them away from "bad street habits" (jieshi exi). Parents would be punished if their children gathered in the streets to make trouble.[47]

The police watched closely some places where "bad people" could hide, especially those frequented by the lower classes. "Chicken-feather inns" were such locations. As a commercial and cultural center in the upper Yangzi region, Chengdu attracted many visitors daily, resulting in a booming trade for innkeepers. Accommodations in Chengdu fit into three categories: "chicken-feather inns," "guesthouses," and "official hotels." Chicken-feather inns, which were primarily places for the poor, beggars, and vagrants, were usually located near the East City Gate. They were regarded as havens for criminals. Guesthouses were commonly for merchants, while official hotels served both officials and merchants. There were more than three hundred inns in late-Qing Chengdu, which may give us an idea about the number of travelers in Chengdu. The chicken-feather inns, however, were the main target of police control. Under the new regulations, those who stayed in chicken-feather inns had to report their native places, ages, occupations, and reasons for coming to Chengdu. The innkeeper was to report any suspicious people to the local branch of the police. Inns were to refuse service to prostitutes, gamblers, and "people who did not have luggage and arrived at night." Patrolling policemen inspected these inns every morning and evening; after the evening inspection the inn was to shut its doors and not allow anyone else in. The inn could not open its doors before the policemen came to count the number of lodgers in the morning.[48] We lack evidence on how this policy was enforced, but one can assume that the measure may have been abandoned for logistical reasons. Because there were many such inns scattered all over the city, it would have been almost impossible for policemen to keep track of each lodger.

Besides enforcing the new measures of control, the police also provided some much-needed services, including a more efficient fire-fighting system. Fire was a constant threat in Chengdu. Newspapers from the era are full of reports on the destruction caused by fires. In 1903, according to *West China Missionary News*, "there was a big fire on one of the most important business streets, right in the center of the city." Buildings on both sides of the street were destroyed for more than 100 yards. The fire resulted from "the explosion of a kerosene lamp left burning while people slept." Just a week later, "another fire broke out not far distant from the scene of the first." Foreigners in particular noted the inadequacy of fire-fighting procedures and equipment. In 1905, an enormous conflagration on Great East Street underscored the need for new equipment; as one bystander noted, "rude fire engines"—"water dragons"—now went rattling through the streets. Unlike Hankou, which had experienced a revolution in fire fighting with the introduction of the hand-drawn fire engine at the end of the eighteenth century, Chengdu depended on huge "emergency vats" on the streets until a new fire-control system was established in the early twentieth century.[49]

To deal with overcrowded shops in the commercial districts, where fire could be catastrophic, the police enacted regulations to prevent fires, including instructions for storing oil and lighting lamps. The first professional fire brigade was founded and employed more than a thousand people. It took responsibility for putting water in 1,100 huge "emergency vats" on the streets and replacing it regularly, and for investigating all wells and marking them with wooden boards labeled "*Jing*" (well) for use in fire fighting. Upon spotting a fire, watchers clanged bells to alert residents.[50] The brigade often conducted public fire drills for educational and training purposes, and these gradually became popular public performances. In 1909, the police fire brigade burned several thatched cottages built especially for the drill. When the brigade extinguished the fire using water hoses, a large audience applauded their skillful performance. The biggest fire drill was held in the Northern Parade Ground in the late Qing; 1,400 policemen and members of fire brigades took part as more than 10,000 people watched. Four watchtowers also were built at the four corners of the city. On spotting a fire, watchers would raise the alarm by ringing bells.[51]

Despite the inconvenience that the regulations must have caused, some evidence shows that during this period the police force was considered "a good helper" for the neighborhood, especially following a natural disaster or an accident. When the streets were flooded, for instance, the police "once more proved the excellence of their training. They came promptly to the rescue; they systematically distributed biscuits to the families in the flooded areas, and ordered those in the dangerous places to move at once." Also, the police helped settle the frequent disputes that occurred on the streets, a responsibility formerly held by the neighborhood organizations.[52]

The police also dealt routinely with unwelcome human or animal interlopers. A cartoon published in *Popular Pictorial* shows a drunkard making a fool of himself at a teahouse (see Figure 5.8).[53] Like drunkards, the mentally ill were not welcome in public, and their appearance was felt to disrupt public order, especially in crowded areas such as the Flower Fair. A journalist reported that within the first two weeks of the fair that year, he had seen six or seven instances when the police escorted mentally ill people out of the area.[54] Dogs, a constant menace, were also controlled by the police. Reformers particularly disliked that some dog owners would "bring their pets to the Center for Promoting Commerce and Industry, compromising the center's lofty reputation in Chengdu business circles." The dogs, reformers complained, "block traffic and also fight each other at the front gate." It was suggested that violators be fined.[55] A cartoon entitled "Spending Money to Watch the Backs of Dogs," published in *Popular Pictorial*, condemned those who brought their dogs to the theater (see Figure 5.9). The police required all dogs to be registered and to wear around their necks a wooden board issued by the police. If a registered dog was lost, the police

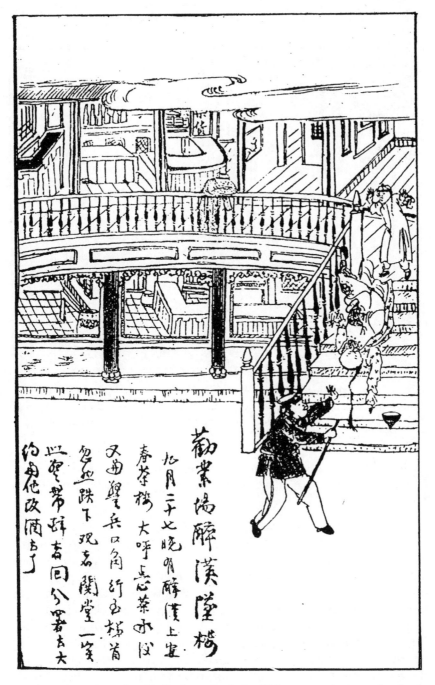

勸業場醉漢墜樓

北月二十七晚有醉漢上宜
春茶樓大呼忘茶水侯
又與巡兵口角行至梯首
忽然一跌下觀者闌堂一笑
此巡警帶辭吾回分署去大
約身他改酒去了

FIGURE 5.8. A Drunkard Falls down the Stairs. This cartoon depicts a drunkard loudly calling for tea and snacks at the Warm Spring Tea Balcony (Yichun chalou) at the Center for Promoting Commerce and Industry. He has an argument with a policeman and then falls down the stairs, to the amusement of onlookers. From TSHB 1909, no. 6.

FIGURE 5.9. Spending Money to Watch the Backs of Dogs. The caption reads: "Good dogs do not get in people's way, and good people do not climb on the stage. This is a dog screen, and these are dog-standing seats. This is a kingdom of dogs." From TSHB 1912, no. 31.

could help find it; otherwise, the police would capture any unlicensed dogs. The owners of dogs that attacked pedestrians were required to pay a fine of one *yuan*.[56]

Restrictions on Spiritual Life. The police tried to regulate not only people's public behavior but also the religious beliefs and activities that had become an important part of everyday life. In premodern times, state authorities always sought to manipulate popular religion; if people displayed "signs of extraordinary devotion, then the officials were likely to step in." To a certain extent, the official ideology met the elites' needs, and thus social reformers joined with state power to change commoners' beliefs. The orthodox view held that commoners' religious beliefs were "superstitious" and "backward" and should be restricted. During the Qing, the government "did everything in its power to limit contact between the common people and non-elite ritual specialists."[57] In the early twentieth century, the police further restricted all religious and folk ceremonial rituals. For example, on the twenty-eighth day of the fourth lunar month, the

birthday of the Medicine King, the police forbade entry to the Temple of
the Medicine King for the celebration. During a drought in the summer of
1914, the local government pasted on all streets posters that prohibited the
ritual of praying for rain. In 1917, although the police did not prohibit the
ritual of praying for rain, they prohibited people from playing the part of
ghosts in the ceremony. During the Medicine King Festival, the police did
not allow the people to burn incense or kowtow either at the Temple of the
Medicine King or in nearby streets.[58]

During the late Qing and early Republic, the police banned certain practices of divination, such as "watching a deity" (guanxian), "visiting hell"
(zouyin), and "drawing an egg" (huadan). People continued to see diviners,
however. Because the reformers were so disappointed in the people's refusal
to abandon "superstitious" beliefs, the police enacted even stricter rules. In
the late 1920s, under pressure from having their businesses sharply restricted, astrologists and diviners wanted to organize and establish an "academic association" to protect their livelihood.[59] The local authority denied
their request, claiming that "astrology and divination have no academic
value." It charged the practitioners with fooling ordinary people, degrad-
ing customs and culture, and damaging society. Therefore, the government
"should restrict all astrologists and diviners" and "abolish superstition"
during the "reformist era." In 1927, city authorities prohibited all witch
doctors and fortune-tellers and also forbade Buddhist monks and Daoist
priests from such practice. The next year, various forms of worship of local
deities were officially prohibited by "a general order from the nationalist
government."[60]

Nevertheless, there is much evidence to show that the police were un-
successful in their attempt to control popular cults. Although the police
forbade the ceremony of the Medicine King, for example, local residents,
especially women, still went to the Temple of the Medicine King to burn incense; in fact, there were so many worshipers that they were forced to set
up altars on the street. When the government prohibited the celebration of
the Dragon Boat Festival, forbidding people from preparing dragon boats
and hiring boatmen for service at the festival, people still gathered in the
River View Tower (Wangjiang lou), a traditional place for the festival. The
Liberating Living Creatures Festival (Fangsheng hui), on the eighth day of
the fourth lunar month, was celebrated by decorating flower boats and
"liberating" living creatures, under the Buddhist custom that regarded the
liberation of birds, fishes, turtles, eels, and snakes as a way of amassing
merit. During the festival, thousands of people gathered on both banks of
the river to watch the creatures being set free, while some poor people took
this chance to earn some money selling fish and animals at good prices.[61]
Despite the prohibition of this activity as a "hundred-year-old bad custom"

and a "decadent custom," commoners kept up the practice. And finally, the police were forced to accommodate the sentiment of the common people. In 1918, the police allowed the Lower Lotus Pond (Xia lianchi) to be used as a "liberating living creatures pond" (*fangsheng chi*).[62]

Social transformation changes people's spiritual life; as Clifford Geertz pointed out, it weakens the traditional ties of social structure and interrupts "the simple uniformity of religious belief and practice characteristic of an earlier period."[63] What happened in early-twentieth-century China provides new evidence to support this argument. In Chengdu, however, police involvement escalated the process. Still, this was not an easy task, and the commoners' lifestyle, religious beliefs, and folk culture demonstrated their strong continuity. The issue of how to treat religious cults was debated among the elites. Although there was a strong inclination to criticize all popular cults, some reformers tried to distinguish between religion and superstition. Moreover, government policies were inconsistent, sometimes harsh and sometimes lenient. In 1919, Sichuan's provincial government approved an appeal by the Sichuan Buddhist Association and vowed to protect the property of temples and nunneries. A public notice to this effect, distributed by the local government, blamed local gentry and heads of communities for such practices as cutting down temple trees and demanding money while falsely citing "public interest" as a reason.[64] As we know, since the late Qing, temple property had been a primary target of local reform movements for financial reasons; therefore, posting public notices protecting this property might reflect a setback for the radicals' policy against popular religions.

Control of Public Leisure

Under the police reform, the commoners' leisure was no longer a "free" activity, and the police could regulate what people watched and listened to for entertainment. The police prohibited performances of "ghostly," "bizarre," "licentious," and "evil" (*yao, dan, yin, xie*) stories. Reformers highly praised this measure, stating that "many licentious activities once practiced in the city of Chengdu are now under control, thanks to the establishment of the police" (see Figure 5.10).[65] When it was reported that a troupe of acrobats was performing "evil plays," the police, yielding to pressure from reformers, banned the performances. The police made several arrests at the Joy Teahouse on the grounds that their performances "harmed local customs" and displayed "unseemly manners." A tricky entertainer, nicknamed "Little Ghost Chen" (Chen Xiaogui) although he was over sixty, performed an indecent game in public places and was accused by the police of "harming people." Previously, martial artists and acrobats could perform in any public space. Now, however, the police required the issuance of a permit before a public area could be used and frequently denied such applications. Traditionally, many blind people made a living by chanting stories and singing folk songs on the street; the practice had been sanctioned by the police, but others were prohibited from doing so. Thus, when people who were not blind, called "rascals" (*wulai*) by the police, sang songs on the street, the police believed that "it would harm local custom" and charged them with "enticing many women to watch." A police regulation banned the activity and threatened these "rascals" with hard labor if they were caught. To bypass this restriction, some pretended to be blind to perform "licentious songs."[66] However, under these restrictive measures, the number of folk performers in Chengdu gradually dwindled.

The teahouse, as the most popular center of public leisure, drew special attention from the police, who sought to supervise them. In early modern Western cities, public places such as taverns, restaurants, theaters, and coffeehouses were "generally on the periphery and therefore reserved for the populace" and were "so well patronised that the government was already

FIGURE 5.10. A Patrolman Chases a Golden Bamboo Clapper Performer. From TSHB 1912, no. 11.

thinking about prohibiting them."[67] The same was true for Chengdu in the early twentieth century, with the police and local government attempting to "civilize" and "modernize" public places. The teahouse immediately became their target. Local authorities constantly criticized teahouses as "disorderly" and sought to control them in the name of preserving public order. Ever since the founding of the Chengdu police in the late Qing, "drinking settlement tea" in teahouses (as described in Chapter 3) had been forbidden. According to Li Jieren's satirical account, "this was the first inconvenience Director Zhou Shanpei of the police gave to the local people, and that was why he was abused by his folks." Although there is no direct evidence to verify Li's comment, one news item in a local newspaper did state that after the police issued a regulation to forbid settling disputes in teahouses in the early Republic, the teahouse guild appealed to the police to make a clear distinction between "settling disputes" and normal chatting. Otherwise, confusion between the two activities would jeopardize the teahouse business. In fact, the practice was never completely extinguished in teahouses and continued to be mentioned frequently in local newspapers.[68]

Just as in the West, where "the commercialization of leisure always attracted criticism as a waste of time,"[69] in Chengdu the elites criticized teahouse-goers for "idly lounging in teahouses all day long" and reflecting Chinese "inertia." The municipal authorities, too, considered teahouses a place of "rumor spreading" and "trouble making," because various kinds of people gathered there and often "did not behave themselves." Teahouses were also criticized for making the students who went there neglect their studies. Performances of local operas in teahouses also became the target of the authorities' attacks. After the 1911 Revolution, the provincial government forced the Joy Teahouse to close; one local newspaper supported the action, saying "watching local operas is nothing but wasting time."[70]

In the late Qing, soon after the establishment of the police force, they issued the first "Regulations for Teahouses." The regulations required teahouses to register with the police and banned them from allowing such activities as gambling, bird fighting, and practicing the rituals of secret societies. Teahouse entertainment also came under police control. Storytellers were to notify the police before performing, and those whose stories were deemed "licentious," "evil," or "bizarre" were to be expelled. Teahouses were no longer allowed to expand into the streets. Patrolling policemen were to be notified when disputes occurred in teahouses, and teahouses were required to allow policemen to enter to investigate. All teahouses had to close by eleven o'clock in the evening. If a proprietor failed to turn the lights off after the third watch (one o'clock in the morning), the police would investigate. In their "Rules for Surveillance and Patrol," policemen were told to give teahouses careful scrutiny. The teahouse regulations may be seen as part of the elite's efforts to control public space, a phenomenon that was similar in some ways to the situation in the United States. Roy Rosenzweig found in his study of an American city that "leisure time became an arena of class struggle in which workers and industrialists fought over who would control life outside the workplace."[71] Basically, although the Chengdu police had conducted some measures of reform in the late Qing, they did not carry out aggressive and harsh policies on teahouses, and this moderation was appreciated by local elites and therefore drew their positive participation. And actually many of the moderate regulations that were enacted were backed by local elites.

During the early Republic, however, teahouses were central to the government attack on popular culture. In 1914, some merchants planned to build a new theater in the prosperous commercial district of New Street (Xin jie), combining a teahouse, bathhouse, restaurant, and barbershop. Although local authorities approved the project, the police later stopped it, citing "security," "customs," and "hygiene." The real reason, however, was to limit the development of teahouse theaters, because the police believed that Chengdu already had too many, reflective of the city's lamentable taste for the "excessively luxurious." Also, they believed "bad" operas were "diseases" that degraded social customs and the intellect.[72] In 1916, the police issued rules controlling teahouse theaters, banning so-called "licentious operas." According to this rule, performances could not contain any disapproved language or behavior; all operas in teahouses were to end by ten o'clock during summer and autumn and by nine during spring and winter. Under this new regulation, the occupancy of teahouses was even restricted, ranging from 100 seats for a small teahouse to 400 seats for a bigger one. More seats could not be added without permission.[73] In 1921, comic dialogues (*xiangsheng*) were again prohibited in teahouses because of their alleged "licentious" and "dirty" language. This increasing control of city dwellers' personal lives was a common phenomenon in the early Republic; in Shanghai, for example, the police force's interference "represented the new state's effort to create a civil culture."[74]

Another common complaint was that teahouses were crowded and dirty. When late-Qing hygiene reforms occurred, the police demanded that teahouses keep the room, grounds, and tables clean. In the early Republican era, further regulations were issued that covered items of sanitation, such as prohibiting barbers and pedicurists from serving customers at their seats. A few new hygiene regulations for teahouses were promulgated in the 1920s and 1930s, laying out standards of sanitation for water, cups, floors, tables, and chairs. They stipulated that cups must be boiled and spittoons and sanitary toilets provided. Also, the police required teahouse workers to wear uniforms and numbered badges, and forbade people with lung, venereal, skin, and other infectious diseases from working in teahouses.[75]

As public leisure increasingly came under the control of the Nationalist government,[76] teahouses in Chengdu suffered unprecedented attack. A new regulation permitted only one teahouse per park, shut down some establishments in areas that had many, and shortened their business hours to six daily. An even more radical campaign against teahouses was waged, limiting their numbers, hours, and number of patrons. Each professional guild was allowed to have only one teahouse; only one teahouse was allowed in each harbor, station, or park, and all others were to be shut down. Teahouses were allowed to be open only from nine in the morning until noon and from six to nine in the evening. Young students, women and children, government clerks, army personnel, and vagrants were not permitted inside; merchants were restricted from going to teahouses that were not associated with their guilds.[77]

Of course, many people, including social reformers, opposed such radical regulation because it brought unprecedented disruption to citizens' customary lives. Critics pointed out that teahouses had traditionally met people's social needs. Like other public facilities such as inns, wine shops, and coffeehouses, teahouses had both negative and positive aspects; the government should not squelch them without taking the positive functions into account. They also noted that frequenting teahouses was relatively economical compared to drinking wine and coffee. In addition, illegal activities were not exclusive to teahouses; if teahouses were closed, they would simply take place at other private or public places. Teahouse-goers were criticized for wasting time and spreading rumors, but these activities could take place elsewhere as well.[78] Unlike in the late Qing, when social reformers endorsed most government-sponsored reform projects, the Republican government's projects were received much less enthusiastically. The disagreement between local reformist elites and the Nationalist government over teahouses was in a sense emblematic of wider schisms that developed between them over time. The split over the teahouse issue was just a reflection of the deterioration of the overall relationship between the government and local elites during this period. The fact that state power increasingly reached into the bottom of the community and its social life seriously jeopardized the elite's traditional leadership for ordinary people.[79]

The teahouse was a microcosm of the society. It has been misunderstood not only by scholars but also by the general public. In the early twentieth century, teahouses were thought to be places for the idle; therefore, the most common accusation against teahouses was that they encouraged people to waste time. Along with other social transformation in China came changes in the very concept of time,[80] but this new understanding was largely limited to "modernized" and "Westernized" elites. Most ordinary residents retained the concept of time that had prevailed for centuries. How they used their time depended on many factors: personal habits, education, occupation, family background, economic status, and so on. In the teahouse, a scholar might find inspiration for his writing; a merchant might make a business deal; a student might learn about the society beyond his textbooks; a member of a secret society might make contact with other members; and a casual worker might find employment. And, of course, many petty peddlers, performers, and craftsmen made their living there. Therefore, distinctions between the idle and the busy were mutable and overlapping. In the teahouse, a man who looked idle might be busy, and vice versa. Idleness and industry were each part of the rhythm of daily life, and the teahouse accommodated both. It was one of the few public spaces available to urban residents for public life; even after the emergence of other "modern" gathering places, teahouses remained the most affordable option for urban commoners. This phenomenon also tells us that for Chengdu, as Susan Davis found for modern American cities, "industrial progress did not immediately destroy older urban and agrarian work rhythms."[81] The persistence of the teahouse exemplified the vitality of Chengdu's popular culture.

Limitation of Success

It might be said that in Chengdu the police were an early form of municipal government. Police duties extended far beyond the contemporary basic responsibilities of maintaining public security and social order. The police in Chengdu were not specialized in their duties, which led to inefficiencies. The police had a stake in almost all public matters, from public order and the city poor to fire control and hygiene, until 1928, when the municipal government was established. The police's involvement at least opened a path for managing urban issues that previously were the domain of neighborhood and charitable organizations, as well as guilds. Transferring these matters to the police, in fact, weakened the influence of the street- (or neighborhood-) and community-level organizations. Although the police force was unable to handle all issues well, it indeed took the first step toward establishing a quasi-municipal administration.

The reformers partially achieved their goal: Chengdu indeed established a new public order in the early twentieth century. Missionary J. Vale admired this change and said, "the police force, as at present organized, is a great improvement to the old Tithing System, and gives great satisfaction to all concerned." He believed that the people of Chengdu had "nothing but praise for the system: they are quick to perceive the advantages the system affords and appreciate the promptness with which petty troubles are dealt with. Under the old system no case could be heard under a week or ten days, but now every case is attended to on the day the plaint is filed."

The streets, he also noticed, became quieter and cleaner, and thieving was "much reduced owing to the police patrol at night."[82]

It is difficult to say whether Vale's opinion truly reflected the commoners' position, although the social reformers could claim some achievements. Vale, as a missionary from the West, naturally admired most Western-inspired reforms and tended to see them in a positive light. When Western missionaries admired police regulation of the city, they revealed their own cultural prejudice. They believed that there was a need for "some regulating in this land where life is of so little value and so many abuses occur!" Therefore, they welcomed this "new feature in Chinese life." Other visitors had a similar impression. According to Yamakawa, the new programs unquestionably enhanced the appearance of Chengdu, which was cleaner than other cities he had visited. In the 1920s, foreigners had a similar opinion, that "the city is clean, orderly, with an efficient police."[83] Nevertheless, any major change brings multiple responses. In American cities of the same time, reformers had a hard time getting working-class people to accept their projects. And when they tried to limit and redefine what constituted acceptable behavior among the lower classes, "their intentions were not easily realized" and their efforts "often met with unenthusiastic responses," because these measures "harassed" the people who "used the street's rich resources."[84] Social reformers in Chengdu met a similar situation; their achievements did not bring happiness to most commoners, in fact, but only more restrictions. Many government regulations affected not only commoners' everyday life but also their livelihoods.[85]

Actually, commoners accepted or rejected street reforms based on their personal interests. Pedestrians, for example, might embrace traffic control, but those whose livelihoods depended on access to the street, such as sedan-chair carriers, ox-cart drivers, and hawkers, would likely be less accepting. Taking beggars, gamblers, prostitutes, and thieves off the street was welcomed by many residents, but not by those removed. Theatrical troupes also opposed measures prohibiting "licentious" and "violent" operas because of the potential loss of audiences and income. Furthermore, those measures that were carried out by force understandably provoked popular resentment. That is why Chengdu Police Director Zhou Shanpei was widely criticized and despised by many before and even after the collapse of the Qing dynasty. Guo Moruo, a major modern Chinese intellectual who experienced early-twentieth-century Chengdu, tried to explain the reason: it was because "a repressive body that carried out extreme regulations had emerged overnight in the formerly diffuse society."[86] For the people who made their living on the street, in particular, more regulations meant more difficulty in earning a living. It is no surprise that they struggled to defend their established claim to the street.

Part III

COMMONERS AND LOCAL POLITICS

6   *The Struggle for the Street*

In early-twentieth-century Chengdu, the street was often used for political purposes, and it became an arena for power struggles. The politicization of the street is the focus of Part III of this book, which attempts to analyze the unprecedented involvement of commoners in local politics by exploring how their struggle for the street transformed street culture into street politics. And we will also see that public power struggles took place between different groups and in complicated ways. The focus of this chapter is the conflict that always existed between elites and commoners and among commoners themselves. The main argument of this section is that access to public space has always been the subject of conflict as people struggled to pursue power, their livelihoods, and, of course, the mundane functions of daily life as well. The lower classes cultivated unique strategies to maintain their access to public space in an unequal society.

In Chengdu, conflict assumed different forms: some conflicts were everyday disputes; some occurred over use of streets; some involved class struggles, while some occurred only among the lower classes; some were between individuals, while some caused mass violence. Most conflicts, however, took the form of disputes between individuals, which, as described by James Scott, "make no headlines" and have "rarely any dramatic confrontation."[1] Although commoners in Chengdu seldom planned, much less carried out, organized protests, they used forms of everyday resistance to express dissatisfaction and maintain their space. Therefore, conflict was part of daily life, despite the close relationships that formed between neighbors, as discussed previously. In fact, conflicts between members of the same family were commonly carried out in public. Many conflicts, however, resulted from disputes over the use of public space, including such mundane issues as seats in a teahouse. Furthermore, townspeople always believed that they had the privilege of using public space and tried to exclude those from the country; a similar situation also developed in relationships between Chengdu natives and immigrants. Even Manchus and Han families who lived in Chengdu for generations were culturally and physically segregated, resulting in hostility.[2] The people at the bottom of the society—coolies, prostitutes, and beggars—often simply refused to accept their fate and struggled for their own space.

In the early twentieth century, conflicts over the street increasingly took place between local authorities, including officials and social reformers, and the commoners who were the primary occupants of the street and the principal targets of reform. Commoners inevitably resisted the increased restrictions on public space that affected their customary ways of making a living and their recreation. During this period, commoners had to deal with many new regulations imposed by the police in addition to routine business operations. When change jeopardized their everyday lives and livelihoods, ordinary people were forced to struggle to survive. Urban reform further restricted women's appearances in public and exacerbated sexual discrimination. To claim their space in the streets, theaters, and other public places traditionally occupied by men, women challenged both new regulations and the traditional norms, eventually changing both.

Disputes: From the Family to the Neighborhood

Domestic conflicts on the street provide an excellent historical perspective from which to examine the relationships among families, neighbors, and communities. Because living space was limited, the everyday affairs of ordinary families often extended into the streets, transforming private matters into public ones. For instance, a wife who was beaten by her husband might run into the street for help, where neighbors or passersby might intervene and she could air her misfortunes publicly. Indeed, neighbors often became involved in family disputes. In one instance, when a couple beat the wife's elderly mother unconsciousness on the street, the neighbors tied up the two culprits and delivered them to the police. Another story tells of the "unusually ferocious" Woman Liu, who lived in East Office Gate (Dong yuanmen). She often abused her mother-in-law and fought with her husband. Neighbors "defended her mother-in-law against this injustice" and forced Woman Liu to sweep the street as punishment; "all spectators laughed at her."[3] Some stories reveal the relationship between "bad men" and their neighbors. Hu Zhongrong was regarded as a "swindler," and after his father publicly denounced his ways to protect the family from ill repute, Hu became the object of street gossip. Hu married a prostitute, who stood in their doorway each day to entice youngsters. Because young people visited her "in an endless stream," Hu accumulated quite a bit of money. This conduct angered their neighbors, causing one to paste a satirical matched couplet on Hu's door: "The door was opened in spring, summer, autumn, and winter; customers come from east, west, north, and south" (*menying chun xia qiu dong, ke'na dong xi nan bei).* Neighbors commonly used this traditional form of cultural expression to air grievances.[4] These stories offer us good examples of how domestic matters became public issues and how neighbors voluntarily collaborated to ensure harmony. Indeed, they regarded settling disputes in the neighborhood as a duty.

The close proximity that fostered relationships among neighbors also led to disputes. Such disputes as children's fights, belongings that blocked public passageways, or gossip about private affairs could result in verbal abuse and even physical violence. However, conflicts more often arose over issues of property ownership and debt. In one case, two brothers argued loudly on the street over property that their father had left them, causing elites to "worry about people's morality." Another case was even more bizarre: two men publicly fought over who could claim one *wen* of copper lying on the ground, causing one man to hit the other on the head with an oil jar.[5] Disputes over money and property could have more serious consequences. Two people in Green Dragon Street (Qinglong jie) who argued over the purchase of a garden soon turned violent, and one of them was beaten to death. Some altercations could even develop into mass violence. Early one morning, a fight broke out among a few dozen people and spilled over to adjacent neighborhoods; most participants ran away when the original two involved were arrested. The cause of this ruckus was a minor dispute between the sugar traders on East Great Street and the cap traders on Provincial Administration Commissioner Yamen Street (Buzheng ya).[6] Disputes of this magnitude could not be resolved within the neighborhood, and the police had to get involved. Before the police force was established, heads of *baojia*, the street, or the neighborhood mediated violent disputes. If an incident involved immigrants, heads of guilds or native place associations were sought for settlement.

Petty theft and gambling caused the greatest concern. There were many petty criminals who came from various backgrounds, and, of course, most were poor, or what some historians call "marginal men," vagrants without steady work. Robert Antony found that most petty crimes were committed by hired laborers, boatmen, porters, peddlers, watchmen, servants, and even the semiskilled, such as itinerant barbers, carpenters, tailors, healers, singers, actors, and monks. These people "lived on or near the margins of respectable society, earning only a subsistence living."[7] In Chengdu, petty thieves were usually unemployed and unskilled outsiders, who regarded the streets as a prime source for ill-gotten booty. The police, however, gradually established a presence; as one folk writer described, "the policemen stand their guard on the street day and night, and thieves are scared and hidden." The reality, however, might have differed considerably, because thieves generally are persistent in their motivation to steal. Such public gathering places as the annual Flower Fair provided them with great opportunities for profit. Some thieves were pickpockets, known locally as "red money thieves" (hongqian zei), while some stole rice bowls, hardware, and other merchandise.[8]

Thieves often organized into groups for self-protection. The police once caught a group of about twenty thieves and sent them to do forced labor as punishment. In another case, police found a child carrying a big bag containing clothing valued at more than 100 taels of silver, which led them to a ring of thieves. In the summer of 1914, when drought caused the price of rice in Chengdu to skyrocket, rice carts were routinely stolen along the roads from the rural markets to Chengdu. According to the newspaper, the thieves were "idle young men" who colluded with their fellow bandits. As missionary G. E. Hartwell described, these thieves usually had a "king" as their leader who was "most probably in the employ" of a magistrate. The "king" was considered a "half beggar" and "half servant to the officials." If the bandits were "reached within three days of a robbery . . . the goods might be found; after that, the booty was divided, the yamen runners getting their share."[9] This report suggested that thieves also tried to establish connections with officials to obtain protection or expand their range of opportunities. There is no other direct evidence to prove the relationship described by Hartwell, but it is no secret that Qing officials lacked the personnel and financial resources necessary to provide adequate protection and depended on some existing powers to maintain social stability. Although thieves' organizations, unlike beggar organizations, were illegal, local authorities often looked the other way as long as they did not cause major trouble. This strategy of governing had already existed in Chinese cities for quite a long time and extended to many groups, such as the Sworn Brothers and the beggars. Of course, this tacit understanding was often broken when social and political situations changed, such as through the transfer of a magistrate.

Although gambling was a prime target of social reformers and the police, it was not easily eradicated; no reform could quickly supplant the associated lifestyle that had emerged over centuries. As a result, in the early Republic, gambling remained very popular both publicly and privately; gamblers also had a lot of experience dealing with local authorities. The River View Tower (Wangjiang lou) and Wenshu Temple became gambling sites because these quiet and scenic enclaves were not under police supervision.[10] The top of the city wall, outside the city gates, and the riverbanks also became prime spots for gambling and fighting. Once, for example, a young boy was beaten to death on the East City Gate wall during a dispute over gambling. The road out of the North City Gate was a veritable haven for gambling for a time, and gambling stalls lined both sides of the road. Gambling also was common on the street along the West Imperial River

(Xi yuhe). In one case, a group of gamblers scurried away when the police arrived. One man who wore "an expensive leather coat" climbed over the wall, forgetting the river on the other side and landing directly in it. Gamblers eventually became even more brazen. Some people set up gambling stalls on city streets; on the first day of the Chinese New Year alone, the police caught fifty to sixty gamblers in Bao Family Alley (Baojia xiang), and on the second day, forty to fifty in the Duke Luo Temple (Luogong ci). Although the proprietors of teahouses did not dare promote illegal activity publicly, they never pushed to squelch it, either. A reporter for a local newspaper saw gambling everywhere in the Square and Circle (Fangyuan) Teahouse: on the tables, chairs, and even the floors. The ease with which gamblers escaped detection caused Fu Chongju to lament that "the gamblers have remarkable ability and power."[11]

Since the late Qing, local authorities had made an enormous effort to control gambling, but with little success. The reason was clear: gambling had very deep and solid cultural roots, both as a private family leisure activity and also as public recreation among strangers. Furthermore, the distinction between serious gaming and seemingly innocent entertainment such as card games or mahjong was unclear. Although local authorities put a great deal of energy into control gambling, it seems that they did not win this battle.

Classes and Conflicts in the Teahouses

Class distinctions were clearly evident in public places in Chengdu, just as in late-nineteenth- and early-twentieth-century American cities, where the working class dominated public drinking places, and the middle and upper classes generally drank at home, in private clubs, or in exclusive hotels. In China's eastern coastal areas, teahouses had two extremes: the street teahouse was usually a place for the middle and lower classes, and the tea balconies were for high society. In Chengdu, however, teahouses were known for accommodating all social classes. Although "every street has a teahouse" in Chengdu, there were "no high-class teahouses as splendid as those in Shanghai, Canton, and Yangzhou, which only served high society." One of the virtues of Chengdu teahouses was commonly believed to be their "relatively equality." One traveler of the 1930s and 1940s remarked that he did not have the courage to go to street teahouses in other places, but he had no such problem in Chengdu. Members of the elite and lower classes alike could sit in the same teahouse, and nobody cared much about social status.[12]

Although this phenomenon may suggest that in early-twentieth-century Chengdu, as in nineteenth-century Hankou, "class identities seem to have been weak," Chengdu teahouses were not as socially equal as they first appeared. There was inevitable class distinction among teahouses; for instance, the Real Amusement Tea Garden (Zhengyu chayuan) was a place where "high society goes." The guidebook of Chengdu also revealed that teahouses were categorized based on the social status of their patrons.[13] We do not have clear criteria for distinguishing between high-class and low-class teahouses, but according to memoirs, travel notes, and newspapers, *chashe* (tea societies) were usually street teahouses, smaller and geared to a lower-class clientele. *Chalou* (tea balconies), *chayuan* (tea gardens), and *chating* (tea halls), by contrast, were what might be called "courtyard teahouses," usually larger, more expensive, and directed at middle- or upper-class patrons.

Some travelers' descriptions of Chengdu teahouses make this class distinction even more apparent. Yi Junzuo did not see any poor patrons at the high-class Double Fountains (Erquan) Teahouse when he visited in Chengdu in the 1940s. Instead, he noted that "all patrons wore decent and clean clothes and were also decent people." In some teahouses, Shu Xincheng wrote, there were no shabbily dressed people from the lower classes. Except for a few women in fashionable attire, all patrons wore long gowns, and most were middle-aged people "for whom livelihood is no issue, who are beyond school age and have no occupation, and therefore spend their time in teahouses." Also, from Shu's description, we find that even the elegantly dressed patrons were categorized. The rich spent their time "drinking there, eating there, and napping there." They read newspapers and discussed news, recited poems, ogled women, and even "exchanged experiences of adultery." When their stomachs were full and they felt tired, they lay on the bamboo chairs and fell asleep. When they woke up, it was sunset and time to go home for dinner. After dinner, they went to the theater. The poorer patrons usually did not eat in teahouses but merely drank tea and napped there.[14]

The small teahouses behind the main streets were the domain of the poor. By 1931, there were around five hundred third- and fourth-class teahouses that served commoners.[15] They were simple and crude; most consisted simply of a room that opened onto the street and featured low tables and stools. Their clientele included "wheelbarrow pullers, sedan-chair carriers, and other working-class people who were struggling for their livelihood. Between jobs, a teahouse is the only place for them to kill time and rest." *New Chengdu* (Xin Chengdu) expressed sympathy by admonishing, "there is no reason to criticize these laborers for wasting time in teahouses." Although a cup of tea in Chengdu was very cheap, many poor people could not afford even this simple luxury. In a Chengdu tradition, teahouses did not exclude "the poorest of the poor" but allowed them in to drink the tea that other patrons left behind; this was called "drinking over-time tea" (*he jiabancha*). There was even a custom regarding how to drink "overtime tea."[16]

There was obvious social discrimination in the teahouses, some of which derived from old customs and some of which was imposed by the government. In the late Qing and even into the early Republic, actors in local operas were not allowed to drink tea or watch shows in teahouses. Some, however, were courageous enough to challenge this restriction, though they were expelled as soon as they were discovered. Actors in teahouses always drew attention. It was reported that when an actor in makeup was drinking tea in the Pleasure Spring Teahouse, "a group of uneducated people" gathered outside to watch him, blocking the sidewalk until a policeman sent them away. One local newspaper reported that "both the actor and audience are shameless." Because the public's curiosity about actors often caused disruption, the police enacted regulations restricting their public appearance. Seeking a public life of their own, local opera performers established their own teahouses, such as the Small Garden (Xiao huayuan) Teahouse.[17] They undoubtedly felt more comfortable when surrounded by their own kind.

Teahouse life in Chengdu reflected social conflict as well as social harmony, and conflicts could escalate into violence. The teahouse was a place for free talk, but careless talk could lead to fights. In an overcrowded teahouse, people would tussle for seats, causing a local newspaper to comment that one such altercation "was another 'drama' playing off the stage." Often disputes arose when patrons left their seats, only to find them filled when they returned. The police made a rule that "even though a guest has left, the seat should be kept for him if his teacup is still on the table."[18] The performances of local operas in a guildhall were major events, and their huge audiences increased the potential for trouble. During one performance at the Fujian guildhall, for instance, a man was arrested after smashing another man's head. At a show at the same guildhall, which drew "a sea of people," a man described as "extremely agitated" beat a child, arousing public indignation. The police settled the dispute before further violence could take place. On another occasion, the packed audience at a local opera trampled some food stalls; the police were called and arrested those who were rowdy and uncooperative. Conflicts over gambling also were frequent in teahouses. A local newspaper reported that in a dispute over a bird fight at the Pleasure Teahouse, one customer stabbed another with a knife, causing serious injury.[19]

Theft of teacups and other goods was a recurring problem in teahouses. Good teahouses usually used teacups made in Jingdezhen, China's most famous porcelain production site. A poor man could live for days on the money he received for a stolen teacup; however, he would be punished severely if his theft was discovered. Once, the Feather (Yujing) Teahouse caught a middle-aged thief and tied him to the pillar in front of the teahouse; he then confessed that he had an elderly mother to feed and no way to obtain money. Such incidents provided a moment of drama for teahouse-goers; when a waiter caught a poor man stealing teacups and beat him, many spectators cried out: "Beat the shameless one to death." Patrons enjoyed watching such disturbances or "plays" in a public space; this was known as "watching excitement." Teahouses often suffered property damage, and their chairs, tables, and teacups could be destroyed deliberately by patrons for any reason, even one as trivial as the postponement of an announced performance. Once, a fight broke out when over two hundred soldiers were watching a show in the Joy Teahouse; the soldiers smashed the chairs and tables to pieces.[20] But, though teahouses could punish the powerless poor, they were outmatched against powerful soldiers during the warlord era.

The teahouse is a window through which one can understand society and its changes. Data from the early Republic reveal that conflicts and violent incidents gradually increased in the teahouses, where local bullies tyrannized and disrupted teahouse life. Although there are no direct statistics to prove this trend, relevant reports in the local newspapers increased significantly in the late 1920s, but such stories seldom appeared in either the late-Qing newspaper *Popular Daily* (Tongsu ribao) or the 1910s *Citizens' Daily* (Guomin gongbao).[21] From those reports, we can see that hoodlums gathered in the teahouses, harassing attractive women with obscenities.[22] More serious, but rare, incidents involved murder and mass violence. Once, a local tough and forty to fifty of his followers surrounded the Elegant Fountain (Wenquan) Teahouse, near the City God Temple. They beat a young merchant to death, stealing his watch and money. A teahouse, as a public space, was also an arena where local bullies showed off their power. In the Archery Teahouse, for example, several soldiers forced a man to kneel before a young woman and apologize to her. The woman, the wife of a military officer, had ordered a dish of food, but the waiter had given it to her in a rough pottery bowl. She felt humiliated, and her husband sought to avenge himself against the proprietor of the teahouse.[23]

Teahouses often had internal problems, such as disputes among performing troupes, patrons, and landlords.[24] Teahouses also frequently became an arena for struggle over livelihood, as we see in this episode, which took place at the Wind and Cloud Pavilion (Fengyun ting) Teahouse in 1928:

Ma Shaoqing had an agreement with Woman Wu, the owner of the Wind and Cloud Pavilion Teahouse, which gave him the privilege of operating a tobacco business there. One year later another tobacconist who envied Ma's good business persuaded Wu to end the agreement, but Ma, who paid the rent on time and was not in debt, refused. One night, before the teahouse closed, when Ma was not there, Wu had the workers inventory teacups, lids, and saucers. They found a tea setting [a single teacup, lid, and saucer] in Ma's cabinet. Wu claimed that her teahouse had lost over a hundred tea settings, and she demanded that Ma compensate her for all of them. But Ma accused Wu of lodging a fake accusation against him in order to take back the rent.[25]

The owner Wu, the tobacconist Ma, and the other tobacconist were ordinary urbanities, all trying to make a living through their own devices. That these kinds of arguments and struggles happened nearly every day tells us that conflicts of economic interests constantly emerged among commoners themselves. But commoners often fought with the upper classes for their livelihood as well. For example, the actors of the Long Pleasure (*Changle*) Troupe went to the teahouse guild to accuse their master of cheating both the teahouse in which they performed and the actors, describing his "many bad habits" and "malpractice."[26] Many such disputes resulted from employers' exploitation, such as pushing performers to work long hours and paying low wages; in some cases, actors simply refused to perform when conflicts could not be resolved.

The opera reform of the late Qing made it extremely difficult for theatrical troupes to make a living. It prohibited so-called "licentious" and "violent" operas; since theatrical troupes depended on these kinds of operas, however, they used every means to keep performing them. Some troupes gave the operas different titles, but some kept the old titles "without scruples." Fu Chongju bemoaned the fact that "theaters are full of enthusiastic audiences," and licentious and violent operas were shown day and night. During the Railroad Protection Movement of 1911, martial law was imposed by Governor-General Zhao Erfeng; it prohibited any public gathering, including opera performances. After the establishment of the Sichuan Military Government, performances were still banned. Those who lost their livelihood gathered at their teahouse to discuss a solution. After their application to reopen business was denied, they went to the police station to make an appeal.[27]

In the Republican era, "superstitious" and "licentious" plays became even more popular, despite the government's heavy restrictions. Ironically, the Elegant Garden, a "reformed" teahouse-theater in the late Qing, was criticized for performing "dirty," "licentious" plays. The Joy Teahouse, a pioneer of "new operas" and a symbol of social reform in the late Qing, was charged by the mayor of Chengdu with ignoring the regulation requiring teahouses and theaters to submit their programs three days in advance for government approval. According to a warning from the mayor, the Joy Teahouse often performed "licentious and immoral" operas. Obviously, the Elegant Garden and Joy Teahouse were not the only ones to sponsor this kind of entertainment. The Broad View (Daguan) Teahouse, too, was forced to close for one day as a penalty for such a violation. In 1932, in fact, only one theater followed the advance submission rule, even though the government threatened punishment for violators. Why did theaters take such a risk? The answer is clear: because forbidden operas attracted more patrons. When business slumped, performing these plays was a surefire way to revive it. For example, when the Popular Garden Society Teahouse (Yuanqun she chayuan) suffered a downturn that jeopardized its future, the teahouse-keeper appealed to the "Bureau of the Society" (*Shehui ju*) to be allowed to show "deity plays" for "protecting their livelihood."[28]

Teahouses and theaters not only violated the regulations on performances of local operas, but also tried to expand their use of public space. Teahouses routinely set up tables and chairs in the public space of streets, squares, or parks, especially during the summer, when shade and cool breezes offered comfort. In 1929, the municipal government promulgated a new regulation forbidding teahouses to encroach on public space. All the teahouses in the Smaller City Park, the Central City Park, and Zhiji Temple Park then complained that this restriction would seriously damage business, and presented an appeal to the local government. Their resistance indicates how similar the experience of street culture in Chengdu was to that of industrialized Europe, where it not only was "not killed by the industrial revolution" but instead "flourished as an expression of the economic and political struggles of the new workforce."[29] The theaters in Chengdu, though profoundly affected by the process of modernization in the early twentieth century, survived by adapting to the shifting social and political environment.

Issues of Exclusion

Exclusion and discrimination always existed in Chinese cities, with one ethnic group or occupation flaunting its power against another one. Cases of townspeople bullying country people were common. The existence of exclusion and discrimination caused those who were excluded, bullied, or discriminated against to struggle for their rights. Emily Honig's study of Subei identity in Shanghai revealed tense relations between ethnic groups.[30] The discrimination against Subei people in Shanghai was typical, and a similar case also existed in Chengdu, where, like Shanghai, language, history, and place of origin could cause boundaries between people. Although there was no regional discrimination for a particular group of people in Chengdu, unlike in Shanghai, residents generally scorned Manchus and country people.

Conflicts between the Hans and Manchus were frequent, even though the groups were segregated into different walled areas.[31] There were around 4,000 Manchu households, and nearly 19,000 Manchus, residing in Chengdu, almost all in the Smaller City (Manchu City). In writings by local elites, bannermen were always described negatively. Hatred against those with different lifestyles and culture was passed through the generations.[32] In the late Qing, Manchus became increasingly poor because of their "laziness" and "idleness," according to elites. As one member of the elite class expressed it: "We make a living by ourselves and Moslem families can survive by slaughtering cows. The bannermen have nothing to do but go fishing until sunset." Another elite sounded a similar complaint: "Without doing daily jobs, they take pleasure in playing cards. As soon as they hear the news of a local opera performance at the North City Gate, they go out of the Smaller City one after another." Young elite women refused to enter the Smaller City, due to the "idle," "dirty," and "rude" people who stared at them. In the "Big City," where Han people lived, rumors constantly circulated about assaults on young women in the Manchu City.[33] The language that local writers used to describe Manchus clearly reflected the antagonism between ethnic groups in Chengdu.

Issues of ethnic conflict always become more important during times of political crisis. Mark Elliott's study of Jiangnan garrisons finds that confrontations between Han people and bannermen existed on two levels: "military versus civilian" and "bannerman versus townsman." Both levels expressed "an opposition between superior and inferior in the power structure." There was a similar conflict in Chengdu. Before the 1911 Revolution, the relationship between Han people who lived in the "Big City" and Manchu people who lived in the Smaller City was tense. Li Jieren, in his novel *The Great Wave* (Dabo), describes such conflicts. Hostility between the Han and Manchu people, which had gradually built up over two hundred years, broke out in 1911; the flash point was not the ethnic issue, however, but economic and political conflicts with the Qing government. When Chengdu declared its independence from the Qing, the Manchus in the city heard that many of their counterparts had been killed by Han people in cities such as Xi'an and Jinzhou. They feared for their lives and were determined to defend themselves. Their plan culminated with all women and children committing suicide while the men would fight to the death. Eventually, however, the Manchus surrendered peacefully after the new revolutionary government promised their safety.[34]

Chengdu residents also despised people from the frontier areas, especially the Tibetans, who lived along the western border of Sichuan. Chengdu was a trading center for herbs, furs, and other goods produced in Tibetan areas and a hub for traders traveling from their homeland to other areas of China. Chengdu dwellers considered those from border areas "rude people" or "barbarians." As one account noted, "people in the Chengdu plain like to hire 'barbarian girls' as servants, who look cute with their many small pigtails." A writer mocked the Tibetans from Big Golden Valley (Da jinchuan), Small Golden Valley (Xiao jinchuan), and Tibet, who came to Chengdu every winter to sell yak butter and buy gongs and other Chinese percussion instruments to take back with them. He sneered at them for striking gongs when they inspected them in the shops.[35] For Tibetans, Chengdu was the closest major commercial center for trading and communicating with the outside world, while the Chengdu residents also depended on this business, but economic exchange seems not to have enhanced cultural understanding.

Fernand Braudel studied the complicated relationship between town and countryside and tried to "rediscover one basic language for all the cities of the world." He found that "the uninterrupted confrontation with the countryside [was] a prime necessity of daily life."[36] Chengdu had similar connections with the surrounding countryside. Although a wall enclosed the city, its residents inevitably depended on trade with the areas outside, and a pattern of confrontation and mutual dependence was established. City dwellers, for example, could not enjoy fresh food and cheap labor without workers from the country. Farmers on the Chengdu plain usually did not live in concentrated settlements; instead, each household was located close to its arable land. These people felt isolated and sought contact with others on Chengdu's streets and in its wine shops and teahouses. They also largely depended on town markets to exchange their agricultural products and handicrafts. William Skinner's classic study on marketing and social structure gives us a profound understanding of the living pattern in the Chengdu plain. Farmers toiled in the fields during the busy spring and autumn seasons but worked as itinerant peddlers or itinerant artisans on Chengdu streets during the summer and winter. Therefore, peddlers and artisans from the countryside could be seen regularly on Chengdu streets. Most arrived in the morning and returned to their homes in the evening, but some stayed in inns, especially the "chicken-feather inns," overnight or longer.[37]

City dwellers naturally thought they were superior to country people, mocking them as "stupid," "naive," "rustic," "rural idiots," and "stupid boys," and gossiping or spreading "bizarre" stories about country folks. Even though both lived on the Chengdu plain, they looked dramatically different. A farmer who lived just outside the city wall looked and spoke differently and wore different clothing from a man who lived inside the wall. The rustic clothing of a rural man could draw many curious stares in restaurants or teahouses.[38] The following amply illustrates the gulf between urban and rural inhabitants:

A farmer was drinking tea at a teahouse yesterday. He heard somebody complain: "The Xi'nan [the southwest region, including the provinces of Yunnan, Guizhou, and Sichuan] Policy has harmed our Chengdu people awfully." Then he came up to the person and said angrily: "We in the countryside have suffered even more from the *Xilan* (complete destruction) Policy. . . ." The person saw his confusion, and explained: "I am talking about the Yunnan Policy." Even angrier, the farmer replied: "Regarding the *Yingpan* (military base) Policy, it's even worse." The man saw that he could not make the farmer understand, so he stood up and left.[39]

The Chinese language has many words with identical or similar pronunciations, and because of this, confusions about meaning often arise. When people who speak with different accents converse, the situation is exacerbated. On the surface, this story is about this kind of confusion, but underneath, it is about a "stupid" countryman's inability to engage in "political talk," and further reflects the urbanites' sense of superiority.

On the street, townspeople often bullied their country counterparts. For example, people who lived along the streets might demand that wheelbarrow (*jigong che*, literally "cock carts") pushers, usually country men, pay one or two *wen* as "street passage money," with the excuse that wheelbarrows would damage the streets. Wheelbarrow pushers who did not pay would not be allowed to pass through, or would have to carry their wheelbarrows. Sometimes residents would deliberately place obstacles, such as rocks and broken bricks, on the streets, and some even deliberately pried stone plates from the street in order to prevent wheelbarrows from passing. In addition, disputes between townspeople and country people were much more likely to become violent than those between two townspeople. In one instance, when a peasant's bucket accidentally soiled a well-dressed young man's clothing at the entrance to a city gate, which was always crowded with peasants carrying human waste, the young man beat the peasant cruelly. Passersby tried to calm him and asked the peasant to apologize. In another case, when a funeral procession passed down the street, a participant beat a rice wheelbarrow pusher who blocked his way. This angered pedestrians, who helped the man retaliate.[40] Most conflicts did not have serious consequences, however, even though policemen were usually not available, because pedestrians often voluntarily intervened in the process of settlement through "public power."

In addition to city-country conflicts, confrontations between old and new immigrants were common in Chinese cities.[41] Chengdu had few real natives after it was almost destroyed by the late-Ming and early-Qing wars; the city recovered its prosperity through constant immigration since the early Qing. Although no serious feuds between old and new immigrants were apparently documented, disputes still took place. Many people went to Chengdu to find jobs each year, "but few of them leave," according to Wu Haoshan, "because it is a good place to live."[42] The large number of merchants from other provinces who came to Chengdu gradually settled down and opened their own shops, most of which specialized in one or several kinds of goods. As their numbers increased, they established guilds or organized native place associations. The resulting competition with established Chengdu businesses inevitably caused resistance by Chengdu natives.[43]

Immigration into Chengdu increased dramatically in the late Qing and early Republic. A report from 1917 stated that there had "recently been added 20,000 households," causing residents to worry about "how this spot within the city wall can contain such massive population." Some residents believed that the number of unemployed people had grown after the Qing collapsed, increasing the burden on all residents trying to make a living. Because Chengdu attracted newcomers from "all corners of the land," "the good and the bad were intermingled." Consequently, "the bad," it was said, could hide in crowds and move around freely, "pretending to be good." Thus, some elites appealed to the government to place more restrictions on mobility.[44]

In Chengdu, as in other Chinese cities, problems caused by differences in race, ethnicity, and city of origin were common. Probably, it was the close tie between neighbors that strengthened the distinction between "us" and "others." Chengdu residents did not like "strangers" to change everyday life. Those who were excluded struggled to maintain a livelihood and find amusement in public spaces.

Women's Challenges

In Chengdu, social reformers harshly criticized the public behavior of women. Their criticisms reveal how social reformers viewed women, their appearance in public, and popular culture. Clearly, women's activities outside the home were often deplored. A proverb in *Investigation of Chengdu* (Chengdu tonglan) stated, with considerable exaggeration: "One is crying, the second is always eating, the third is sleeping, the fourth is swallowing opium, and the fifth has hanged herself" (*yi ku, er e, san shuijiao, si tun yangyan, wu shangdiao*). Fu Chongju claimed that 90 percent of Chengdu women liked watching local plays; 80 percent liked playing mahjong; and 70 percent liked visiting temples.[45] All these behaviors, for social reformers, were "bad habits," which should be changed.

The process of social development and the loosening of social restrictions inevitably affected women's public conduct and appearance. The transition from old to new was reflected in women's choice of fashion; for example, some displayed a uniquely personal sense of style designed to draw attention. A Japanese traveler was surprised to see some women sporting "foreign-style clothes" and short hair. Local newspapers often published reports and folk poems that described how women dressed in gowns with high collars, styled their hair, walked hand in hand with their girlfriends, and wore shoes decorated with red. Generally, women's styles were more colorful than ever. Those who liked to wear current fashions were called a *"modeng nülang"* (modern miss). A drawing by Yu Zidan depicts such a girl wearing a fashionable dress, with a short bobbed hairstyle in the "latest fashion," and waving a bouquet of flowers from a rickshaw. Prostitutes were often at the leading edge of fashion trends in late-Qing Chengdu; as a result, "honorable" but fashionably dressed women were mistaken at times for prostitutes. According to one newspaper report, three young women who visited the Center for Promoting Commerce and Industry were suspected of being prostitutes, and a crowd gathered to gawk. Finally, policemen had to call a sedan chair to take them back home.[46]

Besides clothing, the two most prominent indicators of women's stylishness were hair and feet. Although many women still bound their feet, many did not; in particular, female students who "enjoyed freedom without bound feet" began to influence other women by leading a new trend favoring "natural feet."[47] By this time, women spent more time and energy on their hairstyles, and short hairstyles became fashionable. One observer noted, "society has been quite different this year—women with bobbed hair can be seen everywhere in town." In addition, hairstyles from Shanghai became fashionable. A picture in *Popular Pictorial* shows a number of them in the "Shanghai style," reflecting the influence of this new trend.[48] (See Figure 6.1.)

FIGURE 6.1. Beautiful Heads in the Shanghai Style. From TSHB 1912, no. 2.

FIGURE 6.2. A Bisexual (One Hundred Queer-Looking People of Society, No. 6).
This picture mocks "new-fashioned" women with short hair. The inscription reads:
"Neither man nor woman, wearing a covered-forehead hairstyle and clothes edged
with decoration . . . , how can the Republican era tolerate what was prohibited
even during the Qing? If she is a human being, she looks like a female fortune-
teller; if she is a creature, she looks like a cow." From TSHB 1912, no. 22.

On the surface, women probably used fashion to enhance their beauty,
but this action itself required courage, because elites believed that it was
immoral for a woman to deliberately draw men's attention (see Figure 6.2).
Apparently, cultural prejudice played a part in some of the complaints. For
instance, elites mocked young country women who "tried to be 'fashionable' by wearing new hairstyles and decorating themselves with flowers."
The "fashionable" countrywomen's Manchu dresses, leather shoes, and
makeup, and their desire to show off, made many elites uncomfortable.
Some believed that "colorful makeup generates licentiousness" and tried to
shape women's public appearance. The reform newspaper *Popular Pictorial* even called the new hairstyles "hair monsters" (see Figure 6.3). Elites
were convinced that some "rogues" liked to follow and harass "fashionable
women"; they blamed the women as much as the men, and exhorted them
"not to dress up and wear makeup but to show dignity."[49]

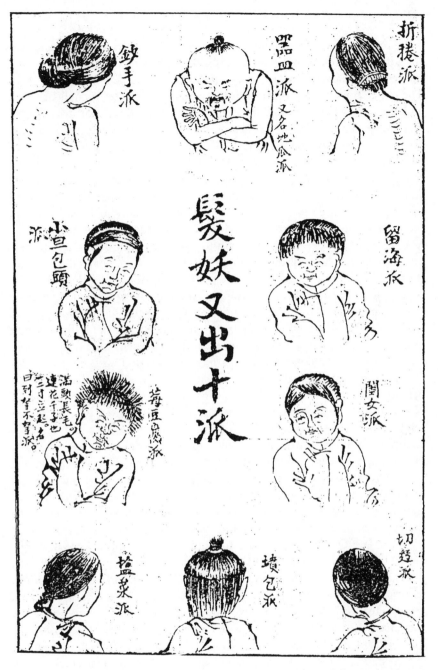

FIGURE 6.3. Ten New Types of Hair Monsters (*fayao*). Top row, left to right: the "handshake," "utensil" (nicknamed "yam bean"), and "folded" types; second row: the "head wrapped as young girl" and "covered forehead" types; third row: the "molded tofu" ("long-erected hair like sticks") and "virgin girl" types; bottom row: the "pickled vegetable," "grave," and "needle" types. From TSHB 1912, no. 36.

In the early twentieth century, women in Chengdu were increasingly showing up in places that were traditionally for men only, such as teahouses and theaters. This, of course, produced resentment in the elite class. The police tried to stop this trend, but women continued to challenge men and the power they retained by virtue of social customs that discouraged women from appearing in public. Up through the late Qing, women were restricted from most public places. Although women were not allowed to enter most teahouses and theaters in the late Qing, some still tried to breach these traditionally male arenas despite the risk of expulsion. For instance, when many dressed-up and made-up women showed up for an opera performance by the Guangdong Guild, the police promptly expelled them. Some young women behaved even more radically in public; one fifteen-year-old girl dressed like a man to drink tea with three male friends but was taken to the police station after her ruse was discovered. Local authorities charged her and her friends with "a serious offense against decency" and punished them accordingly. In another story, when the Shanxi Guild performed a local opera, a young woman dressed in red watched from atop the high wall that separated her home from the guildhall. The audience turned their attention to her, and some began throwing colored balls at her. In the commotion, she fell and was seriously injured.[50] Reformers also disapproved of women visiting temples, and called the police prohibition against women burning incense there "a good regulation." Nevertheless, Chengdu women could not be dissuaded from practicing their religion where they pleased. When banned from the town's temples, they simply went out of town. As a result, suburban temples such as the White Horse Temple (Baima si) and the Three Sages Temple (Sansheng gong) became so crowded that nearby shops enjoyed a boom in business. When many women and men gathered in the White Horse Temple to worship, the street headman grew concerned that there would be trouble and requested the police to prohibit the "mix of men and women."[51]

In the late Qing, however, strictures on women's appearance in public began to relax. In 1906, the Elegant Garden apparently became the first teahouse to allow female patrons, but the police soon forbade them, out of fear that men's harassment of them would threaten the social order. Later, the Joy Teahouse began admitting women, but they had to use a separate entrance. A growing number of women began to frequent teahouses, but the "well-dressed ladies of high society" still refused to tarnish their image in this manner. Indeed, women unwittingly created quite a spectacle at teahouses, becoming the objects of male stares and endless gossip. In the early Republic, more teahouses permitted women patrons, but usually segregated them from men. For instance, the Elegant Garden and Long Spring Teahouse (Wanchun chayuan) reserved special times or days for female patrons. Theaters that admitted women earned several times the profits of those that did not. A local newspaper criticized this phenomenon, saying that men went to theaters not to watch plays but to watch women. In the late Qing and early Republic, the police changed their policies about women's presence in public places, loosening them in some areas but restricting women from areas where incidents often occurred. The River View Tea Garden (Linjiang chayuan) asked the police if it could open its doors to women to counter a decline in business, but the request was denied. A juggling act in a public park attracted large audiences when women were allowed to watch, but this business, too, dropped dramatically after women were barred, and finally the show had to close.[52]

Why did the police and social reformers discourage women's participation in public life? The reasons varied. First, the general relationship between men and women in public was always a sensitive issue. In traditional Chinese society, men and women who were not related were not supposed to appear together in public, and therefore public contact of this nature always drew undue attention. In the past, traditional values and social customs controlled such relationships, but by the early twentieth century, this control had shifted to the police, who remained strongly influenced by custom. For instance, the police enforced separate times for men and women to burn joss sticks at temples. Men could do so from eight to ten in the morning, after which only women were allowed in.[53] In 1913, it was still uncommon for teahouses and theaters to allow male and female patrons to mingle. Women were allowed to enter theaters, but their behavior was highly restricted. For example, the twelve rules listed in "Regulation for Female Seating" dictated women's behavior in everything from applying makeup and changing clothes to acting ostentatiously. Even husbands were not allowed to meet their wives in the balconies.[54]

A second reason women were discouraged from public life related to the local opera, which, according to social reformers, had strayed from its original purpose of promoting loyalty, chastity, and obedience. Reformers condemned female theatergoers for watching licentious programs that taught "immoral" behavior and "heterodox" opinions. Reformers condemned the new notion of equal rights for women as "evil ideas." Notwithstanding this condemnation, women increasingly embraced equality and behaved more openly in public places. Thus, reformers believed that the women who began attending "do not like to watch the new, reformed, and civilized operas. . . . As long as a show has a plot involving adultery, embracing, and other sexual activities, women and men make eyes at each other while applauding."[55] This example also tells us that social reformers, who were supposed to be among the most progressive people in society, still held strongly conservative views about women's appearance in public.

The third reason reflected concern for public order. The police claimed that women would disturb public order, and sought to keep women away or to separate them from men. Indeed, after a play, many "idle people" did gather at the exits to watch well-dressed women patrons from elite families pass by, and policemen had to prevent crowds from gathering. In mixed-sex theaters, as an opera reached its climax, men often stood up to gawk at the women, but the women, according to the complaint of a local newspaper, "tantalized men by laughing loudly." This "disorder" in the theaters was always criticized by the elite class. Again, in order to "avoid trouble," police prohibited women from going to theaters in the Flower Fair.[56] The Center for Promoting Industry and Commerce, too, was cautious about opening its doors to women. One afternoon during the Chinese New Year, five well-dressed young women shopped there, causing a great commotion, because "it was so unusual for so many colorfully dressed ladies to visit the Center together that many people followed them to stare." To prevent trouble, policemen forced them to return home via hired sedan chairs. The women shoppers "were excited when they arrived, but visibly upset when they left," according to a newspaper account. Later, when three well-dressed women shopped at the Center, more than a hundred people gathered to follow them.[57] To prevent these incidents, the police tried to separate women from men in the Center. When the introduction of electric lights drew great crowds to the Center, the police arranged different visiting days for men and women.[58]

The final reason is that reformers still adhered to the traditional patriarchal and hierarchical view of society. The notion of women's equal rights started spreading during or after the New Cultural Movement, as we see reflected in Ba Jin's *Family*. Compared with major Chinese cities like Beijing and Shanghai, Chengdu underwent a much slower process of change because of the city's geographical isolation, which caused it to be less influenced by the West and more conservative in retaining its old social climate and strong local traditions.[59]

There was another kind of women on the streets: they usually came from underclass families, they were less restricted by traditional "women's virtues," and they had courage to fight with men in public. As Fu Chongju described, "poor shrews (*pinjia efu*) often shouted abuse in the streets (*dajie maxiang*)." Their typical stance was called "shape of the teapot" (*chahu shi*), with one hand pointed out and the other planted on the waist. Indeed, it was not uncommon to see women from the underclass insulting each other or even fighting in the streets. Educated people considered them to be "immoral women." Local newspapers often reported their public behavior. One story tells of Yang Zhong, a resident of Office Street (Fu jie), who was addicted to gambling and intimidated by his wife, an "extraordinary shrew." One day, after he lost his clothing in a bet, he sneaked back home to take a quilt for his next wager, but was caught by his wife. She promptly dragged him into the street, "abusing him in every possible way," threatening to send him to the police despite his pleas for mercy. She quit only after the street headman intervened and made Yang Zhong apologize. The local newspaper reported the story saying, "Yang Zhong did not behave himself . . . and he deserved the punishment."

In another report, a dispute arose when a cloth salesman refused to honor the price negotiated earlier with a tailor. The tailor's "shrewish" wife bit the salesman on his hand until it bled, and also threw "dirty stuff" at him. Another case is even more dramatic: when a rickshaw puller with a passenger accidentally knocked down the son of Woman Bai, the wife of a petty peddler, she jumped into the street and punched the offender in the face. The blow was so strong that it punctured his left eyeball, covering his face with blood, and knocked him out. Some lower-class women even dared to confront soldiers. A cobbler's wife, according to a report, regarded by her neighbors as a shrew, slapped a soldier when a dispute occurred. The soldier reported this incident to his officer, and the officer called the head of the guild to the shoe shop to settle the dispute. After determining that the woman was the responsible party, the officer beat her with a tobacco pipe as punishment, and she grabbed a piece of red cloth and set off firecrackers as an apology.[60] These stories demonstrate that there were exceptions to the belief in Chinese families that men were superior to women. The so-called shrews displayed another side of women's behavior, much different from the stereotype of submissive Chinese women. These stories suggest that women, even those victimized in the society, acted according to a host of factors including their culture, folk tradition, personality, and economic status.[61]

Generally, social changes allowed women to engage in more social activities in public. More public places became available for women, including all-female schools, public lecture halls, shopping centers, theaters, and teahouses. In the early Republic, some women caused great excitement by participating in public political gatherings. In the summer of 1916, after victory in the campaign against Yuan Shikai,[62] for example, a memorial ceremony was held; it became a large-scale public entertainment, as more than ten thousand attendees arrived for the event, which lasted several days. The appearance of female students and women was an exciting spectacle for commoners. In the winter of the same year, at another memorial ceremony at Ancestor Hall Street (Citang jie), once again many women were in attendance, drawing a large crowd of "hoodlums" to watch. As a result, local officials ordered the closing of four nearby teahouses to prevent overcrowding.[63]

Some women were held in higher repute than others. He Xifeng, a regular performer at the Elegant Garden, was such an example. Once, when she became ill during a performance, the concerned audience refused to leave until she reappeared on stage. She was also known for donating some of her income to charity.[64] Female students, who led fashion trends and were relatively active in public life, were not only open-minded but were also less tolerant of men's bullying and discrimination. One story in particular underscores this. Two male students followed a group of female students into the Wuhou Temple to gawk at them. The girls harshly condemned the young men, who "scurried off like frightened rats," generating warm applause from bystanders. From the late Qing, with the growth of modern schools, female students enjoyed relatively high social status, and thus some common young girls would pretend to be students. In one account, hoodlums chased one such girl, the sister-in-law of a carpenter, because of her "heavy makeup." Ironically, a policeman did not pursue the hoodlums, at least according to this report, but he did investigate the girl. Her elder sister, the carpenter's wife, claimed that the girl was a student, but when this was discovered to be a lie, the policeman reprimanded the girl harshly. The reporter commented, "Not only did she feel no shame for her indecent appearance, but she also pretended to be a student, which dirtied the pure name of female students. Therefore, she deserved to be reprimanded."[65] The fact that she pretended to be a student is interesting; it is quite obvious that policemen treated female students, who generally came from elite families and enjoyed a higher social status than most women, much better than commoners.

By the 1920s and 1930s, it was no longer novel for women to appear in public, and some open-minded elites began to connect women's public presence with the concept of equality. As one writer remarked, "Social contact between men and women should be made in public, to show that men and women are equal. Where can one find such a place? The Reform (Weixin) Teahouse allows men and women to mingle." Another local scholar described the mix of new and old elements in the street: "Women are still binding their feet but men wear short hair; the people share both conservative and reformist ideas." In this period, the teahouse seemed to symbolize women's struggle for equality with men, as described in one account: "Drinking tea in the teahouse in the park, men and women enjoy equality," and they could even "stay together freely." Streetcars in Chengdu, as well, provided "a more comfortable place than rickshaws for men and women to sit together." Society had become more open: "Socialization has become a part of public life, and it is not necessary to lock harassers of women outside the gate of the Flower Fair."[66] In teahouses, women not only became regular customers but also joined the workforce and participated in social activities there. In his diary, Wu Yu reported seeing a waitress in the Virtue and Wisdom (Yizhi) Teahouse on Warm Spring Road. Customarily, poor women had earned a living mainly as wet nurses, house servants, seam-stresses on the sidewalks, matchbox makers, fortune-tellers (*guapo*), and so on. Now women began to enter some male-dominated occupations, al-though some conservative elites still felt uncomfortable with this shift.[67]

Although we cannot say that at this moment women finally enjoyed an equal right to public space, they had indeed expanded their presence in public. The teahouse best indicated women's changing social status. From the nineteenth century, when they were not allowed to enter teahouses, to the early twentieth century, when they gained some admittance, to the 1920s, when they were frequent patrons, there was increasing acceptance of women in public places.

Prostitutes: Old Livelihood or New Life?

Prostitution in Chengdu can be traced back as far as the Ming dy-nasty, when courtesanship and prostitution became popular and visiting brothels was not a serious moral issue. At that time, many intellectuals even regarded frequenting high-level courtesans as fashionable.[68] This prac-tice was widespread not only in the Jiangnan area but also in isolated re-gions such as Chengdu. According to a fifteenth-century account, "the east-ern part of Chengdu has many pavilions along the Brocade River (Jinjiang), and young girls serve guests wine to cheer them. The guests lose their way returning home when they wake up from a drunken stupor." Another record narrated: "by the river are many small chambers, where native girls sing Sichuan folk songs. Under the shining moon, the river is as bright as day, and the merchants can not help lingering there." Besides elites and mer-chants, lower-class laborers also frequented such places, as a folk poem de-scribed: "The sky is clear and willow trees turn to green after heavy night rain. Since the Brocade River has risen, many ruffians who work in salt boats have nothing to do but go to the chambers by the river and visit prostitutes." Other accounts from the Qing period described similar activ-ities: "Young people go to New Alley (Xin xiangzi), the bank of the Imper-ial River (Yuhe), and the Temple of Sichuan King Street (Shuwang miao) to visit prostitutes." Prostitutes usually had high visibility in public: "they wear elegant shoes and socks and travel everywhere in the city. Townspeo-ple are used to seeing well-dressed prostitutes and are not surprised at their appearance."[69]

In late-Qing Chengdu, the selling of sexual services by women remained popular, and became a target of social reform (see Figure 6.4). Local peo-ple called prostitutes "*biaozi*" (whores) or "*lanchang*" (bitches). Here as in Shanghai, the professional names of prostitutes were "meant to invoke both

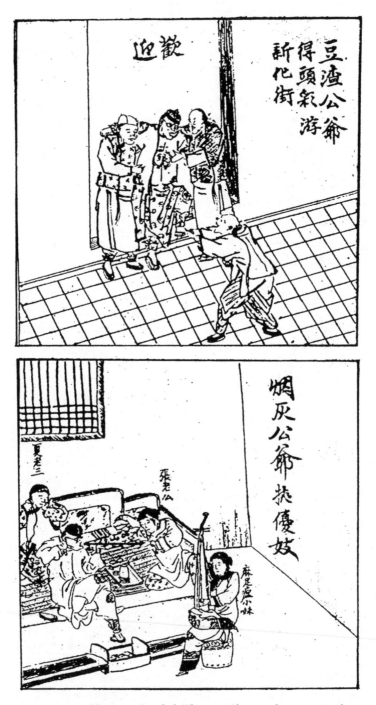

FIGURE 6.4. Visiting a Brothel. The two Chinese characters in the upper picture read "Welcome!" In the lower picture, the professional names of the prostitutes are given. From left to right they are Xia Three (Xia Laosan), Smallest Zhang (Zhang Laoyao), and Plague Sister (Majiaowun Xiaomei). These were real women who were well-known prostitutes in late-Qing Chengdu. From TSHB 1909, no. 5.

sensual pleasure and literary associations." All prostitutes in Chengdu had professional names, such as "Golden Butterfly" (Jin Hudie) and "Lotus Yang" (Yang Hehua). Fu Chongju accused these prostitutes of seducing young men and entrapping women, and published their names in his *Investigation of Chengdu* (Chengdu tonglan) in an effort to warn people to stay away from them. He even suggested that rules should prohibit prostitutes from wearing certain clothes that might be confused with student uniforms.[70] In contrast to gambling, which had been banned outright, prostitution was not prohibited but increasingly restricted. In 1906, the police labeled 325 brothels "supervised households" (jianshi hu), and a wooden board inscribed with the three characters "*Jian Shi Hu*" was hung on brothel doors to distinguish them from ordinary households. Social reformers used concrete examples to warn residents of the miserable consequences of frequenting brothels. One newspaper article concluded that because "prostitutes are merciless, brothel-goers should take a lesson" from them. They especially emphasized that mourners should be prohibited from visiting brothels, because such behavior betrayed traditional morality.[71]

In order to "rescue women from evil places," authorities opened the "House of Reformed Prostitutes" (Jiliang suo). This new organization recruited prostitutes and taught them "self-esteem," reading, and mathematics in the hope of transforming them into "graceful ladies" who could find another livelihood. In return, the women in the program were required to do work, such as knitting socks, to supplement income for the House. By 1909, more than sixty prostitutes had been recruited and educated; to begin life anew, thirty of them chose to get married. The prostitutes, it was reported, "gradually changed their lifestyles and regretted their past." Ironically, even though society discriminated against prostitutes, many men were interested in marrying them.[72] It was reported that most married ex-prostitutes were "doing well" and that some even returned to the House of Reformed Prostitutes to recount their own "success stories."[73]

Prostitutes usually gathered in Persimmon Garden (Shizi yuan) Street, a red-light district regarded by reformers as "filthy" and "lower class." Under urban reform, it was renamed "Newly Civilized Street" (Xinhua jie). Poor women, even in the reformist era, faced the threat of being seduced or forced into work there, and there were many cases of this reported in the local newspapers. Professional brothel brokers, universally regarded as "evil people," were arrested and sent to labor camps. These incidents occurred frequently in the early Republic.[74] Many elites resented the policy of legal prostitution. One Chengdu citizen criticized the effort to reform prostitutes in a satirical folk poem: "Newly Civilized Street represents the reform of street prostitutes, where the fragrance of rouge spreads. The officials supervise them for taxes, so that procuresses are treated as merchants." The police, however, began stipulating which people could and could not visit brothels, making it clear that students "should follow ritual and law," soldiers "should follow military rule," and young men "should care about their health." No members of these groups were allowed to enter a brothel. Prostitutes who violated the regulation could be punished and forced out of the area.[75]

Prostitutes who truly wanted to "do what is proper," however, faced numerous obstacles. Those who left the brothels and got married still retained a reputation as "former prostitutes." In one case, a former prostitute opened a shop on a corner of Perpetual Prosperity Alley (Yongxing xiang) and did well. However, after a "fight for the woman" occurred in her shop, "a decision was made by the public" to move her shop. In another case, the shopkeeper of a small business fell in love with a prostitute and rented a house in preparation for having a family. When they went to the police station to get a marriage license, the police not only refused to issue one but also forcibly sent the woman to the House of Reformed Prostitutes, claiming that her decision to marry violated regulations. This decision proved tragic, unfortunately; the heartbroken man went insane when he learned he could not marry his beloved. Thus, many women who quit prostitution found it difficult to live a normal life. Those who could not survive finally returned to the old business. Some, however, were successful in marrying senior officials or members of the gentry as a strategy to gain security and protection.[76]

Many prostitutes tried to offer their services surreptitiously by mingling with other households. Local residents appealed to the police to remove prostitutes from the neighborhood, but were told it would be difficult because Newly Civilized Street and the House of Reformed Prostitutes were full. However, the police recognized that it was inappropriate to allow prostitutes and residents to mix and promised to remove them as soon as possible. From these reports it can be inferred that brothels prospered in late-Qing Chengdu, and a large number of women depended on them for income. During the late-Qing urban reform, prostitutes concentrated on Newly Civilized Street and Five Baskets Hill (Wudan shan). As prostitution increased during the early Republic, prostitutes moved to areas where there was more room and taxes could be avoided. Even the local government planned to find new spaces where prostitutes could live. During the street war of 1917, many prostitutes fled for their lives and moved in with ordinary households. This led to considerable confusion, as customers mistook "good families" for brothels and entered unannounced. Therefore, the police eventually moved prostitutes back to their assigned locations. Prostitutes had to be legally registered, and illegal or "secret" prostitutes would be sent to the police as soon as they were caught.[77] Lower-class prostitutes concentrated in Newly Civilized Street and Five Baskets Hill, but upper-class ones lived throughout Chengdu, plying their trade in inns, restaurants, and wine shops. In general, residents supported the establishment of a separate area for prostitution. When the police planned to move "native prostitutes" to the area of Brick Memorial Archway (Zhuanzha paifang) and Fragrant Herb and Fountain Street (Chaiquan jie), area residents were opposed. They claimed that the neighborhood had more than a thousand shops and several thousand artisans and apprentices who worked during the day but were free at night; if prostitutes moved in, the workers would be likely to frequent brothels. In addition, residents feared that brothels would become hiding places for criminals, jeopardizing security in the area.[78]

Despite society's generally hostile attitude toward them, some prostitutes apparently never tried to hide their activities and in fact challenged the established use of the street. Nevertheless, most prostitutes simply tried to lead the same kinds of lives as ordinary residents. Some would wear student uniforms, which attracted crowds of curious onlookers, to the point that elites wanted to regulate what they wore. Prostitutes ignored the regulation that prohibited them from sitting in sedan chairs with their patrons, despite the threat of fines from the police. When two prostitutes violated the rule against entering the Flower Fair, they were expelled. Two other prostitutes were stopped outside the Green Goat Temple as they attempted to enter. Prostitutes were forbidden to enter theaters and teahouses, but some of them still challenged this rule, although they would be subject to public humiliation and arrest if caught by the police.[79]

Many prostitutes did not appreciate the effort by the elite and the police to "make them good" and continued to ply their trade, enduring in the process reformist castigation as "strange in dress, vulgar in speech, and thick in make-up." Some women, however, voluntarily became prostitutes. The elite claimed the lesson was that "husbands should not let their wives have freedom." Yang Laosan, a well-known prostitute in the late Qing, got married, but when her husband ran out of money to support her, she returned to her former trade. Her husband did not like it, and got into a fight with one of her customers.[80]

Whereas some prostitutes attempted to mingle with ordinary people, others made an effort to flaunt themselves in public. Their constant challenge of social mores through their dress and public behavior led elites to call for "restricting such behavior." What was the nature of this public behavior and public appearance? A local newspaper gave a description:

Recently, prostitutes who wear odd makeup and dresses wandered the streets. Two shared a rickshaw, glancing about and teasing superciliously. . . . If a prostitute walks down the street, there are sure to be two or three well-dressed frivolous youngsters following behind. . . . A prostitute dressed in neither Chinese nor Western style, and in neither men's nor women's clothing, a hairstyle with a big queue, a green sunshade cap, golden glasses, a Chinese-style leather coat, blue pants, a Western-style hair ribbon, a large green sweater, and green shoes. She kept her hands on her waist, laughing and swearing while walking along the street. A well-dressed young man followed her respectfully and submissively. . . . When they passed the gate of a branch of the police station, the police stopped her and scathingly denounced her. They forced her to take off her glasses and sunshade cap, and immediately hired a sedan chair to send her home. The prostitute remained calm, however, although the young man was upset.[81]

This story tells how prostitutes sometimes challenged social mores. Prostitutes knew exactly what people thought about their presence in public and what behavior would provoke the ire of local elites. As an underclass, constantly regulated and policed, prostitutes used this tool from their limited resources to claim their right to public space.

There was constant talk of abolishing prostitution in Chengdu. In the late 1920s, when other major cities were carrying out prostitution reform, some elites in Chengdu suggested two steps: first, to prohibit women from becoming prostitutes, and second, to ban all existing prostitutes from plying their trade. But some reformers argued that if economic issues were not resolved first, "registered prostitutes" likely would just become "secret prostitutes." In the Republican period, the issue of prostitution was never fully resolved.[82]

City of the Poor

Any big city contains a "social geography" that reflects class segregation.[83] In Chengdu, most of the poor lived in the west of the city, prostitutes concentrated in Persimmon Garden (Shizi yuan), and folk performers lived in the eastern part of the city.[84] In the Manchu area (the Smaller City), "the streets were broad, unpaved, and muddy; the people, especially the women, were badly, even slovenly dressed."[85] Class distinctions could be seen almost everywhere. There was a sharp contrast between sedan-chair carriers and their passengers, between "decent" customers and beggars who ate customers' leftovers at a restaurant, between coolies and their employers, and between street-house residents and residents of a compound-house. The gap between the rich and the poor in shared public spaces can easily be seen in the writings of premodern elites, who clearly categorized people into disparate worlds. Therefore, an author could not resist asking: "It is really mysterious to me that the eastern part of the city is rich while the western is poor. Why is there such an obvious distinction between the rich and the poor within the same city?"[86] For the less fortunate, the Chinese New Year was not always a happy time. As the holiday drew near, the poor worried about their livelihood: "When they discuss how to make some money for the holiday, debt collectors are already at their front doors." During the holiday, "listening to the sound of striking drums with sorrow and worrying about future, they have no cup of wine served on the table although it is the Chinese New Year. All they can do is pray for God's blessing."[87] But in these accounts, we can also detect clearly that some elites criticized social inequality and empathized with the poor.

For modern observers, the street can be the best place to gain insight into the life of the poor (see Figure 6.5). Unfortunate people liked to tell their tragic stories publicly—a man losing his money, or a poor person being beaten by a local bully, or a person's family member becoming ill—in order to obtain sympathy and help from pedestrians. As a Western observer noted, "For the study of life in a large center, no place is more suitable than the capital of a province, for there you generally get everything to perfection—the pomp and show of the richer classes and the degradation and poverty of the poor." This accurately expresses Chengdu's class distinctions. On the streets, one could often see poor coolies lying on the ground, sick or dying. More than once, a poor man died in the teahouse while drinking tea or a coolie fell unconscious on the street from starvation, but other patrons thought the man was simply resting.[88] Missionary Vale pointed out that "one of the strangest and cheapest devices" that peddlers and peasants used to attract the attention of passersby was to "stick a piece of straw or bamboo twisted into a ring." But Vale also observed a "poor coolie going along the street with a ring of straw in his pipe, the last article he would sell, thus proclaiming to passers-by that he had been reduced to the lowest step but one—beggary." Some of the poorest people had nothing to sell but themselves. During a famine, Vale found that one man was "walking along the street with a piece of straw in his queue, thus offering himself for sale." Vale considered this "a most pathetic sight."[89] After the Qing collapsed, the livelihood of the Manchus in Chengdu became a major issue. Because the Manchus lost their "banner grain" and most lacked other skills for making a living, they were thrown into a state of constant hunger and cold. Some young women who could not otherwise survive turned to begging on the street, prompting a newspaper to conclude, "the bitter life of banner people has reached an intolerable point."[90] They indeed faced severe racial discrimination and economic pressure in the early Republic.

There are no reports of large-scale food riots, but accounts of starving people stealing grain were common. During the warlord era, many from famine-stricken areas gathered outside the West City Gate, and whenever a rice peddler would pass by, they would break the bags, take some rice, and run away. Some vagrants offered to help push the carts uphill, only to break the bags and steal some grain. In the early 1920s, as the poor saw

FIGURE 6.5. Behind the Main Streets. Pictured is a small alley where poor people lived in the late Qing. Only the center of the alley was covered with paved stones; these were used by "cock wheelbarrows." From Wallace 1907: 64.

their opportunities to earn a living slip further beyond their grasp, they organized into groups of several dozen, to search for food anywhere. Once, more than ten poor women suddenly snatched all the pancakes from a pancake shop in South Festival Street (Huifu nanjie) and gobbled them while escaping. In restaurants, hungry people stood behind the patrons and "wolfed down" their leftovers as soon as they finished, even while the waiters desperately tried to expel them.[91]

Poor people often were bullied by powerful and rich men in public places. In his "Song for Wailing a Rickshaw Puller," Liu Shiliang recounted just such a story:

[Passenger:] "Run faster, rickshaw! I will meet my friends today: first I'll visit Newly Civilized Street [brothels] and then go to the River View Tower to drink wine with prostitutes. After that I will go to Mao Family Compound (Maojia gong-guan) in Nine Arches Bridge to play cards."

[Puller:] "The distance will be 20 *li* [about seven miles] and the fare will be one *diao* of coppers."

[Passenger:] "Who are you to tell me the price? How dare you look down upon me! I am not a commoner, and I am going to teach you a lesson! It is shameless for a rickshaw puller to argue the price. Damn you! You escape from military service only to become a rickshaw puller." The passenger slapped the rickshaw puller's face. The puller did not dare speak, and his face was pale like a dead man's. The police did not come to apprehend the culprit and the puller could not help crying.[92]

Liu Shiliang's story vividly describes how difficult it was for rickshaw pullers to make a living and reveals the class differentiation that was often cruelly manifested by the rich onto the poor. During this period, the police were weakened by military force and had become inadequate to control local bullies, unlike its power in the late Qing. Commoners did not gain sufficient protection from law enforcement, but they used some means of daily resistance as the "weapons of the weak"; writing matched couplets was one way to air their anger. One couplet expressed poor people's animosity toward an unequal society: "You laugh at me because I am poor, but the rich suffer misfortune in the end."[93]

Sedan-Chair Carriers and Their Daily Resistance. The streets of Chengdu thronged with various kinds of coolies: back carriers, shoulder carriers, water carriers, and sedan-chair carriers. Just as rickshaw pullers in Beijing "represented poverty and social dislocation," so did the sedan-chair carriers in Chengdu (see Figure 6.6). A close look at this group could provide us a better understanding of the survival strategies of lower classes and also their daily methods of resistance. In Chengdu, sedan-chair carriers and beggars were the groups with the most visibility on the streets. The sedan chair was the primary mode of public transportation, and sedan-chair carrying was a very popular and tradition-laden occupation in Chengdu. Chengdu had more than 490 sedan-chair shops in 1916; calculating only ten carriers for each shop, the total number would have been near 5,000.[94] There were several models of sedan chairs, including three- or four-man closed chairs, open chairs, and rattan chairs. The poles of a three-man sedan were adjusted to distribute the weight evenly. After 200 or so steps, the second man rested on the upright pole he was carrying. For a long journey, or if the passenger was heavy, a four-man sedan was required.[95]

To be sure, carrying sedan chairs was very strenuous, but carriers still tried to have fun by showing off their skills. Their styles of carrying were categorized as "plain" and "arch." The latter involved carrying passengers as high as the eaves and was considered "dangerous." Some patrons liked to ride the sedan chairs of the arch style to show off as well, acting complacent when sedan-chair carriers dashed madly down the street. When fast-moving carriers carried passengers using the arch style, they frequently not only knocked down pedestrians, sometimes causing injury, but also often fell down themselves. The style of the sedan chairs and the antics of their carriers created lasting impressions on visitors. A missionary wrote that the city "is full of officials, both in and out of office, who move about

FIGURE 6.6. Sedan Chairs and Carriers. From Davidson and Mason 1905: 35.

the streets in sedan chairs carried at a great speed. The chairs were peculiar in that the long poles were curved, with the body of the chair resting on top of the curve. When carried, such a chair is held well above the heads of the crowd."[96] Sedan-chair carriers spoke in jargon, which helped maintain working harmony and also alleviated boredom. The rear carriers listened to the front men's rhymed couplets that warned of the dangers ahead, and the rear men acknowledged that they understood. The rhymed couplets often included humorous words and jokes. For example, when children were in the way, the lead carrier might call out, "Little plaything, cries at night," and the rear carrier would reply, "Tell his ma to hold him tight." Alternatively, "Cloud in the sky," and the reply, "Below a person close by." For puddles: "Here a river, a river doth flow," and the rear man responded, "Each for himself must over it go." When the road was dangerous: "Steep slope, slippery dip," and in reply, "He who has legs will not slip."[97]

According to a Japanese observer, well-to-do families had their own sedan-chair service. "*Daban*" were sedan-chair carriers hired by the wealthy for long-term service. Although their situation was better than that of carriers who picked up business on the street, they were still socially disparaged. In *Investigation of Chengdu* (Chengdu tonglan), sedan-chair carriers were described as rude and reckless, running into pedestrians, deliberately rocking the chair to make the passengers uncomfortable, filching items from street stalls, and even fighting in the masters' places of business to make the masters "lose face." Just as the rickshaw pullers in Beijing "exhibited in the public performance of their job" and "produced a politics of the street," sedan-chair carriers in Chengdu behaved in a way that expressed dissatisfaction with their living and working conditions and, indirectly, protested their oppression. Nevertheless, like their powerless counterparts in Beijing, they did not display the collective strength of working-class communities.[98]

Some local newspaper reports documented the sedan-chair carriers' misery and the social discrimination they endured. Although the carriers expressed their power through their conduct on the street, they would frequently be targets of harassment, insults, and even physical attacks. Street rogues in particular often caused trouble for sedan-chair carriers. In one instance, two carriers were hauling a woman when two hoodlums suddenly pushed their shoulders in an attempt to make the sedan chair overturn, resulting in a serious fight. Even a dog running down the street could cause unexpected results. In the *Popular Pictorial*, a drawing with the caption "A Dog Knocks Down a Woman's Sedan Chair" depicts a sedan-chair carrier and a woman sprawled on the ground after a dog ran across the narrow street and knocked them down, leaving onlookers agape.[99] (See Figure 6.7.) A report entitled "The Ghost Derides Sedan-Chair Carriers" (*jiaofu bei gui yeyu*) in the *Citizens' Daily* (Guomin gongbao) told an even more bizarre story:

Near midnight, as two sedan-chair carriers with an empty chair passed Osmanthus Flower Alley (Guihua xiang), a man wearing a straw cap and straw sandals asked them to carry him to the edge of the Imperial City. They carried him, passing several streets, but inadvertently stepped into the Imperial River. Fortunately, some people with torches passed over the bridge and heard the sedan-chair carriers calling out in their typical rhymed couplet, "stepping left, stepping right," in the river. They called out and shined their torches on the river, and the carriers seemed to be awakened from a dream. They opened the curtain, but found nobody in the sedan chair and wondered to each other, "did we meet a ghost?"[100]

The most interesting part of this anecdote is the comment of the serious newspaper the *Citizens' Daily* that "this ghost was so mischievous that it played a joke on the poor sedan-chair carriers." We do not know what to make of this tale, but there are only two possibilities. One is that the story is true, and someone with the ability to coordinate such a stunt did it to ridicule the carriers. The other is that it never happened, and the story was fabricated by someone who wanted to use the lower classes as an object of ridicule. In Chengdu, many folk stories center on the supposed stupidity of country folks, women, and uneducated people. This tale is probably an example of this kind of folk story.

The distinction in social class between sedan-chair carriers and passengers was obvious. The carriers, in the eyes of the elite, represented not only poverty but also inferior morality. They complained about all aspects of the

FIGURE 6.7. A Dog Knocks Down a Woman's Sedan Chair. This picture shows the "arch" style of sedan chair. We can also see a money shop, the gate of a residential compound, a food peddler, a policeman, a shopkeeper, a doorkeeper, and several pedestrians. The words on the shop's sign read "Exchange silver taels here," and the character on the door of the residential compound reads "Happiness." From TSHB 1909, no. 5.

carriers' appearance and behavior. They criticized them for carrying lice and, especially during the summer, having offensive body odor. Some newspapers printed stories bearing hostile headlines such as "Detestable Sedan-Chair Carriers" and "Evil Sedan-Chair Carriers." They reported that the carriers did not obey traffic rules and that they demanded high fares, especially from newcomers and country people, whom they often "bullied" and "abused." Because disputes regarding sedan-chair services were frequent, the police established "official fares" for all distances traveled on Chengdu streets and issued "fare books." "People welcome such a policy," the reformers claimed, stating that "it could reduce many disputes." In fact, sedan-chair carriers often encountered situations in which passengers refused to pay the arranged fare, thus causing disputes. Some carriers asked to be paid in advance, but others worried that this would cause them to lose potential passengers. To avoid undue competition, each sedan-chair guild established its own area of business and sought to prevent "illegal carrying" within these boundaries. However, because the zones for some guilds were vague, disputes were common.[101] Apparently, sedan-chair carriers were forced to cope not only with their own passengers but also with competition from other carriers. Their allegedly "impudent" manner reflected the difficult environment in which they struggled to survive.

The Kingdom of Beggars. If we try to observe the urban poor, beggars, the most visible and unfortunate people on the streets, probably would be the best subjects.[102] In Chengdu, as in all other Chinese cities, beggars depended on the streets for survival. In their long history, they had become a unique group and formed their own organizations, methods of survival, and lifestyle. When famines or natural disasters occurred in rural areas, the number of beggars increased dramatically. Missionary Edward Wallace wrote that when entering Sichuan in the late Qing, he saw "beggars in all stages of emaciation crowd the roads near the towns." According to the missionary J. Vale, the number of beggars in Chengdu at that time reached at least 15,000, not including those living in the various almshouses and other institutions for the poor and elderly. Alexander Hosie wrote of the situation when he arrived in Chengdu in the late nineteenth century: "Hundreds of beggars crowded the eastern suburb of the city, and it was with difficulty that we pushed our way through the mass of rags and dirt which held the bridge." Traditionally, local officials and charitable organizations made efforts to control and help panhandlers. In the late Qing, the local government offered rice gruel to between 20,000 and 30,000 beggars once or twice a day at the North and East City Gates. Some, however, simply pretended to be beggars to get rice to feed their pigs and chickens. According to Vale, after receiving their "allotted portion in the morning, the beggar population streams into the city, principally from the north and east gates, . . . and commence[s] the day's rounds, using bells, rattles, or any other device they please, to attract the attention of the shopkeepers or householder to their wretched condition."[103] Under the control measures of late-Qing urban reform, the number of beggars dropped dramatically, only to rise again in the early Republic. From the East Gate Bridge to the Single Arch Bridge, the streets were dirty and crowded with beggars, who gathered in clusters of eight to ten. Each of the chicken-feather inns in this area accommodated more than one hundred such people, most of them younger than twenty.[104]

Among the poor, it was said, the weak become beggars while the strong become thieves or robbers. Young boys and girls lived with their parents in filthy beggar houses and "naturally [grew] up as professional beggars." Calamities such as famine, floods, sickness, and fire reduced many to begging for a living.[105] Others became beggars because of problems brought on by gambling, smoking opium, or drunkenness. As Vale remarked, "It is not an uncommon sight . . . to see beggars sitting in groups gambling or drinking." The plot of Ba Jin's novel *The Rest Garden* (Qiyuan) was based on the experience of a real person, his uncle, and told how a large property owner became a beggar. Because of his gambling, he finally ended up in the Two Deities Nunnery, dying under miserable circumstances.[106] There were many similar stories in real life, we see from local newspapers and other accounts. A rich man who owned two compounds and five houses was a gambler, an opium user, and a frequenter of brothels. He eventually lost everything and became a beggar. When he finally died penniless on the street, a kind old man paid 500 *wen* to hire a night watchman to bury his body out of town. In another example, Liao Zhuo came from a wealthy family that eventually went bankrupt. When his father died and left him no property, he was forced to beg. He was subsequently elected to represent the beggars in the area of East Imperial River Street, primarily because of his family background. Some shops, it was said, asked him to write commercial signs because of his excellent calligraphy.[107]

Beggars lived miserable lives. They were often forbidden to live inside the city and thus entered the city when the four city gates opened early each morning. Then they scavenged for food in garbage or tried to find a menial job such as carrying heavy loads. They were forced to leave the city at night and slept under the eaves of temples, in graveyards, by rivers, or under bridges. As a folk poem described, "they suffer from hunger and cold at the bank of the river and even the living seem dead." The North City Gate became another gathering place for beggars. When the economy worsened and the price of rice rose, beggars often received nothing to eat for a whole day; at night they expressed their bitterness, moaning, crying, or even screaming because of intolerable hunger. A journalist told of seeing a naked beggar moaning, with only his hand to cover his genitals, saying that he had a sexual disease. The beggar groveled for money but got only revulsion and scorn. The reporter called it "an offense against decency."[108]

Winter was particularly difficult for beggars. As Vale witnessed, "after a severe wintry night it is no uncommon sight to see three or four corpses lying on the bridge outside the east gate." These sights were so common that residents seldom took notice. Another Western missionary, G. E. Hartwell, saw streets crowded with beggars "covered with filthy sores, leprosy, itch, and naked apart from a ragged apron of matting or coarse hemp cloth."[109] To avoid freezing to death, they sought any means to get warm, one of which was gathering hot ashes left by small food stalls. Stalls that sold food contained a big clay stove used for cooking, and at day's end many vendors simply left the stoves on the streets, precipitating a rush by beggars to fight over the hot ashes. Their fighting often damaged the stoves, resulting in constant disputes between beggars and food peddlers. Each winter, many beggars froze to death on the street. Usually, a resident who was eager to "accumulate merit" would offer a meager coffin of four rough boards nailed together, called "four boards." The beggar's body would be carried to some part of the graveyard that extended for miles outside the city. Two other beggars usually carried the coffin in exchange for a token payment. To bury the bodies, Vale found, "No tombstone is erected to his memory, no name is recorded either on stone or on any register, and worst of all, from the Chinese point of view, no one is left to offer mass for him or secure his release from the torture of Hades." In some cases, very ill beggars were mistakenly regarded as dead and carried out of town for burial. One beggar, for example, was believed dead and carried from where he lay on Red Temple Street near the North City Gate. When the beggar was found to be still alive, neighbors were surprised at his "regaining life."[110]

Beggars did everything imaginable to survive. In Chengdu, it was customary that whenever a family had a ceremony for either a wedding or a funeral, beggars could come to the door and ask for food and money. There was even "an unwritten law" that any beggar could "demand cash from every shop on the second and sixteenth of each month." A shopkeeper would consider this a tax that "he more or less readily pays, but [he] may ignore the most urgent appeals on all other days unless the beggar becomes a nuisance at his door, a thing which he consistently endeavors to be"[111] (see Figure 6.8). Reformers regarded this as a "bad custom," and it was eventually forbidden by the police. To reap the highest rewards from begging required a good strategy, and Chengdu scribes documented many interesting tales about this. One beggar, surnamed Li, lived with a group of fellow indigents by the Imperial River. Being young and healthy, but shabbily dressed, he received little sympathy from pedestrians or from waiters

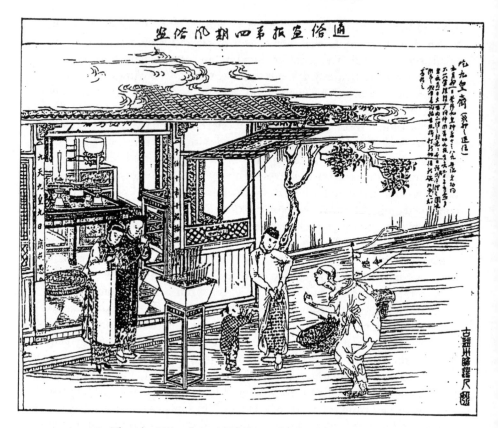

FIGURE 6.8. The Abstaining from Meat Festival (*Chi jiuhuang zhai*, literally "eating nine emperors' diet"). Festivals always offered a good opportunity for beggars to ask for money from residents. This picture shows a man begging and carrying a flag that reads "Grand Nine Emperor Festival" (*Jiuhuang shenghui*). From the twenty-ninth of the eighth lunar month, all restaurants and itinerant kitchens cleaned up their stoves, pans, bowls, etc., and pasted yellow paper couplets on them. For nine days people abstained from meat (some did it for half a month and some even for twenty days); at home, people burned yellow candles and kowtowed (see CDTL 1: 552–53). The couplet on the gate in the picture reads: "Nine heavens, nine emperors, nine days of abstaining from meat; ten numbers, ten gods, ten grains for making a circle." From TSHB 1909, no. 4.

in restaurants, who considered him to be lazy. One day, an old beggar gave him advice: "There is a blind, old woman living alone at the corner of Horse Riding Street. Why don't you carry her on your back and claim that she is your mother? You will become a 'dutiful son' while begging with 'your mother.' I guarantee you will get enough to eat if you do so." Li "saw the light" and did what the old beggar suggested. From that moment on, the "dutiful son" carrying his blind, old "mother" on his back was a familiar sight in Chengdu. On crowded street corners, he would seat his "mother" on a pedestal and feed her leftovers. His "filial piety" gained such immediate renown that people brought food and money just to get a glimpse of the "Dutiful Son Li" who "begged to feed his mother."[112]

Beggars were not always peaceful but often were involved in robbery, picking pockets, and blackmail; any passersby and petty peddlers could become their victims. They frequently snatched food and hats from pedestrians on the streets; for instance, as one peddler sold peaches at the South Gate Bridge, more than twenty beggars grabbed the peaches and ran away while eating them. Some mendicants, called "fierce beggars," used special trickery to force households to give them food or money. They might scratch at sores until they bled, then accuse a dog of causing the injuries to extort money from the dog's owner. If money was not forthcoming, they might lie on the ground and pretend to be dying. Finally, a leader from the beggars would be invited to mediate, and the household would have to pay a settlement.[113]

Many mendicants did not beg exclusively but survived by other means as well. According to Vale, 20 percent of the beggars "by one means or another, seek to make a living, and only beg to supplement their scanty earnings." Beggars with the skills to make toys could use their time making windmills, whistles, and dolls for sale "at remarkably cheap rates." Some collected feathers and made cane-handle brushes (a sort of duster), while others gathered discarded cigar butts at teahouses, inns, and opium dens for sale to tobacconists. Many of them collected cinders from teahouses and restaurants and sold them to small itinerant kitchens.[114] Clever panhandlers devised every possible scheme to obtain food. Before electric fans were introduced, Chengdu restaurants became stifling in the summer. In the 1920s, one would often see the same beggar with his children, each carrying a big cattail-leaf fan, in the restaurants around East Great Street. Usually, the father would begin fanning a well-dressed customer and then would move on to another customer while one of his children continued to fan the first. After the customers finished dining, they would give their leftovers to the servants, sometimes along with a few cents. It was said that the beggar who first made a living this way was nicknamed "Master Wind" (Fengshi). For younger beggars, carrying flags "in street processions or in the retinue of the magistrates or high provincial authorities" provided more regular work. A funeral or wedding was "always preceded by a long procession of these dirty urchins, who for the time being are dressed in green, red, or some other striking colors, with queer conical-shaped hats upon their heads." Contemporary society may find it difficult to imagine shabbily dressed beggars walking in the processions at weddings and funerals of decent families, but this was once a widely recognized custom.[115]

"Lotus chatting" (*lianhualuo*) was another way of begging and became the most popular beggar's performance. Panhandlers performed it at street corners and in front of shops, restaurants, and teahouses to earn a little money. During the Chinese New Year celebrations, they knocked on doors of households up and down the street to get "happy money" (*xiqian*) by performing happy songs. A writer from the time noted that pork butchers usually gave them leftover morsels for their performance, so that some beggars collected quite a few pounds of meat. Their performances might include various stories from real life and sometimes might even reflect political ideas.[116]

Beggars' organizations played an active role in their survival. Beggars usually belonged to an established group ranging from thirty to fifty people and organized under an acknowledged leader, or "king," who was "recognized by the local magistrates" and was responsible to the authorities for panhandlers' public behavior. In the late Qing, residents often saw a "king" of beggars standing on a bridge outside the East City Gate and "levying a tax upon his followers when they went out of the city." Luo Yongpei was head of the beggars in the areas of Three Righteousness Temple (Sanyi miao), Canon Factory Square (Paochang ba), Zhongshan Street, West Great Wall Street (Daqiang xijie), and Long Peace Street (Yongjing jie). His gimmick was his "business card." The formal imprinted title was that of "watchman," and on the back his other "specialties" were listed: preparing and burying corpses; locating illegitimate children; burying dead infants; hanging curtains that read "woman in labor" on the doors of public lavatories; and other businesses. He was as busy "as an official who holds many positions" and even had to appoint fellow beggars as assistants.[117] This story tells us that some beggars existed in a gray area between begging and free labor. They could provide some unique social services, which did not exist in normal professions. From this perspective, we can ascertain that in Chengdu, like in Shanghai, "begging became an urban occupation."[118]

Beggars were always expelled from public places, such as neighborhoods, streets, restaurants, and teahouses, so they had to find some places to live and to organize their own community. They usually chose abandoned land. In the early Republic, some panhandlers, using bamboo sheds as fortresses against the elements, occupied an abandoned graveyard near the City God Temple at the North City Gate. Others soon joined, and they eventually formed a "beggars' village." In 1919, a group of philanthropists raised money to build houses for the indigent, and later this area was called the "House for Wandering People" (Xiliu suo). The leader of these beggars was Zhao Zhanyun, who had built his reputation by "taking up the cause of injured persons" and engaging in charitable acts such as sharing leftover food with ill and disabled beggars, women, and children. Whenever the leader of the community found a corpse on the street in the area of the North City Gate, he would hire Zhou and his followers to bury it, and whenever a family needed assistants for a funeral or wedding, they also called on Zhou. The reward included enough morsels from the table so that he and his followers could have a "big meal" afterward.[119]

The organized beggars even had the courage to challenge local powerful men. One story describes how beggars interrupted a military officer's party. In 1928, a division commander of the Sichuan Army planned a huge banquet in celebration of his fiftieth birthday, and several streets near the Thunder Deity Temple (Leishen miao) were decorated with colorful paper, sheds, and lamps for this purpose. Many important people in Chengdu joined the celebration. Just as the banquet was about to start, however, an enormous procession of more than 300 beggars, including women carrying babies, passed by with a large sign that read: "Wishing you happiness as great as the East Sea and life as long as the South Mountain" (furu Donghai, shoubi Nanshan). The party crashers seated themselves at the several hundred dining tables along the river and waited for the banquet. Although the division commander was accompanied by his armed soldiers, he could not direct them to shoot the "humble guests" on his birthday. So, to compel the beggars to leave peacefully, the division commander's adjutants had to negotiate with the beggars' designated representatives. The interlopers left after it was agreed they would receive twenty baskets of leftovers, two vats of wine, and one hundred wen each.[120]

As we saw in Chapter 5, the police launched an aggressive campaign against beggars in the early twentieth century, which herded them into government workhouses. For some beggars, however, street life was attractive enough that they refused to look for legitimate work and detested living in the workhouses. We previously noted that those who "idled about and did no decent work" were taken off the street and forced to work. Often, as Vale found, "boys just starting on this life have been rescued; they have been washed and clothed and properly cared for a few months or perhaps a year," but as soon as they had an opportunity "they turned back to their old life of freedom and begging, evidently preferring this to the restraints of civilization." Many beggars tried to run away from the workhouses. Policemen told runaways that inmates in the workhouses got plenty to eat, but even this promise held little appeal.[121]

The reasons that beggars preferred street life were numerous and complicated, but one obvious factor was the loss of freedom experienced in the workhouses. Of course, some preferred a life of wandering and truly were unwilling to do "decent work"; society accused these of "laziness." The elites looked askance at beggars, as reflected in several cartoons in the Popular Pictorial (Tongsu huabao). One, entitled "Hard to Get Rid of Them," satirized beggars and their methods for obtaining free meals. Another, entitled "Generals Who Extend Their Arms" (shenshou jiangjun), criticized panhandlers for begging for food and stealing rather than doing honest work, and for snatching pancakes on the street with their "long arms."[122] (See Figure 6.9.) No doubt beggars were scorned by the city dwellers because they looked dirty, lazy, and "shameless." An article in a local newspaper expressed a common opinion held by the elite toward the beggar:

During the Chinese New Year I prepared some coppers and intended to give them to beggars on the street in order to gain some psychological peace, and also to make the poor happy. I came back from the streets with all my money, because I changed my mind when I saw that many panhandlers were strong young men who did not want to work for benevolent people would give them money. Therefore, giving them money was harmful to them. I suggested that benevolent money should be collected together to build some workhouses and schools for the poor.[123]

In the early Republic, the police prohibited begging on the street, but gave the elderly or disabled identity cards that could be used to receive relief. Some continued to beg, however, even though the penalty was suspension of their cards. Those who were able to work but still begged along the streets and shops were regarded as "humiliated by their own actions and shameless" and were pursued by the police. The police ordered all districts to send beggars to the workhouse. Sometimes more than a hundred beggars would arrive daily, so within only a few days, the workhouse had no room for new arrivals.[124]

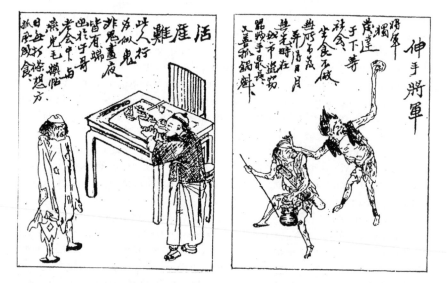

FIGURE 6.9. Two Cartoons about Beggars. At left: "Hard to Get Rid of Them"; at right: "Generals Who Extend Their Arms." Such depictions show the elites' attitude toward beggars, satirizing them for panhandling and stealing rather than doing honest work. From TSHB 1909, no. 6.

Generally, there were two kind of beggars: those who had lost their ability to make a living because of illness, old age, or disability, and those who regarded begging as a "profession" and did not want to do hard work. Chengdu residents seem to have treated these two kinds of beggars differently. They gave sympathy, understanding, and even help to the first group but despised the second. Government policies also treated the two differently. When the government was unable to offer financial support for the first group, it at least gave them the "right to beg." The government constantly tried to take the second group off from the street, however, and make them into "decent workers." These measures resulted in new strategies to deal with new social conditions. Despite their rules and regulations, the police were not successful in removing beggars from the street. Beggars used their limited resources to resist these efforts, and somehow managed to survive on the street.

7 Street Politics

As Chinese cities were being politically transformed in the early twentieth century, Chengdu developed an unprecedented connection with national politics. This chapter explores how the reformist and revolutionary movements drew the street and commoners into their political orbit; how street culture was transformed into street politics; and how both elites and commoners redefined their public role mainly through addressing conflicts between the state and commoners and between the state and elites. We will see that during this period—although street culture, public space, and street life continued—the street was no longer just a place for livelihood, everyday life, and amusement, but became an arena for political conflict as well. Commoners' activities on the street were exploited to further local political struggles.

Elite reformers regarded commoners as a volatile element, and believed social order would be stabilized if they could gain control of the street, where commoners conducted many of the activities of everyday life. In addition, reformers sought to manipulate commoners for political gain. Therefore, the urban reform movement would benefit if the street could be brought into the sphere of local and even national politics, and if street culture could develop an overtly political orientation. In the late Qing, urban elites had tried to increase their influence on the masses through such measures as public readings and lectures, book lending, and reforms of local opera. Even though elites typically scorned the lower classes, preferring to frequent "the circles of gentry, merchants, and students," they nonetheless wanted to insinuate themselves into that class by providing leadership. Urban commoners traditionally had little interest in local politics, but the sweeping social transformation under way forced their participation. On the one hand, elites attempted to exploit commoners to further their political agenda and to mobilize in the political struggle for local rights against the central government; on the other hand, however, commoners also spoke on their own behalf and promoted their own economic interests, especially when their interests were threatened.

The 1911 Revolution and other political movements in the early Republic deepened Chengdu residents' involvement in national politics while simultaneously contributing to the destabilization of public order. Chengdu, like other Chinese cities, suffered disasters ranging from heightened militarism and economic distress, "but it continued to display its particularities of custom and consciousness." Thus, the city "was neither wholly representative of China's condition in the 'warlord era' nor wholly atypical."[1] The chaos of the early Republic and the new presence of various military and political powers seriously disrupted the familiar patterns of street life, at times even turning the street into a battlefield. At the same time, the street became a more visible arena for political protest, giving rise to many sensational "social dramas." Of course, the experience of Chengdu people in the early Republic was similar in many ways to that of other Chinese; in Chengdu, however, street politics also adopted some highly local characteristics, which developed in tandem with the city's street culture.

From the late Qing on to the 1920s, the relationship between the state, elites, and masses changed constantly. In terms of using public space for local political purposes, commoners and elites had a complicated relationship that was under the influence of national and local politics: sometimes united and sometimes split. This relationship was often determined by interactions of the state and elites. In other words, elites, as the agency between the state and ordinary people, shifted their positions between the two ends to suit their own interests. When state policies were to strengthen their leadership in local community, elites would support the state and participate in the new programs against commoners; otherwise, they would oppose or remain neutral about new measures and policies. During the period of the late-Qing New Policies, the state and local elites collaborated to conduct urban reform and to regulate commoners, but when state power jeopardized local political and economic interests, the elites and the masses united to protest—such as against the policy of nationalizing railroads, which triggered the 1911 Revolution. After the revolution, both the warlord and Nationalist governments abolished the traditional reliance on local elites for social control, imposing their power directly on communities. Whereas in the late Qing the local elites led commoners, in the early Republic this control fell to government hands. As a result, the elites increasingly lost their role and influence in community life, and thus became less enthusiastic toward the government's new programs.

In the late Qing and early Republic, various social groups played a role in local politics. In addition to traditional organizations such as charitable establishments, native place associations, and guilds, many new organizations emerged in the late 1890s, when the wave of the national reform movement reached Chengdu. In the early twentieth century, in promoting the New Policies, a much larger number of voluntary and professional organizations were established, including the Society of Sichuan Learning (Shuxue hui), the Chengdu Chamber of Commerce (Chengdu zongshang hui), the Office for Judgment of Commercial Disputes (Shangshi caipan suo), the Society of Studying Current Laws and Regulations (Xianxing faling yanjiu hui), and the Association for Education in Sichuan (Sichuan jiaoyu zonghui). With the development of self-government, the Chengdu City Council was established; it had sixty members elected by residents, with offices in charge of education, hygiene, road construction, the economy, public affairs, and consultation.[2] Although these elite organizations played an important role in influencing local politics through their participation in the reformist movements, this study will focus instead on the use of public space and the role of commoners.

In the field of Chinese history, the focus has been primarily on how elite thought influenced politics,[3] but little work has been done about the relationship between popular culture and local politics, an exploration of which could give us an opportunity to observe social transformation from another angle. Political uncertainty deteriorated public order and gradually damaged the stability of the neighborhood and community; conflicts increased between sexes, classes, and ethnic groups throughout the city. We should also realize, however, that political changes opened up the relatively isolated society and brought new social, economic, and cultural elements as well. Postrevolutionary Chengdu provides an excellent example of how politics can influence everyday life and underscores the importance of including politics in the study of popular culture.

The Creation of Public Political Space

Social reformers wanted to create a new and progressive city by transforming the appearance and culture of the streets, but they also wished to gain political advantage by influencing popular opinion. For example, reformers viewed the mundane issues of sanitation, traffic control, begging, gambling, and prostitution through the broad lens of "civilization." Fu Chongju acknowledged that his Investigation of Chengdu "satirized current society and customs" in an effort to compensate for the failure of state-sponsored social reform efforts. He hoped that his work would "promote progress." Thus, he intended his book to be part of a comprehensive campaign to "enlighten the people." In another effort to reach the lower classes, Fu also established the Enlightenment Colloquial News (Qimeng tongsu bao) in 1902. The News used local dialects to popularize reform ideas among commoners. Social reformers believed that enlightening people meant emphasizing scientific progress and hard work and curtailing all "bizarre talk" about gods and other "superstitions" that were the foundation of Chengdu's cultural legacy. Freed from such fantasies, the people could concentrate on "useful things" such as agriculture, industry, and business.[4]

Social reformers established various organizations to help achieve this goal. In 1910, the Provincial Assembly passed a resolution establishing the "Popular Educational Society" (Tongsu jiaoyu she) to promote reading among the public. Like the *Investigation of Chengdu* (Chengdu tonglan), the Society was created to "eradicate the roots of social disorder" through popular education, including storytelling, local operas, and public lectures, and to stop the spread of "wicked ideas." The Society planned to gather stories and dramas, select some for revision and translation as foreign-language books, and translate into the vernacular selected works from classical Chinese literature. The elites hoped that "uneducated commoners" would be enlightened so that they "would not stand in the way of the New Policies and would not harm public security." Fu also established the "Society of Newspaper Readers" (Yuebao gongshe), which collected nearly a hundred journals and newspapers from Sichuan and other provinces. The Enlightenment Bookstore (Kaizhi shuju) opened a lending service of Chinese and foreign books. In 1911, the Sichuan Bureau of Educational Affairs (Chuansheng xuewu gongsuo) established a library at the site of the old Examination Hall (Gongyuan) for the purpose of providing books to local residents in order to "promote civilization . . . and cultivate decorum and beneficial customs."[5]

Reformers also used public lectures as a platform for changing customs (see Figure 7.1). They adopted the methods of sacred-edict preachers, but altered the contents. In 1904, for instance, some elite women lectured in Jade Dragon Street (Yulong jie) on the importance of unbound feet and distributed more than 100,000 copies of the "Don't-Bind-Feet Song" (*Wu chanjiao ge*). They may have been preaching to the converted: by 1909, 30 to 40 percent of Chengdu women already had "big" (i.e., unbound) feet. Jeffery Wasserstrom has emphasized that in this culture, "giving a speech" was just like "acting" in the theater and was "an important source of political metaphor in modern China."[6] Indeed, through these public lectures, local elites could be said to have performed "political opera," which had a deep impact on public life. The form of public speech was similar to traditional storytelling, but the contents were changed from historical events, legends, and romances to current issues of society. This new use of the street became a major tool of the political struggle later.

Although social reformers spoke of providing "enlightenment," what they actually emphasized throughout the reform was a combination of localism and nationalism in an effort to make Chengdu appear progressive to the rest of the world. These patriotic underpinnings also facilitated the leadership function over commoners that the elite class assumed during political

FIGURE 7.1. A Public Lecture. The characters on the pillar read: "General Association for Public Lectures in Sichuan." From TSHB 1912, no. 28.

movements. More accurately, "patriotism" meant a devotion to Chengdu, the hometown that figured prominently in the writings of the local intelligentsia. One local intellectual, for instance, wrote that "Sichuan overlooks China, and Chengdu is the center of Sichuan, with fertile lands, rich natural resources, a large population, well-developed silk production, many historical sites, and beautiful scenery. It is the hub of transportation coming from or going to Shaanxi, Gansu, Hunan, Hubei, Yunnan, Guizhou, Qinghai, and Tibet."[7] In late-Qing and early Republican literature, in such florid descriptions there was also the implication that Chengdu held a special position in China, reflecting the elite's strong local pride.

Chengdu's inhabitants were, to a significant extent, self-conscious "urbanites," regardless of social class. In the preface to his *Investigation of Chengdu*, Fu Chongju indicated his own self-consciousness:

As a resident of Chengdu, what I say about Chengdu is more substantial than what outsiders say. As a person who lives in Chengdu, what I say about Chengdu contains more truth than what visitors say. As a person who has experienced life here, what I say about Chengdu reveals more truth than hearsay. What I say about Chengdu is based on facts, not empty talk; what I say about Chengdu is based on actual experience, not the second-hand descriptions found in classic books.[8]

Many of the chapter titles in *Investigation of Chengdu*, such as "Chengduese of Chengdu," "Women of Chengdu," and "Chengduese Personality and Customs," underscored Fu's identity as a Chengdu citizen, just as his criticisms did.[9]

Since the late nineteenth century, awareness of and pride in provincial traditions had been important, and local elites made use of them in promoting the politicization of the city and public space. In contrast to most other agrarian societies, in China the families of those who left rural areas to work or study elsewhere most often stayed behind. As a result, "a man's class membership might change; his membership in his native local system persisted." Many Western scholars have concluded that China did not develop cohesive urban communities because of this characteristic. Although at first glance it appears that the "Chinese urban dweller legally belonged to his family and native village in which the temple of his ancestors stood and to which he conscientiously maintained affiliation," in fact, many of Chengdu's citizens were born and reared there and most families had lived in the city for a lifetime or even for generations. Whether consciously or unconsciously, most residents considered themselves distinctly "Chengduese." Fu Chongju's statement cited above clearly expresses his identity as a "Chengdu citizen."[10] This self-consciousness and patriotism became a basis for commoners to participate in the movement to protect local interests.

Mobilizing Commoners

Some political mobilization had occurred at the street level before the 1911 Revolution, when organized protests such as antiforeign demonstrations, armed attacks by unorthodox sects, strikes, bannermen's riots, and revolutionary uprisings became a constant force on Chengdu's streets. One prominent incident, a market strike, took place in June 1905, when a gang of men marched down East Great Street and drove "the hawkers of various wares who habitually line that thoroughfare to their homes, forbidding any to sell under penalty of pounding and destruction of his property." All shops were shut, and petty peddlers were forced to cooperate. "A street peddler who ventured out had his stand smashed and it seemed as though a riot was imminent." This market strike protested a new tax requiring each residential compound and shop to pay anywhere from 500 to 1,000 coppers monthly. "This addition to their burden of taxation the people felt they could not bear." In November 1907, more than four thousand members of the Sworn Brotherhood Society (Gelaohui) planned to attack Chengdu. The uprising failed when the plan was revealed as the rebels were lying in wait on Small India Street (Xiao tianzhu jie), Peaceful and Fluent Bridge (Anshun qiao), and the Tea Market (Chadianzi). In 1909, when Shanghai merchants boycotted Japanese goods, propaganda flyers that rallied more support reached Chengdu.[11]

In the summer of 1911, the Qing government decreed the nationalization of all local railroads, and a mass movement for railroad protection broke out in Hunan, Hubei, Guangdong, and Sichuan.[12] Wei Yingtao, in his groundbreaking 1981 study of the Railroad Protection Movement, pointed out that the movement was led by the "Constitutional Faction of Gentry," and later the Sworn Brotherhood played an important role in military uprising. In my 1993 study on social transformation in Qing in the upper Yangzi region, there is a substantial discussion on the issue of how social changes built a foundation for the Railroad Protection Movement and the 1911 Revolution. I argued that the changes in the economy, political and educational systems, social organizations (secret societies and new professionals), and ideologies made the radical revolution possible.[13] In this section, however, I make a new attempt to examine this movement, this time from the angle of popular culture, and to reveal how street culture and rituals were used to mobilize the masses.

As soon as the Qing government announced the policy of nationalizing railroads, Chengdu residents quickly recognized that this was "a matter of life-and-death" and vowed to "give our lives to protect our railroad."[14] The streets became a huge "stage" during this political struggle, with public meetings the most popular method for mobilizing ordinary citizens. A mass meeting that the railroad company held at its headquarters on Yue Mansion Street (Yuefu jie) "became a stream of people," with about five thousand participants, according to one estimate, and was probably the largest public political gathering in Chengdu since the anti-Christian movement in 1895.[15] Several well-known elites made speeches explaining how the right to control the railroads shaped the fate of the nation. When the meeting reached its climax, "all participants wept from the bottoms of their hearts, including the policemen who were keeping order." As soon as the Railroad Protection Association was set up, representatives were chosen to go to Beijing to petition the central government. A large-scale ceremony was held at the Southern Parade Ground to send them off, at which the representatives swore they would not return if they did not achieve their goal. At that moment, "the people both on the stage and in front of the stage cried and applauded." At another mass meeting, an elementary school boy representing his classmates gave a speech suggesting that each student contribute two *wen* per day to the movement, and all present responded with great emotion. An old man stepped onto the stage and held the boy, weeping and saying, "our struggle for the rights of the railroad is for the sake of our little brothers like him." Everyone in the crowd of ten thousand wept bitterly, it was reported, and some policemen even cried out in support of the movement: "we [police-men] are Sichuanese and we are also patriotic men."[16] Clearly, the local elites were skilled at using public gatherings as a means of shaping public sentiment and spreading propaganda for their political goal, a tool that was used with great success in mobilizing the masses.

For the first time, reformers and commoners joined in the same political organization—the Sichuan Railroad Protection Association (Sichuan baolu tongzhi hui). Their common interests brought various groups and classes together; at least at this moment, the gap between social classes became narrower. The many branches of the association were organized according to neighborhood, occupation, and social group. The Peaceful Street (Taiping jie) Association, the Women's Association, the Student Association, the Silk Guild Association, and even the Beggar's Association sprang up like "bamboo shoots after a spring rain." Shopkeepers organized the "One Cash Association" (Yiqian hui), each member of which contributed one *wen* daily to the Railroad Protection Association.[17] Some guilds, such as those for lumber and silk, also organized occupational "one cash associations"; the silk guild alone attracted more than two hundred members in just a few days. Within a short time, associations could be found on every street. According to a local newspaper, within a single day the Muslims in Chengdu organized more than twenty associations.[18]

The Sichuan Railroad Protection Association conducted the largest campaign of propaganda ever held in Chengdu. According to the missionaries, "public speakers" took up "prominent positions on busy streets." The *Newsletter of the Sichuan Railroad Protection Association* (Sichuan baolu tongzhihui baogao) gained wide distribution, with a circulation of up to fifteen thousand copies per issue. Every day, readers crowded around the walls where newsletters had been pasted to discuss the latest developments. In addition, the elites tried to appropriate the street by any means possible to rally the masses. Their tactics included posting political flyers in all public spaces, delivering public lectures, and sponsoring popular entertainment including such "lowbrow" performances as "golden bamboo clappers" and "drum stories." A special advertisement was created for public lectures, which announced the place, time, and names of the lecturers and urged all members of the gentry, merchants, and residents to attend. Lectures were held in local temples, including the Three Righteousness Temple (Sanyi miao), Fire Deity Temple (Huoshen miao), Yanqing Temple (Yanqing si), and the Literacy God Temple (Wenchang gong).[19] Thus, traditional places for religious observance were transformed into places for political mobilization.

Commoners responded to the call by taking part in a market strike, which started in August. All shops were shut down and all trades were discontinued. The whole city was like a clock that had stopped ticking:

The sound of gongs and drums in the Joy Teahouse and Elegant Garden, the pure singing in other teahouses, the cries of business in Drum Tower Street, and waiters' voices in restaurants all disappeared. Even the noise of the weaving machines on Half Street (Banbian jie) and Horse Riding Street, and the jingling of hammers in the jewelry stores on Golden Ware Street (Dajin jie), which could be heard throughout the day, were stopped. The hawkers also stripped the goods from their sheds and stalls.[20]

The city had never known such stillness. Like people in any urban area, residents were accustomed to the noise and rhythm of daily life. The strike adversely affected the livelihoods of many commoners, especially peddlers and coolies, yet they were powerless to resist the will of the majority. Partly in compensation for these commoners' lost income, reformers organized a relief bureau (shiji ju) under railroad company management to dispense money and rice to more than thirty thousand poor city dwellers. After the September massacre (described below), all shops were forced open by order of Acting Governor-General Zhao Erfeng. Initially, this order met "stubborn resistance," but it could not last. Under both political and economic pressure, all shops opened within a few days, beginning with the shops on East Great Street, Horse Riding Street, and some other main streets, and followed by the shops on smaller streets.[21]

The elites' attitudes toward commoners gradually began to change. Previous to this movement, local elites had always disparaged what they considered the inferior moral values and intellects of commoners. At this time, however, the elites had to admit to being "touched by what poor people in the lower order of society are doing." Commoners eagerly joined the associations, attended public meetings, and contributed money. A sedan-chair carrier donated his hard-earned money to the movement, proclaiming that "coolies are citizens, too." Popular performers also sent delegates to the association to show their support. The residents of North Summer Sock Street held banners and knelt in the mud to present a petition to Acting Governor-General Zhao Erfeng as he passed by.[22] The collective impact of these actions made elites recognize the potential strategic value of commoners in the political arena. Even the patriotism demonstrated in their common support of the Railroad Protection Movement, however, could not completely bridge their differences in personal interests, beliefs, and values. The reformers, despite their success in rallying the masses against the state's railroad policies, were primarily concerned with getting the state to accept their demands; they were hardly willing to destroy the social order they had managed for so long. For commoners, the struggle soon expanded

to include issues of increased economic opportunity and an improved social environment as well as greater use of public space. These differences
explain why the affiliation between the upper and lower classes in Chengdu
was doomed. As soon as the 1911 Revolution erupted throughout China,
the unity between them was broken.[23]

Revolutionary Ritual

Religious rituals, festivals, ceremonies, and public entertainment can
play a role in radical social change. Community leaders might use customs
to mobilize citizens against state power; as Emily Ahern has argued, "citizens could use religion and ritual to oppose political authorities." What
happened in Chengdu in 1911 provides a perfect validation of Ahern's argument. During the Revolution, Chengdu entered a period of unrest in
which traditional religious rituals were used to serve political purposes and
elites and commoners alike participated in local politics in unprecedented
numbers. Lynn Hunt, in examining the relationship between politics and
culture in the French Revolution, pointed out that political activities were
not just for seeking economic and social interests; by appropriating political language, political images, and everyday political practices, revolutionaries reconstructed society and social relations. In the process of political
movement, they formed new social and political relations. Their struggle
"forced them to see the world in new ways." Like the French Revolution,
the 1911 Revolution in Chengdu to a certain extent was rooted in traditional popular culture, but the popular culture itself was transformed as it
was forced to confront new phenomena. Furthermore, in this movement,
under the influence of local politics, the traditional community became a
sort of "political community" in the sense of the political fights or revolutionary struggles described by Richard Sennett, in which street culture is
drawn into the political arena.[24]

Chengdu commoners were customarily wary of those who urged them
to join rebellions or support a political cause. This attitude changed, however, after the elite used popular religion and street culture as a tool for mobilization. As in the French Revolution, when "symbolic practices, such as
language, imagery, and gestures, became an important part of the political
culture," in Chengdu during the Railroad Protection Movement similar
symbolic constructs—powerful weapons, indeed—were evident everywhere.
Commoners occupied all the streets and, with elites' support, built "altars to
the Guangxu Emperor" (*Xianhuang tai*), who died in 1908 and was considered an important proponent of local ownership of Sichuan railroads. The
elite issued "memorial tablets" by the tens of thousands for the deceased
emperor, which were displayed in all households and shops within days.

Also, matched couplets were pasted on their doors, reading "national policies follow public opinion; railroads should be run by local people" (*shuzheng gongzhu yulun; tielu zhungui shangban*)—a phrase take from the Guangxu emperor's edicts. On every street, people burned incense and worshiped at altars day and night; the whole city bubbled with noise.[25] A foreign witness vividly described the scene:

Every house in the city was placarded with a slip of yellow paper marked "Spirit Tablet of the Late Emperor Kuang Hsu [Guangxu]," with quotations from his edicts granting the right of railway construction to the merchants of Szechuan [Sichuan]; and across most of the principal thoroughfares platforms were erected, on which were placed mastheads containing portraits of his late Majesty, with vases, incense pots, and the other paraphernalia of a commemorative altar. Some few of these platforms were barely five feet above the street, but most were high enough to allow pedestrians to pass.[26]

Obviously, building altars, erecting memorial tablets, and worshiping on the streets were not simply acts of ritual practice but of political protest as well. The masses used street altars, for example, as a means of challenging governmental power and expressing their anger against officials, who did not dare show disrespect for the deceased emperor by passing the altars while riding a horse or sitting in a sedan chair. As Acting Governor-General Zhao acknowledged, "There are emperor's tablets in the sheds on all Chengdu streets. Sedan chairs and horses are unable to pass. Any attempts to travel in sedan chairs or ride horses on the street will give the masses an excuse to oppose the officials. They have the emperor's tablets as their amulet." Religious rituals on the street, like parades in American cities, were thus "public dramas of social relations," which could act as "the field of power relations." Sacred altars and memorial tablets, like the tricolor cockade and patriotic altars of the French Revolution, "were sanctified by their use" in the new ritual. It should be noted, however, that the goals of the two revolutions were quite different. Whereas the French revolutionaries consciously struggled to cut off the French past and to build the foundation for "a new national community," the Chinese urban reformist elites limited their goals to local economic interest alone.[27] Even so, the Railroad Protection Movement was still an unprecedented step in the public politics of Chengdu. Even though local elites did not attempt to oppose the central government, this was the first time that they organized the masses to challenge state power.

These public rituals reflected the elites' strategy and their belief that religious ritual was the best weapon for their struggle. They made no attempt to go any farther, however. Like the French revolutionary regime that "tried to discipline popular political festivity,"[28] from the beginning of the Railroad Protection Movement, Chengdu elites tried to avoid violent confrontation by designing a plan of "civilized protest for the railroad." The public notice of the Railroad Protection Association emphasized that "the matters our association should pay most attention to are (1) preventing rebellion, (2) keeping social order, and (3) making the masses know that these two things are important." Another public announcement was directed at restraining the masses: "(1) No gathering on the street, (2) no rebellion, (3) no attacking churches, (4) no humiliating officials and government, (5) oil, salt, firewood, rice, and all other food should be sold as usual." When elites tried to mobilize commoners, they stressed that "this is a political movement, and foreigners and their property will be protected."[29] These documents show that the elites tried to keep the movement as a "rational" and "reasonable" force for stabilizing the lives of Chengdu residents, even while confronting state power.

What caused the movement to develop into a full-fledged "rebellion" against the Qing government was the so-called Chengdu massacre, which took place in September of 1911. On the ninth of September, Acting Governor-General Zhao arrested Luo Lun, a major leader in the movement, and eight others, shocking the whole city. Groups immediately gathered to demonstrate, and "they were soon followed by thousands of the populace, raising the same cry." Men, women, and children "with sticks of lighted incense in one hand and yellow paper spirit tablets of the Emperor in the other, pressed toward the Viceroy's yamen, weeping and wailing, all crying: 'give us back our Loh-lun [Luo Lun]; give us back our Loh-lun.'" They petitioned for their leaders' release. Although previously street performances had appealed only to the lower classes, elites now played a crucial role in occupying the streets. City dwellers had never before seen such a spectacle: policemen led the way, followed by many gentry wearing long gowns, and behind them, enormous numbers of commoners in short jackets.[30] Urban elites and commoners together acted out a vital social drama on the public stage.

The demonstration ended tragically. Although the people presented their appeal by "begging and kowtowing," the local government "slaughtered them brutally." In the blink of an eye, Zhao ordered his soldiers to open fire in front of the governor-general's yamen; people ran away, doors of shops and households slammed shut, and mothers cried frantically for their missing children. The yard in front of the yamen was emptied except for more than twenty bleeding bodies and scattered debris that included shoes and broken memorial tablets. Zhao's cavalry even rushed into the crowd while shooting. Zhao had also sent his soldiers to guard street corners and prohibited people from coming and going. Most of the participants were laborers, artisans, and other members of the lower class. Twenty-six of the victims were identified: sixteen were weavers, carvers, apprentices, tailors, and peddlers.[31]

The massacre resulted in a direct confrontation between the people and the government, and the initially peaceful Railroad Protection Movement exploded into violence. As one eyewitness pointed out, "The ferocious New Army depended on guns to maintain order, but this only made people so angry that they snatched the guns from them, fighting without fear." To prevent rebellion and stop communication with the outside world, Zhao Erfeng imposed martial law and shut the city gates. However, the massacre had dispelled any illusions about the Qing government, and the people expressed their passion in various ways. Some wrote comments on Zhao Erfeng's public notices: "Why did you kill many ordinary people?" and "The government has made the common people rebel," and "Our people must struggle with our lives!" On some backstreets and alleys, residents tore off the public notices or splattered them with red paint. They invented a new tool, which they called the "river telegraph" (*shui dianbao*), to communicate with the outside world: tens of thousands of small wooden boards, on which were written accounts of what was happening in Chengdu, were put in the rivers. The boards were soon found all over Sichuan. Foreign observers praised this "clever invention."[32] In the meantime, people began to organize a military force, the Railroad Protection Army (Baolu tongzhi jun), which gathered outside the Chengdu city wall in preparation to capture Chengdu. Most of the soldiers were members of the Sworn Brotherhood Society, carrying swords, spears, and red flags. They came from the counties near Chengdu in groups as large as several thousand and even tens of thousands. The city was anxious and restless, and panic spread like wildfire.[33]

After it had declared the independence of Sichuan, the new revolutionary government struggled to restore public order.[34] The new Sichuan Military Government, a mixture of urban elites and Qing provincial officials, issued regulations for public gatherings: "the gathering meeting" had to be "an activity with a certain goal," such as a public lecture, or "political and critical meetings." Organizers of such meetings were required to tell the police in advance about the purpose of the meeting, the meeting time and place, the backgrounds and addresses of organizers, and the number of attendees expected. The police had to approve nonpolitical gatherings as well. Many groups were denied the right to political assembly, among them Buddhist monks, Daoist priests and other members of the clergy, teachers and students of middle and elementary schools, men under eighteen, all women, former prisoners, and illiterate people. These regulations gave the police much more authority to control public political gatherings, of course. They were instructed to oversee or investigate all such activities, could deny admittance to anyone who refused to obey, and could end any lecture that had rebellious content, caused trouble, or offended "public decency."[35]

Nevertheless, this period witnessed magnificent spectacles in street politics. Two drawings from the period are particularly vivid: one shows Governor Yin Changheng of the Sichuan Military Government leading his army
out the south gate of the Imperial City at the start of his "Western Expedition."[36] The other depicts artillery troops marching out the South City Gate.
Both are expansive views that show an enormous and powerful army, horses,
flags, guns, cannons, and crowds of spectators. The captions tell us that several thousand people gathered to send off the troops at the South City Gate.
From these pictures, we can also see that social organizations were very
active, judging from the display of their banners, which had slogans such
as "all legal organizations" (*ge fatuan*), "citizens' organization" (*mintuan*),
"journalists" (*baojie*), and so on.[37] (See Figures 7.2 and 7.3.)

The strong role of street culture in the political movement, especially in
the Railroad Protection Movement, however, does not suggest that street
politics determined the movement's success. Previous studies have pointed
out the crucial role of military uprising. An exploration of street politics in

FIGURE 7.2. The Departure of Governor Yin's Western Expedition. From TSHB
1912, no. 11.

FIGURE 7.3. The Departure of the Artillery Troops. From TSHB 1912, no. 28.

the movement is meant to extend our understanding of this political move-ment from elites' activities and leadership to commoners' experiences—from the superficial waves of politics to the undercurrents below. It also provides a new angle to observe this movement and the relationship be-tween reformist elites and ordinary people.[38] The year 1911 symbolized commoners' political participation and the transformation from street cul-ture to street politics, which radically affected their daily lives. From then on, the streets were frequently used for political purposes, and ordinary residents were forced to live in the shadow of relentless power struggles. Although street culture and street life, to a considerable extent, survived the era of chaos, the social environment deteriorated to the point that it could not be restored.

Chaos

The greatest change in the early Republic was that residents had to go about their daily lives in an environment of constant chaos. A foreign observer in the 1930s believed that Sichuan had been "at one time after the Revolution one of the most bandit-ridden provinces of China."[39] Chengdu, a bustling political and economic center, was surely not the worst place in early Republican Sichuan, but the suffering caused by recent social turmoil was still very much in evidence. Chengdu dwellers could never have pre-dicted that the 1911 Revolution would turn out to be only the beginning chapter in a long period of turmoil.

During the Revolution, when the Qing troops were out of control, "sol-diers were given the liberty of the streets," carrying guns and bayonets as they wandered about in tyrannical gangs. These soldiers, according to some, looked very odd: some wore "hero ties" (yingxiong jie) on their foreheads and colored pants; some had hair that reached below their ears; some wrapped their legs like actors in a local opera.[40] On the eighth of December, a large group of soldiers went to the Imperial City, temporary headquarters of the new government, to demand their pay. Before they could enter, mem-bers of the government, including the new governor and vice governor, fled for their lives. The angry soldiers attacked the Great Qing Bank (Daqing yinhang), one of Chengdu's biggest banks, as well as two others. Then they looted the Center for Promoting Commerce and Industry: "in an incredibly short time, the mob headed by the soldiers had cleared every shop on the street, upstairs and down." The mob shattered glass display cases and tossed much of their contents into the street. Later that afternoon, soldiers looted East Great Street, Chengdu's most prosperous district. Their main goal, however, was money: "Late into the evening, smaller bands of soldiers, still carrying their rifles and bandoleers of cartridges, visited many of the larger compounds of the city, demanding and receiving dollars or lump silver." At night, pawnshops became common targets of these bandits, who set fifteen or sixteen fires throughout the city. "Shooting continued almost for the whole night," and "there was little sleep for anyone." The city gates were not closed during the night, and many soldiers fled with their booty. Chengdu suffered extensive damage. "Much of the silver had been melted in the fire, and had run into great masses, mixed with ashes and burned wood." As Robert Kapp pointed out, this looting of the provincial treasuries deprived subsequent government leaders of the financial means to stabilize the province.[41]

Early Republican Chengdu became a world of soldiers. The streets were occupied and controlled by one or another warlord's army, which took over local security by patrolling streets and neighborhoods. Many soldiers were stationed in Chengdu, and numerous veterans lived there. They soon became the most powerful forces in the city and a constant disruption to daily life. Soldiers brazenly committed all kinds of outrages in public places. Often, for example, they kidnapped coolies, sedan-chair carriers, and rickshaw pullers off the streets to work as forced laborers. Coolies were so terrified that they ran from any soldier who requested their service. To deal with this, the Chamber of Commerce requested that each sedan-chair shop provide four men for military service. Soldiers took not only lower-class men but other residents as well, even street headmen and teachers, as forced laborers.[42] They often occupied temples to use as their barracks. In the 1920s, a Japanese visitor observed soldiers at the Green Goat Temple cooking on the altars, sleeping in the main hall, and hanging their laundry to dry between the pillars. Many people, especially young local toughs, pretended to be soldiers to partake of their various privileges. Consequently, military uniforms and collar badges became highly sought merchandise. Some military officers' servants and even some children wore uniforms as an "honor." The army had to make a rule prohibiting this, and the police ordered all tailor shops not to make military uniforms for anyone.[43]

Social turmoil weakened the power of the police, whose failures further exacerbated disorder on the street. In the early Republic, various powers maintained public security, including the police, military police corps, local militia (*mintuan*), and the army. However, the police force was essentially ineffectual; it is even described in one account as a "puppet" organization. At times no police would even report for duty, and local toughs began to impose their own brand of tyranny on the street. The Chengdu police themselves became targets for assault, robbery, and even murder. One account reported that after killing a policeman, the murderous soldiers shouted, "we send you to Heaven to be a guard." Even more ironically, a powerful group damaged Police Society headquarters (*jingjie hui*). Consequently, police officials often stayed away from danger, to the extent that some were accused of failing to investigate disputes.[44] Some policemen not only failed to protect ordinary citizens but also abused their power, which heightened citizens' anxiety. For example, some used the pretense of searching for opium to enter households and take private property. Moreover, many local toughs pretended to be policemen in order to rob residents. Some policemen who used drugs even entered the opium dens in their jurisdictions to indulge while on duty.[45]

Even though some on the police force were presumably sincere in their commitment to duty, their task was made much more difficult when the troublemakers were soldiers, and violent conflicts were inevitable. During the Flower Fair, for instance, when about eighty students from an all-girl middle school went in through the entrance for women, a couple of soldiers cut in the line, blocking the girls. After policemen asked the soldiers to step out of the line and enter through the men's entrance, several more did the same thing again. When an argument broke out, one of the soldiers blew the whistle to signal an "emergency muster." Immediately, dozens of soldiers appeared and began fighting the police, even assaulting them with benches from nearby vendor stalls. Two other policemen tried to calm them down, begging, "Sirs, please just walk in as you like through the entrance for women," and asking the policemen who were there first to apologize to the soldiers. The soldiers, however, shouted, "Beat them! Beat them!" They took the policemen's knives and tore off their uniforms. For a moment, the Fair was engulfed in chaos. The army posted a notice at the Fair warning all soldiers not to disrupt public order and that violators would be punished. The army also sent a military police team to supervise the soldiers while in public.[46] Thus, the absence of a powerful law enforcement entity contributed to the further deterioration of everyday life.

Social turmoil brought another disastrous element to Chengdu residents—bandits. After the 1911 Revolution, the number of robberies skyrocketed as the number of bandits swelled and their tactics became more brazen. In the early years of the Republic, the robbery problem emerged on the outskirts of Chengdu and then spread into the city proper. Once, more than a hundred gun-toting uniformed bandits—whom residents mistook for a local army—marched into the streets outside the North City Gate, accompanied by trumpets and drums. They plundered the area for four hours, robbing and burning houses. The suburbs of Chengdu were thus marked as dangerous areas, and bandits continued to rob and shoot patrons in teahouses.[47] Nobody in Chengdu felt safe as the incidence of robbery increased dramatically.

Of course, military authorities enacted harsh punishment for offenders; public executions and the public display of the heads of decapitated criminals became a means by which local authorities sought to control criminals or attack political opponents as well. In premodern China, executions often represented a "public death ritual" that powerful authorities used to intimidate the masses. They were always carried out in crowded markets, to "execute one as a warning to a hundred." In early Republican Chengdu, public executions were frequent, and like public executions in ancient times, the condemned prisoners were first paraded through the streets (see Figure 7.4), as described here:

At the head of the procession, eight buglers sounded a sorrowful call, followed by a battalion of soldiers carrying guns. In the middle of the procession were the condemned men, shackled and stripped above the waist, kneeling on rickshaws. While some continuously cried "I'm innocent" throughout the procession, others took this chance to make public speeches and show their courage. Following them were more armed soldiers and officers, including the officer in charge. The movement of the procession always attracted many bystanders to follow and watch.[48]

Generally, the procession wound its way along East Great Street, exited the city through the East City Gate, and then passed along East Purple

FIGURE 7.4. Executing a Forger. The condemned man is paraded through the street. The characters on the wooden board read: "Cutting Off Forgers' Heads." From TSHB 1912, no. 43.

Street (Zidong jie) and Yearly Harvest Alley (Nianfeng xiang) to Lotus Flower Pond (Lianhua chi). This route included one bridge, aptly named the "Losing Soul Bridge" (Luohun qiao). The public execution ground, near the Lotus Flower Pond and Earth Buddhist Nunnery (Dizang an), was also site of a mass graveyard. On execution days, people gathered there to watch, and petty peddlers sold their goods and food. Often, a dramatic scene ensued when an execution was to take place. One report told of a convict who refused to leave the cage in which he had been paraded through the streets to be led to the gallows, and then bit the executioner's hand when he tried to drag him out. This made the executioner so angry that he hacked the prisoner to death on the spot.[49] Space at the nunnery was rented as temporary storage for coffins until they could be transported for burial, quite a lucrative enterprise for the nuns. Those who did not have relatives to take their bodies were buried in a nearby public graveyard by beggars hired for the purpose by heads of local *baojia*. Because the corpses were wrapped only with broken mats, it was said that many stray dogs lived on the remains.

In the early Republican period, however, because military authorities wanted to draw larger crowds and to intimidate "bad people," executions were often held within the city, in front of the police station or, in the 1920s, even in the commercial district of Warm Spring Road and Smaller City Park. This public ritual led to some problems. Social reformers, who criticized the practice as unnecessarily brutal and detrimental to public sanitation, recommended that a permanent execution ground be established. In 1927, just as military forces were about to execute a felon in Sun Yat-sen Park, the government requested that the event be moved out of town.[50]

The public display of the heads of decapitated criminals—a practice usually reserved for the most notorious felons—became a favorite strategy of military authorities. In 1916, for example, after the bandit Wu Renjie was executed, his head was put in a wooden cage and hung for three days on the East Gate Bridge. Then it was moved in turn to the West City Gate, North City Gate, and South City Gate, to "threaten other bandits and please the people." During the war of 1917, the Yunnan Army hung four heads on the wall of the Imperial City. In 1928, the government abolished public executions and the display of heads.[51] These ancient "death rituals," however, lingered for quite a long time following the ban. Such brutal punishment was not only a result of severe crimes but also a by-product of the ongoing political and military struggle, and a constant reminder for ordinary residents that they were living in a horrible world.

An Age of Rumors.   Social disorder intensified the scrutiny and spread of rumors. During the late Qing and early Republic, public gathering places were rife with gossip, which became an indicator of the extent of social unrest. A missionary observed:

There was some little flutter for a time among the Chinese in the teashop about the rumored British occupation of Tibet. The teashops are all kept busy these weeks by the rumored order for the cutting of the queue. . . . Then that a young man on a certain street has cut his queue in anticipation, etc. But there can be no manner of doubt as to the sentiment of the Chinese public on the matter.[52]

By the spring of 1910, however, rumors had assumed more ominous undertones, and rumor control was a constant task for the police. Many rumors circulating in Chengdu concerned the removal of people's organs and body parts. The police arrested five people who confessed they had concocted the stories purely for the sake of sensationalism. To punish them and warn others, the police strapped yokes on their shoulders and paraded them through the streets, then included their confessions in a public notice warning that all rumormongers would be punished severely. Another man was arrested on similar charges in the Fortune and Longevity Teahouse when he gossiped with a stranger who, unluckily for him, was an undercover police detective.[53] After the Revolution, the prevalence of wild rumors reflected Chengdu's social instability. One rumormonger, for example, was executed after being found guilty of drawing black lines—regarded as signs of the plague—on paving stones. Rumors of imminent attacks by bandits were frequently reported in newspapers and were the most disturbing to local residents; therefore, the police tried very hard to find their origin. For example, when the police heard on the street that a gang of bandits had come to Chengdu, they sent many secret agents to teahouses and wine shops to collect intelligence.[54]

Rumors circulated quickly when the old order had been destroyed but a new one had not yet been established to replace it. It was believed that both "high society" and "low society" contributed to the spread of rumors but that the elite bore more of the responsibility: "high society makes rumors for social status and reputation; lower society makes rumors for money. The former is a driving force for the latter, and their common point is greed." An editorial in a local newspaper stated that in the late Qing, people spread rumors because they felt psychologically threatened, but in the early Republic, they sensed impending disaster, and thus rumors were even more prevalent. Political instability created a hotbed for political rumors; the same newspaper reported that people were "badly frightened," like "a bird startled by the mere twang of a bowstring." Indeed, rumors of all kinds were so widespread that just one day after a local newspaper published an editorial on "stopping rumors," it published the rumor that the price of salt would go up, creating a rush on the purchase of salt. Occasionally, of course, "rumors" turned out to be true. In 1916, a rumor was spread in the area of the South City Gate that soldiers had stolen rice from rice shops. Consequently, all rice shops in the area closed down immediately. The police claimed that this was a rumor and that they would try to find the source, but there is considerable evidence that this rumor might have been true. Moreover, local authorities often abused their power, suppressing criticism by punishing so-called rumormongers. As a result, any "political talk" or even "street gossip" (*jietan xiangyi*) could be called a rumor and thus forbidden.[55]

During the early Republican era, false alarms—locally called "gusts of ground wind" (*dipifeng*)—were frequent, causing extreme panic. Social disorder made residents feel unsafe. On the crowded street, any untoward incident could cause people to panic and run for their lives. However, many such occurrences were just "gusts of ground wind." A family set off firecrackers during a funeral near the Green Goat Temple, for example, frightening everyone within earshot. One evening, just after the street war of 1917, "a gust of ground wind" blew through Xu Mansion Street (Xufu jie) and Along City Wall Street (Shuncheng jie); "all streets became chaotic at once," stalls and shops slammed shut, people dashed down the streets, and the price of sedan-chair transportation soared immediately. Even policemen disappeared from their stations. Later, people learned that the cause of this false alarm was a simple dispute between two sellers of rice straw, in which a drunkard was knocked down, then ran like mad, shouting "Fighting! Fighting!" That same day, a soldier discharging his gun caused a "gust of ground wind" in the area of the Yard of the Imperial City and all nearby streets, including Provincial Military Commander Street (Tidu jie), East Imperial Street (Dongyu jie), and West Imperial Street (Xiyu jie).[56] These reports underscore the insecurity and fear that had become part of everyday life.

During times of unrest, virtually anything could provoke feelings of distrust against society at large. City dwellers felt especially vulnerable to criminals—often outsiders—who roamed the streets. Reports of children being kidnapped by strangers abounded, and outsiders were considered the prime suspects. A report under the headline "Horrible News: A Child's Tongue Was Cut" in the *Citizens' Daily* proves this point. The article stated that a child was found half-naked and bleeding on East Office Street (Dongfu jie), and, when asked what had happened, he was unable to reply because he was missing half his tongue. The police sent him to the hospital and sought to identify the culprit. The next day, a follow-up story revealed that the boy's tongue was intact; in fact, the child suffered a mysterious ailment that caused him to accidentally bite his tongue during periods of "madness."[57] Another bizarre story also reflected the pervasive feelings of insecurity and horror:

Yesterday, a police officer spotted a man carrying an uncovered wooden coffin, containing the body of a little girl, past the front gate of the Bureau of Investigation (Tanfang ju). The officer immediately suspected the man of intending to bury the girl alive and began to follow him. On the corner of Upper Street (Shangsheng jie), the policeman got a closer look at the man's flustered face and heard a child crying "mommy" from the box, so he apprehended him and brought him back to the Bureau of Investigation. The man explained that as he was bringing the wooden coffin to town, an old friend asked him to take his ailing daughter to the hospital on Peaceful Bridge Street (Ping'an qiao). To do so as expeditiously as possible, he carried the girl in the coffin. The police immediately found her parents and confirmed that his story was true.[58]

In addition to being a good example of the era's widespread anxiety, this story also reveals some of Chengdu's cultural and social beliefs. The sight of a man carrying a coffin—which indicated "death"—on his back through the crowded streets inevitably piqued the curiosity of bystanders. Inhabitants worried about anything unusual in a city where people gathered from "all corners of the land," and even a minor incident could trigger panic. That this simple misunderstanding could cause such turmoil indicates the psychological difficulties that Chengdu residents experienced during this period of chaos.

Street Wars

Evidence has shown that the collapse of the Qing dynasty did not improve the lives of ordinary people but only resulted in more anxiety and misfortune. Indeed, a much worse catastrophe awaited Chengdu residents than the upheaval wrought by bullying soldiers and rampant bandits after 1911. When soldiers looted the city during the 1911 Revolution, a missionary philosophized that "revolutions do not happen every year, and there are better times ahead." He never expected that the nightmare had only just begun and that military struggles would escalate in Chengdu. During the National Protection War of the anti-Yuan Shikai campaign during 1915 and 1916, "Szechwan (Sichuan) became the principal battleground in the war against Yuan Shih-k'ai." When the battle spilled into the streets of Chengdu, frightened residents hid in their houses and shops stayed closed. Teahouses became a barometer of social order and political stability, and their opening or closing signaled to residents the relative level of safety. In his diary, Wu Yu wrote that he went out of his house only after he confirmed that "the teahouses have been opened." He even went to a teahouse with friends after hiding at home for many days while "the shops on all the streets were still closed."[59] This anecdote tells us that even during times of great danger, people sought opportunities to socialize at their favorite teahouses.

Victory in the anti-Yuan Shikai campaign did not bring peace to Chengdu but sowed the seeds of a bigger calamity. Chengdu residents suffered even greater disasters in 1917, when two wars broke out within the city, the first

between the Yunnan and Sichuan armies in May, and the second between
the Guizhou and Sichuan armies in July. The first war lasted over a week
and resulted in more than ten thousand deaths and injuries and the burning of several thousand civilian homes. The loss of property came to more
than ten million *yuan*. During the second war, the Guizhou Army set fire to
a large area around the South City Gate that was already lying in ruin.[60]
More than six thousand houses were reduced to ashes, and the loss of property totaled several million *yuan*. Chengdu lost two-thirds of its prosperous
areas, and refugees numbered more than ten thousand. The *Citizens' Daily*
claimed, "such an unheard-of calamity had not happened for several hundred years."[61]

The claim was true. This was the first time since the late-Ming Zhang
Xianzhong Rebellion that Chengdu streets had become battlefields. When
the Yunnan Army controlled the northeast part of Chengdu, according to
the *Citizen's Daily*, its troops took anyone affiliated with the police or the
Sichuan Army to the city wall and shot or stabbed them to death. Their
bodies were thrown into the moat outside the city wall; outside the Military City Gate (Wuchengmen) alone, charitable organizations buried more
than two hundred bodies. Beggars who tried to take clothes from the bodies discovered that some of the victims were still alive, but Yunnan soldiers
crushed them to death with rocks and threw the bodies into the river. Soldiers even used civilians as shields when they tried to capture an enemy position, resulting in the deaths of many innocents.[62]

During the war, residents endured constant horror. Soldiers guarded the
streets and brazenly took whatever they wanted; "ordinary people did not
dare resist." When the Sichuan Army tried to capture the Imperial City,
soldiers climbed onto the housetops for better aim. An appeal from forty-
eight families on East Imperial River Street alleged that the soldiers of the
Yunnan Army shot residents and then set fire to the houses with kerosene,
destroying them all. The soldiers of the Yunnan Army rushed into a teahouse on Central Mansion Street, which was full of merchants, in an effort
to capture forced laborers. The merchants escaped and tried to hide in
nearby shops, but twenty or thirty were captured. When the soldiers went
to the Center for Promoting Commerce and Industry for the same purpose,
the people had no place to hide and ran into a branch station of the police.
The forty or so policemen who were there escaped out the back door when
they saw the soldiers breaking in, but two were eventually captured.[63] We
can only imagine the horrors that awaited ordinary citizens when even the
police were unable to protect themselves.

During one battle with the Sichuan Army, the Guizhou Army ordered all
residents to open their doors, and they robbed the houses while shooting
at their enemies. Many residents moved to the countryside to escape the
ever-present dangers of life in Chengdu. Those who had nowhere else to go

pasted notices on their doors that said either "This house has been robbed and is empty" or "There is no money or clothing here after several robberies." When the southern region of the city was burned, refugees ran to other areas. They saw tragic scenes on the way: people trying to escort the old and young, carrying boxes, bags, and chickens, with some even leading pigs and cattle, some fleeing in horse carts, others in sedan chairs. Refugees were everywhere; when churches were deemed relatively safe, they served as refugee shelters. Temples also provided safe havens; the Duke Ding Temple (Dinggong ci) and the West Temple (Xilai si) alone accommodated between three and four thousand.[64]

The street wars of 1917 left very deep wounds for Chengdu residents, but they also imbued them with a sense of perseverance. Hard times also increased their dependence on each other and pushed them to unite in the face of common issues and common enemies; for these reasons, the traditional organizations were able to survive and still play a crucial role in the local communities and local politics. During this period, public space for ordinary people was dramatically decreased, and their very lives were frequently threatened. To ensure their safety, they tried to find a way to stabilize community life. Without economic power and social reputation this task was difficult to achieve, however, so their traditional leaders—local elites—took this responsibility.

Citizens' Self-Protection

Chinese urban communities always featured some sort of local security system, especially during times of social chaos. When Chengdu fell into disorder during the 1911 Revolution and early Republic, and the government was no longer able to maintain public security, residents organized for self-protection. This is documented first during the looting of 1911, when residents tried to stop soldiers from entering the four city gates and confronted those who carried booty out of town. To bypass this scrutiny, some soldiers pretended to be women riding in sedan chairs; some hired prostitutes as bogus wives; and some put their loot into coffins and pretended to hold funerals. Most loot was taken either by boat to the south or via sedan chair or horseback to the north. At this time, the "public harbor" of secret societies on each street played an important role in organizing local militia, raising funds from the residents, and assuring that someone from each household took his turn on night watch.[65]

In the early Republic, baojia, in which households simply watched over each other and reported suspicious activity, was still the basic local security system. When this method proved ineffective in the early Republic, residents of the same street organized into "neighborhood militias" (tuanfang) to which each family contributed money. The militias also took over some police responsibilities, such as searching for opium and weapons. As an unofficial force that was often involved in "official affairs," however, militias inevitably clashed with the police, with local authorities seeking to restrict neighborhood militias. When a crisis arose, local authorities appeared to support neighborhood militias, but then would attack them after the crisis subsided. For example, when the anti-Yuan Shikai war broke out in Yunnan in 1916, spread into Sichuan, and approached Chengdu, residents were encouraged to organize into militias, but they were disbanded immediately after the situation stabilized.[66]

During the street wars of 1917, residents largely depended on these unofficial organizations for their security. Indeed, they had few other alternatives when the police could offer only meager protection against bandits plundering the city. The heads of more than a hundred streets appealed to the city council for a permit to form neighborhood militias. Their activities were founded on the street, and they formed a united front with other streets in the neighborhood. The street head would collect money from each household to hire two night watchmen to guard each end of the street and be in charge of opening and closing the gates. If robbers approached, the guards would beat on a bamboo board to alert residents. The neighborhood militias also required all households to prepare sticks, each about four and a half feet long and over an inch in diameter, with iron heads, to be used for defense. Individual households were required to have four of these sticks, and those living in compounds, one per family. Large homes along the street were required to have two, and small homes, one. Households also were obligated to purchase sticks for those who could not afford them. As soon as an alarm was sounded, the residents were required to bring their sticks out into the street to resist the robbers, or else face punishment. The organization also required all households to prepare lanterns with the name of the street on them, for use when needed. At night, all households hung lanterns outside their doors. To prevent invaders, some street gates were closed, and paving stones were piled up to block passage. During the times of greatest danger, each street would also hire a dozen or so poor men as guards, with residents paying to treat any injuries that occurred.[67]

Organized night watch programs became a regular practice throughout Chengdu in the 1920s. These programs could cause dissatisfaction when they added to the burden of daily life or when the street heads abused their power. In the 1920s, Li Jieren wrote a short story about citizens' self-protection programs in Chengdu, in which he realistically described a night watch:

There are still some pedestrians at the moment just after dark, but until the second watch [11 o'clock at night] the only things that can be seen clearly are lights outside the doors and more than thirty night watchmen. They all sit silently outside the main gate of the God of Wealth Temple, accompanied by seven to eight large lanterns, on which is written "neighborhood militia of so-and-so street." There is a lamp on the table, on which is written "catching robbers." Seven or eight of these watchmen are older than fifty, and sent by the mansions; there are over a dozen apprentices who are older than sixteen and sent by shops. All these people work very hard during the day, and still have to get up at dawn even though they do night watch. The rest are seven to eight middle-aged men, usually artisans, who have no apprentices to be sent and have to do this duty by themselves.

. . .

One of them suddenly becomes angry, spitting and complaining, "Damn night watch! This is done simply to make us miserable! We make our living in the day, but have to stay awake all night. We cannot stand any more. Even if we were iron men, we could not do this for ten days or half a month."

His words arouse a lot of sympathetic responses. Everyone blames the street head for making people do this arduous task. "This is really outrageous: Tomorrow we are going to ask him why he makes us serve night watch on such a cold night while he is sleeping with his concubine! He said self-protection, but why does he not come out! We are just residents of this neighborhood, not his bodyguards!"[68]

The issue of the night watch thus reflected another distinction between the upper and lower classes. Li Jieren's critical attitude toward self-protection and street headmen and the inequality among citizens is evident from this account. Nevertheless, this story paints a vivid picture of how a typical neighborhood organized for protection.

Organization of night watches also demonstrated that neighborhoods could still respond to such social crises as wars, banditry, and other external threats. On the one hand, ordinary residents needed someone to organize self-protection, but on the other hand, such an activity caused a great inconvenience, which could worsen the relationship between local leaders and commoners. After the wars of 1917, bandits and soldiers remained a constant threat, and residents tried to establish a more reliable system of self-protection. As a result, in 1928, all leaders of local militias from all areas of Chengdu gathered to discuss standardizing community security and agreed to establish a "communal military power" (minzhong wuli).[69] Although there is no evidence to show that such a power was successfully established, the mere discussion of this issue demonstrated that community organizations were still functional. However, it was during 1928 that the municipal government of Chengdu was established, symbolizing the end of traditional organizations' domination over the community.

Public Politics and "Secret Politics"

Political turmoil directly or indirectly influenced the use of public space. During and immediately after the revolutionary movement, public life began to adopt a different face. The context of leisure in public places was often disrupted by political uncertainty and shifts in political power. As we have seen, the teahouse served as a microcosm of society, clearly reflecting the changes of the period, including political ones. At the eve of the 1911 Revolution, for instance, teahouse patrons, both the idle and the busy, were inevitably engaged in local politics. As Han Suyin wrote in her autobiography: "You know how our Chengdu is: an old, old city, trees, flowers, literature, old bookshops, a quiet city, proud of its age, its history. But . . . at the end of May 1911, it was uneasy, irritable, anxious, the teahouses in the public gardens and on the streets exuding unease. An anxious city, poised for rioting." According to Han's father, teahouses changed during the Railroad Protection Movement from places of quiet retreat to centers of political debate and related activities. The call "I buy tea" was now a virtual "clarion call for an immediate drift of diverse loiterers, small groups coalescing into larger ones, some even standing to listen as debates went on concerning the nationalization question and the railway loan; and silently they would drift apart again, then on to another teahouse, to hear another man expound."[70]

If teahouses were arenas for open discussion, they were also a resource for the local government to collect intelligence on antigovernment agitation. Local authorities often sent agents to eavesdrop in teahouses. "About the crowded teahouses went the spies of the Manchus. In the open-air spaces, under the trellised honeysuckle dripping fragrance and shade, between the harmony trees and the bamboo groves, agents of the dynasty loitered, sipping tea, listening to the talk of the scholars." During the early Republic, warlord and local governments used the same means to ferret out so-called destructive people. The government, to a large extent, thwarted the free flow of conversation in public places. One regulation, for example, required teahouse proprietors to secretly notify the police of patrons with non-Sichuan accents who discussed military affairs and "looked like a spy"; in return, they would receive ten *yuan* if the police apprehended the suspicious patron. Because the government often used the intelligence collected from teahouses against ordinary people, most teahouses took the precautionary step of displaying this public notice: "*Xiutan guoshi*" (Do not talk about national affairs). Then again, the government tried to bring its own politics into the teahouses by requiring such establishments to hang portraits of Sun Yat-sen and Chiang Kai-shek, as well as display the "Party Members' Principles of the Guomindang" (*Dangyuan shouze*) and the "Pledge of the Citizen" (*Guomin gongyue*). Urban reformers, however, denounced this requirement as "dictatorship."[71]

Entertainment in the teahouse was also increasingly politicized; public performances adopted a strong political orientation promoted by both elites and the government. In the past, for instance, traditional local operas had

mainly dealt with romance, the supernatural, or orthodox values such as filial piety, chastity, and loyalty, but this began to change with the introduction
of "political operas." In 1912, the Joy Teahouse performed the Sichuan
opera *A Story of the Blacks Recovering Their Rights* (Heiren guangfu ji),
based on the American novel *Uncle Tom's Cabin*. Advertisements in the local newspaper for this opera stated:

Our teahouse has been trying to reform local operas and promote social development. This is an age of racial competition and the survival of the fittest. Therefore,
we present the special *Story of the Blacks Recovering Their Rights*. . . . This play
tells a tragic story about the Blacks who lost their motherland and their honor and
tried to recover their rights. It is a moving and touching story, intended to inspire
our own racial thought and patriotic zeal.[72]

Obviously, the Chinese understanding of the famous American novel was
colored by their own political situation. The Chinese title was even changed
to reflect current social and political attitudes in China. Before the 1911
Revolution, *Uncle Tom's Cabin* had been translated into Chinese and sold
in Chengdu under the title *Heiren yutian lu*, literally "The Blacks Crying to
the Sky." It was also used by revolutionaries to campaign against Manchu
rule, and the performance of this opera was an emotional expression of the
Han people's ideology after the overthrow of the Manchu regime.

   Although traditional local operas still dominated the stage after the 1911
Revolution, their subjects changed from gods, ghosts, and love to revolutionary stories. Social reformers made a great effort to subvert the dominance of
traditional local operas. They were hostile toward the theater, believing that
theaters degraded morality. They accused theaters of "presenting their programs as educational in name, but in fact teaching licentiousness." They
also worried that the morality that "took a hundred years to form would
be destroyed within one day." Some schools even prohibited their students
from attending the theater to avoid "bad influences." New intellectuals organized the New Opera Evolution Society (Xinju jinhua she) to focus on
the reform of local operas. Its aim was no less than to "instruct people's
minds, change customs, evaluate society, help education, promote the idea
of a republic, and stabilize the nation." The Society planned to build a
moving stage in the Joy Teahouse and follow the European and American
style by using modern methods of stage setting. After *Uncle Tom's Cabin*,
other Western novels were transformed into local operas, most of which
had an obvious political orientation. One of them was *Passionate Hero*
(Duoqing yingxiong), a Polish love story that explored the interaction of
love and politics, patriotism and selfishness, and heroes and "ugly" politicians. A new theater called the Newly Reformed Theater (Gexin xin juyuan)
in the Tasty Teahouse performed plays that criticized society and old customs as well as inspired audiences to consider marriage reform.[73]

Modern dramas were also introduced. After Zeng Xiaogu, a pioneer of the "New Drama Movement" (*xinju yundong*), returned to Chengdu from Japan in the early Republic, he organized the Spring Willow Drama Society (Chunliu jushe) to challenge the traditional Three Celebrities Society (Sanqing hui). The Three Celebrities Society was the most influential local opera organization, attracting large audiences with its traditional programs. At the other end of the continuum, the Spring Willow Drama Society performed "dramas in the latest fashion" (*shizhuang xi*), which recounted heroic stories of the Republican revolution, reflecting a very strong political orientation.[74] During the New Cultural Movement, the "curtain drama" (*mubiao ju*), a so-called "new" or "civilized" drama (*wenming xi*), became popular. The performers of these new plays were students in various schools who were interested in portraying "antifeudalism." The Drama Society of Nineteen (Yijiu jushe), a professional modern drama organization, was established in the early 1920s. Besides revolutionary plays, it also performed Western dramas such as Shakespeare's *The Merchant of Venice*. In 1925, the Institute of Popular Education opened a theater in the Smaller City Park, where two troupes—the Society of Beautification (Meihua she) and the Society of Arts Studies (Yishu yanjiu she)—took turns performing modern dramas for free two or three nights a week. These dramas used Sichuan dialect, which was well received by the local people. Based on the success of these societies, the Association of Modern Drama (Juxie) was organized in 1926. Under its aegis, Chinese and some foreign modern dramas were performed, including Ibsen's *A Doll's House*. Notably, social reformers promoted a modern drama entitled *Forced Marriage* (Qiangzhi hunyin), which criticized the "vicious society" and explored "social worms," such as opium smokers, gamblers, hooligans, and prostitutes. They commended this play as a "civilized modern drama" (*wenming huaju*) and believed that it was "going along with world trends" and a "driving force for reform." At the same time, local authorities also promoted so-called "revolutionized entertainment" and built a new theater, a cinema, a music hall, and a dance hall and sponsored a play on the history of Sun Yat-sen's revolution.[75] Apparently, both social reformers and local authorities, who regarded performances as tools for education and political change as well as amusement, pushed forward the politicization of entertainment during the early Republican era.

Secret Politics. Whereas collective activities in streets were "public politics," the activities of the Sworn Brotherhood Society in teahouses might be called "secret politics." Sichuan was one of the most active areas of the Sworn Brotherhood Society (called "Paoge" in Sichuan, literally "Gowned Brothers"), whose power in Chengdu expanded dramatically in the late Qing and early Republic. It is estimated that in 1947, 70 percent of the men belonged.[76] The ongoing social unrest gave secret societies a great opportunity

to expand their power and influence. After the 1911 Revolution, they played
an increasing role in local politics. For a short period during the 1911 Revolution, secret societies were allowed to conduct their activities openly;
prior to that and subsequently, they were prohibited by both the Qing and
Republican governments. However, their power continued to expand, and
at the time the Chinese Communists took over China, their political influence had reached unprecedented highs. This section does not attempt to
fully examine the secret societies in Chengdu but mainly concentrates on
their clandestine activities in public places, especially in the teahouses, and
the resulting cultural phenomena.

In contrast to Shanghai's notorious Green Gang, Chengdu's Gowned
Brothers often played a positive role in the community. As Kristin Stapleton stated, "Whereas Du Yuesheng stood over the unruly Shanghai community, whip in hand, to stir up or suppress trouble as it served his purposes to do so, Gelaohui organizations permeated communities throughout
western China, forming a common ground from which to resist reformist
pressure from political activists perceived as outsiders."[77] During the late-
Qing and early Republican eras, both central and local governments banned
the Gowned Brothers, but in the Chengdu area and especially in some
nearby small market towns, the Gowned Brothers controlled local society,
managing teahouses, wine shops, and inns as their "harbors" or headquarters. These places became the unofficial power centers of many communities, and behind closed doors members also oversaw illegal businesses such
as drug trafficking, gambling, and prostitution. There were two kinds of
Gowned Brothers: "professional" and "semiprofessional." "Professional" members depended on gifts or donations from recruiting efforts, ceremonies, birth-
days, weddings, and funerals. Some professionals also demanded broker
fees on transactions involving the sale or purchase of land, shops, and other
businesses, while others managed gambling or opium dens. "Semiprofessional" Gowned Brothers were free to choose any occupation but barbering,
and were usually partners in the ownership and management of theaters
and restaurants in order to help control local hoodlums and soldiers who refused to pay.[78] Leaders of the Gowned Brothers usually regarded certain
streets as their own turfs. They established their headquarters in teahouses
or other places and took responsibility for maintaining public peace, resolv-
ing conflicts, and protecting the area's economic interests.[79]

Although local authorities banned the organization, its activities were
common on the streets and in other public places such as teahouses, opium
dens, restaurants, and theaters. In the late Qing, police regulations identified the Gowned Brothers as "groups of people who look rough," "wear
strange clothes," or "gather in a suspicious way." Under long-term pressure from the Qing government, the Gowned Brothers developed a unique

activist style that enabled them to survive and even expand. For instance, they created their own argot, which Fu Chongju's *Investigation of Chengdu* (Chengdu tonglan) discussed under the subtitle "The Paoge Languages of Chengdu." Most of the Gowned Brothers' activities occurred underground, but for a short period—just after the 1911 Revolution broke out—their activities were made public. "Public harbors" were set up on almost every street, with members coming and going with guns and swords. Many householders posted a red label on their doors, on which was written the name of the "public harbor" to which it belonged. In 1914, however, the central government set out to disband the Gowned Brothers, because it believed it to be the root of social disorder. The police ordered all teahouses, restaurants, wine shops, and inns to sign an agreement prohibiting any activities of the Gowned Brothers in their establishments.[80]

The government never successfully extinguished the Gowned Brothers; indeed, their power actually increased during the Republican period. Most Gowned Brothers were headquartered in teahouses, some of which were dedicated exclusively to their activities. A sign or a lantern with "so and so society" (*she*) or "so and so 'public harbor'" (*gongkou*) was hung outside a teahouse, to indicate that it was the headquarters of a branch of the Gowned Brothers. The income of the teahouses supported the Gowned Brothers' activities. Because the organization was so influential and powerful, it attracted all sorts of people, from coolies to senior officials and even military officers and policemen. According to an investigation undertaken by the Chengdu Police Station, there were 130 branches of the Gowned Brothers in Chengdu before 1949. Of these, the addresses of 119 headquarters were identified, and 36 of these were in teahouses. All others were only marked as being located on "so and so street," and it is likely that many of these also had their headquarters in teahouses. Even if some teahouses were not public harbors, their proprietors usually joined the organization for protection. Teahouses were often forced to contribute money or provide free tea and boiled water to people who were powerful locally, but the teahouses opened or protected by the Gowned Brothers, warlords, and others were not harassed.[81]

Teahouses became the best places for communication within and between members of different branches of the Gowned Brothers. For the sake of unity, all members participated in celebrations during traditional events or the organization's special events, such as the "Ghost Festival" (*zhongyuan hui*), the "Reunion Festival" (*tuanyuan hui*), and the "Guandi Festival" (*Guandi hui*). Besides these occasions, the members of each branch would meet every three days at the teahouse to discuss business matters. The tea at these meetings was paid for by the branch, so the meetings were always well attended and were nicknamed "tea duty" (*chashao*). The sight of people acting mysteriously in Chengdu teahouses, usually because they were conducting Gowned Brothers business, became common. If a member of the Gowned Brothers wanted to meet his counterparts in a different area, he usually sought them out at a teahouse. After entering, he would sit on the right side of an empty table. When provided a cup of tea, he would not drink it, but leave the lid on the saucer and sit quietly to signal that he was looking for fellow members. Waiters understood this signal immediately and might casually inquire: "From far away?" The newcomer would reply with his name and his harbor's name. The teahouse keeper, "who is familiar with this ceremony," would report immediately to the controller of the local branch, who would appear and ask "a series of questions to the refugee, who must reply in appropriate, extremely technical terms."[82]

A common means by which members of the Gowned Brothers contacted other members was to play "teacup formations" (*chawan zhen*), which was an alternative to their secret language. When a head of the Gowned Brothers came out to meet an outsider, he would put his teacup directly opposite to that of the outsider; this was called the "benevolent formation" (*renyi zhen*) or the "two dragon formation" (*shuanglong zhen*). There was even a poem about this formation: "It is the cause of so much happiness that two dragons play in the water, like Han Xin visiting Zhang Liang; brothers meet here today, drinking tea before discussing matters."[83] If a member went to another "public harbor" to ask for help, he would set up the "single whip formation" (*danbian zhen*): a teacup facing the mouth of a small teapot. If the host agreed to offer help, he would drink the cup of tea; if not, he would spill the tea on the ground. A small teapot facing three cups of tea arranged in a line was called "challenging tea" (*zhengdou cha*) and was an invitation to compete. If the opponent accepted the challenge, he would drink all three cups; if he refused, he would only drink the middle one.[84] All of these secret protocols reflected a unique political culture that developed in a special niche of society. The casual observer would feel that he was watching a unique performance when two Gowned Brothers performed such a ritual, which became part of teahouse culture. These mysterious actions separated members from other people and piqued ordinary people's curiosity. Furthermore, their puzzling behavior was a means of survival as well as a challenge of local power.

The development of secret societies depended on two important factors: their own ability to succeed and the social and political environment that enabled their success. During their long struggle with the government, members of secret societies created all kinds of techniques to deal with official suppression. They had a great ability to adapt to and develop within the harsh social and political environment, even using it to attract members. When ordinary people felt helpless, secret societies offered some protection and comfort. Because such a function challenged official power, local government tried to control secret societies, even though efforts to do this accomplished little.

Popular Protests

With the increasing politicization of everyday life, the incidence of popular protest on the street—a "collective action directed by elements of the general population against political or economic power-holders"—also increased and became more prominent through the use of placards, public lectures, and political demonstrations. In premodern Chengdu, anonymous placards on the street had been common, posted by people who felt misjudged or mistreated, and primarily in regard to personal matters. This traditional means of protest was adopted by social organizations to express their opinions in the early twentieth century. A critic of this phenomenon said, "for whatever matter, they would put up their posters throughout the city." Some posters were no longer anonymous but carried names such as "all people in the so and so circle," an effort that was criticized as "bleat and bluster." In addition, public lectures given by various social organizations became popular, leading to the establishment of professional societies such as the Society of Public Lecture in Sichuan (Sichuan yanjiang zonghui) and the Public Lecture Society for Women's Education (Nüzi jiaoyu yanjiang hui), whose meetings often attracted a few hundred participants (see Figure 7.1).[85] Public lectures became a symbol of political mobilization and became very powerful in influencing the masses. In this process, elites could successfully impose their political ideas on commoners.

During and after the 1911 Revolution, every aspect of one's appearance, including clothing and hairstyle, was considered fodder for revolutionary practice. Any "revolution," however, is received differently by different people, and any change could meet resistance, even those that were considered "sweeping the dirty customs away," such as new fashions in clothes and cutting queues. When some radical elites suggested abandoning the old style of clothing, many were opposed, saying that it was an attempt to follow the "foreign style" rather than Han tradition. As a compromise, the government issued a public notice allowing people to decide for themselves. They could continue wearing their current clothing, except for official Qing caps and uniforms. At this time, cutting the queue became a sign of revolution. The queue was a symbol of the Manchu's domination of the Han people, and therefore, after the Qing collapsed, the new government ordered everyone to have his queue cut. In fact, this order sometimes met resistance and could become a source of conflict. A countryman, dubbed "a rural fool" by a newspaper, was ordered by a policeman to have his queue cut on the street. He refused, and then when the policeman forcibly cut his hair, he became so angry that he knocked the officer to the ground. The fight drew many observers. Nevertheless, during this period various styles could be seen: some men cut their queues; some kept them; some wore the ancient style; some wrapped their hair in cloth; some wore sunshade caps; some wore foreign-style caps. The "hero tie" of soldiers, mentioned above, was also a product of the era. However, the queue generally was the object of criticism. Labeled "A drawing to wake up society" (*jing-shi hua*), a drawing in the early Republican *Popular Pictorial* (Tongsu huabao) illustrated how the hairstyle could bring trouble(see Figure 7.5). Radical political movements like both the French Revolution and the 1911 Revolution in China brought about changes in fashion, in which "certain aspects of personal decoration might signal adherence or antipathy to the Revolution."[86]

Teahouse "free" talk gives us rare insight into commoners' thoughts and feelings about society, although historians of China have so far neglected this source. In teahouses, conversations would flow freely. One conversation between two men in a teahouse, reported in a newspaper, was typical. One man complained: "In these days there are so many 'new things'—new society, new fashion, new ideologies, new vocabulary; we don't want to follow the new trends, but we don't have an 'old' one to keep." The other laughed and responded sarcastically: "I don't believe people who wildly boast about the new things; they can only lure naïve, inexperienced youngsters. . . . Haven't you heard enough empty promises? Have you enjoyed any happiness since 1911?"[87] Although the report did not reveal the men's identities or social status, it is clear that they were dissatisfied with their situation and used this conversation to vent their resentment. The report also confirms that it was an age of transition, when the "old" had been destroyed and the "new" was filling the void. These men did not like new things, but their resistance was provoked by promises that had been broken repeatedly. That the promised "bright future" never arrived made them turn their anger to everything under the "new" banner of the elite reformers, revolutionaries, and the government. Complaints about social realities also appeared in folk literature of the era. The story of the man who pretended to be wealthy and whose cat stole his piece of meat, told in Chapter 3, is a good example, underscoring that expressing complaints and resentments was a routine part of teahouse life.

Because "the promise of the Chinese Revolution of 1911 had never been fulfilled," some commoners became social critics or political dissidents. Liu Shiliang, keeper of a small bathhouse, was one example. His initial concern for the poor turned into an effort to reveal the darker sides of all Chengdu society and culminated in a challenge to the power of local authorities. His weapon of choice was folk literature: he expressed his criticism through many bamboo-branch poems, folk songs, and matched couplets. For example, Liu used the practice of binding women's feet as a metaphor to criticize the new political system: "Nowadays, large shoes are commonly worn, but why, if one's feet are already bound? It's just like the form of our nation these days: a dictatorship inside, with a Republic around." Another of Liu's folk poems expressed similar animosity for the so-called Republic: "Everybody says the Republic will bring people happiness, but in fact we have more sorrow; the people are suffering wars and repeated famines, and commoners have no way out of their distress."[88] Other commoners railed

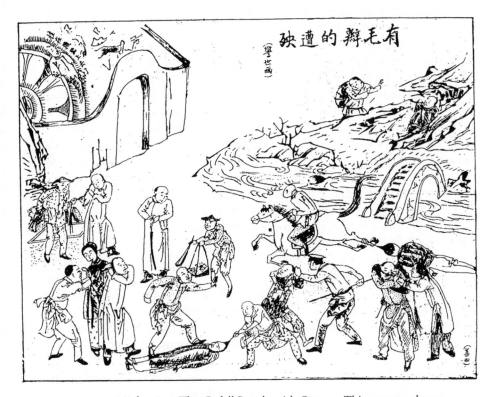

FIGURE 7.5. Misfortunes That Befall People with Queues. This cartoon shows how having a queue can lead to trouble. Somebody can easily seize a man's queue during a dispute, we see, no matter whether it was between a man and a woman, a policeman and a civilian, or a peasant and a city dweller. At top left, one man's queue gets caught in a machine, and on the right, another man's queue has been tied to the leg of a horse, forcing him to be dragged along the ground. From TSHB 1912, no. 41.

against not only the political system of the warlord era but also the abuse of power by some community leaders. Although the street headman became an elected position after the Qing collapsed, some tried to manipulate the elections in favor of their preferred candidate, "in the name of the public"; some candidates were even local toughs.[89] Therefore, conflict inevitably arose between ordinary residents and street heads, as we saw above in the discussion of the night watch program.

Direct confrontations over the use of urban space also took place between residents and the local government. For example, commoners strongly opposed the construction of Warm Spring Road (Chunxi lu) in the 1920s, because it required the dismantling of many residential houses and shops. The area from Central Mansion Street to Horse Riding Street had been the Yamen of the Surveillance Commissioner, which was abandoned after the overthrow of the Qing (see Map 4). Many poor families had moved to the area, building shelters and opening small shops, and gradually transformed it into a small alley. In 1924, the warlord governor Yang Sen undertook the project of building Warm Spring Road to open the route to traffic and commerce. Yang forced residents in the area to move and sent his army to destroy their sheds, houses, and shops, making them understandably anxious. Simultaneously, other street construction was begun that resulted in the demolition of other shops and teahouses. Keepers of small teahouses appealed to the guild for help, and all teahouses went on strike to resist the project. Because of the disruption caused by the construction, the celebration of the Chinese New Year that was sponsored by the Chamber of Commerce every year had to be canceled. To protest the project, after the road was completed Liu Shiliang wrote a matched couplet: "The new road has been built; when will the governor go away? Since all residents' houses have been dismantled, we wish that the general would leave here as soon as possible."[90] This couplet was posted secretly in Salt Market Corner (Yanshi kou), the city's most prosperous area, and in two days word had spread throughout the city. The couplet provided an outlet for the commoners' anger. People predicted that Yang would not be able to stay in Chengdu.[91] This is probably another example of how street culture was transformed into street politics. Unlike during the 1911 Revolution, when such a transformation was led by local elites, now commoners played a positive role in street culture, perhaps indicating their deeper involvement in local politics.

In political movements, however, students were still the most prominent force. Whenever national or local politics reached a turning point—such as over the issue of the Shandong peninsula in 1919, or Sichuan's demands for self-government in 1920, or China's participation in the Washington Conference in 1921—students would take their protests to the street in an effort to "wake up our countrymen." Anniversaries of major political incidents always brought many propaganda troupes delivering lectures. During the 1920s, although antiforeign movements no longer provoked large-scale mass violence, isolated incidents were frequent. In one case, after a demonstration against Japan, more than two hundred people, called "a mob" by the Japanese, destroyed property in the Japanese consulate.[92] Students' reactions to national and international politics reflected the close tie between Chengdu and the world beyond. Although students' activities might have had an impact on the lives of commoners, there is little evidence to indicate that the two forces united, as they had during the Railroad Protection Movement.

Whereas students tended to focus mainly on national issues, commoners began to unite to fight for their own economic interests. In 1909, the textile workers of Chengdu, organized by the Three Emperors Society (San-huang hui), and the textile workers' guild went on strike for higher wages. They received support from the God of Wealth Society (Caishen hui) and the Society of One Hundred Deities (Baishen hui), but local authorities quickly moved to ban the strike. When striking workers wandered about and shouted slogans on the streets, the police accused them of disturbing the peace and threatened punishment. Similarly, teahouse keepers also organized through their guild to protect their interests. Customarily, local charitable organizations depended on the teahouse-theater tax; under the rule made by the police, one day's income each month went to these organizations. In 1917, theaters collectively refused to pay the tax, saying that charitable donations should be voluntary. After the police forcibly collected a new tea tax and beat and arrested teahouse keepers and workers in 1928, the teahouse guild organized a strike to demand a tax cut. The guild also represented its members in negotiations with the police and appealed for public support. Teahouses increasingly became the sites of social, economic, and political struggle, so much so that some people described them as "battlefields."[93] An essay in *Current Affairs Weekly* (Shishi zhoubao) titled "Chengdu in May" listed numerous protests in Chengdu in that month alone. First, book merchants opposed to a new mail tax struck with the support of various occupations. Then, all shops went on strike against a new shipping tax and demanded that the government release the imprisoned president of the Chamber of Commerce. Finally, many workers demonstrated for higher wages. The author dubbed May 1928 "a revolutionary May" and said, "workers of Chengdu obviously have their own consciousness." In the 1920s, laborers also began to establish their own organizations. These included the Autonomous Labor Association in the Area of South City Gate (Nanmen laodong zizhi hui), the Association of Mutual Aid for Printing Workers (Yinshua jie laodong huzhu tuan), and the Association for Ten Patriotic Laborers (Laodong jie aiguo shiren tuan). The presence of these new organizations underscored that fact that Chengdu workers had begun to develop a class consciousness, which David Strand has termed the "sprouts of unionism."[94]

Of course, until the late 1920s, the popular protests in Chengdu were relatively small in scale, unlike those in political or economic centers such as Beijing and Shanghai. However, there is no question that in the early Republic individuals in Chengdu were gradually coming together to take collective action, forever changing not only street life but also urban political culture in general. Increasingly, groups with a political agenda wrested control of the street from ordinary commoners. As a result, street culture lost some of its old elements while gaining some new elements. Although mass movements no longer assumed the large scale of the Railroad Protection Movement, the proliferation of street political activities was a constant reminder of the resentment that ordinary people felt toward the new political system and social reality.

8 Conclusion

During the period from 1870 to 1930, Chengdu, like other Chinese cities, experienced a dramatic alteration through reform, revolution, and the tyrannical rule of warlords. In this transformation, public space was restructured, Chengdu came under systematic urban management, conflicts between citizens and state power increased, the relationship between commoners and local elites was redefined, and popular culture and elite culture began to interact more closely. After all these changes, the street, street life, and street culture were never the same.

Although there was no large-scale demolition of public space during the late-Qing reform, some old sites were transformed for new public use and some new public places were built. After the 1911 Revolution, however, tremendous physical change took place, because of the destruction of the wars, on the one hand, and the implementation of radical ideas in urban planning, on the other. Because the wars had destroyed a considerable portion of the city, the construction of homes, streets, temples, and government offices brought the city a new appearance. Implementing their new ideas, local authorities and inhabitants deliberately tore down the ancient city wall and opened more city gates to improve traffic flow; gradually, Chengdu's most visible structure disappeared in front of the very eyes of its residents.

In this study, we have seen the transformation of urban management. Prior to the early twentieth century, state power had scarcely affected everyday life, because of the absence of a municipal administration. Public space in traditional Chengdu had been relatively "free," with considerable popular autonomy regarding its use. The basic unit of control, the street or neighborhood, took responsibility for its own affairs, with little government involvement. These voluntary associations played an important role in organizing residents' public life. Although in Chengdu there were three levels of official administration—for the province, the prefecture, and two counties—each had large populations scattered across vast territory to manage, and none really focused on the city. The state did seek to manipulate ordinary people through celebrations and other ritual ceremonies, but its power was very weak by the time it reached this local level. In the late Qing, however, the police force, as a representative of state power in the city, increased its involvement in everyday life. Street culture and common-ers' public life underwent significant transformation, which touched every-thing from the people's public role to the relationship between ordinary people, local elites, and the state. Street life was no longer freely conducted but was increasingly regulated by an unprecedented variety of policies and procedures. Thus, the state had begun to extend its power into the com-munity; in the early Republic until 1928, when the municipal government was established, Chengdu was largely controlled by military power, which filled the power vacuum left when the imperialist system collapsed.

This study has examined the importance of public life in one isolated city—Chengdu, where inhabitants shared a common identity as "Chengdu people." The evidence presented demonstrated Chengdu's strong commu-nity consciousness, in Richard Sennett's words: "the 'sense of community,' of a society with a strong public life, is born from this union of shared ac-tion and a shared sense of collective self." In Chengdu, such a sense of col-lective self was clearly displayed in a variety of organized community ac-tivities. Based on this solid foundation, the residents of Chengdu were able to develop a "collective identity," as William Rowe found it in his study of Hankou: "a style of community self-management" and "the strength of ur-ban community ties," which "was actually growing over the course of the early modern period." Max Weber, in his analysis of Chinese community, held that Chinese cities lacked a well-developed urban community, a view that has dominated scholarship about Chinese urban society.[1] Rowe, how-ever, has proven that such a community existed in China. Because of Han-kou's special role as a commercial center, the city can hardly be viewed as representative of Chinese cities. The present study of Chengdu, which was more important administratively and less important commercially than Hankou, supports Rowe's criticism of Weber.

Even though Chengdu people shared a common cultural tradition, daily life there inevitably brought forth conflicts, as it does elsewhere. Examining the competition for the use of the street in Chengdu highlights the compli-cated relationships among the elites, the common people, and local author-ities. Past scholars of Chinese urban history have stressed conflicts between elites and commoners and between the state and commoners, but little has been done to date regarding conflicts among commoners themselves. This study has found that although commoners had close ties in community life, they also struggled for public space, the opportunity to make a living, and other economic interests. In commoners' struggles for the streets, two pat-terns of behavior were revealed. First, there were issues of exclusion be-tween social groups. Natives wanted to maintain their privileges regarding the use of public space, while newcomers tried to carve out their own niche for survival. Second, most disputes could be resolved in the street or neighborhood through mediation, either by neighbors who volunteered their services or by their designated street heads.

In this study, I have stressed the complicated relationship between urban commoners and local elites, which progressed through four stages between 1870 and 1930 and reflected changes in both local politics and street culture. In the first stage—that is, the pattern of traditional urban society—elites dominated the organizations of the streets and neighborhoods and played leadership roles in local community life. In general, the relationship was one of mutual dependence; elites needed commoners' support to establish their leadership, and commoners needed the authority of the elites to organize community life. This relationship became the foundation for the city's autonomy, as discussed in Part I.

The second stage began with the New Policies, when the elites used the power bestowed by the state to implement urban reforms that mainly targeted the poor. Commoners responded in various ways, depending on their own economic interests. Indeed, as major occupants of public space, they benefited from new theaters, shopping centers, and parks. However, as public space was increasingly restricted by local authorities, who were supported by social reformers, commoners found it increasingly difficult to earn a living and engage in recreational activities, and they struggled to regain control of the street. Furthermore, women's freedom in public was granted not by elites or local authorities but by women who challenged tradition, and by social developments resulting in part from the increasing influence of Western culture. All of these struggles reflected the political transformation in the early twentieth century and changes in the relationships between elites, commoners, and public space. In the process of social transformation, street culture was not only the basis for commoners' shared identity but also a weapon through which they simultaneously resisted the invasion of elite culture and adapted to its new social, economic, and political structures. Although common people suffered more restrictions, there was no evidence to show that they withdrew or attempted to withdraw from public space. Instead, they challenged the regulations and struggled for continued use of public space. In early modern Western cities, as Richard Sennett observed, people gradually sought to "flee" the public arena in search of more meaningful experience "in the private realms of life, especially in the family," resulting in a "profound dislocation which capitalism and secular belief produced."[2] Contrary to what Sennett described, public life in Chengdu went in the opposite direction: people sought to escape the dreariness of family life and joined in shared common activities even as the public space allotted to them shrank. This is indicated by the importance these residents attached to the constant pursuit of public life.

The third stage was short, but it was a significant turning point for the public roles of both commoners and elites during the 1911 Revolution. Whereas commoners had been targeted by the joint force of elites and the state during the New Policies in the late Qing, they united with local elites against the state when the state jeopardized their common interest. Urban elites were involved more directly in popular culture than ever before, striving to create a new city image and to lead public opinion while gradually drawing commoners into the orbit of local politics. In their attempt to "enlighten" and mobilize commoners against the state, elites transformed street culture into street politics, providing the basis for commoners' unprecedented participation in political movements. In this process, both commoners and reformers redefined their public roles. For centuries, commoners had had no voice in municipal politics, although they comprised the majority of Chengdu residents. To elites, the dynamics of social "progress" in the late Qing and early Republic had always involved the "gentry," "merchants," and "students," but not the anonymous "masses." Although commoners often used their public behavior to express dissatisfaction, they seldom had a chance to speak as a cohort. Nevertheless, commoners on the street did not always act passively—reformed, regulated, and policed as they were by the elite and state power. They struggled against the elites and other authorities for their survival and livelihood; the challenges that women and the poor posed to the use of public space provide a good example. The revolutionary movement brought about an important change in the use of the street; for the first time, commoners used the streets for organized political protest as well as for commerce and leisure activities. Commoners, it turned out, were not so easily controlled once they were "enlightened," mobilized, and marched into the political arena.

The fourth stage in their relationship was the early Republican era, when the social and political situation changed dramatically. During this period, elites' influence on commoners declined; military force and state power directly reached through the community to the common people. However, although elites were no longer strong leaders of the local community, common people still needed their leadership when social crises emerged and the state was unable to protect them. Commoners also had to rely on the financial support and social leadership of the elite for ensuring their livelihood, especially during times of economic and political instability. Elites tried to maintain social stability and to ensure normal urban life and undertook some measures for self-protection. Social reformers were at odds with state power on the issue of the reform of popular culture, especially when the state conducted radical measures. They better understood local popular culture and had a different attitude toward the radical changes. During the early Republic in particular, urban elites reacted against the state's efforts to extinguish street culture rather than "reform" it. The elites emphasized their urban society's special features and disagreed with the government's plans. Whereas the government imposed ever-stricter controls and increasingly radical "reforms" on street culture, the elites, despite their criticisms of various ills of popular culture and their support of reforms, generally preferred to work within the existing system. Why they adopted such an attitude is not difficult to understand: public life permeated their own existence, and they understood the virtues of public space as well as its vices. Thus, the main reason that radical government controls failed was probably that they lacked wholesale support among local reformers. That is also why street culture was so persistent. Early in the Republic, in contrast to their enthusiasm for social reform in late Qing, Chengdu elites were no longer uncritical proponents of reform, especially the more radical ideas. This phenomenon reflected the intense relationship between local elites and state power.

From this study, we have seen both the changes and the continuities in Chengdu's street culture, which interacted with elite culture throughout the early twentieth century. Studies of the relationship between popular culture and state power have taken two opposite approaches: one emphasizes cooperation, and the other, opposition. Perry Link and other scholars have pointed out that "ideas and values expressed in words include official ideals, but also extend far beyond them," whereas Helen Siu has declared that within community and domestic rituals, "local society actively cultivated a symbiotic relationship with the state culture rather than opposed it."[3] Despite their different emphases, these studies note that the dominant class was sufficiently flexible to allow those outside it to develop their own culture. This study has shown that in Chengdu officials did not generally oppose commoners' activities on the street, instead often joining in them. At the same time, state power was strong and resilient enough to promote a national culture, as reflected in studies by James Watson on Tianhou, David Johnson on temple festivals, and Prasenjit Duara on Guandi. The state could influence popular culture in various ways, such as through promotion, as with the cult of Tianhou, or through direct participation, as with temple festivals in Shanxi, or simply by attempting to destroy it, as with Guandi in North China.[4] This study has examined all forms of influence by revealing how social reformers, under the auspices of the state, reformed and refined street culture, how state power suppressed and attacked street culture, and how street culture resisted the various assaults. Although each of these ways—promotion, participation, and demolition—could be seen during the reformist and revolutionary periods (such as initiating local opera reform, reorganizing the Flower Fair, and attacking popular religion), the use of official capacity to destroy popular culture, especially popular religion, dominated. How to evaluate and deal with the popular culture were constant priorities for the government and local authorities. No regime, it seems, from the Qing on, was able to work out a successful accommodation.

In Chengdu, the role of the state was often expressed through social reformers; as I have discussed, some reformers held positions of authority in the police department and local government. During the era of social and cultural transformation, the state sought to promote elite culture and constrain popular culture. Street life in late-Qing and early Republican Chengdu revealed constant friction between popular culture and elite culture. In their "civilizing" mission, social reformers of the elite class targeted the lower classes and their customs. During the process of transformation, some features of street culture were lost, while some new ones emerged. Some religious rituals (such as praying for rain), popular entertainment (such as puppet shows), and occupations (such as water carriers) gradually disappeared. At the same time, street culture began to have some new features: fairs promoting industry, shopping centers, theaters, electricity, streetlights, running water, motor vehicles, and so forth. As quickly became apparent, commoners did not always benefit from such reforms. Some new projects and policies seemed to improve commoners' material and cultural life, but did not always have the intended results. Furthermore, commoners did not readily accept the changes and fought to maintain what they considered the most pleasant aspects of their previous lifestyle. Even when they accepted change, they still clung to their cherished customs, which in a very real sense comprised their only legacy for future generations. Although street culture was no longer the same, many of its traditional features survived. People still used streets as spaces for commerce, everyday life, and amusement, even though these activities were regulated. And teahouses were still the most popular leisure space for commoners despite constant measures of reform, control, and outright assault by the government.

Political transformation did not bring advantages to ordinary people, but rather more disasters. The new Republic had been envisioned as a coming "era of law," characterized by "civilized appearance" and "peace and high morality," but these enthusiastic revolutionary dreams failed to be realized. When many aspects of society turned out contrary to people's expectations, many began to question the current political system and society. People often nostalgically compared the situation before the Revolution with that afterward, complaining that afterward "the good might be changed and the new might be abandoned." For most urban commoners, the nature of ideology and political systems was not important; they simply longed for a return to relative peace and stability. As someone remarked, "During the autocratic era, which was criticized as a 'barbarous age' by 'civilized' elites, ordinary people could walk out of the door safely after nightfall and could have a good night's sleep. After the autocracy was overthrown by the 1911 Revolution . . . no one could not fall asleep at night because of constant threats." And elites, too, were dissatisfied with the social situation and felt that the moral degeneration of the society was increasing day by day.[5]

Chengdu people began to examine the "disasters of the revolutions" (*geming zhihuo*) after they endured the 1911 Revolution, the Second Revolution (1913), the Anti–Yuan Shikai Campaign (1916), and the street wars (1917). Clearly, most were weary of the constant disruptions and terror they brought. Indeed, people lived so long in an era of unrest that they lost any sense of social stability.[6] The established order of society was replaced by the uncertainty of never-ending "revolutions," in which changes in the local power structure were almost routine. Commoners' everyday lives and means of livelihood had never been so tightly linked with local politics. For commoners, the transformation of public space was merely a means for local elites and authorities to grab a larger share of the power and profit. Dramatic political changes in the city brought more misery and unrest than benefit to the lower classes, regardless of which side they stood on.

In the past, we knew little about how political movements affected ordinary people's everyday lives, but this study explores alterations that occurred at both the catastrophic and the microscopic level, resulting from sometimes invisible factors. Historically, Chengdu had been a relatively isolated but peaceful city, where ordinary citizens had access to a greater shared public space and thus enjoyed greater freedom to pursue work and amusements. The social transformation expanded the political arena tremendously while decreasing the commoners' space for everyday use. The "modernized" city brought better roads, newer facilities, and more fashionable amusements, but only at the staggering price of the sacrifice of centuries of traditional lifestyle. Furthermore, the reconstruction of urban space and street life too often neither served the commoners' real needs nor allowed them access to its benefits. Ultimately, most Chengdu residents gained few benefits from the political and social transformation, but they were able to continue their public life and street culture, although both were permanently altered.

REFERENCE MATTER

Character List

Well-known names and terms, such as Shanghai, Hankou, and Gelaohui, are omitted.

Ancha si (street)	按察司(街)
Anlesi chashe	安樂寺茶社
Anshun qiao	安順橋
ba	壩
Ba Jin	巴金
baba xi	壩壩戲
baiguo deng	白果燈
Baihua tan	百花潭
baihua yanyi	白話演義
Baihua zhuang	百花莊
Bailaohui (teahouse)	百老匯 (茶館)
Baima si	白馬寺
Baishen hui	百神會
Baita si	白塔寺
baitai	拜台
baixiang	拜香
Banbian jie	半邊街
bandeng xi	板凳戲
bangbang hui	棒棒會
bangbang xi	棒棒戲
Banji tang	半濟堂
Baofeng yuqian	暴風雨前
Baojia ju	保甲局
Baojia xiang	包家巷
baojie	報界
Baolu tongzhi hui	保路同志會
Baolu tongzhi jun	保路同志軍
baoshi	寶市
baozheng	保正
basheng shoushi	八省首事
Bei dajin jie	北打金街

Bei jiaochang	北較場
Bei shuwa jie	北暑襪街
Beicheng gongyuan	北城公園
beidan xi	被單戲
Beimen dajie	北門大街
benjie shouren	本街首人
bi	婢
bian huofo	變活佛
biaozi	婊子
Boji jie	簸箕街
buzheng bushi	不正不實
Buzheng si (street)	布政司 (街)
Buzheng ya (street)	布政衙 (街)
caishen	財神
Caishen hui	財神會
canshi	蠶市
cezi	測字
cha boshi	茶博士
chachuan	茶船
Chadianzi	茶店子
chafang jiushi	茶房酒肆
chaguan	茶館
chaguan jiangli	茶館講理
chaguo	茶國
chahu shi	茶壺式
Chaiquan jie	苣泉街
chake	茶客
chalou	茶樓
chang duitaixi	唱對台戲
Changle (troupe)	長樂 (戲班)
Chaokou	吵口
chapu	茶鋪
chashao	茶哨
chashe	茶社
chashi	茶肆
chashi	茶室
chating	茶廳
chating	茶亭
chawan	茶碗
chawan zhen	茶碗陣

chaye gonghui	茶業公會
chayuan	茶園
Chehuang ba	扯謊壩
Chen Bixiu	陳碧秀
Chen Xiaogui	陳小鬼
Chengdu	成都
Chengdu chaye tongye gonghui	成都茶業同業公會
Chengdu daoyou	成都導游
Chengdu gushi	成都故事
Chengdu minjian wenxue jicheng	成都民間文學集成
Chengdu tonglan	成都通覽
Chengdu xinwen	成都新聞
Chengdu zong shanghui	成都總商會
Chengfang siling bu	城防司令部
Chenghuang chujia	城隍出駕
Chenghuang hui	城隍會
Chenghuang miao	城隍廟
Chenghuang pa	城隍壩
Chengshou jie	城守街
Chengshou yamen	城守衙門
Chengshou ying	城守營
chi jiangcha	吃講茶
Chi jiuhuangzhai	吃九皇齋
chi lanqian	吃爛錢
chonghuang xi	蟲蝗戲
Chongqing duli	重慶獨立
Chongxiu Chengdu xianzhi	重修成都縣志
Chuanbei luogu	川北鑼鼓
Chuansheng xuewu gongsuo	川省學務公所
chugong	粗工
Chunhua jie	純化街
Chunliu jushe	春柳劇社
Chunqi huayuan	純溪花園
chuntai	春台
chuntai xi	春台戲
chunxi	春戲
Chunxi lu	春熙路
Cihui tang	慈惠堂
cishan yuan	慈善院
Citang jie	祠堂街
Cunren tang	存仁堂

da daoqin	打道琴
Da jinchuan	大金川
da lianxiang	打連響
da qingjiao	打清醮
da weigu	打圍鼓
da wenjiao	打瘟醮
Da'an (gate)	大安 (門)
daban	大班
Dabo	大波
Dacheng	大城
Daci si	大慈寺
Daguan (teahouse)	大觀 (茶館)
dagu	大鼓
dagushu	大鼓書
Daishu jie	代書街
daizhao	待詔
dajie maxiang	打街罵巷
Dajin jie	打金街
danbian zhen	單鞭陣
danda hutu	膽大糊涂
dandan ban	擔擔班
"Dangyuan shouze"	党員守則
Daqiang xijie	大牆西街
Daqing yinhang	大清銀行
dazayuan	大雜院
Deng Yukun	鄧玉昆
dengshi	燈市
dianguang xi	電光戲
dianshu	電术
diao (money)	吊 (錢)
die qian houzi, ma qian gou;	爹牽猴子, 媽牽狗;
qian dao hebian da liulianliu	牽到河邊打柳連柳
Dinggong ci	丁公祠
Dingzi jie	丁字街
dipi	地痞
dipifeng	地皮風
Diyi chalou	第一茶樓
Diyilou (teahouse)	第一樓 (茶館)
Dizang an	地藏庵
Dong jiaochang	東較場
Dong yuanmen	東轅門
Dongdajie	東大街

dongfang	冬防
Dongfu jie	東府街
Donghua men	東華門
Dongyu jie	東御街
Dongyuan (teahouse)	東園 (茶館)
Dongzi kou	洞子口
Doujitai chapu	斗雞台茶鋪
doukouwang lingguan	斗口王靈官
douyar	豆芽兒
Du Yuesheng	杜月笙
Duanli men	端禮門
dudu	都督
Duoqing yingxiong	多情英雄
duoshen	觶神
Duoshen hui	觶神會
Erquan (teahouse)	二泉 (茶館)
Erxian an	二仙庵
eshao	惡少
Eshi xiang	鵝市巷
Fangchun (teahouse)	訪春 (茶館)
Fangji (teahouse)	方記 (茶館)
Fang Pei	放裴
fangsheng	放生
fangsheng chi	放生池
Fangsheng hui	放生會
Fangyuan (teahouse)	方園 (茶館)
fangzhi	方志
Fanshi (street)	藩司 (街)
fatuan	法團
fayao	法妖
Fencao hu	糞草湖
fengci hua	諷刺畫
Fengshen yanyi	封神演義
Fengshi	風師
fengtu	風土
Fengyun ting (teahouse)	風云亭 (茶館)
Fu Chongju	傅崇矩
Fu jie	府街
Fude ci	福德祠
Furong chalou	芙蓉茶樓

Furong cheng	芙蓉城
Furong ting (teahouse)	芙蓉廳 (茶館)
furu Donghai, shoubi Nanshan	福如東海, 壽比南山
Fuxing jie	福興街
Fuxing men	復興門
gaiwan cha	蓋碗茶
Ganshu	甘肅
Gao Baxi	高把戲
ge fatuan	各法團
geming zhihuo	革命之禍
gengfu	更夫
Geshuo ge (teahouse)	各説閣 (茶館)
Gexin xin juyuan	革心新劇院
gong	公
Gong laochong	攻癆蟲
gongguan	公館
gongkou	公口
gongshu	公署
Gongyuan	貢院
guan	館
guanbi minfan	官逼民反
Guandi hui	關帝會
Guandi miao	關帝廟
Guanghua jie	光華街
Guangsheng miao	广生廟
guanshen	觀神
guanshi	管事
guanxian	觀仙
Guanyin	觀音
guapo	卦婆
Guhua xiang	桂花巷
guihua xi	桂花戲
guiku zhuyi	跪哭主義
guishi	桂市
Guizhou	貴州
Gulou	鼓樓
guntu	棍徒
Guo Moruo	郭沫若
Guomin gongbao	國民公報
"Guomin gongyue"	國民公約

haicha	海察
Han Xin	韓信
he jiabancha	喝加班茶
He Manzi	何滿子
He Shui Xiang Cha	河水香茶
He Xifeng	何喜鳳
He Yuqing	何玉卿
hehua chi	荷花池
Heiren guangfu ji	黑人光復記
Heiren yutian lu	黑人吁天錄
Heming (teahouse)	鶴鳴 (茶館)
Heshang jie	和尚街
Hongbu jie	紅布街
honglong	烘籠
Hongmiaozi jie	紅廟子街
hongqian zei	紅錢賊
Hongzhao bi	紅照壁
Houzi men	后子門
Hu Zhongrong	胡仲榮
huadan	畫蛋
huadanzi	花擔子
huadeng	花燈
Huahua chating	華華茶廳
huahui	花會
Huaiyuan (teahouse)	懷園 (茶館)
huajiao dapi	花轎打屁
Huang Xing guashuai	黃興掛帥
Huang Zhi	黃芝
Huangcheng	皇城
Huangcheng bianjie	皇城邊街
huangtang	荒唐
Huanxi an	歡喜庵
huapozi	花婆子
huashi	花市
Huawai chalou	花外茶樓
Huaxing (teahouse)	華興 (茶館)
Huaxing jie	華興街
Huayang (county)	華陽 (縣)
Huayang xianzhi	華陽縣志
Huguang guan	湖广館
Huifeng chashe	惠風茶社

Huifu (street)	會府 (街)
Huifu beijie	會府北街
Huifu nanjie	會府南街
huiguan	會館
hundan	混蛋
huojiao	火醮
huopai	火牌
huoqian	火錢
Huoshen miao	火神廟
huqin	胡琴
hutong	胡同
Ji Zou Rong	祭鄒容
jia	甲
Jia Shusan	賈樹三
jiaban cha	加班茶
jiang geyande	講格言的
jiang shengyude	講聖諭的
jianghu pianzi	江湖騙子
jianghu yisheng	江湖醫生
Jiangjun yamen	將軍衙門
Jiangqiao (gate)	江橋 (門)
jianjiao qingshui	建醮請水
jianjiao qiufu	建醮求福
jianshi hu	監視戶
jiaochang	較場
jiaofu bei gui yeyu	轎夫被鬼揶揄
jiazhang	甲長
jie	街
jie lingguan	接靈官
jieban	街班
jiechai	街差
jiedao	街道
jiefang	戒方
jiefang	街坊
jiefang linju	街坊鄰居
jiejao	街轎
jieshi	街市
jieshi exi	街市惡習
jietan xiangyi	街談巷議
jietou	街頭
jietou xiangwei	街頭巷尾

jiewar (or gaiwar)	街娃兒
jiezheng	街正
jiezhong	街眾
jigong che	雞公車
jijiao shen	雞腳神
Jiliang suo	濟良所
jimao dian	雞毛店
Jin Hudie	金蝴蝶
Jinchun chalou	錦春茶樓
jingchang	精唱
Jingjie hui	警界會
jingshi hua	警世畫
jingui	金圭
jingxi zizhi	敬惜字紙
Jinhua jie	金華街
Jinjiang	錦江
Jinjiang qiao	錦江橋
jinqianban	金錢板
jinshi	錦市
Jinshui (river)	錦水 (河)
Jinyan ju	禁烟局
jinzhouzhou	京肘肘
Jipin hui	濟貧會
jiuhuang shenghui	九皇盛會
Jiulou sheji	酒樓設計
jiushi	酒市
Jiuyan qiao	九眼橋
Junping jie	君平街
Juxie	劇協
juzheng	局正
Kaizhi shuju	開智書局
kehen	可恨
Kejia xiang	科甲巷
kewu	可惡
Keyuan (teahouse)	可園 (茶館)
Ku wugeng	哭五更
Kuli bingyuan	苦力病院
laba	喇叭
Lan zhaopai	爛招牌
lanchang	爛娼

langzhong	郎中
Lao She	老舍
Lao ximen	老西門
laoda	老大
Laodong jie aiguo shiren tuan	勞動界愛國十人團
Laoruo feiji yuan	老弱廢疾院
Leishen miao	雷神廟
li	里
Li Decai	李德才
Li Jieren	李劼人
Li Laojun	李老君
li yi lian chi	禮義廉恥
Li Yueqiu	李月秋
Liang yuan (teahouse)	梁園 (茶館)
Lianhua chi	蓮花池
lianhualuo	蓮花落
lianhuan bao	聯環保
Liao Er	廖兒
Liao Zhuo	廖灼
Lichuan chashe	麗春茶社
Lihua jie	梨花街
lin	鄰
lingyi	領役
Linjiang chayuan	臨江茶園
linju	鄰居
linli	鄰里
Liu Bang	劉邦
Liu fang (teahouse)	留芳 (茶館)
Liu Shiliang	劉師亮
liulianliu	柳連柳
liumang	流氓
liuxin shixue	留心實學
liyuan	梨園
longdeng	龍燈
Longmenzhen	龍門陣
loushi	陋室
Luo Lun	羅綸
Luo Yongpei	羅永培
Luogong ci	駱公祠
Luoguo xiang	羅鍋巷
Luohun qiao	落魂橋

Luomashi (street)　　　　　　騾馬市 (街)
Lütian (teahouse)　　　　　　綠天 (茶館)
Lüying ge (teahouse)　　　　　綠蔭閣 (茶館)

Ma Shaoqing　　　　　　　　馬少清
mai goupi gaoyao　　　　　　賣狗皮膏藥
maidayao　　　　　　　　　　賣打藥
Majiao wen Xiaomei　　　　　麻腳瘟小妹
Malu yi chuicheng, wen duli,　　馬路已捶成, 問督理,
　heshi caigun; Minfang yi chaijin,　何時才滾; 民房已拆盡,
　yuan jiangjun, zaori kaiche　　願將軍, 早日開車
Mancheng　　　　　　　　　滿城
Manglixian (teahouse)　　　　忙里閑 (茶館)
Maojia gongguan　　　　　　毛家公館
Mawang miao　　　　　　　馬王廟
Mawangmiao jie　　　　　　馬王廟街
Meiguo huodong dianxi　　　美國活動電戲
Meihua she　　　　　　　　美化社
meishi　　　　　　　　　　梅市
meisu　　　　　　　　　　美俗
Meng Lijun　　　　　　　　孟麗君
Mengjia xiang　　　　　　　孟家巷
menshen　　　　　　　　　門神
menying chun xia qiu dong,　　門迎春夏秋冬,
　ke'na dong xi nan bei　　　　　客納東南西北
Mianhua jie　　　　　　　　棉花街
Miaogao lou (teahouse)　　　妙高樓 (茶館)
Ming yuan (teahouse)　　　　茗園 (茶館)
minge　　　　　　　　　　民歌
mintuan　　　　　　　　　民團
minzhong wuli　　　　　　　民眾武力
modeng nülang　　　　　　摩登女郎
Mozi jie　　　　　　　　　磨子街
Mozi qiao　　　　　　　　　磨子橋
mubiao ju　　　　　　　　幕表劇
muzhouzhou　　　　　　　木肘肘

Nan shamao jie　　　　　　南沙帽街
Nan shuwan jie　　　　　　南署襪街
Nanmen laodong zizhi hui　　南門勞動自治會
Nao Guangzhou　　　　　鬧广州

Neicheng	內城
Nianfeng xiang	年丰巷
Niangniang hui	娘娘會
Niangniang miao	娘娘廟
Niushi kou	牛市口
nüguanggun	女光棍
Nüzi jiaoyu yanjiang hui	女子教育演講會
pa wandour	炮碗豆兒
paizhang	牌長
Pang Huifang	龐惠芳
pao jianghu	跑江湖
Paochang ba	炮廠壩
paoge	袍哥
paoge daoyou	袍哥倒油
pigun	痞棍
Ping'an qiao	平安橋
pinghua	評話
pingshu	評書
pinjia efu	貧家惡婦
pinmin	貧民
Pinxiang chashe	品香茶社
pipu	皮鋪
pofu	潑婦
pubao	鋪保
puhu	鋪戶
pumian	鋪面
Qian Liancheng	錢廉成
Qiangzhi hunyin	強制婚姻
qianlu	錢爐
Qianshan suo	遷善所
Qiao Erjie	巧二姐
Qigai gongchang	乞丐工廠
qimeng	啓蒙
Qiming diandeng gongsi	啓明電燈公司
qingbao shaonian	輕薄少年
qingchang	清唱
qingdao fu (Qing Dao Fu)	清道夫
qingjiao hui	清醮會
qingjiao xi	清醮戲

Qinglian xiang	青蓮巷
Qinglong jie	青龍街
Qinglong xiang	青龍巷
Qingshi qiao	青石橋
qingshui	請水
Qingsongting chayuan	青松亭茶園
Qingyang chang	青羊場
Qingyang gong	青羊宮
qingyin	清音
Qingyuan (gate)	清遠 (門)
Qingyun an	青云庵
qionggui	窮鬼
qiongku	窮苦
qiren	旗人
Qiwu ju	旗務局
Qixiangju (teahouse)	其香居 (茶館)
Qizhi yuan	啓智園
Quangong hui	勸工會
Quangong ju	勸工局
Quanye chang	勸業場
qudi kehen zhi jiaofu	取締可恨之轎夫
Qunxian chayuan	群仙茶園
Randing jie	染錠街
Ranfang jie	染房街
ren	仁
renfan	人販
renshi	人市
rentiao zilaishui	人挑自來水
renyi zhen	仁義陣
Runansi songqin guofu	汝南寺送親過府
Sandao jie	三道街
Sandong qiao	三洞橋
Sanhuang hui	三皇會
Sanqing hui	三慶會
Sansheng gong	三聖宮
sanxian	三弦
Sanyi miao	三義廟
Sha Ding	沙丁
Seishin jijo	西清事情

Shaanxi jie	陝西街
Shamao jie	沙帽街
Shang heba (street)	上河壩 (街)
Shang lianchi (street)	上蓮池 (街)
Shang xinjie	上新街
Shangjie jieyan suo	商界戒烟所
Shangsheng jie	上陞街
Shangshi caipan suo	商事裁判所
Shangwu ju	商務局
Shangye chang	商業場
shanren laoye, guoba shengfan	善人老爺, 鍋巴剩飯
shanshi	扇市
Shaocheng	少城
shaodeng	燒燈
shaojie	燒街
shaoxiang	燒香
she	社
Shedehui (teahouse)	射德會 (茶館)
Shehui ju	社會局
Shen tongzi	神童子
Sheng junshi jingcha ting	省軍事警察廳
shengcheng xinwen	省城新聞
Shengqing chayuan	聖清茶園
shengxun	聖訓
shengyu	聖諭
Shenshou jiangjun	伸手將軍
shequ	社區
Shifang (county)	什邡 (縣)
shihu	市虎
Shiji ju	施濟局
shiliu men	十六門
Shina shōbetsu zenshi	支那省別全志
Shinshu shina shōbetsu zenshi	新修支那省別全志
Shisen-shō soran	四川省綜覽
shishi hua	時事畫
shizhuang xi	時裝戲
Shizi yuan (jie)	柿子園 (街)
shou	壽
shouhuang	收荒
shoujiu	守舊
Shu	蜀

Shu Xincheng	舒新城
shua baxi	耍把戲
shua shizi longdeng	耍獅子龍燈
Shuang huaishu jie	雙槐樹街
Shuang zhazi jie	雙柵子街
Shuanglong chi zaotang	雙籠池澡堂
shuanglong zhen	雙龍陣
Shuhou zhu	蜀后主
shui dianbao	水電報
shui duangong	水端公
Shuijing jie	水井街
shuiqian	水錢
shuixian	水線
Shuncheng jie	順城街
Shuo weixin	説維新
Shuwa jie	暑襪街
Shuwang miao	蜀王廟
Shuwutai (teahouse)	蜀舞台 (茶館)
Shuxue bao	蜀學報
Shuxue hui	蜀学會
Shuyou xinying	蜀游心影
shuzheng gongzhu yulun,	庶政公諸輿論,
tielu zhungui shangban	鐵路准歸商辦
Sichuan baolu tongzhihui	四川保路同志會
Sichuan baolu tongzhihui baogao	四川保路同志會報告
Sichuan jiaoyu zonghui	四川教育總會
Sichuan junzhengfu	四川軍政府
Sichuan wenshi ziliao xuanji	四川文史資料選輯
Sichuan wenxian	四川文獻
Sichuan yanjiang zonghui	四川演講總會
Sichuanren fu Henanren qian	四川人服河南人牽
sida jianghu	四大江湖
sida mentou	四大門頭
song tongzi	送童子
Suiyinping	碎銀瓶
sushen xi	蘇神戲
Taihehen (teahouse)	泰和亨 (茶館)
Taiping jie	太平街
Tanfang ju	探訪局
Tang minghuang	唐明皇

tangguan	堂倌
taofushi	桃符市
Taoran ting	陶然亭
Tianfu jie	天福街
Tianyashi (street)	天涯石 (街)
tiao yachong	挑牙蟲
tiaowu buxi she	跳舞補習社
Tidu jie	提督街
Tiejiao xiang	錢腳巷
Tonghui men	通惠門
Tongle (troupe)	同樂 (戲班)
Tongren tang	同仁堂
Tongshun jie	通順街
Tongsu huabao	通俗畫報
Tongsu jiaoyu she	通俗教育社
Tongsu ribao	通俗日報
tongyuan	銅圓
Tongzi jie	童子街
tuanfang	團防
tuanyuan hui	團圓會
tudi (diety)	土地 (神)
tudi hui	土地會
tudi shen	土地神
tudi tang	土地堂
Tushu ju	圖書局
Waidong jie	外東街
Wanchun chayuan	万春茶園
Wangjiang lou	望江樓
wanglairen, dengbude, zaici xiaobiao	往來人, 等不得, 在此小便
wanglairendeng, bude zaici xiaobiao	往來人等, 不得在此小便
wankua zidi	頑胯子弟
wannian tai	万年台
Wanxian	万縣
Wei Guo Qiu Xian	為國求賢
Wei Yingtao	隗瀛濤
Weixin chaguan	維新茶館
wen (money)	文 (錢)
wen caishen	文財神

Wen Yuanshuai	溫元帥
Wenchang gong	文昌宮
Wenhua (teahouse)	文化 (茶館)
Wenmiao qianjie	文廟前街
wenming	文明
wenming gun	文明棍
wenming huaju	文明話劇
wenming jiao	文明腳
wenming mao	文明帽
wenming xi	文明戲
Wenquan (teahouse)	文泉 (茶館)
wenshen	瘟神
wenzu	瘟祖
"Wu chanjiao ge"	勿纏腳歌
Wu Huanzhang	吳煥章
Wu Renjie	巫人杰
Wu Song	武松
Wu Xian	吳暹
Wu Yu	吳虞
Wu Yuncheng	吳云程
Wuchengmen	武城門
Wudan shan	五擔山
Wuhou ci	武侯祠
wulai	無賴
Wutong miao	五童廟
wuye liupi	無業流痞
Xi yuhe	西御河
Xi'an	西安
Xia dongdajie	下東大街
Xia heba (street)	下河壩 (街)
Xia Laosan	夏老三
Xia lianchi (street)	下蓮池 (街)
Xia xinjie	下新街
xiang	巷
xianghuang	響簧
xiangsheng	相聲
xiangshi	香市
Xianhuang tai	先皇台
Xianju chashe	閑居茶社
Xianxing faling yanjiu hui	現行法令研究會

Xiao beimen	小北門
Xiao dongmen	小東門
xiao gou yao xiayu	笑狗要下雨
"Xiao guafu shangfen"	小寡婦上墳
Xiao huayuan chashe	小花園茶社
Xiao jinchuan	小金川
Xiao nanmen	小南門
xiao ti zhong xin	孝悌忠信
Xiao tianzhu jie	小天竺街
xiaodan	小旦
xiaowozhe wufei qiongkun, facairen zongyao beishi	笑我者無非窮困,發財人總要背時
Xiaoyi hui	孝義會
Xiaoyuan (teahouse)	曉園 (茶館)
Xichenggen jie	西城根街
xifu tianguan	禍福天官
Xihechang	西河場
Xihua men	西華門
Xilai si	西來寺
xilan	稀爛
Xiliu suo	棲流所
ximenqian	喜門錢
Xi'nan	西南
Xin Chengdu	新成都
Xin dongmen	新東門
Xin jie	新街
Xin nanmen	新南門
Xin shijie (teahouse)	新世界 (茶館)
Xin shisi niangniang	辛十四娘娘
Xin xiangzi	新巷子
Xin ximen	新西門
Xinglong xiang	興隆巷
xingmu	醒木
Xinhua jie	新化街
Xinju jinhua she	新劇進化社
xinju yundong	新劇運動
xiongxi	凶戲
xiqian	喜錢
Xiqu gailiang hui	戲曲改良會
xishen	喜神
Xiutan guoshi	休談國事

Xiyuhe	西御河
Xiyuhe jie	西御河街
Xiyujie	西御街
xizi defu, xizi yannian	惜字得福, 惜字延年
xizi gong	惜字宮
xizi hui	惜字會
Xu Xilin ci En Ming	徐錫麟刺恩明
xuanjiang hui	宣講會
Xue Tao	薛濤
Xuedao jie	學道街
Xufu jie	許府街
yachi yachi jin yachi; shoubiao shoubiao lan shoubiao; you zhenzhu, you ma'nao, you shanhu, you chahu	牙齒, 牙齒, 金牙齒, 手表, 手表, 爛手表, 有珍珠, 有瑪瑙, 有珊瑚, 有茶壺
Yandao jie	鹽道街
Yang Hehua	楊荷花
Yang Laosan	楊老三
Yang Xiong	楊雄
Yang Zhong	楊忠
yangfangzi zoulu	洋房子走路
yangjiao deng	羊角燈
yangma	洋馬
yangmiao xi	秧苗戲
yangqin	洋琴
Yangyi Yier	揚一益二
Yangyuan chashe	養園茶社
Yangzhou taiji	揚州台基
Yanhui gongzhu	烟灰公主
yanjie yanxi	沿街演戲
yanliang shijie	炎涼世界
Yanqing si	延慶寺
Yanshi kou	鹽市口
yao, dan, yin, xie	妖, 誕, 淫, 邪
Yaochaji	藥茶記
yaoshi	么師
yaoshi	藥市
Yaowang hui	藥王會
Yasheng hui	亞聖會
yelaixiang	夜來香

yexing piao	夜行票
Yi Junzuo	易君左
Yichun chalou	宜春茶樓
Yidong qiao	一洞橋
Yijiu jushe	一九劇社
yiku, ere, sanshuijiao, situnyangyan, wushangdiao	一哭, 二餓, 三睡覺, 四吞洋烟, 五上吊
Yin Changheng	尹昌衡
ying caishen	迎財神
ying xishen	迎喜神
Yinghui (gate)	迎輝 (門)
yingpan	營盤
yingxiong jie	英雄結
Yinshuan jie laodong huzhu tuan	印刷界勞動互助團
yinxi	淫戲
yinyang xiansheng	陰陽先生
yinyuan	銀圓
Yiqian hui	一錢會
Yishu yanjiu she	藝術研究社
Yizhi (teahouse)	益智 (茶館)
Yongjing jie	永靖街
Yongni (teahouse)	咏霓茶社 (茶館)
Yongquan (teahouse)	涌泉 (茶館)
Yongxing xiang	永興巷
you baibing	游百病
Youhai jiaoyang gongchang	幼孩教養工厂
youmang jieji	有忙階級
Youxian (teahouse)	優閑 (茶館)
youxian jieji	有閑階級
Yu Zidan	俞子丹
Yuanqun she chayuan	園群社茶園
yuanwai	員外
Yuanxiao jie	元宵節
Yuebao gongshe	閱報公社
Yuefu jie	岳府街
Yuelai chaguan	悅來茶館
Yuelai juchang	悅來劇場
yugutong	魚鼓筒
Yuhe	御河
Yuhuang guan jie	玉皇觀街
Yujing (teahouse)	羽經 (茶館)

Yulong jie	玉龍街
Yuqing jie	餘慶街
yuzhao huolin	預兆獲麟
Zeng Binkun	曾秉昆
Zeng Xiaogu	曾孝谷
zhafu	柵夫
Zhang Laoyao	張老么
Zhang Liang	張良
Zhang lihong	張莉紅
Zhang Mapo	張麻婆
Zhang Shixian	張士賢
Zhang Xuejun	張學君
Zhao Erfeng	趙爾丰
Zhao Zhanyun	趙占云
zhaohun daji	招魂大祭
zheng (character)	正 (字)
zhengdou cha	爭斗茶
Zhengyu chayuan	正娛茶園
Zhenliu (teahouse)	枕流 (茶館)
Zhijisi gongyuan	支磯石公園
zhiqian	紙錢
zhiri gongcao	值日功曹
Zhong dongda jie	中東大街
Zhong Kui	鐘魁
Zhong Xiaofan	鐘曉凡
Zhong xinjie	中新街
Zhonghua tianzheng guo	中華天正國
Zhongshan jie	中山街
Zhongyuan hui	中元會
Zhou Shanpei	周善培
Zhou Xun	周詢
Zhou Yuji shi Daizhou	周玉吉失岱州
zhuang shuiyan	裝水烟
Zhuanlun zang jie	轉輪藏街
Zhuanzha paifang	磚柵牌坊
Zhubao jie	珠寶街
zhuqin	竹琴
Zhushi jie	珠市街
zhuzhici	竹枝詞
zi	字

Zidong jie	紫東街
ziku	字庫
Zitong jie	梓橦街
Zong shanghui	總商會
Zongfu jie	總府街
Zouma jie	走馬街
zouyin	走陰

Notes

1. Braudel 1975: 441.

2. Certeau 1984: 23.

3. William Edgar Geil's book on China's provincial capitals translated Chengdu literally as "perfect capital" (1911: 287), which, to a certain extent, expressed the character of the city. The area surrounding Chengdu is the focus of G. William Skinner's classic work about marketing and social structure (1964–65).

4. Walmsley 1974: 2.

5. Bird 1987 [1899]: 10. Many Western travelers had similar impressions. Ernest Wilson wrote: "The plain of Chengtu [Chengdu] is the only large expanse of level ground in the great province of Szechuan [Sichuan]; it is also one of the richest, most fertile, and thickly populated areas in the whole of China" (1929: 112). A similar passage appears on p. 68.

6. Shi Jufu 1936; Wang Di 1993: 78; Hubbard 1923: 2; Wilson 1929: 121. For more figures, see Stapleton 1993: 32. Another heavily populated inland city was Chongqing; I estimated that it had 340,000 to 350,000 residents in 1910 (Wang Di 1989b: 70–71).

7. Bird 1987 [1899]: 345; Wilson 1929: 121; Chizuka 1926: 230.

8. Yang Xie 1804: 42; Sichuan sheng wenshi guan 1987; Zhang Xuejun and Zhang Lihong 1993: 36; Wang Di 1993: 52–59.

9. Rowe 1989: 144; 1990: 321; Rankin 1986: chap. 3; Zelin 1990: 105.

10. Bird 1987 [1899]: 350; Ba Jin 1985 [1932].

11. Ginzburg 1982: xv; Hershatter 1993: 117–18.

12. During the Qing, Chengdu County and Huayang County co-managed the city (Sichuan sheng wenshi guan 1987: 12). Chengdu did not have a formal municipal government until 1928.

13. Originally published by Chengdu tongsu baoshe in 1909–10 and reprinted in two volumes by Bashu shushe in 1987.

14. Hu Tian 1938; Zhou Zhiying 1943.

15. Kanda 1905, 1936; Tōa Dōbunkai 1917: vol. 5, Shisen-sho (Sichuan province); Tōa Dōbunkai 1941: vols. 1 and 2, Shisen-sho (Sichuan province).

16. Ginzburg 1982: xv.

17. Archives have been considered the most reliable source, but Philip Kuhn has cautioned scholars that they "are not necessarily verbatim transcripts of what a suspect said. They must be considered government documents and viewed with due skepticism" (1990: 270).

18. CDTL 1: 2.

19. Huang 1985: chap. 2.

20. Johnson 1990, 1994, 1995; Ng 1994; Berling 1989; Arkush 1990.

21. Certeau 1984: 23.

22. Bamboo-branch poetry can also be considered a form of traditional Chinese narrative literature distinct from lyric poetry (Levy 1988: 3). The emergence of bamboo-branch poetry probably was attributable to "the rise of realism in Qing poetry" (Lo and Schultz 1986: 9, 21).

23. This collection includes 850 folk stories and 759 folk songs and poems (a total of 1.7 million Chinese words), which are chosen out of 53,000 pieces with a total of 24 million Chinese words (Chen Haodong and Zhang Siyong 1991: 3).

24. Chevalier 1973: chaps. 3 and 4; Sennett 1977: chap. 8.

25. Stapleton found many photos taken by early missionaries in the Museum of Toronto; these are included in her book *Civilizing Chengdu* (2000).

26. CDTL 1: 283-98, 402-58. Qian Liancheng's drawings also depicted street people in the early nineteenth century (1985 [1820s-50s]).

27. Skinner 1964-65, 1977.

28. Faurot 1992; Zhang Xuejun and Zhang Lihong 1993; Stapleton 1993, 1996, 1997a; Wang Di 1993, 1998a, 2000a. Kakehi (1987) published a book on Chengdu and Chongqing that serves as an introduction of history and culture for popular readers rather than an academic study.

29. Stapleton 2000: 2-3.

30. For Chinese definitions of these terms, see *Xiandai hanyu cidian*, *Xinhua zidian*, and *Xiandai hanying cidian*. It is also useful to compare the English-language definitions to the Chinese definitions. In the *American Heritage Dictionary of the English Language*, "street" is defined as "a public way or thoroughfare in a city or town, usually with a sidewalk or sidewalks." This definition does not emphasize the houses at the sides, however, as the Chinese definition does. "Neighborhood" is defined there as "a district or area with distinctive characteristics" and also "the people who live near one another or in a particular district or area." This dictionary defines "community" as (a.) "A group of people living in the same locality and under the same government"; (b.) "The district or locality in which such a group lives"; (c.) "A group of people having common interests"; (d.) "A group viewed as forming a distinct segment of society" (Pickett et al. 2000). The definition of the word "street" in *Webster's Dictionary* is close to the Chinese word "*jie*": "Originally, a paved way or road; a public highway; now commonly, a thoroughfare in a city or village, bordered by dwellings or business houses" (Porter 1913: 1424). The same work defines "neighborhood" as "a region the inhabitants of which may be counted as neighbors," or "the inhabitants who live in the vicinity of each other" (p. 969), which is almost the same as the Chinese definition.

31. Sennett 1977; Duis 1983; Rosenzweig 1983; Peiss 1986; Brennan 1988.

32. Certeau 1984; Heller 1984; Sennett 1977; Davis 1988: 29-30, 34; Ryan 1990: 92.

33. Sennett 1977: 17.

34. Rowe 1990: 315.

35. Duis 1983: 3.

36. Yinong Xu has just published a study of urban planning in Suzhou, which focuses on urban physical space. See Xu 2000.

37. Whyte 1981 [1943]; McEligott 1983; Stansell 1986: chaps. 9 and 10; Davis 1988.

38. Strand 1989; Esherick and Wasserstrom 1990; Wasserstrom 1991. In 1998, Michael Dutton published *Streetlife China*, which focuses on political control in contemporary China. Although this book does not necessarily focus on "street life" as its title claims, it is a good source for understanding the relationship between politics and everyday life in contemporary China.

39. Gernet 1962; Ng 1994; Yeh 1995; Lu 1999a: 294–95.

40. Generally, popular culture is created and shared by ordinary people, whereas elite culture—also called "high culture"—is created and shared by the dominant class. The creators of popular culture, however, no longer consist exclusively of people from the lower classes but may also include well-educated elites. Therefore, some scholars of American popular culture have concluded that a history of popular culture is also "a history of intellectuals" (Ross 1989: 5).

41. Johnson, Nathan, and Rawski 1985: x. David Johnson warned that although popular culture and elite culture are useful concepts, they might cause confusion if one does not understand them in terms of the complex reality of the society being studied. He suggested that social classification of late imperial Chinese society was based on three factors: education, privilege, and economic status. Using these dimensions, Chinese society could thus be divided into nine different cultural groups (1985a: 56).

42. Gramsci 1985: 195; Gans 1974: 24.

43. McDougall 1984a: 279; Smith 1991: 6, 1994: 262. James Watson also concluded that late imperial China "had a remarkably high level of cultural integration." State power, he pointed out, played an important role in imposing "a kind of unity on regional and local-level cults" (1985: 292–93). Kwang-ching Liu suggested that elite culture can cultivate popular culture, and that many creators of popular culture were well educated, pointing out, for instance, that popular religion "had long flourished peaceably alongside Confucianism" (1990: 2). David Johnson stated that legends, myths, stories, and other artifacts of popular culture are disseminated orally among ordinary people, and in the process "certain values are deliberately inculcated by a dominant social group" (1985a: 35). Barbara Ward found that economic status or class was not a differentiating factor within local operas, which transmitted both orthodox and heterodox values among ordinary people (1985: 187).

44. Link, Madsen, and Pickowicz 1989b: 5; Rowe 1989: 173. David Arkush's study of rural proverbs demonstrated the separation of popular culture and elite culture, and he believed that "the evidence from proverbs seems to show that peasant acceptance of orthodox values and beliefs was limited" (1990: 331). Local operas, especially performances by itinerant troupes, could often escape the elite's control, some scholars have concluded (Tanaka 1985).

45. Esherick 1976; Schoppa 1982; Rankin 1986; Esherick and Rankin 1990a; Roger Thompson 1995; Stapleton 2000; Xiaoqun Xu 2001. However, a few works on nonelites have been published, including Emily Honig's studies of female workers in cotton mills and of Subei people (1986, 1992), Gail Hershatter's studies of workers and prostitutes (1986, 1997), Weikun Cheng's study of actresses (1996),

and Madeleine Dong's study of jugglers (1999), but almost all focused on a few major cities and dealt only with a particular social group. Li Hsiao-t'i has studied the movement to "enlighten" the lower classes in the late Qing, but the subject was still elite activists, not ordinary people (1998).

46. Braudel 1975: 430.

47. Rowe 1989: 78–79; Yeh 1992: 191; Link 1981: 5; Certeau 1984: 1–3; Chevalier 1973: chap. 3; E. P. Thompson 1974.

48. Stapleton 1993: 308; Esherick 1976: 66–69. In her study of the Chinese YMCA, Shirley Garrett adopted the term "social reformers," but her focus on the religious (1970) differs from what I discuss in this book. I also frequently use the term "elites" or "local elites" to refer to the counterparts of commoners. Unlike "social reformers," the term "elites" is often loosely used in this study. They could be "any individuals or families that exercised dominance within a local arena," to use the definition of Joseph Esherick and Mary Rankin (1990b: 10). They were not necessarily wealthy, powerful, or modernized and Westernized, but they did attempt to influence commoners economically, socially, culturally, politically, or mentally.

49. Wang Di 1987a: 122–29; Gao Chengxiang 1990: 483. For the details of his activities in establishing the Sichuan police, see Stapleton 1993 and Stapleton 2000: chap. 3.

50. According to some sources, there were 57 students from Sichuan in Japan in 1904; in 1905, 393; and in 1906, 800. In 1909, the number of modern schools in Sichuan reached 9,900, with more than 340,000 students (Wang Di 1993: 456, 479).

51. Scholars of European history have closely examined this issue, especially the relationship between popular culture and the French Revolution; see, for example, the explorations of the cultural origins of the Revolution by Robert Muchembled (1985) and by Roger Chartier (1991) and also the investigations of the links between politics, culture, and class in the Revolution by Lynn Hunt (1978, 1984) and by Mona Ozouf (1988). The connections between street culture and local politics in Chengdu have both similarities to and differences from the French experience.

CHAPTER 2: THE STREET

1. *Baojia* were approved by the county magistrate, who was usually not involved in community affairs. The *baojia* organized ten families into a *pai*, ten *pai* into a *jia*, and ten *jia* into a *bao*, the heads of which were called, respectively, *paizhang*, *jiazhang*, and *baozheng*.

2. For example, Ba County (Baxian) had 235 officials and clerks in its yamen in late Qing, but the total population was over 990,000 (Wang Di 1989c: 315; 1993: 362). Although we do not know the exact number of officials and clerks in Chengdu and Huayang counties, I assume that the ratio of clerks and population would not differ significantly. Total population of both counties in the late Qing was 850,000 (Shi Jufu 1936: 9). For the most recent and comprehensive study of county clerks, see Reed 2000.

3. Zhou Xun 1987 [1936]: 17.

4. Stapleton 2000: 45.

5. Braudel 1975: 396.

6. Naquin 1976; Esherick 1987. Anthropologists have conducted some studies of the role that popular religions play in community solidarity; for example, see James Watson's analysis of the "Empress of Heaven" (1985).

7. A number of scholars of Chinese urban history have examined public activities in the cities. See Hershatter 1986; Rowe 1989; Strand 1989; Perry 1993; Wakeman 1995b; Goodman 1995. Among them, William Rowe and David Strand pay particular attention to the analysis of public space. Rowe has examined the urban space of Hankou from the broader structural view of "urban ecology," examining such matters as property, spatial structure, land assignment, residence patterns and neighborhood formation, and public places. Strand, however, focused more on the uses of urban public space, especially for the rickshaw men of Beijing. See Rowe 1989: 64–87; Strand 1989: chaps. 2 and 3.

8. The importance of time should be emphasized. Despite continuous development of urban commerce and cultural life throughout the nineteenth century, until the early twentieth century the basic use and management of the street remained virtually unchanged. Unlike political transformations, which can be pinpointed to a specific event and time, cultural trends are often visible only after a long period. Therefore, it is unnecessary, and indeed often impossible, to chart the chronology of social change.

9. Regarding the city wall and gates of Chinese cities, see Chang 1977 and Yinong Xu 2000: chap. 4.

10. CDTL 1: 16; Torrance 1916: 19; Wilson 1929: 122. However, one source says that the wall was 22.8 *li* in circumference (Sichuan sheng wenshi guan 1987: 97).

11. Hubbard 1923: 12–13.

12. Yamakawa 1909: 96; GMGB Apr. 19, 1916; Hubbard 1923: 14.

13. Torrance 1916: 19; Sichuan sheng wenshi guan 1987: 95.

14. Chang 1977: 96–97.

15. The closing time was frequently changed; at different times it was 6:30, 7:30, or 11:00 P.M. After 1928, the city gates were no longer closed at night (Qian Ren 1928: 105).

16. Yang Xie 1804: 42–43; CDTL 1: 31; Sichuan sheng wenshi guan 1987: 97. Therefore, the Smaller City was also called Mancheng ("Manchu City") or Neicheng ("inner city"). Foreigners sometimes called it the "Tartar quarter" or "Tartar garrison" (Bird 1987 [1899]: 45; Wilson 1929: 122).

17. Bird 1987 [1899]: 45; Elliott 1990: 40. Fernand Braudel, for example, was incorrect when he wrote, "The system was all the more foolproof in China in that everywhere the square of the Tartar town stood next to the Chinese town and watched closely over it" (1975: 383).

18. Lin Kongyi 1986: 135; Yamakawa 1909: 98–99; Yokoyama 1940: 149, 224. The North Gate of the Imperial City was called Houzi men (Rear Gate); the East Gate, Donghua men (East China Gate); and the West Gate, Xihua men (West China Gate). The South Gate was the main one (Yamakawa 1909: 98–99). I have checked all sources, including some old maps, but found that the South Gate did not have a name. On some old maps, the gate is just marked "Huangcheng" (Imperial City). However, in the Ming dynasty, the South Gate was called "Duanli men" ("Formal Rite Gate"; see Sichuan sheng wenshi guan 1987: 89). After the Qing was

overthrown, whether to keep or abandon the city wall became an issue of much public concern. Eventually, it was destroyed, perhaps because it has so often been regarded as a symbol of backwardness. For more on this issue, see Chapter 4.

19. Wilson 1929: 120. Marco Polo not only described the bridge itself but also emphasized the connection between bridges and commerce: "The city is watered by many large streams, which, descending from distant mountains, flow around and pass through it in a variety of directions. These rivers range from half a mile in width to two hundred paces [about a thousand feet], and are very deep. A great bridge crosses one of these rivers within the city. It has on each side a row of marble pillars that support a roof constructed of wood, ornamented with paintings of a red color, and covered with tiles. Throughout the whole length also there are neat compartments and shops, where all sorts of trades are carried on. One of the buildings, larger than the rest, is occupied by the officers who collect duties and a toll from those who pass over the bridge. From this bridge, it is said, His Majesty received daily the sum of a hundred bezants of gold" (Polo 1961 [1271-95]: 145-46).

20. Susan Naquin has recently published her massive study of Beijing temples, which is intended "to expand our understanding of the range and variety of roles that temples could play in Chinese society and to establish the importance of religion in general" (2000: xxi).

21. Wu Haoshan 1855: 69; CDTL 1: 25-32; Sichuan sheng wenshi guan 1987: 305. The word for "street" is pronounced *jie* in Mandarin Chinese and *gai* in Chengdu dialect, while the very small, narrow streets and alleys were usually called *xiang*, or *hang* in Chengdu dialect. The alleys in the Smaller City, however, were known as *hutong*. The public squares and yards were called *ba*.

22. Hubbard 1923: 16-17; Wilson 1929: 123. Chengdu was nicknamed "Hibiscus City" (Furong cheng), because hibiscus blossoms were found throughout. In the words of one bamboo-branch poem, "The city wall is tall and rugged, and hibiscus flowers permeate the area" (Yang Xie 1804: 42; Dingjinyan 1805: 60). In Chengdu, the tradition of planting hibiscuses can be traced back as early as the Later Sichuan King (Shuhou zhu) era of the Five Dynasties and Ten Kingdoms (907-79), and the city has maintained this practice ever since. After completing the reconstruction of the city wall in 1783, the governor-general of Sichuan ordered the planting of the flowers throughout the city (Huayang xianzhi 1934: 1420-21). Consequently, daily life in Chengdu for centuries has had a strong association with the hibiscus.

23. Gernet 1962: 49.

24. Wang Di 1993: 259-64.

25. In order, they were the Lantern Fair (*dengshi*), Flower Fair (*huashi*), Silkworm Fair (*canshi*), Brocade Fair (*jinshi*), Fan Fair (*shanshi*), Fragrant Incense Fair (*xiangshi*), Jewelry Fair (*baoshi*), Osmanthus Flower Fair (*guishi*), Medicine Fair (*yaoshi*), Wine Fair (*jiushi*), Wintersweet Flower Fair (*meishi*), and Spring Festival Couplets Fair (*taofushi*).

26. Qing Yu 1909: 181-84; Liu Yuan ca. 1790: 129.

27. Dingjinyan 1805: 62; Wang Zaixian ca. 1850: 134; Wu Haoshan 1855: 72; Yamakawa 1909: 184-85; Qing Yu 1909: 181.

28. CDTL 1: 25-32; Wilson 1929: 123. Gauze Hat Street featured costume shops that catered to local operas and was a favorite among performers. The Small

East City Gate (Xiao dongmen), the Goddess Temple (Niangniang miao), and the Peaceful and Fluent Bridge (Anshun qiao) boasted an assemblage of florists, popular because they were conveniently close to temples. It was said that a thousand baskets of flowers were sold there daily, but there were still "not enough for Buddhist altars." Wood-sculpture artisans were usually located on Salt Circuit Intendant Street (Yandao jie), and framers of artwork could be found on Provincial Administration Commission Street (Fanshi). People went to the shops on Surveillance Commission Yamen Street (Ancha si) to buy silk and satin (Yang Xie 1804: 47; Dingjinyan 1805: 60–61, 67). Festival Street (Huifu) was a gathering place for antique dealers and sellers of bronze, wooden, and ceramic Buddhist statues. Coffins were sold at more than twenty shops on Water Well Street (Shuijing jie) and Double Scholartree Street (Shuang huaishu jie), near the East City Gate. Education Circuit Intendant Street (Xuedao jie) was the center for the book business. Yokoyama Tsuneo wrote that he bought eighty-two sets of books on Education Circuit Intendant Street, most of which were about the geography of Sichuan, Tibet, and the Yangzi River (1940: 147). The Single Arch Bridge (Yidong qiao) outside the East City Gate was a clothing market (GMGB July 25, 1914; Chizuka 1926: 233; Yokoyama 1940: 147; Ye 1996: 96–101). The most famous shops were frequently mentioned in bamboo-branch poetry: the Benevolent Hall (Cunren tang), which had the best Chinese medical herbs; the Half Relief Hall (Banji tang), which sold eye ointment; and the Universal Benevolent Shop (Tongren tang), which had the best Chinese medicine. "If you ask where to find the best pair of scissors, everybody tells you to go to the 'Bad Sign' (Lan zhaopai)" (Dingjinyan 1805: 60–61; Wu Haoshan 1855: 72–73). Such a phenomenon still exists in today's Chengdu, where commercial streets can be found specializing in clothing, food, electronics, construction materials, and so forth. Such specialization has increased; now there are separate streets for cell phones and computers. In the area of food, there is even a street only for hot pots.

29. All stalls that sold beef were located in the Yard of the City God (Chenghuang ba) and Iron Leg Alley (Tiejiao xiang) (CDTL 1: 388). A folk poem goes, "The groceries of Drum Tower Street (Gulou jie) cannot be found on any other streets; huge numbers of used items fill Festival Street, and the people in front of the yamen of the Provincial Administration Commissioner (Buzheng ya) are liars who sell bogus medicine" (Wu Haoshan 1855: 74).

30. The night market was located on East Great Street (Dongdajie), and spread from the City Guard Yamen (Chengshou yamen) to the Salt Market Corner (Yanshi kou).

31. CDTL 1: 275–76. Many bizarre and often funny stories originated from the night market. In *Popular Daily*, one with the strange headline "Selling Human Feet in the Night Market" told of a reporter finding a pair of human feet, covered with mud, in a "ground stall" (that is, where a peddler put goods on the ground for sale). Upon closer inspection, he discovered that the feet belonged to a sleeping apprentice who had been hired to watch the space. The writer commented, "How could the shopkeeper make any money by hiring such an apprentice?" (TSRB Sept. 8, 1909). The story not only described the way people looked at the night market but also revealed the Chengdu sense of humor.

32. Yang Xie 1804: 49; Chen San 1988: 95–98; Wilson 1929: 123; Hubbard 1923: 17.

33. Hubbard 1923: 17–18.

34. Bird 1987 [1899]: 350. Chengdu's geographical location is the reason for this. It was very difficult to transport goods from the lower Yangzi region to the upper Yangzi region due to the Three Gorges pass. This channel, notoriously difficult to navigate, caused many boats to overturn each year, thus increasing transportation costs. It was not until the end of the nineteenth century that the first Western steamship finally succeeded in reaching Chongqing, a major harbor city in the upper Yangzi region (Wang Di 1993: chap. 2).

35. For more on the origin, meaning, and social impact of the God of Wealth, see Von Glahn 1991. This process is similar to that in nineteenth-century American cities, where the development of trade inevitably promoted a culture of commerce, "merchants of leisure," and a "local plebeian culture" (Couvares 1983: 124).

36. Maniai 1898. I can find this only in its Chinese translation, titled "Maniai you Chengdu ji" (Maniai's notes on travel in Chengdu), which was published in the *Chongqing News* (Yubao), 1898, no. 9.

37. Bird 1987 [1899]: 349–50.

38. Bird 1987 [1899]: 349–50; Wilson 1929: 122.

39. Yamakawa 1909: 95.

40. Hartwell 1921: 5–8.

41. Chizuka 1926: 223, 230. Chengdu had several other prosperous commercial areas. A similarly broad busy street led for a half mile from the South City Gate directly into the city, angling first to the right and then to the left and finally leading straight into the south entrance to the Imperial City. "Shops with homes behind line these streets continuously on each side." From the West City Gate, a curved street lined with shops and houses led inward more than a mile. No such straight street going from the North City Gate existed, but there was the Arcade, "a group of buildings, situated about a mile straight east of the central part of the old capital, and occupied by a variety of retail shops, much as in American cities" (Hubbard 1923: 17).

42. CDTL 1: 275–76. Sending salesmen door to door was another strategy to increase sales. Many other "itinerant" businessmen were sent by shops to sell goods door to door. They usually chose to visit large compounds where many households or a rich family lived. The *Zhao Erxun Archives* contains a registry of everyone who came to the door of the governor-general of Sichuan. In just two days in 1909, people from more than twenty shops appeared, among them sellers of clocks, silk, hats, paper, brush pens, coal, oil, medicine, clothing, groceries, fur, and silver. Most of them were "were not allowed in and left" (*Zhao Erxun dang'an* 1909, vol. 507).

43. Xing Jinsheng 1902–32: 164. A similar description can also be found in an account written by a foreign visitor (Sewell 1971: 98).

44. Braudel 1975: 386, 427.

45. These "street houses," also called "shop houses" (*pumian*), were usually used by businesses, teahouses, wine shops, and inns. Rent was very expensive in the main commercial streets, such as in East Great Street, City Guard Street, Education Circuit Intendant Street (Xuedao jie), Green Stone Bridge, and Central Mansion Street (Zongfu jie) (Yamakawa 1909: 96; CDTL 1: 303).

46. Sewell 1971: 86–87.

47. Studies of urban residence patterns began to be made as early as the end of the nineteenth century; one such was Jacob Riis's *How the Other Half Lives* (1924

[1890]), on the tenements of New York. Historians have just started to examine Chinese urban history, in particular, the relationship between city dwellers' living space and urban commerce (Rowe 1989: 77–83; Lu 1995). The focus here, however, is on how urban commoners used the street as their everyday space.

48. CDTL 1: 303; Ba Jin 1985 [1932]; GMGB May 21 and May 23, 1917.

49. CDTL 1: 380; Sewell 1986: 38.

50. Since ancient times, city dwellers looked to the street for entertainment. Thirteenth-century Hangzhou, for example, had "numerous entertainments which the townspeople could enjoy in the streets," such as jugglers, marionettes, shadow plays, storytellers, and acrobats. Large popular theaters were to be found "where people of all conditions met and jostled together." The variety of available entertainment made "a vivid contrast with the poverty in the countryside and the hard, monotonous and frugal life of the peasants" (Gernet 1962: 55).

51. Peng Maoqi ca. 1810: 131; Wu Haoshan 1855: 73, 77; Hershatter 1986: 184; Cheng 1996: 200; Dong 1999.

52. Wu Haoshan 1855: 72. In early-twentieth-century New York, many working-class people enjoyed dancing during their leisure time. Although for ordinary Chengdu people, like their counterparts in New York, "recreation meant street life" (Peiss 1986: 167), they had no dance halls or, indeed, any public dances at all. This was partly because Chengdu did not have a tradition of public dancing, and though its citizens enjoyed watching dance performances, they never danced themselves. Another important reason, however, was that most people carefully avoided associating with performers, who occupied a lower social status.

53. Yamakawa 1909: 96; Dingjinyan 1805: 64; Xing Jinsheng 1902–32: 164; Yang Xie 1804: 49.

54. A missionary gave a vivid description of children playing with kites: A country boy was flying a fish kite with overlapping red scales over the river. Guided by a city boy, a lean hunting kite suddenly darted out, with a sharklike shape. At intervals along the string pieces of glass were glued, providing a sharp cutting edge. The city boy expertly wound his string several times around the string of the country boy's fish kite. Then, with a gentle tug, the city boy cleverly cut the string of the other kite, bringing down both the hunter and its prey within the city wall (Brace 1974b: 225–26).

55. CDTL 1: 287; Sewell 1986: 18.

56. Bird 1987 [1899]: 346; WCMN 1910, no. 7: 11. Regarding antiforeign sentiment in Sichuan, see Wyman 1997. Wearing magical charms was not unique to Chengdu. According to the North China Daily News, the rumors of queue-clippers "spread like a panic through the city. . . . Grave men are to be seen walking along the streets with their tails hanging down over their shoulders in front. Others are tenderly carrying them in their hands, and evince considerable anxiety on the appearance of a foreigner or any suspicious-looking character. . . . Nearly all the children carry [a magical charm] in a red bag at the lapel of their dress or have it written on a piece of yellow cloth and tied into their hair" (Aug. 4, 1876, cited in Kuhn 1990: 237–38n26).

57. Feng Yuxiang 1890s: 142; Yang Xie 1804: 46, 55; Liu Yuan ca. 1790: 128–29; Wu Haoshan 1855: 70; Li Jieren 1980 [1937]: 33; Xiong Zhuoyun, 85 years old, interview by author, Joy Teahouse, June 22, 1997.

58. GMGB July 31–Aug. 5, 1912; Ward 1985: 187; Tanaka 1985: 149.

59. Johnson 1989: 31, 34; Zhou Xun 1987 [1936]: 61–62.

60. Goodman 1995: 28.

61. Wu Haoshan 1855: 70, 76; Dingjinyan 1805: 60; Yang Xie 1804: 57.

62. Davis 1988: 5; Turner 1984; Johnson 1989: 29; 1990: 45–49.

63. The tea-drinking tradition has long been noted by both Japanese and Western observers, whose travel notes, investigations, and memoirs usually contained their impressions of Chinese teahouses. See Fortune 1853; Nakamura 1899; Davidson and Mason 1905; Inoue 1921; Hubbard 1923; Tōa Dōbunkai 1941; Sewell 1971; Takeuchi 1974; Brace 1974a; Service 1989; and Naitō 1991. American scholars of modern Chinese urban history have pointed to the multiple social functions of teahouses, but to date they have provided no in-depth studies. See Skinner 1964–65: 27; Hershatter 1986: 185; Rowe 1989: 60, 196; Strand 1989: 58; Perry 1993: 22; Wakeman 1995a: 112; Goodman 1995: 17. One major reason for this lack is the difficulty of finding sources. Although I faced the same problem, I found that the teahouses in Chengdu offer perhaps the richest source of this kind of information because, as I mentioned above, so many people left personal accounts of their experiences in them. In addition to various newspaper reports about teahouses, I have benefited from travel notes left by both Chinese and foreign travelers and from sources uncovered in my own field investigations and interviews. Chinese scholars have published a number of books on tea culture, but almost all treat this topic as a cultural curiosity rather than a tool of historical analysis. See Chen Jin 1992; He Manzi 1994; and Gang Fu 1995. Scholars have only begun to study Chinese tea culture and teahouses. See Meserve and Meserve 1979; Suzuki 1982; Nichizawa 1985, 1988; Evans 1992; Shao 1998; and Wang 2000b. Although Nichizawa's article on Chengdu teahouses before 1949 is basically a summary of Chen Maozhao's memoir "Teahouses in Chengdu" (*Chengdu chaguan*), he was probably the first non-Chinese scholar to focus on Chengdu teahouses. The most interesting part of his 1988 article is a description of the revitalization of Chengdu teahouses after the Cultural Revolution. Compared with other subjects in Chinese social and cultural history, scholarship on teahouses is sparse.

64. Zhang Fang 1995: 96; Li Jieren 1980 [1937]: 43, 126–27, 153–55, 189, 251, 378, 414, 1057–60, 1327, 1464; Sha Ding 1982 [1940]; 1963: 206.

65. There were 599 by 1935. One source says that there were around 120,000 teahouse patrons per day in 1935 (CDTL 2: 253; GMGB Jan. 15, 1931; Yang Wuneng and Qiu Peihuang 1995: 731; Qiao Zengxi, Li Canhua, and Bai Zhaoyu 1983: 20). According to the 1938 *Guidebook of Chengdu* (Chengdu daoyou), the large teahouses could serve 200 to 300 patrons and the small ones, several dozen (Hu Tian 1938: 69). Shu Xincheng estimated that in the 1920s teahouses accounted for 10 percent of the shops in Chengdu (1934: 142). A 1941 report from the Chengdu Municipal Government counted 614 teahouses; they ranked fifth among employers of all occupations in the city (Chen Maozhao 1983: 178). The Teahouse Guild of Chengdu counted 598 teahouses at the end of the 1940s (Gao Shunian and Wang Yongzhong 1985: 110). Some estimates for the number of Chengdu teahouses are even higher. One author concludes that in 1942 there were more than 1,600 teahouses both inside and outside Chengdu (Yao Zhengmin 1971: 18). An-

other article claims that there were more than 1,000 teahouses before 1949 (Jia Daquan and Chen Yishi 1988: 366). I have not found official records that confirm these figures. If the figures are accurate, I assume that they include the teahouses found in the small market towns surrounding Chengdu. On the numbers of tea-houses and teahouse-goers, also see Wen Wenzi 1990: 452; Xue Shaoming 1986 [1936]: 166.

66. Tōa Dōbunkai 1941: 631; Lin Wenxun 1995: 141; Evans 1992: 7–16; Wang Qingyuan 1944: 29; Shu Xincheng 1934: 142.

67. Couvares 1983: 124; Davis 1988: 29, 37; Brennan 1988: 312; Nasaw 1993: 6.

68. Rowe 1989: 86.

69. Coffeehouses in Europe emerged in the seventeenth century, but in America saloons did not emerge until the nineteenth century (Leclant 1979; Duis 1983). In China, teahouses appeared much earlier, at least as early as the Song dynasty (960–1279) (Gernet 1962: 36, 46, 47, 49; Freeman 1977: 159–60; Evans 1992: 62–66). No material about teahouses in Song-era Chengdu has been found, but *A Record for Festivals* (Suihua jilipu), from the Yuan period (1279–1368), stated that Chengdu had "teahouses and wine shops" (*chafang jiushi*). While customers drank tea, singers entertained them with "tea poems" (*chaci*) (Fei Zhu n.d.: 2–4).

70. Wang Qingyuan 1944: 34–35; Zhou Xun 1987 [1936]: 24. This book frequently mentions units of Chinese currency. *Wen* (cash) is the most basic unit, which roughly corresponds to "cents," though they are not identical. In the late Qing, the exchange rates were one silver dollar (*yuan* or *yinyuan*) to one hundred coppers (*tongyuan*), and one copper to ten *wen*. However, coppers were constantly devalued from the late Qing to the Republican period. In the 1910s, the rates were one silver dollar to about 1,500 to 2,000 *wen*, and in the 1920s, one silver dollar to about 2,000 to 3,000 *wen*.

71. Xue Shaoming 1986 [1936]: 166; Jiang Mengbi, 78 years old, interview by author, Joy Teahouse, June 21, 1997; Yang Wuneng and Qiu Peihuang 1995: 731.

72. Chen Maozhao 1983: 182.

73. Regarding such activities in the teahouse, see Chapter 3.

74. Chen Maozhao 1983: 183; Jiang Mengbi, 78 years old, interview by author, Joy Teahouse, June 22, 1997; GMGB Aug. 14, 1929; Yu Shiming, 73 years old, interview by author, Joy Teahouse, June 21, 1997; Wang Qingyuan 1944: 34.

75. Chen Maozhao 1983: 185; Cui Xianchang 1982b: 101–2.

76. Xing Jinsheng 1902–32: 165; Chen Maozhao 1983: 185. According to one memoir, if the total cost of tea, coal, labor, and rent were regarded as a single unit, the profit would equal 2.5 to three units; in other words, a teahouse could reasonably expect a profit equal to between two and three times the original investment (Chen Maozhao 1983: 185). This estimate seems overly optimistic. In 1910, the investors in the Joy Teahouse received 1.67 taels for every ten-tael investment and 0.8 percent interest per month. Thus, the interest the investors received in 1909 added up to a 60 to 70 percent return on their investment (TSRB Aug. 3, 1911). Of course, such a high return would indicate the potential for high profits in the teahouse business. Like most other businesses, however, teahouses were affected by declines in the overall economic environment. A 1931 report by the teahouse guild revealed that more than forty teahouses had gone out of business in one season

(GMGB Jan. 15, 1931). Nevertheless, since the original purpose of this report was to appeal to the local government to reduce the teahouse tax, it is quite possible that the guild exaggerated their problem.

77. Chen Maozhao 1983; Cui Xianchang 1982b.

78. The well-known modern drama *Chaguan* (Teahouse), by Lao She, described society and people in 1930s Beijing (Lao She 1978).

79. Chen Jin 1992: 30–31.

80. Fang Xu ca. 1900: 144; Yang Xie 1804: 47; Dingjinyan 1805: 63.

81. Chizuka 1926: 338; GMGB May 8, 1918; Zhou Chuanru 1926: 91, 95; Xu Xinyu 1985: 15; Shu Xincheng 1934: 170. In a 1938 entry in his diary, Wu Yu, a well-known anti-Confucian scholar active in the New Cultural Movement, wrote that on Sundays a teahouse next to the river by the West City Gate could sell as many as seven to eight hundred cups of tea, because "there are many leisurely teahouse-goers" (Wu Yu 1984 2: 775).

82. GMGB Mar. 5, 1919; Xu Xinyu 1985: 2.

83. Goodman 1995: 104; CDTL 1: 279; TSRB Feb. 11, 1910.

84. Chen Maozhao 1983: 187; Chen Jin 1992: 32–33; Cui Xianchang 1982b: 94; Wen Wenzi 1990: 453; Zhou Xun 1987 [1936]: 24.

85. Geertz 1973: 168; Davis 1988: 45; Grimes 1982: 274; Johnson 1995; Watson 1985: 308; Siu 1989: 122; Wang 1995.

86. GMGB Mar. 18, 1916.

87. Death rituals were sometimes connected with national political affairs. In 1908, Chengdu residents participated in the national mourning in the provincial capital after the Guangxu emperor and the empress dowager died in succession. During that period, all red objects were covered with white and blue paper or cloth as part of the mourning ritual. White cotton was draped over all gateways, and slogans were written on white paper instead of the usual red. The red strips on sedan chairs were repainted or were covered with white or blue cotton. Even red buttons on hats were changed to blue or black. All policemen and soldiers wore white cotton sashes, and students were given five days of holiday. Music was forbidden for a hundred days (WCMN 1908, no. 12: 19).

In addition to participating in death rituals in the imperial period, Chengdu residents also had an opportunity to observe a memorial ceremony during the new Republican era. After the National Protection Army's victory over Yuan Shikai's troops in 1916, the military and local government held a large-scale memorial ceremony for the war dead, known as the "Great Calling Souls Memorial Ceremony" (*zhaohun daji*). All households were required to fly the national flag, hang colorful lanterns, and set up altars for worship. A public altar was also built in the Smaller City Park for the ceremony. When the ceremony was held there, more than a hundred Buddhist monks participated, and "unusual noise and excitement" spread throughout the area (GMGB Aug. 10, 12, and 15, 1916). This Republican death ritual was a new style of "mass ceremony," while it incorporated some traditional performances, such as monks' chanting. Beginning in the late Qing, such public memorial ceremonies often turned into political protests and became key incidents in modern Chinese political history (see further discussion in Chapter 7).

88. On at least one occasion, a funeral and wedding were held together, which seems bizarre to modern sensibilities. A girl named Liu, who lived in Great North

Gate Street (Beimen dajie), became very ill, and taking medicine did not cure her. While unconscious, she dreamed that a long-bearded man in ancient clothes came to her, claiming to be the God of West River Town (Xihechang) near Chengdu and saying he had drawn a lot entitling him to marry her. She told this dream to her parents before she died, and they interpreted it to mean that she had gone to be with the City God. Therefore, they prepared her dowry and a colorful sedan chair and sent them with her portrait, accompanied by music, to the City God Temple. Along the way, joss sticks were burned, and people thronged to celebrate the City God's marriage. The elite, however, condemned this ceremony as "too stupid" (GMGB Apr. 9, 1914). Many who were curious about a dead girl "marrying" the City God watched the procession. This story indicates the powerful influence of the City God in commoners' lives and beliefs. Even if local authorities and elites opposed such supposedly "superstitious" rituals, people still felt free to conduct them in public places.

89. Yang Xie 1804: 52; Wolf 1974.

90. Dingjinyan 1805: 68; CDTL 1: 552–53; TSHB 1909, no. 4.

91. Most Chinese festivals were based on seasonal events, such as the Spring Festival (*Chunjie*, celebrated on the first day of the first lunar month, and also called "Chinese New Year") and Pure Brightness Day. Others, such as the Liberating Living Creatures Festival (*Fangsheng hui*, on the eighth day of the fourth lunar month) and the Medicine King Festival, emerged from folk tradition. In contrast to most Western countries, whose holidays contained notions of both national ceremonies and popular religion, in China fairs were developed at the local, not national, level.

92. "Joy cash" is sheets of red paper; it is also called "joy door cash" (*ximenqian*).

93. Wilentz 1983: 39; Grainger 1917a: 5–10; Liu Yuan ca. 1790: 125; Lin Kongyi 1986: 80. The passage of time, in hours, days, and seasons, was always recorded in poetry (Zumthor 1990: 121). As the most important festival in China, the Chinese New Year always fascinated bamboo-branch poets, who wrote many poems about it, describing the festival's setting, atmosphere, participants, and various activities. Some of these descriptions cannot be found in other written sources.

94. WCMN 1905, no. 3: 57.

95. Yang Xie 1804: 43; Qing Yu 1909: 184; Liu Yuan ca. 1790: 127–30; Xing Jinsheng 1902–32: 164; Grainger 1917a: 10.

96. Grainger 1917a: 10–11; CDTL 1: 202–03, 206; Yang Xie 1804: 43.

97. Liu Yuan ca. 1790: 126–27; WCMN 1905, no. 3: 57; Vale 1906, no. 11: 262; Grainger 1917a: 8.

98. Regarding the relationship of neighborhoods, Hanchao Lu has offered a detailed description of Shanghai. See Lu 1999a: 218–42.

99. GMGB June 11, 1929.

100. CDTL 1: 549; GMGB Apr. 14, 1918; Feb. 8, 1919; Dingjinyan 1805: 61.

101. During lunar eclipses, for example, Chengdu people protected themselves from devils by setting joss sticks on the street, kneeling under the moon, and beating basins and vats, while Buddhist monks and Daoist priests clanged bells. The whole city was noisy (GMGB June 5, 1928).

102. Grainger 1917c, no. 9: 13–14.

103. GMGB June 9, 1917.

104. GMGB June 13, 1917. In this ceremony, the dragon was important in representing the change of seasons. In winter, the people played "fire dragons," while in summer they played "water dragons" (GMGB June 18, 1914).

105. R. Watson 1985: 36-54; Yang 1961: 58-80; Wolf 1974; Freedman 1966; Ahern 1973; DeGlopper 1977; Harrell 1982; Strauch 1983.

106. DeGlopper 1977. However, some anthropologists stress official involvement because, as Emily Ahern points out, "the existence of gods who were not officially recognized could lead to direct confrontations between the strength of popular cults and the strength or determination of official opposition" (1981: 84). I discuss this issue later in this chapter.

107. Zhou Xun 1987 [1936]: 17; Grainger 1917a: 9. According to former magistrate Zhou Xun, "all the street heads joined secret societies," and therefore they were able to control "all sorts of people, so that robbery and thefts became rare" (1987 [1936]: 17), but I have not found more evidence to support this claim. In the late Qing, gates were closed at the third *watch* (one o'clock in the morning). The closing time, however, changed depending on the political climate. Sometimes the gates of streets were closed as early as nine o'clock in the evening, on the beating of the first *watch* (STJZ I-9; Xiong Zhuoyun 85 years old, interview by author, Joy Teahouse, June 22, 1997). In the early twentieth century, local communities still managed the street gates, although under police regulation. According to the new rules, no one except officials and soldiers could pass through the gate after midnight. If a family hosted a special occasion that continued past midnight, such as a wedding or a funeral, a "night pass" (*yexing piao*) was required from the policeman patrolling their street (Grainger 1917a: 9).

108. This phrase is common even today among Chengdu residents.

109. GMGB Feb. 9, 1928.

110. Grainger 1917b: 9-10; Hartwell 1921: 13. This activity ultimately resulted in a violent and widespread anti-Christian movement. "Owing to the fact that the riots of 1895 having commenced during the observance of this custom, the practice has been suppressed" (Grainger 1917b: 9-10). Regarding this incident, see also Wallace 1903: 59-63.

111. Grainger 1917a: 5-10.

112. WCMN 1905, no. 1: 11-12.

113. Qing Yu 1909: 181; Yang Xie 1804: 44; Feng Yuxiang 1890s: 141.

114. GMGB Feb. 16, 1919; Zhou Xun 1987 [1936]: 60.

115. Ba Jin 1985 [1932]: 162.

116. GMGB Feb. 14, 1922; Ba Jin 1985 [1932]: 165.

117. TSHB 1909, No. 6; GMGB Apr. 9, 1919; Dingjinyan 1805: 62; Wu Haoshan 1855: 74; Yang Xie 1804: 55; Grainger 1917b: 12.

118. Weber 1958: 96; Rowe 1989: 176; Zhong Maoxuan 1984: 147.

119. Johnson 1985b: 434-43; Dai Wending 1998: 380.

120. Cohen 1990; Grainger 1918b: 5; Yang 1961: 81.

121. Chongxiu Chengdu xianzhi 1873: 2; Grainger 1918b: 5; GMGB May 19, 1928; Zhou Xun 1987 [1936]: 63; Xing Jinsheng 1902-32: 164. The patron deity associations, which were affected by the construction of new roads, ceased their ac-

tivities for a few years during the early Republic. Furthermore, the police prohibited building stages on the streets because they "interrupted traffic." In 1928, the custom was revived, however, and all streets built stages in the name of celebrating the birthday of the patron deity. Spectators watched local operas performing there for a whole day, blocking traffic (GMGB Aug. 23, 1928).

122. Consequently, street floods became more frequent. In the spring of 1914, for example, streets in the northwestern part of the city and the western Smaller City became "canals," and residents were forced to use wooden boards as flotation devices. There are more descriptions of street floods from the same year. In the summer, Chengdu was said to have experienced its most severe flooding: "The streets became rivers," water levels in some streets reached a few feet, and all houses in the areas of the southeastern city wall, Ancestor Temple Street, and the Smaller City were flooded. At East Gate harbor, a key transportation site, floodwaters rushed from higher-lying areas, overturning several boats and killing more than ten people. Residents along the rivers rushed to higher ground, and ferryboats were enlisted as the primary means of transportation. In one day, more than thirty bodies floated through the Nine Arches Bridge (Jiuyan qiao), along with enormous amounts of debris, including furniture, firewood, cattle, suitcases, and clothing. The flood even caused the collapse of parts of the city wall, injuring or killing some residents whose homes abutted the city ramparts (GMGB Mar. 27, Aug. 20, Aug. 26–27, 1914). For more flood reports, see also GMGB Oct. 1, 1917. The danger from flooding worsened, and by the 1940s, many streets were routinely flooded (Sichuan sheng wenshi guan 1987: 455).

123. GMGB July 17, July 31, Aug. 20, Aug. 27, 1914; Mar. 19, 1916; Sept. 27, 1928; Huayang xianzhi 1934: 230–61.

124. Goodman 1995: chap. 3; Rowe 1984: 337–38; Wang Di 1989b, 1989c. In Chengdu, established groups of merchants often dominated certain businesses. People from Fuzhou, for example, opened porcelain shops, and Jiangxi people controlled local banking. Chengdu natives wove brocade, and Shaanxi people repaired everyday objects (Xing Jinsheng 1902–32: 164).

CHAPTER 3: STREET LIFE

1. Hartwell 1921: 5. According to the "Investigation Table of Chengdu Customs" (Chengdu fengsu diaocha biao), the largest number of men worked as artisans and the second largest number as traders, whereas women in the lower classes most often worked as assistants in handicraft shops or household maids (Chengdu shi shizheng 1930, 25–27). Sedan-chair carriers, prostitutes, vagrants, and beggars also largely depended on the street for their living; I give a detailed discussion of them in Chapter 6.

2. This phenomena was not unique to Chengdu or even to China; we find that in the industrial cities of America, the streets in large part belonged to members of the working class (Stansell 1986: 203). Some historians of China have commented on the relationship between streets and lower-class people. According to Richard Smith, "the people who displayed their strength and swordsmanship in public places were almost invariably of low social status" (1994: 262). In his *Rickshaw Beijing*, David Strand describes how rickshaw men struggled to earn a living on the

street (1989: 38–43). Gail Hershatter, in her *The Workers of Tianjin*, demonstrates the relationship of workers' daily life with food vendors, streetside doctors, and various folk performers (1986: 182–87).

3. This pattern was unlike that of nineteenth-century industrialized cities in the West, where "people living in different places in the city lived different kinds of life," and where the workplace was usually distinct from the living place (Sennett 1977: 221).

4. Hanchao Lu has studied peddlers in modern Shanghai. See Lu 1999a: 198–217.

5. Vale 1906, no. 10: 237.

6. Vale 1906, no. 10: 237. The rhythm of urban life in seventeenth- and eighteenth-century Paris would have seemed very familiar to a Chengdu dweller. According to Braudel, "A whole book could be written on the Halles in Paris and their offshoot." He described "the regular dawn invasion of the town by bakers from Gonesse; . . . the five to six thousand peasants who came in the middle of every night half-asleep on their carts" to bring vegetables, fruit, and flowers into the town. He depicted the hawkers shouting: "Live mackerel! Fresh herrings! Baked apples!—Oysters! Portugal, Portugal! (i.e., orange)." In such a city, "the ears of the servants on the upper floors were well attuned to get their bearings in the midst of these noises and not to go down at the wrong moment" (Braudel 1975: 390). From past scholarship, we have seen many comparisons of the political, economic, social, and cultural differences between premodern West and China, but we have not paid enough attention to their similarities. It is interesting to contemplate how people who lived in such different parts of the world had created such similar urban commercial cultures.

7. Vale 1906, no. 10: 237; CDTL 1: 397. The seller of ribbons, silk thread, and other notions for women beat a small drum with a handle attached. The vendor of trinkets, bangles, and jade rings carried a small brass gong. The seller of needles and cottons used a combination of a small brass gong and a drum. A brass gong was affixed to the top of the drum and was struck by the same handle, so that it sounded simultaneously with the drum (Vale 1906, no. 10: 237–38). The appearance of these street vendors remained the same until the 1920s and 1930s, as we learn from William Sewell's descriptions (1986: 80).

8. Yang Xie 1804: 51.

9. In Chinese, this would be: *Yachi yachi jin yachi, shoubiao shoubiao lan shoubiao; you zhenzhu, you manao; you shanhu, you chahu* (Yu Xun, 73 years old, interview by author, Joy Teahouse, June 21, 1997).

10. Cui Xianchang 1982a: 86–92; Yuan Han 1992: 108–11.

11. Sewell 1986: 120. Many bamboo-branch poems described them. As one poem said, "buying snacks in the spring suburb gives you pleasure." Another local poet wrote: "Vendors of soft bean curd and bean jelly pass through the streets every day. My little daughter likes their hot pepper and she still complains even though her food is covered all over with hot pepper powder" (Yang Xie 1804: 47; Xing Jinsheng 1902–32: 165).

12. Liu Keji 1996: 98–101; Vale 1906, no. 11: 261; Sewell 1986: 121–24.

13. Sewell 1986: 82; CDTL 1: 390, 397–98; Vale 1906, no. 11: 260.

14. Vale 1906, no. 11: 259. Huang Shangjun, an editor in a publishing house who grew up on East Great Street, told me that next door to his home was a tea-

house, and he saw itinerant tobacconists doing business there even in the 1950s and 1960s (Huang Shanjun, 42 years old, interview by author, Sichuan Publishing House, June 26, 1997). In his novel *The Great Wave*, Li Jieren described how an itinerant tobacconist served his customers (Li Jieren 1980 [1937]: 154-55).

15. Vale 1906, no. 11: 259. These warmers caused many fires every winter. See Chapter 6.

16. Sewell 1971: 125; GMGB May 26, 1917; Aug. 15, 1922; CDTL 1: 397, 399. These techniques were considered fraudulent, and elites sought to prohibit them.

17. CDTL 1: 399-401.

18. CDTL 1: 399-401; Sewell 1986: 48, 64, 68, 144-61. The writers of bamboo-branch poetry wrote about various working people. One described a stone-carver: "Old Cao is well known for his statue making, and his statues of gods are of high quality. The statues of Buddha and ghosts he makes look alive with a variety of faces" (Yang Xie 1804: 50). Some poets focused on artisans' daily life: "Weaving workers always eat cheap vegetables, so they go to buy bean sprouts early every morning, and they always get drunk during a festival." Another characterized butchers of cattle and goats, saying "they wear unique clothes and also are cruel-hearted" (Dingjinyan 1805: 63; Wu Haoshan 1855: 70, 74).

19. CDTL 1: 393-94; Sewell 1986: 2.

20. Li Jieren 1980 [1937]: 413-14; CDTL 1: 389.

21. There may have been exceptions. A photograph from the era shows a water carrier wearing shoes, but he might have been a well-water carrier (see Figure 3.3).

22. Sewell 1986: 1; He Manzi 1994: 214-15; Wu Xiaofei 1994: 9-14.

23. In 1735, a missionary wrote about Beijing: "People who fill these streets . . . not counting various groups, one hundred or two hundred strong, who gather here and there to listen to fortune-tellers, conjurors, singers and others reading or telling some tales conducive to laughter or pleasure, or even to charlatans who distribute their remedies and demonstrate the wonderful effects thereof" (quoted in Braudel 1975: 426-27). Braudel considered this passage to be typical of the crowded streets and markets in China's major city.

24. Rowe 1989: 22.

25. Wang Di 1993: 235; Mair 1985: 354-55; Davidson and Mason 1905: 48; Grainger 1918a: 5.

26. Fang Chongshi and Shi Youshan 1989: 17-19.

27. Wang Qingyu 1992: 303-4; Luo Shang 1965: 22. Someone later said that the word for storytelling was *"pinghua"* (reviewing historical romance). A folk story explains the origin of the term. Late Qing storytellers always hung a white square lantern, on which was written "so-and-so *pingshu*," listing their programs and schedule. *"Pingshu"* was popularly used to mean "storytelling," but literally it means "reviewing books." According to the folk story, once when Zhong Xiaofan was telling stories at a teahouse near the governor-general's yamen, Governor-General Zhao Erfeng happened to pass by and see Zhong's lantern, on which was written "Zhong Xiaofan pingshu." Zhao felt uncomfortable with Zhong's claim of "reviewing books," because in his view such a job should only be done by scholars, not by lower-class folk entertainers; he ordered him to change it. To avoid trouble, Zhong, who was the president of *Yasheng hui*, the guild of storytellers in Chengdu, asked all storytellers to stop using *"pingshu"* and use *"baihua yanyi"* (literally

"vernacular historical romances") instead. Later, and until the 1950s, *"pinghua"* was the word used (Luo Ziqi and Jiang Shouwen 1994: 59–60).

28. Grainger 1918a: 5–6; Xing Jinsheng 1902–32: 165; Sewell 1971: 86–87; Zhou Zhiying 1943: 225; CDTL 1: 293; Luo Ziqi and Jiang Shouwen 1994: 61.

29. Meng was a leading character in the well-known Yuan (1271–1368) drama of the same name.

30. Chen Haodong and Zhang Siyong 1991: 403–4. Storyteller's tales also appeared in bamboo-branch poems, one of which said that local people love to listen to Wu Xian's storytelling, but "he performs for a day and is idle for half a day" (Dingjinyan 1805: 62).

31. Dingjinyan 1805: 62; Xing Jincheng 1902–32: 165; Sewell 1986: 140–41; Zhou Zhiying 1943: 220–21, 224; Di Fan 1966: 23; Buck 1978: 34.

32. For example, people could go to the New World (Xin shijie) Teahouse to hear Li Decai play dulcimer, to the Lotus Pavilion (Furong ting) for Jia Shusan's bamboo dulcimer, or to the teahouse near to New South Gate for Li Yueqiu's ballads. Someone who wanted to watch Zeng Binkun's vocal imitations could go to a teahouse at the South City Gate in the morning or to the Sacred and Pure (Shengqing) Teahouse in the afternoon. Zeng would hide in a cloth-covered cage and imitate the voices of various persons, birds, and animals; he also told humorous stories (Zhou Zhiying 1943: 22; Chen San 1989: 60–61). In the late Qing and early Republic, Magician Gao (Gao Baxi) hung a wooden sign outside a teahouse in Green Dragon Alley (Qinglong xiang) announcing that anyone wanting him to entertain at a birthday celebration or a wedding could contact the teahouse. Other popular forms of entertainment, such as storytelling, comic dialogue, and drum stories, also were common at teahouses throughout Chengdu (Zhang Dafu 1981: 109; Wen Wenzi 1990: 457; Che Fu 1995: 1–6). Some teahouse performers were educated, to some extent. Zhang Shixian, a well-known local opera performer, loved reading and writing poetry and often stayed on in teahouses or wine shops to discuss classic essays of the Tang (618–907) and Song (960–1279) dynasties with customers. Another performer, Zheng Shuangcai, was good at painting (Yang Xie 1804: 54).

33. Grainger 1918a: 6–7; CDTL 1: 295; Luo Shang 1965: 22.

34. Grainger 1918a: 7–8.

35. In Chinese, this is: *"Die qian houzi, ma qian gou; qiandao hebian da liulianliu"* (Xiong Zhuoyun, 85 years old, interview by author, Joy Teahouse, June 22, 1997). *Liulianliu*, a form of folk performance, was criticized as licentious show. See further discussion in Chapter 4.

36. Sewell 1986: 20; CDTL 1: 285; Zhou Shaoji, 75 years old, interview by author, Joy Teahouse, June 22, 1997.

37. Shows in the first lunar month were called "Pure Brightness Day ceremony opera"; the second lunar month, "Guanyin opera"; and the third and fourth lunar months, "rice-shoot opera" (*yangmiao xi*). The troupe would take a break for one or two months (i.e., the fifth and sixth months). They resumed their tour at rice-harvesting season in the seventh and eighth lunar months with a program called "insect emperor opera" (*chonghuang xi*). In the ninth lunar month, Guanyin opera was performed again, and then the troupe enjoyed a hiatus in the last two months of the year (Wang Zhihang 1987: 67).

38. CDTL 1: 285; Sewell 1986: 12.

39. Among the sixteen sorts of itinerants, there were "Four Great Itinerants" (*sida jianghu*, literally "Four Great River and Lake Runners"): fortune-tellers, doctors, picture-sellers, and geomancers. The wind itinerant, the fire itinerant, the rank itinerant, and the glory itinerant were called the "Four Great Door Heads" (*sida mentou*) (Vale 1914, no. 3: 28). Other itinerants included the opera itinerant, the horse itinerant, the illusory itinerant, the folk-performer itinerant, the yamen-clerk itinerant, the soldier itinerant, the prostitute itinerant, and the courtesan itinerant. The composition of these categories was very complex. For the fortune-telling itinerant alone, for instance, there were nine male and ten female subcategories.

40. Cheng 1996; Dong 1999. Fu Chongju, in his *Investigation of Chengdu*, wrote that these people made a living through "deceitful tricks" and recounted sixty-six of them, telling interesting, detailed stories about how some of them conducted their practices (CDTL 1: 463–500).

41. Accounts of itinerants cheating people were common in local newspapers (Zheng Yunxia and Jiashu 1989; CDTL 1: 459–500; TSRB Mar. 27 and 31, 1909). This study does not attempt to study the serious Chinese martial artists, who were legendary characters in Chinese literature. Unlike those who performed martial arts on street corners or in public squares, they did not depend on the streets to make their living.

42. Vale 1914, no. 2: 29; CDTL 1: 464.

43. GMGB Dec. 29, 1914; July 28, 1917. Incidents in which tricksters pretended to be customers to deceive shopkeepers occurred frequently. See a similar report in GMGB Jan. 14, 1917.

44. Vale 1914, no. 3: 29.

45. Sewell noted: "Chengdu was a place through which many of the old traditional herbs passed on their way to all parts of China, and abroad to wherever Chinese live." The various herbs and medicinal plants were "collected chiefly in spring and then carried across the plain by lines of carriers jogging along together" (1986: 176).

46. CDTL 1: 195, 394; Sewell 1986: 84, 176.

47. Sewell 1986: 128; CDTL 1: 460, 462. How could the diviner win the trust of the sophisticated and unsophisticated alike? A story relates how a fortune-teller nicknamed "Divine Boy" (Shen Tongzi) became famous. He usually frequented a few teahouses in the Smaller City Park, where he was besieged by enthusiastic patrons. His reputation as one who could predict the future was established when he pointed out a secret mark on the skin of an officer who had asked him to tell his fortune. The officer was so impressed by this "divination" that he believed anything Divine Boy said. Someone later remarked that Divine Boy had noticed the mark when he accidentally saw the naked officer in a public bathhouse (Yang Huai 1982: 67). Perhaps the real insight of this story is that fortune-tellers were expert at collecting all the information they needed. There are many stories about fortune-tellers in folk literature. See Xu Shiwen 1983; and Cheng Ji and He Chun 1982.

48. Dingjinyan 1805: 62; Yang Xie 1804: 50; Sewell 1986: 128–29.

49. Smith 1991: xii, 9, 269. But Smith points out that this answer is not convincing: "one reason for a persistent interest in divination—not only in the West but throughout the world—is that regardless of how powerful science may be as an explanatory tool, it is not very emotionally satisfying" (1991: 283). Smith is of

course right to criticize the simple conclusion and to attempt to find more complicated and profound factors, but it is hard to deny a cause-and-effect relationship
between the appearance of more sophisticated scientific knowledge and the decline
in divination.

50. CDTL 1: 550; Yang Xie 1804: 46; GMGB Mar. 12, 1914; Mar. 17, 1922;
Apr. 13, 1928.

51. Grainger 1917c, no. 9: 14; Katz 1995: 1; Benedict 1996.

52. GMGB July 1, Nov. 8, 1914; CDTL 1: 553; Grainger 1917b: 6.

53. CDTL 1: 465, 556; Yu Xun, 73 years old, interview by author, Joy Teahouse, June 21, 1997. The enormous number of people who "took clerical garb to
evade the law" caused the government to be concerned about social stability. Philip
Kuhn has pointed out, "To the bureaucratic mind, wandering beggars of any sort
threatened public security. People without homes and families were people out of
control" (Kuhn 1990: 44).

54. Grainger 1917c, no. 9: 10; no. 11: 10; CDTL 1: 393.

55. GMGB May 26, 1928; Li Qiao 1990; Wang Mingming 1997: 224–25;
CDTL 1: 393.

56. Ko 1994; Mann 1997: 3–4.

57. See Ba Jin 1985 [1932]; Li Jieren 1980 [1937]; Lin Kongyi 1986.

58. Bird 1987 [1899]: 346. Some folk poems give an opposite notion of the
"norm." For example, we all believe that in traditional society the Chinese preferred sons to daughters. But one poem gives a different opinion: "While many
families who have ten sons are still starving, the families who have five daughters
are enjoying their life. Having more sons is less favorable than having more daughters because daughters have a higher value than sons" (Wu Haoshan 1855: 75).
Therefore, at least in Chengdu at that moment, the social value of women was not
as low as we might think.

59. Liu Yuan ca. 1790: 127; Yang Xie 1804: 44–45, 53; Chen Kuan 1911: 151;
CDTL 1: 559; Feng Jiaji 1924: 86.

60. Dingjinyan 1805: 61, 66; Yang Xie 1804: 44.

61. Yang Xie 1804: 46; Dingjinyan 1805: 64; Wu Haoshan 1855: 75; Feng
Yuxiang 1890s: 142. A poem recounted a elite hostess's daily life: "After carefully
combing her hair and making up, she goes to the market, followed by a little servant boy, to buy rice, vegetables, oil, salt, soy source, vinegar, and firewood." We
even find a description of opium-addicted women: "It is a disaster that opium
spreads all over China; young girls lie on the beds until noon. They are addicted to
opium and must sell their golden jewelry for it" (Wu Haoshan 1855: 73–76). Some
accounts do not clearly indicate class. A poet described women planting trees: "In
spring, women joyfully visit the tool market at the Silkworm Fair. After purchasing
small hoes, they plant mulberry trees by the bridge at sunset" (Qing Yu 1909:
181–82). We can see the relationship between women and flowers from another
poem: "The Hundred Flower Pond (Baihua tan) is located across the Hundred
Flower Village (Baihua zhuang), where a red house stands in the shadow of green
trees. As soon as the lady of the house hears a flower seller passing her gate, she
calls to buy tuberoses (yelaixiang)" (Peng Maoqi ca. 1810: 131). Women and the
tuberose were always closely connected. Another bamboo-branch poem, written a

century later, drew a similar picture: "She wears fashion and a beautiful hairstyle, enjoying cool wind created by fanning after she finishes embroidering. As soon as she hears a flower vendor pass her home, she calls out to buy tuberoses" (Xing Jinsheng 1902–32: 165).

62. CDTL 1: 397–98. Fu did not tell why and how they "seduced" women, but it was commonly believed that such people liked to gossip and boast of their own "immoral" experiences when plying their trade (Dingjinyan 1805: 61). The local newspapers occasionally reported that "a so-and-so woman was seduced into becoming a prostitute" (GMGB July 22, 1914).

63. Dingjinyan 1805: 60; Lin Kongyi 1986: 123; Wang Di 1998a: 44.

64. Ironically, the reforms of the early twentieth century increased the restrictions on women's behavior. For instance, the police prohibited the traditional practice of staying overnight at the Green Goat Temple on the fifteenth day of the second lunar month, the birthday of Li Laojun, who was considered one of the founders of Daoism, out of concern about the "mixing of men and women" (CDTL 1: 549). Reformers seemed to have had more conservative views on women's public activities than the purveyors of folk tradition did. For further discussion, see Chapter 5.

65. Chen Jin 1992: 12–13; Shu Xincheng 1934: 142–43; Xue Shaoming 1986 [1936]: 166; Hubbard 1923: 17.

66. Zheng Yun 1981: 82–83; Yu Xun, 73 years old, interview by author, Joy Teahouse, June 21, 1997; Chen Jin 1992: 32. Travelers also were told of another "Three Plenties": plenty of teahouses, plenty of *gongguan* (walled residential compounds), and plenty of small restaurants (Yao Zhengmin 1971: 17).

67. Hu Tian 1938: 62; Yi Junzuo 1943: 194.

68. Here we discuss only patrons. Actually the busiest people in a teahouse were the waiters, who embodied the teahouse culture. Sichuan people call teahouse waiters "*tangguan*" (teahouse officials) or "*yaoshi*" (small masters) or even "*cha boshi*" (masters of tea, literally, "Dr. Tea"). Why were they called *cha boshi*? According to He Manzi, the name came from the Tang (618–907) and Song (960–1279) periods, when the custom of calling various occupations by official titles emerged. For instance, the doctor was called *langzhong* and the landlord, *yuanwai* (He Manzi 1994: 155–56). While in American cities the saloonkeeper was the "highly visible person" (Duis 1983: 141), in Chengdu social influence, or the "spirit of the teahouse," rested not with the teahouse-keepers but with the waiters. It was they who took care of all patrons, greeting them by name and guiding them to their seats, asking what kind of tea they preferred, adding boiled water frequently to teacups, keeping tables clean, giving change accurately, and treating all customers courteously (Chen Maozhao 1983: 183–84). Waiters had to be alert and attentive at all times, so that they could answer a call from a customer immediately. Their reactions had to be very fast. Gradually, waiters' speech took on a highly distinctive style. At peak times, patrons could hear the waiters' greetings and answers rising one after another, mixing with the background noise and the general excitement. Patrons did not mind the noise; instead, it added to the fun for them.

The waiter was also expected to handle special situations appropriately. Just to receive payment from patrons, a waiter needed considerable knowledge. For example, consider this common situation: a patron entered a teahouse and ran into his friends. To show his wealth, generosity, or respect, he would tell the waiter that he would take care of all payment even though his friends' tea had already been paid for. The waiter had to decide whether to return the money to his friends and to receive money from him. This decision depended on a number of social factors, including the patrons' social status, age, and status as outsider or insider and as a regular or irregular customer. If the teahouse was also a meeting place for a secret society, the waiter had to deal with the members from different branches with secret gestures and argots (Cui Xianchang 1982b: 100–101; Luo Shang 1965: 21). A folk poem describes the teahouse waiters vividly as "not going out of the gate though walking a thousand *li* per day; not governing people though being 'officials'; having a pocket full of money in the day, but nothing at night" (Chen Haodong and Zhang Siyong 1991: 1569).

The waiter's most prized skill was providing boiled water for patrons. He would carry a large purple bronze kettle in one hand and balance a pile of tea utensils (often more than twenty settings) on the other. He would stop a distance from a table, distribute saucers in front of each patron, and put a teacup onto each saucer. He could not afford to make the mistake of giving a customer the wrong kind of tea. Then, standing two or three feet from the table, he would pour boiling water into each cup from the kettle. Then he would step forward and hook each cup lid off the table with his little finger to cover the cup. The whole process had to be neatly done in one step, and not a drop of water could spill on the table (Wen Wenzi 1990: 454). Foreign visitors remarked on the skill required by waiters. One rhapsodized about "the row of new long-spouted tin kettles, all shining and boiling away on the range at the back of the tea-shop; and the pride and the skill with which the scalding water was poured from a height on to the green leaves in the bowls" (Sewell 1971: 119). Customers felt as if they were watching a magician's performance while enjoying their tea.

69. Davidson and Mason 1905: 86; Sewell 1971: 15; Rosenzweig 1983: 49; GMGB Mar. 22, 1930.

70. Pedicurists usually worked in teahouses and used a small, square wooden board as their sign (CDTL 1: 383).

71. Li Jieren 1980 [1936]: 340.

72. Kasson 1978; Rosenzweig 1983; Nasaw 1993; Peiss 1986.

73. Yang Huai 1982: 67; Cui Xianchang 1982b: 96; Zhou Zhiying 1943: 236; CDTL 1: 297. This type of event often drew large audiences who enjoyed watching for free. Some who later became professionals started their careers in such informal teahouse operas (Wen Wenzi 1990: 455; Jinghuan and Zheng Ronghua 1982: 133).

74. Rowe 1989: 60; Wen Wenzi 1990: 454; Zhou Zhiying 1943: 246.

75. GMGB Apr. 9, May 10, 1917; Feb. 20, 1922. Chapter 7 gives an analysis of teahouse speech.

76. Chen Haodong and Zhang Siyong 1991: 1443.

77. Sennett 1977: 107.

78. Yerkovich 1977: 192; Abrahams 1970: 293; Scott 1985: 282.

79. Yi Junzuo 1943: 104; Lin Kongyi 1986: 113; Wang Qingyuan 1944: 34.

80. Vale 1906, no. 11: 260; Cui Xiangchang 1982b: 97–98; He Manzi 1994: 193.

81. Wang Qingyuan 1944: 35; Zhou Zhiying 1943: 251; Sewell 1971: 73.

82. Brace 1974a: 245; Li Jieren 1980 [1936]: 339; CSSN 1927: 511–12; Cui Xianchang 1982b: 98; Chen Jin 1992: 59.

83. Local literature is filled with such situations (see Zhong Maoxuan 1984: 59; Li Jieren 1980 [1937]). As one folk poem remarked, "When friends or relatives run into each other on the street, it is polite to invite each other to a teahouse" (Wu Haoshan 1855: 70). It is amazing that this tradition has survived to current times among some Chengdu people. During my field research in the summer of 1997, when I made appointments with some elders for interviews, they asked me to meet them in teahouses.

84. Hu Tian 1938: 69–70; Yi Junzuo 1943: 194; SSSD: 34–35; He Manzi 1994: 193; Sewell 1971: 131–32; GMGB Oct. 17, 1929; Yang Huai 1982: 67; Wen Wenzi 1990: 456–57.

85. TSRB May 15, 1910; GMGB Sept. 11, 1914.

86. Han Suyin 1965: 228–29.

87. Davidson and Mason 1905: 86; Hubbard 1923: 17. In coastal areas, we find that teahouses have a similar function. See Suzuki 1982; Goodman 1995: 17; Shao 1998.

88. Huang 1996; Davidson and Mason 1905: 86.

89. Sha Ding 1982 [1940]: 147.

90. Davidson and Mason 1905: 86.

91. Li Jieren 1980 [1936]: 338.

92. Wen Wenzi 1990: 455; He Chengpu 1986: 351; GMGB July 24, 1914; June 10, 1928; Li Jieren 1980 [1936]: 338.

93. Rankin 1986: chap. 3; 1990; Rowe 1989: chaps. 3 and 4; 1990; Strand 1989; Huang 1993.

CHAPTER 4: RESHAPING THE STREET AND PUBLIC LIFE

1. This contrasts with social reforms in nineteenth-century America, which usually were initiated by religious groups (Walters 1978: chap. 1).

2. For more information about the New Policies and their impact on society at both the national and local levels, see Esherick 1976, chaps. 2–4; Rankin 1986, chap. 6; Thompson 1995; Wang Di 1984, 1987b, 1987c, 1987d, 1988, 1989a. On the New Policies in Sichuan, see Wang Di 1985, 1986, 1992, 1993. Stapleton's recent book offers an extensive analysis of the New Policies at both the national level and in Chengdu, and regards these reforms as an important stage of nation building and municipal administration (2000: chap. 2).

3. TSRB Aug. 18, 1909. Wenming was an old Chinese term, but since the late Qing, it had generally been seen to mean "culture from the West," and therefore, many things from the West would be considered "wenming," such as "wenming gun" (Western-style walking stick), "wenming xi" (modern drama), "wenming mao" (Western-style caps), and "wenming jiao" (natural, unbound feet).

4. For instance, they mocked those fooled by "tooth-worm pickers" (tiao ya-chong), who came primarily from Fengyang in Henan province. Previously, most people had believed that tooth decay was caused by worms. A tooth-worm picker tricked his customer by hiding a worm in his hand and then claiming he had plucked it from a tooth (Dingjinyan 1805: 65; Wu Haoshan 1855: 74; Yu Xun, 73

years old, interview by author, Joy Teahouse, June 21, 1997). Members of the elite class also ridiculed the vanity of some townspeople: "Wearing beautiful clothing and carrying a huge jar, he told others that he brought back wine from a neighborhood store, but in fact what he bought was rice." Whereas one might boast of being able to afford a luxury such as wine to create a sense of superiority, rice was a staple of everyday life. We find a similar story in the same account: "Carrying a bag, he passed through the eastern streets and then walked up the western streets. People asked him what he had, and he claimed that he had bought peaches, although what he actually had was bean dregs" (Wu Haoshan 1855: 77).

5. Yang Xie 1804: 44, 57; Wu Haoshan 1855: 70.

6. CDTL 1: 272–73; GMGB Mar. 24, 1914. For more discussion on the "Chinese and Dogs Not Admitted" signs, see Bickers and Wasserstrom 1995.

7. Of course, we cannot say that all elites shared the same opinion of commoners. A few did recognize the virtues of common people. In their writings, we often find references to the kind deeds of commoners, in contrast to the prevailing view of commoners as brutes. In one news story, for example, when a poor old Manchu woman, who had no living kin, jumped into the river, she was rescued by a passerby who gave her money and paid for a sedan chair to take her home. In another, when a child fell into the river while playing, a patron of a nearby teahouse saved his life. In a third, after a pedestrian suffering from sunstroke lost consciousness on the street, a resident gave him medicine. When the grateful man brought his rescuer food—chicken and some snacks—the next day, the rescuer refused to accept it. Coolies were generally considered by elites as having low moral standards. Another story relates, however, that when a coolie who was helping a family move found a wallet containing more than twenty yuan—an enormous sum for the poor man—he returned it to its owner. This act inspired a writer to surmise: "great men and rich men struggle for power and profit, which means that they are higher in knowledge but lower in morality; it is the people who have less knowledge who hold high values or morality" (GMGB Apr. 14, 1913; Apr. 3, 1916; June 23, 1917; June 30, 1922).

8. GMGB Apr. 6, 1917; Zhou Zhiying 1943: 225; CDTL 1: 190.

9. Zhiqian was perforated paper that symbolized money. Wishing the deceased to have money to spend in the other world, people would burn it at funerals or in the annual ceremony of sweeping the gravesites.

10. GMGB May 4, 1914; TSRB June 6, 1910; Qing Yu 1909: 184.

11. TSRB Mar. 31, 1909.

12. Xing Jinsheng 1902–32: 165; TSRB Aug. 26, 1909.

13. Ba Jin 1985 [1932]: 355.

14. Duara 1988b: 792; 1991: 75; CDTL 1: 547, 549–53; Sichuan ziyiju 1910: 61.

15. TSRB Apr. 22, 1909; Apr. 27, 1910; Feb. 14, 1914; CDTL 1: 380.

16. TSRB Sept. 19, 1909.

17. TSRB Oct. 18, 1909.

18. SCGB 1904, no. 10; 1905, no. 32; TSRB Nov. 18, 1909; Chen Zuxiang and Jiang Mengbi 1982: 144–59; Xiao Han 1986.

19. Xiao Han 1986: 43.

20. TSRB June 15, Oct. 1, 1909; Feb. 17, 1910; Lin Kongyi 1986: 149–50.

21. TSRB July 22, 1909.

22. TSRB July 22, 1909.

23. SCGB 1906, no. 3; Sichuan Chengdu diyici 1906; TSRB Mar. 24, 1910; Sichuan sheng wenshi guan 1987: 459; Wang Di 1993: 266–70.

24. Some accounts described that people participated enthusiastically in such activities despite heavy rains. Actually, local people claimed to love the spring rains. One proverb proclaimed that "a spring rain is worth as much as oil." In his book *Eighteen Capitals of China*, William Edgar Geil quotes the saying on the title page of the chapter about Chengdu (1911: 287). A bamboo-branch poet wrote, "Mist and rain make fragrant mud shine" (Qing Yu 1909: 181).

25. Chen Kuan 1911: 151; Wang Di 1993: 266–70.

26. GMGB Feb. 23, Apr. 10, 1913; Apr. 1, 1914; Mar. 2, 1919; Apr. 10, 1928.

27. There were many private gardens in late-Qing Chengdu, but only five gardens were open to the public. See CDTL 1: 24–25.

28. Sichuan sheng wenshi guan 1987: 461; Li Jieren, 1980 [1937]: 120–21; GMGB Apr. 17, June 1, 1913; June 18, July 11, 1914.

29. Gramsci 1985: 380; TSRB July 27, 1909; Apr. 12, 1910.

30. Tanaka 1985: 148; STJZ II-2; CDTL 1: 277, 279; TSRB Apr. 29, 1910.

31. See Chapter 7 for additional discussion of reformed local operas.

32. GMGB Mar. 14, 1917; TSRB Apr. 12, 1910.

33. CDRB Nov. 9, 1904; CDTL 1: 284; Wang Di 1998a: 52; TSRB July 27, Sept. 17, Oct. 19, 1909.

34. CDTL 1: 277; GMGB Sept. 7, 1912; Zhou Zhiying and Gao Sibo 1987: 55.

35. TSRB Aug. 24, Sept. 17, Sept. 27, 1909; TSHB, 1909, no. 3; GMGB Apr. 11, 1913; July 22, 1914; Sept. 3, Sept. 17, 1915; Oct. 4, Nov. 20, Dec. 13, 1927; June 30, 1928; WCMN 1906, no. 1: 28; Zhou Zhiying 1943: 226–28.

36. The trend could be seen in a complaint from a local writer: "I do not understand why some people admire foreign things, express happiness upon buying foreign goods and praise their quality" (Wu Haoshan 1855: 77).

37. Yamakawa 1909: 103. Regarding the impact of foreign goods on the society, see Wang Di 1993: 281–95. On the one hand, the need for some traditional handicrafts was diminished, but on the other hand, some new handicrafts emerged. Also see Wang Di 1993: chap. 5.

38. TSRB July 23, July 30, 1909; Mar. 5, 1910; CDTL 1: 134; Lin Kongyi 1986: 213.

39. CDTL 1: 307; Li Boxiong 1988: 29–30; GMGB Oct. 4, 1917; Lin Kongyi 1986: 206. However, the reconstruction of public space caused public resistance. This issue is discussed in Chapter 7.

40. Xiao Han 1986: 43; TSHB 1909, no. 5; Wu Xiaofei 1994.

41. Include Upper New Street (Shang xinjie), Middle New Street (Zhong xinjie), Lower New Street (Xia xinjie), Central Mansion Street (Zongfu jie), and Middle East Great Street (Zhong dongdajie).

42. Xiao Han 1986: 42; TSRB Oct. 20, 1909; Wang Di 1993: 332–33. Another modern convenience that appeared in Chengdu at this time was the telephone. Although we have no details on how it developed, a 1909 newspaper report states that when telephone poles were erected by the police, who wanted to use them to

better respond to natural disasters and crime, rumors spread that telephones would bring bad luck to the city. The police issued a public notice instructing people not to believe the rumors (TSRB Oct. 18, 1909). Unfortunately, no follow-up reports are available regarding this topic.

43. Sennett 1977: 161; CDTL 1: 112, 272–73; 2: 71; WCMN 1906, no. 1: 28; TSHB 1912, no. 17.

44. GMGB Sept. 15, 1916. Qin Shao (1997) has studied the significance of the clock tower in early-twentieth-century Nantong.

45. GMGB July 23, Nov. 15, 1914; June 13, 1918; Jan. 9, 1922.

46. GMGB May 23, 1917; Apr. 19, 1919; GMGB Jan. 10, Aug. 2, Nov. 12, 1913; Sichuan sheng wenshi guan 1987: 98–99. These gates had alternative names: Tonghui men was also called New West City Gate (Xin ximen), Wucheng men, New East City Gate (Xin dongmen), and Fuxing men, New South City Gate (Xin nanmen).

47. GMGB Jan. 12, 1915.

48. GMGB Mar. 15, 1913; Jan. 23, 1918; Feb. 16, 1919; May 5, June 19, July 24, 1917; Zhong Maoxuan 1984: 202. More than 2,000 invaders occupied the Imperial City and used it as a fort during the war (see details in Chapter 7).

49. Sichuan sheng wenshi guan 1987: 100, 421; GMGB May 27, 1917; June 19, 1917; Feb. 16, 1919.

50. Sewell 1971: 101; Zhong Maoxuan 1984: 25.

51. Cited in Kapp 1973: 57–58.

52. Stansell 1986: 194–97; Rosenzweig 1985: 225; Kasson 1978: 98; Brennan 1988: 269–310; Storch 1982b: 3. Joseph Gusfield, in his book *Symbolic Crusade*, argues that middle-class reformers participated in the temperance movement in order to secure their own social status and to serve as examples so that their ideals would dominate the customs of the lower classes (1963: chap. 2). Social reformers in Chengdu reflected a similar motivation.

CHAPTER 5: STREET CONTROL

1. On the early history of the Chengdu police, see Stapleton 1993; 1997a; 2000: chap. 3; Wang Di 1993: chap. 8; 1994. In the early Republic, the police force frequently changed names under different political and military powers. In the early 1920s, it was called the "Bureau of Capital Military Police" (*Sheng junshi jingcha ting*), and in the late 1920s it became the "Headquarters of City Defense" (*Chengfang siling bu*) (GMGB May 29, 1922; Dec. 23, 1927). On the *baojia* system, see Chapter 2 above and Wang Di 1993: 376–80. For more on street headmen, see Stapleton 1993: 151–52, 179–84.

2. CDTL 1: 388–89; WCMN 1904, no. 5: 126; GMGB Apr. 17, 1914. After Zhou, however, management of the police became so loose that some elites questioned the policemen's education and morality. They pointed out that if policemen were uneducated and of poor moral character, they would abuse their power and disrupt the lives of law-abiding citizens (GMGB Apr. 17, 1914).

3. CDTL 1: 201, 308, 300–301, 372; Raeff 1983: 5.

4. CDTL 1: 193, 301, 389, 390, 392, 393, 394; STJZ I, II, III; Vale 1904, no. 5: 110.

5. See Stapleton 2000: 126–34. Stapleton's analyses of these issues are basically limited to the late Qing period.

6. This phenomenon is entirely different from the situation when the People's Republic was established in 1949, when the communist municipal government enforced policies about public space.

7. The police also tried to control households. They enacted a restrictive code, which required all heads of households, whether living in compounds or in houses on the street, to register their name, age, place of birth, occupation, and the number, names, and ages of other male and female family members and servants. One copy of the form was to be filed at the nearest police station and another was to be hung on the home's door. Residents who were suspected of crimes but against whom the police had no evidence were required to put "supervised boards" on their doors (STJZ I-1). There is no direct evidence to show if this rule was actually enforced. The police conducted a census in 1910 under the order of the Department of Civil Affairs (Minzheng bu) of the central government (Wang 1993: 592–93; Stapleton 2000: 135).

8. STJZ I-7; TSRB Mar. 6, 1910; GMGB Sept. 9, 1914.

9. The selling of frog meat, for example, was prohibited because the peasants who hunted frogs cut off the skin, making the meat spoil quickly. Some beef shops sold spoiled beef to street peddlers at a discount, exposing the people who purchased it—mostly the poor—to harmful bacteria and disease. To rectify the situation, the police issued a public notice prohibiting the sale of unsafe beef. In another example, pork became smelly by afternoon during the summer months, and some butchers tried to sell it by way of a lottery, offering the winner half a kilogram of "smelly pork" at a discounted price. The police eventually outlawed this practice as well, citing gambling as well as sanitation concerns. Some meat peddlers sold at a discount meat from diseased pigs, horses, and cattle, and many people who ate it became ill. The police tried to find the peddlers, and if they did, they threw the meat into the river publicly and punished the sellers. See STJZ III-3; TSRB July 21, July 23, Sept. 11, 1909; Apr. 29, 1910; GMGB Sept. 5, 1914.

10. STJZ I-8; TSRB Nov. 1, 1909; GMGB June 26, 1914.

11. CDTL 1: 390–91.

12. TSRB Mar. 2, Apr. 14, 1910; GMGB May 20, 1914; Wen Shu, Wu Jianzhou, and Cui Xianchang 1984: 15–27.

13. Maniai 1898; CDTL 1: 562; Hartwell 1921: 24.

14. CDTL 1: 199–200, 563; TSRB Aug. 27, 1909.

15. Vale 1904, no. 4: 86; STJZ III-2. Street sweepers' social status was not as low as one might expect; because they were hired by the police, they considered themselves "official employees." An article in one local newspaper accused a street sweeper of 'bullying common people." It reported that a street sweeper had dashed madly down the street and struck a woman and her children with his garbage cart. Not only did he fail to apologize, but he also hurled verbal abuse. His behavior provoked anger from residents and pedestrians (GMGB Mar. 17, 1914).

16. Hubbard 1923: 16; GMGB Dec. 2, 1928.

17. Stapleton mentioned that in 1906 the police issued instructions to standardize the construction of public lavatories (2000: 136–37).

18. STJZ III-1; TSRB May 9, 1910; GMGB Apr. 1, July 29, 1914; Apr. 6, 1917.

19. Regarding immigration in the early Qing, see Wang Di 1993: chap. 2.

20. TSRB June 17, 1909; Ba Jin 1985 [1932]: 338–39; Wang Tianshou 1991: 50.

21. Quoted in Nasaw 1993: 8.

22. WCMN 1903, no. 5: 76; GMGB Mar. 1, 1917; CDTL 1: 200.

23. Xiliang, 1905; WCMN 1903, no. 5: 76.

24. Both standard Chinese and the local dialects have many words for "bad men." In Hankou, William Rowe found *pigun* (toughs), *dipi* (local toughs), *guntu* (ruffians), and *zhongchen* ("loyal ministers")(1989: 218). Except for the last example, these words were also common in Chengdu residents' vocabulary. Chengdu people also had many other words to describe hoodlums, such as *duoshen* (literally "evil deities"), *eshao* (brutal young men), *liumang* (hooligans), *qingbao shaonian* (frivolous boys), *wulai* (rogues), *hundan* (bastards), and *wuye liupi* (unemployed and wandering ruffians). Those from rich families were called *wankua zidi* (profligate sons of the rich). The term *duoshen*, which is found only in Chengdu dialect, was the most frequently used term (Liang Deman and Huang Shangjun 1998: 124).

25. Woman Gao, the wife of a laborer who lived in Three Lanes Street (Sandao jie) in the Smaller City, was victimized by several "immoral bastards," who peeped at her, took other liberties with her when her husband was at work, and beat her when she resisted (GMGB June 16, 1914). One of the rascals was named Wu Huanzhang. After his name was revealed in the newspaper, a famous local lawyer with same name was so angered that he demanded that the newspaper clear his name (GMGB June 18, 1914).

26. GMGB Mar. 10, Mar. 15, Mar. 19–20, 1917; STJZ II-3.

27. TSRB July 10, Aug. 4, 1909; Chen Kuan 1911: 150–51.

28. TSRB Oct. 12, 1909. A similar story appeared in the same paper: Yao, a local hooligan, led several of his followers to the brothels on Meteorite Street (Tianyashi)—a "red light district"—every day to drink and eat. The reformers condemned Yao and his men as "shameless," appealed to the police to eliminate them, and also criticized prostitutes for "loving to be their slaves." See TSRB Oct. 2, 1909.

29. GMGB May 31, 1913.

30. GMGB Aug. 16, Oct. 2, 1914; Mar. 11, 1919. One such story is particularly interesting: a hooligan grabbed the foot of a sedan-chair passenger, thinking the passenger was a woman, but instead, the foot turned out to belong to the magistrate of Huayang County. As a result, the man was punished severely (GMGB July 12, 1914).

31. TSRB Dec. 10, 1909; GMGB Dec. 29, 1927. Once, more than ten men, old and young, poor and rich, were forced to kneel at the site of the Flower Fair merely because they tried to enter through the female entrance. Among them, the reporter noticed, there was even "a man wearing intellectual-style glasses and a silk gown" (GMGB Mar. 26, 1919).

32. GMGB Mar. 21, 1919. Such punishment seems improbably harsh. I was skeptical about "two thousand times" and assumed that it was a mistake of "twenty times" or, at most, "two hundred times." In an earlier date's *Citizens' Daily* (Guomin gongbao), however, there was another report that a "hooligan" was beaten two thousand times with a "big wooden board" simply because he touched a woman's hand (GMGB Mar. 20, 1919). I wonder if the newspaper exaggerated the severity of the punishments.

33. Since the issue of opium has been discussed by my previous work (1993: 641–43) and by Stapleton (2000: 133–34), I will not repeat the discussion here. The following gives a brief description of the situation: Sichuan had been one of the biggest centers of opium cultivation in China, providing users with a ready supply. Opium production in Sichuan was the most extensive in all of China; in 1906, it totaled 238,000 *dan* (1 *dan* = 60 kilograms), out of 584,800 *dan* in all of China (Li Wenzhi 1957: 457). For more about opium cultivation in Sichuan, see Wang Di 1993: 153–55. Social reformers and local governments thus conducted a campaign to restrict opium use. A 1903 police regulation prohibited women, youths under age twenty, students, and soldiers from entering opium houses. After 1907, the local government conducted a more aggressive policy forbidding opium; the Bureau for the Prohibition of Opium (*jinyan ju*) was established in Chengdu, and all opium houses and opium equipment shops were ordered to close. Policemen searched everyone entering the city gates and destroyed all opium equipment found in brothels. They also prohibited opium equipment in public spaces (STJZ I-11; SCGB 1907, no. 6; TSRB July 21, Aug. 1, 1909). In the meantime, programs to help addicts were established in the name of social reform. The police built a hospital for opium addicts, and the Chamber of Commerce set up the Merchants' House for Opium Addiction Recovery (Shangjie jieyan suo) and requested all shops to register their employees who used opium. Employees who did not quit smoking opium and who refused to enter the house were to be fired; otherwise, the shop owner would be punished. Within a year, more than two thousand merchants quit smoking opium, it was reported (SCGB 1909, no. 11). In the early Republic, however, opium consumption surged under loose administrative oversight and political instability, as powerful warlords took over the opium trade.

34. Wang Di 1998a: 41; CDTL 1: 200, 298–302, TSRB Mar. 19, 1910.

35. TSRB June 30, July 3, 1909.

36. TSRB Aug. 26, Sept. 1, Oct. 27, 1909; Mar. 13, Oct. 21, 1910.

37. We will come back to this issue in Chapter 6.

38. Walters 1978: 173–74, 197, 200; SCGB 1906, 15; *Huayang xianzhi* 1934: 331–41; GMGB June 21, 1913; May 6, 1914.

39. Vale 1907, no. 9: 6–7; no. 10: 8; STJZ I-2; *Sichuan xuebao* 1905, no. 5; Xiliang 1959: 646, 648; SCGB 1906, no. 28. Stapleton pointed out that in fact most beggars fled the city for the suburbs (2000: 26–27).

40. Vale 1907, no. 9: 7; no. 10: 7–9; Jiang Yungang 1943.

41. Vale 1907, no. 10: 7–9.

42. The issue of beggars' resistance is addressed in the next chapter.

43. STJZ I-5; Wallace 1903: 43; GMGB Feb. 21, 1913.

44. The "winter defense" began in the post-Taiping era. In winter, grain prices rose and rural refugees would flock to the cities. Thus, in winter officials paid special attention to local security and relief. Such activities gradually became institutionalized. Also see Rowe 1989: 129–30 for discussion of the winter defense in nineteenth-century Hankou.

45. GMGB Jan. 7, Mar. 14, 1916; Feb. 25, 1917.

46. CDRB Aug. 8, 1909; GMGB Jan. 10, Apr. 15, 1918. In the ruins, one reporter wrote, fifty to sixty children played a game of war, throwing rocks and bricks at each other while constantly shouting "Kill!" The game of "leapfrog,"

though very popular, was forbidden by the police, because children sometimes fell and were injured as they jumped over their playmates' bowed backs (TSRB Aug. 6, 1909; GMGB May 18, 1917).

47. CDTL 1: 201; GMGB Apr. 15, May 13, 1918.

48. GMGB Aug. 13, 1912; CDTL 1: 276; STJZ I-1.

49. WCMN 1903, no. 3: 45; 1905, no. 12: 258; Rowe 1989: 164; TSRB Apr. 13, 1910.

50. TSRB July 18, 1909; CDRB Aug. 11, 1906; CDTL 1: 58. After a local fire brigade put out a fire in a shop on East Great Street, the keeper of the shop went to the police station to express his apologies and offer to pay for a *huojiao*, a ceremony in which Daoist priests performed a fire-prevention rite. The police responded that a *huojiao* would do nothing for fire control; however, the money would help purchase a few emergency water vats (TSRB Mar. 14, 1910).

51. TSRB Oct. 26, 1909; *Chengdu zhi tongxun* 15: 10; CDRB Aug. 11, 1909.

52. WCMN 1907, no. 9: 20. In another case, a woman carrying a child dropped her money; when a man identified as a "laborer" picked it up, a policeman who saw him made him return it. Another story is about a young man on a horse who knocked over an old woman. After pedestrians stopped the young man, the old woman stood up and said she was uninjured. A policeman confirmed this but still ordered the young man to hire a sedan chair to take her back home. The poor woman said, "I don't want to take the sedan chair but would rather get 200 *wen*." The policeman replied, "200 *wen* is useless," and persuaded the old woman to take the sedan chair (GMGB Mar. 24, July 13, 1914).

53. TSHB 1909, no. 6. Another case in point is Gao Laoyao, a shop owner in the area of the Nine Arches Bridge who often drank to excess, behaving crudely and using foul language. Once, a policeman expelled him from a restaurant because he punched the cook and the waiter. In another report, a drunken man charged into the First Tea Balcony (Diyi chalou), shouting loudly, and was subdued only after policemen arrived. "If not for his expensive clothing," *Popular Daily* commented, "he would have been taken to the police station" (TSRB Nov. 1, Dec. 21, 1909).

54. A former official, for example, fired because of his addiction to opium, eventually went insane. One day, with stick in hand, he dashed into the street, announcing that foreign lamps were not allowed, and broke two. He then ran to the office of the local administrators, planted himself in front of the gate, and refused to leave, only to be removed later by three policemen before an inquisitive crowd (TSRB Sept. 23, 1909). Another instance of irrational conduct occurred at the Flower Fair. Policemen discovered a man speaking and behaving strangely and promptly escorted him to the station for "compromising public security." Later, it was learned that he had mental problems (GMGB Mar. 10, Mar. 23, 1914).

55. Once, as a customer was enjoying his lunch in a restaurant, the shopkeeper's black dog bit his leg until it bled, for example. Those who brought dogs to public places were often criticized by elites (TSRB Oct. 26, Oct. 28, 1909).

56. CDTL 2: 348.

57. Johnson 1995: 46; 1989: 25; Smith 1991: 221.

58. TSRB June 6, 1910; GMGB June 24, 1914; June 19, 1917.

59. The efforts that traditional occupations made to organize in Shanghai are discussed in Xu 2001: chap. 7.

60. TSRB Sept. 2, 1909; GMGB Nov. 16, 1927; Dec. 10, 1928; Huayang xianzhi 1934: 399–401.

61. TSRB June 6, 1910; GMGB May 3, May 17, 1914; Grainger 1917b: 8; CDTL 1: 549; *Chongxiu Chengdu xianzhi* 1873: 2; *Huayang xianzhi* 1934: 413.

62. GMGB May 13, 1913; May 3, 1914; May 6, 1918. One "benevolent person" bought 600 turtles and, after having their shells carved with Chinese characters, released them into the pond, by one account (GMGB May 13, 1918).

63. Geertz 1973: 148.

64. GMGB May 17, 1914; Feb. 9, 1919.

65. STJZ I-5; TSRB Dec. 10, 1909.

66. TSRB Feb. 6, Feb. 26, Sept. 27, Nov. 22, Dec. 17, 1909; Mar. 22, 1910.

67. Braudel 1975: 434.

68. SSSD: 6; Li Jieren 1980 [1936]: 338–39; GMGB July 8, 1914; Mar. 6, 1917.

69. Duis 1983: 4.

70. Zhou Zhiying 1943: 246; SSSD: 18–19; GMGB Aug. 4, 1912.

71. STJZ I-10, I-12; Shengyuan jingqu zhangcheng n.d.: 27; Rosenzweig 1983: 225.

72. GMGB Apr. 27, 1914.

73. For example, 400 seats were permitted for the Cluster Deity (Qunxian), 200 for the Joy, 150 for the Sichuan Theater (Shuwutai), 120 for the Elegant and the Tasty, and 100 for the Long Spring (GMGB Dec. 26, 1916).

74. GMGB Dec. 26, 1916; Dec. 10, 1921; Wakeman 1995a: 20.

75. Wang Qingyuan 1944: 36–37; CSSN 1927: 510–11; Wang Di 2001.

76. Wakeman has made a profound study of this issue in Shanghai (1995b).

77. Jia Daquan and Chen Yishi 1988: 369; SSSD: 20–23.

78. SSSD: 14–20.

79. Chapter 7 discusses this issue in greater detail.

80. Yeh 1995; Shao 1997.

81. Davis 1988: 36.

82. Vale 1904, no. 6: 126.

83. Vale 1904, no. 5: 110; Yamakawa 1909: 95; Wilson 1929: 122.

84. Peiss 1986: 164; Davis 1988: 29–30.

85. For instance, the warlord government forced public bathhouses to replace traditional Chinese wooden tubs with Western-style porcelain ones, which, at that time, had to be imported from the West or Japan. This policy immediately devastated the bathhouse business. Liu Shiliang, owner of the Double Dragon Pond Bathhouse (Shuanglong chi zaotang), faced bankruptcy and finally had to close his business when he discovered he lacked the capital to purchase the foreign tubs (Zhong Maoxuan 1984:86).

86. Zhou Shanpei 1957; Guo Moruo 1978 [1929]: 187; Li Jieren 1980 [1937]. Kristin Stapleton has given a similar explanation: "Zhou was disliked because of his zeal for reforming public behavior in the city" (2000: 110).

CHAPTER 6: THE STRUGGLE FOR THE STREET

1. Scott 1985: 36. This situation is unlike, though not entirely, the one described by Richard Cobb in his book *The Police and the People*, which states that the principal weapon of the common people is "collective violence" (1970: 86). Indeed, in

both Western and Chinese cities, riots—especially food riots—were very common. See Cobb 1970: 92; Esherick 1976: chap. 4; Perdue 1986; Rowe 1989: 207–11; Bouton 1993.

2. This situation resembled that in Hankou and Xiangtan, where "certain deeper animosities between cultural groups" were frequently displayed at community events such as the dragon boat race (Rowe 1989: 200; Perdue 1986: 190).

3. GMGB Feb. 26, Apr. 2, 1916; Oct. 13, 1917.

4. GMGB Aug. 19, 1914. Neighbors also played a role in stopping crime. A story in a local newspaper explained how a mentally disabled girl escaped being raped. When the headman of Jade Emperor Temple Street (Yuhuang guan jie) saw the young girl wandering at night and discovered her handicap, he became concerned for her security and arranged for her to stay overnight in the night watchman's house. The watchman attempted to rape her, however, and when she screamed, the neighbors stopped him. Angry neighbors tied him up, beat him 200 times on the palms of his hands, and sent him to the police. He was told he was "old, low, and bawdy" and was fired (GMGB Dec. 6, 1927).

5. TSRB Aug. 9, 1909; Apr. 23, 1912. In another story, a waiter in a restaurant on Osmanthus Flower Street (Guihua jie) who was widely known to be "rude and violent" threw a bowl at a customer and split open his head. The incident happened because the waiter mistakenly asked for a payment of twelve *wen* after the customer finished a six-*wen* dish. When the customer protested, the waiter thought that he was trying to "eat illegal money" (*chi lanqian*) and attacked him. The waiter was arrested (TSRB May 20, 1910). "Eating illegal money" was a local phrase that referred to the common practice of sneaking away from a restaurant after a meal without paying.

6. TSRB Oct. 15, 1909; Aug. 2, 1911.

7. Perry 1980: 59–60; Antony 1995: 122.

8. Feng Jiaji 1924: 90; GMGB Mar. 17, 1917.

9. GMGB Mar. 23, May 4, June 23, 1914; Hartwell 1921: 25.

10. GMGB Aug. 19, 1912; Feb. 19, July 29, Aug. 19, Dec. 29, 1914; Sept. 15, 1916.

11. GMGB Feb. 14, 1914; June 5, 1917; Feb. 21, 1918, June 4, 1930; CDTL 1: 299.

12. Rosenzweig 1983: 51; Zhou Zhiying 1943: 247; Suzuki 1982: 530; He Manzi 1994: 192.

13. Rowe 1989: 16; Zhou Zhiying 1943: 247; Hu Tian 1938: 70.

14. Yi Junzuo 1943: 104; Shu Xincheng 1934: 142–43.

15. The more than 620 teahouses in Chengdu in 1931 could be classified into four levels. The first included more than 20 teahouses on the prosperous streets, each of which usually employed more than 20 workers and made more than 200 *yuan* each day from tea sales. The second constituted about 90, each employing a dozen or more workers and earning more than 100 *yuan* in sales. The third numbered around 300, each employing 5 or 6 workers and earning 40 to 50 *yuan*. The fourth, numbering around 200, were one-room teahouses that each employed 3 or 4 workers and made about 20 *yuan* (GMGB Jan. 15, 1931).

16. Zhou Zhiying 1943: 247; Sichuan sheng wenshi guan 1987: 464. When "drinking overtime tea" the rules were to drink only tea that was uncovered, which indicated that the patron had left, and not to drink directly from the cup but use

the lid to ladle out the tea from the cup. In one story, an elderly man recalled drinking "overtime tea" as a young man, when he had just arrived in Chengdu from the countryside to work as a coolie. Once, he was hungry and thirsty but without a job, and the only sustenance he had was "overtime tea." Miraculously, he found a fifty-cent silver coin under a cup-lid, which was enough to feed him for half a month, enabling him to survive (Hao Zhicheng 1997: 39–40).

17. GMGB June 1, 1914; Mar. 13, 1917; TSRB Oct. 21, 1909; Xiao Han 1986: 38; Peng Qinian 1963: 159.

18. TSRB Dec. 21, 1909; May 15, 1910; GMGB Dec. 26, 1916.

19. TSRB Feb. 26, Sept. 1, 1909; Mar. 24, 1910; Aug. 1, 1911.

20. GMGB Jan. 5, 1916; June 12, 1922; Aug. 5, 1930; Zhong Maoxuan 1984: 59, 62.

21. I was able to find one such case in the *Popular Daily*: When a man was drinking tea in the Chicken Fighting Stage Teahouse (Douji tai chapu), his nephew, who was regarded as a local villain (*wulai*), suddenly showed up, punched his uncle in the nose, then ran away (TSRB Aug. 8, 1911).

22. Sometimes, however, hooligans could also be victims. A local newspaper reported such a story: a company commander dressed in civilian clothes went to a teahouse in the North City Park (Beicheng gongyuan) with his wife. When several hoodlums took liberties with her, he ordered his soldiers to assault the hoodlums with truncheons (GMGB June 27, 1929).

23. GMGB July 17, 1928; May 29, Aug. 6, Sept. 24, 1930.

24. TSRB May 3, 1909; GMGB Aug. 30, 1914; Aug. 4, 1916; Jan. 27, July 29, Aug. 1, Aug. 18, Sept. 15, Sept. 16, 1929; May 29, 1930; Tan Shaohua 1984: 120.

25. GMGB Mar. 28, 1928.

26. TSRB Aug. 29, 1909.

27. CDTL 1: 279; Xiao Han 1986: 38; Peng Qinian 1963: 159.

28. GMGB Feb. 1, 1914; Mar. 29, 1916; *Chengdu shi shizheng gongbao* 1930, no. 17; 1932, no. 43; Qian Ren 1928: 106.

29. GMGB June 25, 1929; Aug. 8, 1930; *Chengdu shi shizheng gongbao* 1932, no. 44; Vincent 1982: 40.

30. Honig 1992. For discussion of the struggle for the use of public space, see Chapter 6.

31. Edward Rhoads's recent book (2000), *Manchus and Han*, gives a national perspective on relations between the Manchus and the Han people.

32. Wang Di 1993: 79. Regarding Manchu people in late-Qing Chengdu, see Stapleton 1993: 50–51. Folk writers depicted the Manchu lifestyle of hunting, watching local operas, and fishing. Near the barracks of the western city, townspeople could see the horses of the Manchus grazing on the grassland. An account told of the Chengdu Manchus' other hobbies: "The Manchu families who live by the Western Parade Ground do not favor a luxurious lifestyle, but they buy flowers as soon as they have money. They have to sell those flowers when they cannot afford food" (Yang Xie 1804: 47, 55).

33. Wu Haoshan 1855: 72, 76–77; Li Jieren 1980 [1937].

34. Scott 1985: xix; Elliott 1990: 56; Li Jieren 1980 [1937]; Wei Yingtao 1990: 725–26.

35. Yang Xie 1804: 50, 58; Dingjinyan 1805: 63.

36. Braudel 1975: 374.

37. Skinner 1964–65; Wang Di 1993: chap. 4.

38. TSRB Oct. 28, 1909; GMGB Dec. 9, 1913.

39. GMGB May 20, 1917. A similar story can be found in GMGB May 10, 1917. Such confusions also occurred among city dwellers.

40. CDTL 1: 306; GMGB Sept. 4, 1914; Nov. 8, 1916; July 22, 1922. Rural peasants were easy prey for urban toughs. In one case, a countryman came to Chengdu with 90 taels of silver to pay off his debt to a shop on East Great Street. While en route, several strangers approached him and said they were from his hometown. He joined them for tea, but after smoking a cigarette they gave him he began to feel dizzy and eventually lost consciousness. When he awoke, his silver and the strangers were long gone. These kinds of incidents sometimes had more tragic consequences. For example, a young country boy who went to Chengdu from Hunan to look for his older brother hanged himself after all of his money and clothes were stolen and he was unable to find any information on his brother (GMGB Dec. 9, 1913; May 13, 1914).

41. Perdue 1986.

42. Wang Di 1993: chap. 1; Wu Haoshan 1855: 75–76.

43. A widespread story in Chengdu adds more interesting insight into the tense relations between old and new immigrants. After Shaanxi people became established in Chengdu in the 1880s, they wanted to build their own guildhall for their native place association, but Chengdu people did not like these newly influential traders and initially refused to sell them any land for this purpose. Finally, after much negotiation, the Shaanxi people bought property in a low-lying, muddy area that had to be filled in with rocks and earth before construction could begin. Their plan was thwarted when they were denied permission to transport material from any other areas of Chengdu. The association then called upon all Shaanxi people to bring a bag of dry earth with them from their homeland. Within two years, the wetland was filled (Lu Zhaoyue 1988: 83). This story might overstate the "mean-spirited nature" of Chengdu people and their feud with Shaanxi people, but it reflects the conflict that existed between residents and outsiders.

44. GMGB Mar. 12, Mar. 17, July 22, 1914; July 28, 1917. A story in a local newspaper told how a countryman recognized a man with a "ferocious face" in Mule and Horse Market (Luoma shi) Street as being one of the bandits who had robbed his home in Shifang County (GMGB May 23, 1917).

45. CDTL 1: 112.

46. Chizuka 1926: 233; GMGB July 25, 1914; Mar. 17, 1917; Lin Kongyi 1986: 196; Sewell 1986: 25; TSRB Feb. 20, 1910.

47. GMGB Dec. 2, 1916; Lin Kongyi 1986: 188. Even poor women influenced social trends. Apparently, when one woman with "natural" (unbound) feet carried a heavy load of water through the Center for Promoting Commerce and Industry, her strength drew great attention, and reformers immediately used this incident as an example to promote the "advantage of natural feet" (TSRB Sept. 4, 1909).

48. Lin Kongyi 1986: 196, 214; TSHB 1912, no. 2.

49. Qian Ren 1928: 104; Lin Kongyi 1986: 215; GMGB July 12, 1912; Mar. 23, 1914.

50. TSRB Aug. 9, 1909; May 4, 1910; Aug. 20, 1911.

51. TSRB Aug. 6, Oct. 28, 1909.

52. CDTL 1: 277–79; Li Jieren 1980 [1937]: 1464; GMGB Apr. 25, Oct. 31, 1912; TSRB Aug. 1, Aug. 15, 1911; TSHB 1912, no. 35.

53. GMGB Mar. 21, 1919.

54. Regulations included: (1) no male or female patrons could arrive at the theater more than half an hour before the show; (2) no female patron could put on makeup or change clothes in the balcony (which was reserved for women); (3) no female patron could point to male patrons downstairs; (4) no male patron could go upstairs, even if his wife was there; (5) no male or female patrons, even if they were a couple, could send food or anything else to each other; (6) no boys over thirteen could be taken to the balcony; (7) no female patron could open the curtains that kept the men from looking at the women; (8) no children could lean out of the curtains; (9) the female patrons upstairs and male patrons downstairs could not make jokes, make noise, or throw anything to each other; (10) no male servant boy or husband was allowed upstairs; (11) female patrons could not exchange seats or talk to each other; (12) servant girls could not go downstairs once the show had begun (GMGB Apr. 8, 1913).

55. TSRB Apr. 29, 1910.

56. GMGB May 13, 1913; Mar. 8, 1914; Mar. 2, 1917.

57. TSRB Feb. 17, Mar. 5, 1910. In another case, on the day of the traditional Climbing High to Escape Disease Festival (*you baibing*), two women were assaulted, resulting in police intervention (TSRB Feb. 20, 1910).

58. The policy sometimes caused confusion. On one ladies' night, a policeman stopped an old country woman who was wearing a long blue gown and felt hat. He discovered that the person he was addressing was a woman only when she removed her hat (TSRB Oct. 15, 1909).

59. From Ba Jin's novel, we can also see that women's freedom in public was still pretty much limited (1985 [1932]).

60. CDTL 1: 112–13; GMGB Aug. 2, 1914; Oct. 15, Dec. 9, 1927; TSRB Oct. 27, Dec. 10, 1909.

61. Both Dorothy Ko (1994) and Susan Mann (1997) have pointed out that in traditional Chinese society, women in a certain area or class could live quite different lives from other women, although both authors basically deal with elite women in the Jiangnan region.

62. After Yuan Shikai declared himself emperor of China in December 1915, a National Protection army came to fight the monarchist movement. See Young 1977: chap. 8.

63. Hu Guofu 1916: 160–61; GMGB Dec. 5, 1916.

64. TSRB Aug. 13, 1909. The successful actress had similar counterparts in Beijing and Tianjin during the same period (Cheng 1996).

65. TSRB Oct. 10, 1909; Aug. 15, 1911.

66. Qian Ren 1928: 100; Lin Kongyi 1986: 111, 170, 196, 212. Regarding the stories about the police locking up "hoodlums" for public humiliation, see Chapter 5.

67. Wu Yu 1984 2: 774; CDTL 2: 113. Women even became involved in the traditional male activity of "settling disputes in teahouses." A report from the *Citizens' Daily* (Guomin gongbao) told such a story. A woman nicknamed "Chaokou"

(quarreling mouth) had a fight with Woman Wei over a gambling debt, and Chaokou was wounded. Chaokou gathered more than ten people in the Fountain (Yongquan) Teahouse to settle the dispute, but Wei brought twice that number. As the mediations came to an end, a fight threatened to break out, and Woman Fang, a leader of "women bachelors" (nü guanggun), was asked to step in. "Fang severely reprimanded both sides and ordered them not to fight any more. She also ordered Chaokou to pay the cost of the tea. The two women acceded to the settlement and left with their followers" (GMGB July 17, 1930). This anecdote indicates that women had indeed begun to play an active role in the public space formerly dominated by men.

68. K'ung Shang-ren 1976; Ko 1994. For more information on prostitution in the Song dynasty in the coastal area, see Gernet 1968: 96-100.

69. Xue Xuan ca. 1420: 120; Dingjinyan 1805: 60; Yang Xie 1804: 54.

70. TSRB Mar. 8, 1910; Hershatter 1991: 260. Hershatter's recent book on prostitution in Shanghai is the most complete study of prostitution in modern China (1997). Obviously, social reformers regarded clothing as a symbol of social status and did not want it to be a source of social confusion. More examples can also be found in Fu Chongju's writing, including his suggestion that people from "lower society" be prohibited from wearing leather boots (CDTL 1: 200).

71. CDTL 1: 193, 200. One such story concerned a man who became involved with a prostitute nicknamed "Second Cunning Sister" (Qiao Erjie), who lived just across from the Pine Tree Pavilion Teahouse (Qingsongting chayuan). After the man had become bankrupt from spending all his money on her, she told her servants to turn him away whenever he called (TSRB Oct. 10, 1909).

72. TSRB July 27, Aug. 1, Aug. 2, Aug. 9, 1909.

73. Pang Huifang was one such woman. After reforming and leading a good life, "she once dressed up and brought a servant girl and a servant boy to visit the women in the House and talk about the morality of ceasing to sell one's flesh. Many women were touched by what she said." In another story, a woman named Zhao married a member of the local gentry, and she was able to "keep the way of a decent woman." She and her husband visited the House and donated 20 yuan to it in appreciation (TSRB Aug. 2, Aug. 13, 1909).

74. In one report from the late Qing, a prostitute claimed to the police that she was from a good family but had been trapped in a brothel. The police arranged for her admittance into the House of Reformed Prostitutes. In another report, an old woman allegedly enticed a young girl to become a prostitute. Her mother agreed to take her back, precipitating a family crisis when her brother attempted to beat her to death for her shameful acts. As a result, the police arrested the old woman and sent her to a labor camp (TSRB Aug. 1, Dec. 10, 1909; May 14, 1910). In another, a servant girl went out on the street and was not seen again, and it was later discovered that she had been sold into prostitution by a stranger she met on the street on Five Baskets Hill (Wudan shan). Some unfortunate women were even forced to become prostitutes by their husbands. An "unemployed vagrant," who had come from a late-Qing official family but fell into poverty during the early Republic, beat his wife "black and blue" after she refused to become a prostitute (GMGB June 11, July 22, 1914). Wu Yuncheng, an unemployed man, tried to force his wife into

prostitution, but she refused and voluntarily entered the House for protection. When Wu went to the House to get her, the police stopped him and decreed that she was free to divorce him and marry someone else (TSRB Aug. 7, 1909).

75. CDTL 1: 193–94; Feng Jiaji 1924: 91; TSRB Mar. 8, May 14, 1910. In one case, the police expelled a prostitute nicknamed "Pockmarked Woman Zhang" (Zhang Mapo) from Newly Civilized Street for selling opium. Subsequently, she resurfaced as a madam, although she claimed to be "doing what is proper." She purchased two women and sent them to Newly Civilized Street to be prostitutes, warning them that if they did not earn enough money, she would beat them severely. Following an investigation, she was sent to a labor camp, and the two prostitutes were admitted to the House of Reformed Prostitutes (TSRB Mar. 8, 1910).

76. GMGB Aug. 15, 1922; Dec. 24, 1927; TSRB Dec. 27, 1909. A folk poem mocked: "That lady is which official's wife? Her eyebrows were drawn nicely. To look at her carefully, it seems that I met her in the brothel before" (CDTL 1: 193; Liu Shiliang 1923: 97).

77. TSRB Aug. 3, 1909; GMGB Aug. 6, 1914; Mar. 14, 1917; Mar. 15, 1918.

78. GMGB Sept. 13, 1915; May 9, 1922.

79. GMGB Mar. 5, Mar. 12, Mar. 23, Oct. 7, 1914; Feb. 29, 1916.

80. CDTL 1: 193–94; GMGB July 15, Sept. 22, 1914.

81. GMGB Jan. 19, 1915.

82. Hershatter 1992; 1997: chaps. 10 and 11; GMGB May 9, 1922; Dec. 6, 1927. In the 1930s, prostitution flourished more than ever before. Because many prostitutes came from East China, most of them from Yangzhou, there was a distinction between "native prostitutes" and "Yangzhou prostitutes" (Yangzhou *taiji*), who appeared almost everywhere, from inns, gambling houses, and opium dens to restaurants, teahouses, and theaters (Xiuqing et al. 1988: 57).

83. Ryan 1990: 61.

84. In places like Along City Wall Street (Shuncheng jie), Five Boys Temple (Wutong miao), and Eastern Parade Ground, for example (Yang Xie 1804: 49).

85. Hosie 1890: 86. Compare Fernand Braudel's description of the poor in early modern Naples: "They were so crowded that their life encroached and overflowed on to the streets." A large number of beggars "do not have houses; they find nocturnal asylum in a few caves, stables, or ruined houses." The poor were visible everywhere, "lying like filthy animals, with no distinction of age or sex; all the ugliness and all the offspring which result from this can be imagined." When famine struck, many died in the streets (Braudel 1975: 417). Modern American cities were little different, containing "extremes of wealth and poverty" (Stansell 1986: 198). In nineteenth- and early-twentieth-century Chengdu, one could see almost all the details of Braudel's description of Naples reflected here.

86. Wu Haoshan 1855: 74–75. Another writer expressed a similar sentiment: "On windy and snowy winter nights, people stay at home and wear furs and heavy coats, while the coal peddlers cry out for customers [on the street]" (Dingjinyan 1805: 67).

87. Liu Yuan ca. 1790: 125–26.

88. Vale 1907, no. 4: 8; GMGB May 23, 1912; Sept. 6, 1914; Sept. 4, 1916; May 28, 1922; Nov. 5, 1930.

89. Vale 1906, no. 10: 238. Local newspapers contain many tragic stories involving the poor. A washerwoman committed suicide by jumping into a well, merely because a mosquito net she washed for a customer was stolen. When a man hired by the local army to castrate a violent steed found the horse dying, he slit his own throat with the castration knife. A night watchman in Red Temple Street (Hongmiaozi jie), who lay sick in the watch shed on a cold winter night, put a hand and foot warmer (*honglong*) in his bed to avoid being frozen. As he slept, the warmer turned over, and the resulting fire burned him to death. Because such tragic incidents happened every winter, the police ordered all districts to pay more attention to fire and required all "emergency vats" to be kept filled with water. The police especially noted that for poor families, "hand and foot warmers are not allowed to be put on beds" (GMGB June 21, 1914; Jan. 7, 1916; Mar. 23, 1917).

90. GMGB June 21, 1914; Nov. 10, 1915.

91. GMGB June 30, 1914; Mar. 19, 1916; Feb. 12, July 14, Aug. 25, 1922.

92. Zhong Maoxuan 1984: 51.

93. In Chinese, "*xiaowozhe wufei qiongkun; facairen zongyao beishi*" (GMGB Feb. 10, 1919)

94. CDTL 1: 389, 393–94; Strand 1989: 38; GMGB June 17, 1916. Each shop probably had more than ten carriers. One piece of supporting evidence for this is that in 1916, the Chamber of Commerce asked each shop to provide four carriers for service in the army in order to prevent soldiers from capturing carriers on the street as forced laborers (GMGB June 17, 1916).

95. CDTL 1: 308; Service 1989: 40; Sewell 1986: 102.

96. CDTL 1: 308; GMGB Apr. 1, Oct. 8, 1916; Wilson 1929: 122–23.

97. Sewell 1986: 102. There are more such rhymed couplets in Chen Haodong and Zhang Siyong 1991: 1519–23.

98. Yamakawa 1909: 102; CDTL 1: 309–10; Strand 1989: 38, 46.

99. GMGB Mar. 24, 1916; TSHB 1909, no. 5.

100. GMGB Aug. 25, 1922.

101. CDTL 1: 308; TSRB Oct. 5, Dec. 5, 1909; Mar. 2, 1910; GMGB Mar. 4, May 18, 1917.

102. A few studies of beggars in modern China have been done in the English world, such as Schak 1988; Lu 1999; and Fernández-Stembridge and Madsen 2002. A couple of studies have touched on the issue of beggars in Chengdu; see Wang Di 1998b: chap. 5; and Stapleton 2000: chap. 4. In Chinese, Qu Wenbin published a general history of beggars in China (1990), and some popular books deal with current issues of beggary (Yu Xiu 1999; Liao Yiwu 2001). Several scholars of American and European history have done extensive studies of beggary—see Culbert 1985; Adler 1986; Stanley 1992; Coldham 1992; Fleisher 1995; and Pittenger 1997.

103. Wallace 1903: 16; Vale 1907, no. 4: 9; no. 7: 7; Hosie 1890: 85.

104. GMGB Nov. 29, 1914.

105. The missionary Vale gave a detailed description of how a coolie could become a beggar: "I have known too many cases of coolies who have become beggars within a week or ten days. Suppose an official or merchant engages fifty coolies from Wanhsien [Wanxian, a county in eastern Sichuan] to Chentu [Chengdu], a distance which takes fourteen days to cover. The coolie, when he starts out on the

journey, receives a certain percentage of his pay for expenses en route; he leaves a portion of this, possibly, to support his family, or, as is more frequently the case, to pay off old debts incurred during the days he has been waiting to be hired. If all goes well he will have a small balance to draw on on his arrival at the capital. This, with 'wine money' given by his employer, will enable him to get back to his home by boat or wait until he gets another engagement in some other direction. But, if he becomes footsore or gets a chill by the way, he has to hire a substitute to carry his load, so that, by the time he arrives at his destination he has used up all his money and probably drawn something of his 'return money' from the headman. Having settled with his employer and headman, no one is responsible for him to see that he gets back to his home, and after a few days in a strange city the innkeeper will not allow him to stay in his inn; he has also pawned his last garment, and within a week he is on the street with a bowl and a pair of chop-sticks, using the piteous cry of *shan ren lao ie, ko pa sheng fan* [shanren laoye, guoba shengfan]: 'benevolent sirs, crusts of rice, or surplus rice'" (1907, no. 4: 10-11).

106. Vale 1907, no. 4: 9-10; no. 9: 6; Ba Jin 1989 [1944].

107. GMGB July 14, 1922; Wu Jianzhou and Wu Zhaobo 1989: 27.

108. Zhang Jiqing 1981 [1820s-60s]: 112; Wu Haoshan 1855: 77; GMGB Aug. 6, 1914; July 22, 1922.

109. Vale 1907, no. 7: 8; Hartwell 1921: 24.

110. Wu Jianzhou and Wu Zhaobo 1989: 26; Vale 1907, no. 7: 9; GMGB Mar. 24, 1914.

111. Vale 1907, no. 7: 7.

112. GMGB May 21, 1912; Wu Jianzhou and Wu Zhaobo 1989: 27.

113. CDTL 2: 370; GMGB Aug. 28, 1914; Wu Jianzhou and Wu Zhaobo 1989: 30.

114. Vale 1907, no. 7: 8.

115. Wu Jianzhou and Wu Zhaobo 1989: 29; Vale 1907, no. 7: 8.

116. Liu Yuan ca. 1790: 126. Some beggars used "lotus chatting" as a tool to express their anger about their miserable situation. One case in point occurred after the street war of 1917, when a "mad beggar," whose "face was dark but eyes were bright, looking like a member of a secret society," performed lotus chatting on the street. He was shabbily dressed, with a broken pottery pan and a "dog beating stick" and jumped around, sometimes laughing and sometimes crying, while chatting. His chatter was not the funny stories from daily life that other beggars told; instead, he told of the disaster the warlords had brought to Chengdu and directly mocked the powerful warlords. He even talked about national and international affairs (GMGB May 17, 1917).

117. Vale 1907, no. 7: 7; CDTL 2: 370; Wu Jianzhou and Wu Zhaobo 1989: 27-28. In the past, some poor women used the public lavatories as their "delivery rooms" in order to receive public welfare money.

118. Lu 1999b: 25.

119. Wu Jianzhou and Wu Zhaobo 1989: 28.

120. Wu Jianzhou and Wu Zhaobo 1989: 29.

121. Vale 1907, no. 7: 9; GMGB Jan. 9, 1922.

122. TSHB 1909, no. 6.

123. GMGB Feb. 9, 1919.

124. GMGB May 23, 1912; May 15, May 17, 1914.

CHAPTER 7: STREET POLITICS

1. Kapp 1973: 5.

2. My 1993 book gave a close look at the Chengdu city councils, including their structures, membership, functions, and social impacts. See Wang Di 1993: 403 and chap. 8. Also see Stapleton 2000: chap. 5.

3. Escherik 1976; Schoppa 1982; Rankin 1986.

4. CDTL 1: 4, 546–47.

5. *Sichuan ziyiju* 1910: 61–62; TSRB July 18, 1909; CDTL 1: 340, 358; *Sichuan jiaoyu guanbao* 1911, no. 28.

6. CDTL 1: 112; Wasserstrom 1991: 4–5.

7. CDTL 1: 2.

8. CDTL 1: 3.

9. CDTL 1: 109, 111, 271.

10. Duara 1995: chap. 6; Skinner 1971: 275; Weber 1958: 81–83. In fact, as I noted in Chapter 2, some historians of China have demonstrated beyond doubt that premodern China had indeed formed well-developed urban communities and urban culture. The case of Chengdu also supports this contention. In 1914, the Memorial Monument for the 1911 Sichuan Railroad Protection was built in the Smaller City Park (Sichuan sheng wenshi guan 1987: 461). The monument later came to symbolize Chengdu itself, acting as a significant visual representation of the city's self-image. It also provides tangible evidence against the argument that the lack of "civic monuments" in Chinese cities suggests a lack of "corporate identity" (Mote 1977: 114).

11. Wei Yingtao 1981: 144; 1990: 356–69; WCMN 1905, no. 3: 57; TSRB Nov. 10, 1909.

12. For detailed accounts of this national movement, see Gasster 1978; Zhang Kaiyuan and Lin Zengping 1981; and Wei Yingtao 1981.

13. Wei Yingtao 1981: 2; Wei Yingtao and He Yimin 1983; Wang Di 1993: chaps. 6–10.

14. Zhong Shixiu 1911: 185.

15. For a detailed account of this incident, see Cunningham 1895.

16. Wei Yingtao 1981: 216; SBTB 1911, nos. 8 and 34.

17. This organization originated in East Great Street, spread to South Gauze Hat Street (Nan shamao jie), and later expanded to Virgin Boy Street (Tongzi jie), Chinese Catalpa Street (Zitong jie), and Horse King Temple Street (Mawang miao jie).

18. SBTB 1911, nos. 8, 10, 24, 32, 35; Li Jieren 1980 [1937]: 315. Others included Dyeworks Street (Ranfang jie), Jade Dragon Street (Yulong jie), Shaanxi Street (Shaanxi jie), Yuqing Street (Yuqing jie), Horse Riding Street (Zouma jie), Indigo Street (Randing jie), Junping Street (Junping jie), Peach Flower Street (Lihua jie), Manchu City (Mancheng), Red Shining Wall Street (Hongzhao bi), and Three Ways Street (Dingzi jie). See SXGS 1: 385.

19. WCMN 1911, no. 11: 8; Wei Yingtao 1981: 226; SBTB 1911, no. 2.

20. Shi Tiyuan 1962: 57.

21. CDRB Aug. 31, 1911; WCMN 1911, no. 11: 11.

22. SBTB 1911, nos. 25 and 36.

23. From the discussion that follows, we can see how local elites tried to restrict commoners' activities on the streets as soon as the new government was established.

24. Ahern 1981: 92; Hunt 1984: 12; Sennett 1977: 239.

25. Hunt 1984: 13; Guo Moruo 1978 [1929]: 228–32; Li Jieren 1980 [1937]: 416–19; Zhou Shanpei 1957: 27.

26. Combe 1924: 8.

27. Dai Zhili 1959: 277; Davis 1988: 6; Hunt 1984: 12, 60.

28. Hunt 1984: 61.

29. SBTB 1911, no. 16; Li Jieren 1980 [1937]: 366; SXGS 1: 385.

30. WCMN 1911, no. 11: 10; Li Jieren 1980 [1937]: 41–42; Guo Moruo 1978 [1929]: 259.

31. Lin Kongyi 1986: 186; Min Changquan 1911: 156; Li Jieren 1980 [1937]: 468; Qin Nan 1914: 373; Wei Yingtao 1981: 292. When family members came to claim their bodies, the government forced them to acknowledge that the dead were "bandits," and charged them forty silver *yuan* (Lin Kongyi 1986: 186).

32. Lin Kongyi 1986: 186–87; Wei Yingtao 1981: 294; Li Jieren 1980 [1937]: 41–42, 638; Combe 1924: 9; Guo Moruo 1978 [1929]: 259.

33. SXGS 1: 470; Stapleton 1996: 36. One morning, for example, children playing on the street saw some mounted soldiers riding from the South City Gate and ran away, crying "They are coming; they are coming." Because people were expecting the Railroad Protection Army to invade, this report quickly swept through the streets. Some shouted, "They are coming by the east gate"; others cried, "they are coming by the south gate"; still others said, "the north gate has been broken through." An observer described that, even "men in the hands of the barbers rushed out, with their hair hanging down and their eyes bulging with fright." Later, of course, people recognized this as a false alarm (WCMN 1911, no. 11: 11).

34. For more on the process of the revolution, see Wei Yingtao 1981; Zhang Kaiyuan and Lin Zengping 1981.

35. SXGS 1: 587–88.

36. The Western Expedition was a military campaign under orders from President Yuan Shikai to put down a rebellion in Tibet. See Wei Yingtao 1990: 731–32.

37. Even in such a militaristic environment, people's more mundane needs are evident: an itinerant kitchen is shown on the street, with a couple of men and children milling around. These pictures provide insight not only into urban spectacles but also into local politics.

38. Secret societies became very active when the movement broke out, and they began to cooperate with the revolutionaries to push the movement into military confrontation. See Wei Yitao and He Yimin 1983. Also, elites skillfully promoted sentiments of nationalism among the masses. For more on antiforeign sentiment, see Wyman 1997.

39. Quoted in Kapp 1973: 57.

40. WCMN 1911, no. 11: 20; SXGS 1: 517. The "hero-tie" was a unique hairstyle during the Revolution. Some soldiers, refusing to have their queues cut off after the Revolution, instead tied them around their foreheads and decorated them with a ribbon (Qin Nan 1914: 548).

41. WCMN 1912, no. 4: 20–22; Kapp 1973: 9. The provincial treasury alone lost six to eight million taels of silver (Wei Yingtao 1990: 715).

42. GMGB Feb. 21, 1913; Apr. 22, June 17, June 27, Aug. 9, 1916; Mar. 21, 1917. Accounts of military officers and soldiers bullying Chengdu residents filled local newspapers. In one case, a soldier not only refused to pay for a meal in a restaurant but also abused the proprietor and broke several bowls. In another case, a resident brought a bowl of paint into the city through the North City Gate, and the soldier standing guard accused him of smuggling opium. When the man complained, the soldier lost his temper and hit the man with the bowl, splitting open his head. Similarly, a tailor going past the gate to the Imperial City, which was being used as a military camp, peered inside out of curiosity. A soldier guarding the gate suspected him of being a spy and tied him up. Soldiers' outrageous acts often aroused public indignation. Once, when twenty or so soldiers bullied the proprietor of a silk shop, an angry mob surrounded them on the street. The soldiers used their bayonets to push back the crowd, the frightened bystanders fled, and all shops on this street were closed to prevent more trouble. The police refused to investigate (GMGB Apr. 23, 1914; Sept. 22, 1916; Mar. 17, June 22, 1917).

43. Chizuka 1926: 133; GMGB Apr. 1, 1916; Jan. 10, Feb. 2, 1917.

44. GMGB Apr. 14, Apr. 20, 1913; Mar. 12, Apr. 27, July 11, July 17, July 22, 1914; Mar. 10, 1918; Qian Ren 1917: 162. It seems that during this period, the presence of a foreigner was a more powerful deterrent than the police were. In one case, a soldier rushed into a females-only reception room at the Two Deities Nunnery and fought off the policeman who tried to stop him. A foreigner, however, "came to the soldier and beat him on the back a few times with a horsewhip without saying a word" (GMGB Mar. 17, 1917).

45. GMGB Feb. 25, Feb. 26, 1913; Feb. 21, 1914.

46. GMGB Mar. 10, 1917.

47. GMGB May 12, 1912; Jan. 22, Jan. 26, Apr. 20, 1913; June 25, 1914; May 17, May 18, 1916; Feb. 8, Mar. 24, 1917.

48. Wang Tianshou 1991:51.

49. Wang Tianshou 1991: 50–51; TSRB May 27, 1910.

50. GMGB Mar. 15, 1913; Oct. 10, 1927.

51. GMGB Oct. 30, Nov. 2, 1916; May 9, 1917; Dec. 6, Dec. 10, 1928.

52. WCMN 1905, no. 1: 13.

53. TSRB Apr. 27, Apr. 28, 1910.

54. GMGB May 24, Dec. 22, 1912; Feb. 10, Feb. 12, Feb. 20, June 5, 1917.

55. GMGB May 21, 1913; May 11, May 20, 1914; Jan. 6, Jan. 7, Jan. 10, Aug. 6, 1916.

56. GMGB May 21, 1916; Mar. 10, May 16, 1917.

57. GMGB Apr. 28, 1914; Aug. 18, Aug. 19, 1915.

58. GMGB Aug. 28, 1914.

59. WCMN 1912, no. 4: 22; Kapp 1973: 15; Wu Yu 1984 I: 265–66.

60. GMGB May 5, 1917. The area included Meng Family Alley (Mengjia xiang), Front of Confucius Temple Street (Wenmiao qianjie), Green Lotus Alley (Qinglian xiang), Red Shining Wall (Hongzhao bi), Peach Flower Street (Lihua jie), Mature Straw Lake (Fencao hu), Brocade River Bridge (Jinjiang qiao), East Imperial Street

(Dongyu jie), West Imperial Street (Xiyu jie), Grinding Stone Street (Mozi jie), Splendid Street (Guanghua jie), Purification Street (Chunhua jie), Tibet Rotating Wheel Street (Zhuanlun zang jie), Upper River Beach (Shang heba), and Lower River Beach (Xia heba).

61. GMGB July 29, 1917.

62. GMGB May 5, May 6, 1917; Huang Yanpei 1936: 177.

63. Lin Kongyi 1986: 151–52; GMGB May 7, May 9, May 15, 1917.

64. GMGB July 24, Aug. 18, 1917; Qian Ren 1917: 162–63. In addition to threats of robbery and property destruction, residents faced shortages of food when the regular flow of trade from outside was blocked. Only the Old West City Gate (Lao ximen) remained open for transporting rice, vegetables, and firewood into town. Meanwhile, when invaders eventually infiltrated most of the interior, the circulation of goods within Chengdu was further restricted. The only area where merchants and peddlers could work was the part controlled by the Sichuan Army, from east of Fluent Street (Tongshun jie) to the Imperial City (GMGB July 24, 1917).

65. SXGS 1: 516–17; Qin Nan 1914: 551.

66. GMGB Oct. 13, 1912; June 1, 1913; Feb. 19, Apr. 9, 1914; Aug. 10, 1916.

67. GMGB May 7, May 21, June 28, July 24, 1917. To organize militia groups was a "active" means of self-protection, whereas to send money and food to robbers as a bribe was a "passive" one. Residents employed both strategies. During the street war in 1917, two thousand soldiers of the Yunnan Army settled in the area of Fragrant Herb and Fountain Street (Chaiquan jie), Heavenly Happiness Street (Tianfu jie), and Oriental Purple Street (Zidong jie). When they began to plunder this area, all the shops collected money to buy food to send to them. The residents were trying to "buy protection": the Yunnan Army subsequently made five rules forbidding robbery and rape in this area (GMGB May 6, 1917). Regardless of whether self-protection was "active" or "passive," we find that when a crisis arose, the neighborhood or the street usually dealt with it collectively rather than as individual families.

68. Li Jieren 1947 [1926]: 131–33.

69. GMGB Oct. 3, 1928.

70. Han Suyin 1965: 228–29. Li Jieren's *The Great Wave* (Dabo) gives more detailed and vivid pictures of the teahouses of this period (Li Jieren 1980 [1937]: 43, 126–27, 153–55, 189, 251, 378, 414, 1057–60, 1327, 1464).

71. Han Suyin 1965: 96; Zhong Maoxuan 1984: 91; GMGB Aug. 20, 1917; SSSD: 23, 31; Wen Wenzi 1990: 454.

72. GMGB Apr. 4, 1912.

73. GMGB May 3, June 15, 1914; Feb. 16, Feb. 21, Apr. 12, 1917.

74. The *shizhuang xi* included *Memorial to Zou Rong* (Ji Zou Rong), *Story of Chengdu* (Chengdu gushi), *Independence of Chongqing* (Chongqing duli), *Xu Xilin Assassinates En Ming* (Xu Xilin ci En Ming), *Huang Xing as a Commander* (Huang Xing guashuai), and *Attacking Canton* (Nao Guangzhou) (Zhou Zhiying and Gao Sibo 1987: 53–54).

75. Zhou Zhiying and Gao Sibo 1987: 55–57; GMGB Oct. 15, 1927; Oct. 31, 1928.

76. Wang Di 1993: 545; Liao T'ai-ch'u 1947: 162.

77. Stapleton 1996: 29. For more on the Gowned Brothers, see Stapleton 2000: 197–203.

78. Wen Wenzi 1990: 455; Wang Dayu 1993: 151–52. One elderly Chengdu resident told me that there were no professional barbers in China before the Qing dynasty and that barbering as an occupation emerged in the early Qing only after the government forced Han men to have their hair cut, but wear a queue. Barbers were known as "*daizhao*" (edict carriers), because they hung the imperial edict on cutting hair on wooden boards on their baskets. Thus, they were regarded by the anti-Manchu Gowned Brothers as servants of the Qing government (Zhou Shaojie, 75 years old, interview by author, Joy Teahouse, June 22, 1997). In his novels, Li Jieren also called barbers "*daizhao*" (1980 [1936]: 339).

79. Although Gowned Brothers members were recognized as the leaders in the unofficial local power structure, their influence was still occasionally challenged by lo-cals, as the following story shows: When a small peddler boy insisted that a man who called himself a senior member of the Gowned Brothers pay the price that he offered, the man became angry and said, "How dare you, a little boy, make trouble for me!" and threatened to take him to the police. Their dispute attracted many onlookers. During the argument, the man inadvertently broke two bottles of oil in an adjoining stall, causing the stall keeper to demand compensation before he would allow the par-ties to leave. The spectators made fun of this event, calling it the true meaning of the expression "Gowned Brothers breaking an oil bottle" (*paoge daoyou*), which was a slang phrase that Gowned Brothers used to mean "being forced to apologize for a wrongdoing" (TSRB Sept. 8, 1907; CDTL 2: 48).

80. STJZ I-3; CDTL 2: 47–50; Wei Yingtao 1981: 347; Stapleton 1996; GMGB Jan. 16, Mar. 24, 1914.

81. Shao Yun 1984: 61; "Chengdu shi paoge" 1949–50; Chen Maozhao 1983: 186.

82. Yun Tao 1933: 15; Wang Dayu 1993:147; Liao T'ai-ch'u 1947: 164.

83. Both were well-known generals who helped emperor Liu Bang establish the Han dynasty (206 B.C.–A.D. 220).

84. Wang Chunwu 1993: 65–66; Yang Wuneng and Qiu Peihuang 1995: 741.

85. Rowe 1989: 207; GMGB Apr. 10, Dec. 1, 1913; TSHB 1912, no. 28.

86. SXGS 1: 603–04; GMGB Mar. 23, 1914; Qin Nan 1914: 548; Hunt 1984: 75.

87. GMGB Feb. 20, 1922. A conversation that expressed a similar sentiment was quoted in the same newspaper on an earlier date (Apr. 9, 1917).

88. Sewell 1971: 27; Stapleton 1997b; Zhong Maoxuan 1984: 83. Regarding Liu Shiliang and his writings, also see Stapleton 2000: 242–45.

89. GMGB Feb. 21, 1914; Mar. 30, 1917. According to another report, Zhu, the headman of Outer East Street (Waidong jie), was a local ruffian (*pigun*) who had been arrested several times for gambling and selling opium. In another case, more than a hundred residents (*jiemin*) on Fluent Street (Tongshun jie) accused their street headman of being a "hoodlum" (GMGB Apr. 6, 1917).

90. In Chinese: "*Malu yi chuicheng, wen duli, heshi caigun? Minfang yi chaijin, yuan jiangjun, zaori kaiche.*" The couplet contains a couple of puns: *caigun* could mean either "rolling (on the street)" or "going away"; *kaiche* could mean either "driving a vehicle" or "getting out of here."

91. Zhong Maoxuan 1984: 25, 40–41, 89. Stapleton has given a more comprehensive analysis of Yang. See Stapleton 2000: 220–37.

92. GMGB Dec. 22, 1921; June 1, 1928; Chizuka 1926: 135.

93. TSRB July 28, July 29, 1909; GMGB Mar. 14, 1917; Dec. 11, Dec. 12, 1928; Hu Tian 1938: 70; Yang Huai 1982: 67; Wen Wenzi 1990: 457.

94. Jianqing 1932: 2–3; Zhang Xiushu 1979[1959]: 886; Strand 1989: 162. Some groups and organizations for ordinary people, though "neither fish nor fowl," still displayed some political color. For example, a Daoist priest claimed that he dreamed he was appointed by the Shining Emperor of Tang (Tang minghuang) to save the world. He and his believers prepared for rebellion, making banners emblazoned with the words "Chinese Heavenly Loyal State" (*Zhonghua tianzheng guo*). In another case, an adolescent boy—sent by an "evil sect"—was caught in Chengdu disguised as a girl, purportedly to gather information for an uprising. In yet another case, a rickshaw puller who lived near the South City Gate gathered more than a hundred teenagers, each of whom paid five *yuan* to prepare a dagger or stick, and organized a "stick society" (*bangbang hui*) (GMGB June 16, July 9, 1914; Oct. 13, 1927). These different kinds of organizations all reflected the anxiety and unrest of the lower classes during this period of general social disorder and their efforts to make their views known.

CHAPTER 8: CONCLUSION

1. Sennett 1977: 222; Rowe 1989: 8; Weber 1958: 83.

2. Sennett 1977: 259.

3. Link, Madsen, and Pickowicz 1989b: 7; Siu 1989: 122.

4. Watson 1985; Johnson 1994; Duara 1991.

5. GMGB Dec. 9, 1913; July 9, Aug. 28, 1914; Mar. 28, 1917.

6. GMGB Oct. 20, 1916.

Works Cited

Abrahams, Roger D. 1970. "A Performance-Centred Approach to Gossip." *Man* 5.2: 290–301.

Adler, Jeffrey S. 1986. "Vagging the Demons and Scoundrels: Vagrancy and the Growth of St. Louis, 1830–1861." *Journal of Urban History* 13.1: 3–30.

Ahern, Emily. 1973. *The Cult of the Dead in a Chinese Village*. Stanford: Stanford University Press.

——. 1981. *Chinese Ritual and Politics*. New York: Cambridge University Press.

Antony, Robert J. 1995. "Scourges on the People: Perceptions of Robbery, Snatching, and Theft in the Mid-Qing Period." *Late Imperial China* 16.2: 98–132.

Arkush, David R. 1990. "Orthodoxy and Heterodoxy in Twentieth-Century Chinese Peasant Proverbs," 311–31 in Liu, ed., 1990.

Ba Jin. 1985 [1932]. *Jia* [Family]. Beijing: Renmin wenxue chubanshe. First published in 1932. My translations are based on the version published by Cheng & Tsui Company, 1972.

——. 1989 [1944]. *Qiyuan* [The rest garden], in *Ba Jin quanji* [Complete collected works of Ba Jin], vol. 8. Beijing: Renmin wenxue chubanshe.

Benedict, Carol. 1996. *Bubonic Plague in Nineteenth-Century China*. Stanford: Stanford University Press.

Berling, Judith A. 1989. "Religion and Popular Culture: The Management of Moral Capital in *The Romance of the Three Teachings*," 188–218 in Johnson, Nathan, and Rawski, 1985.

Bickers, Robert A., and Jeffrey N. Wasserstrom. 1995. "Shanghai's 'Dogs and Chinese Not Admitted' Sign: Legends, History and Contemporary Symbol." *China Quarterly* June (142): 444–66.

Bird, Isabella. 1987 [1899]. *The Yangtze Valley and Beyond: An Account of Journeys in China, Chiefly in the Province of Sze Chuan and Among the Man-sze of the Somo Territory*. First published by John Murray in 1899. Reprinted by Beacon Press, 1987.

Bouton, Cynthia A. 1993. *The Flour War: Gender, Class, and Community in Late Ancien Regime French Society*. University Park: Pennsylvania State University Press.

Brace, Brockman, ed. 1974a. *Canadian School in West China*. Published for the Canadian School Alumni Association, n.p.

——. 1974b. "Kites," 225–27 in Brace, ed., 1974.

Braudel, Fernand. 1975. *Capitalism and Material Life, 1400–1800*, vol. 1. Trans. Miriam Kochan. New York: Harper & Row, Publishers.

Brennan, Thomas. 1988. *Public Drinking and Popular Culture in Eighteenth-Century Paris*. Princeton: Princeton University Press.

Buck, David D. 1978. *Urban Change in China: Politics and Development in Tsinan, Shantung, 1890–1949*. Madison: University of Wisconsin Press.

Cai Qiguo. 1972. "Chuanju xiyu" [Sichuan opera idioms]. SWX 2 (114): 28–30.

Certeau, Michel de. 1984. *The Practice of Everyday Life*. Trans. Steven F. Rendall. Berkeley and Los Angeles: University of California Press.

Chang, Sen-dou. 1977. "The Morphology of Walled Capitals," 75–100 in Skinner, ed., 1977.

Chartier, Roger. 1991. *The Cultural Origins of the French Revolution*. Trans. Lydia G. Cochrane. Durham: Duke University Press.

Che Fu. 1995. "Zhou lianzhang chaguan yu Li Yueqiu" [Company Commander Zhou's teahouse and Li Yueqiu]. LMZ 2 (86): 1–6.

Chen Haodong and Zhang Siyong, eds. 1991. *Chengdu minjian wenxue jicheng* [Treasury of Chengdu folklore]. Chengdu: Sichuan renmin chubanshe.

Chen Jin. 1992. *Sichuan chapu* [Teahouses in Sichuan]. Chengdu: Sichuan renmin chuban she.

Chen Kuan. 1911. "Xinhai huashi zhuzhici" [Bamboo-branch poetry on the Flower Fair of Chengdu in 1911], 150–51 in Lin Kongyi, ed., 1986.

Chen Maozhao. 1983. "Chengdu chaguan" [Teahouses in Chengdu]. CWZX 4: 178–93.

Chen San. 1988. "Chamao guangai hechu xun" [Where to find gauze hats]. LMZ 4 (46): 95–98.

——. 1989. "Jiu Rongcheng yiren yipian" [Tales from my memories of entertainers in old Chengdu]. LMZ 5 (53): 59–61.

Chen Zuxiang and Jiang Mengbi. 1982. "Chengdu Quanye chang de bianqian" [Development of the Center for Promoting Commerce and Industry of Chengdu]. CWZX 3: 144–59.

Cheng Ji and He Chun. 1982. "Shen mo, kupian, lipian" [Magic touch, bitter cheat, and reasonable deceit]. LMZ 2 (8): 119–22.

Cheng, Weikun. 1996. "The Challenge of the Actresses: Female Performers and Cultural Alternatives in Early Twentieth Century Beijing and Tianjin." *Modern China* 22.2: 197–233.

Chengdu fengwu [Chengdu folklore]. 1981. vol. I. Chengdu: Sichuan renmin chubanshe.

Chengdu ribao [Chengdu daily]. 1904–11.

"Chengdu shi paoge de yige jingtou" [A view of the Gowned Brothers in Chengdu]. ca. 1949–50. In Chengdu shi gong'an ju dang'an [Archives of the Chengdu police station].

Chengdu shi shizheng gongbao [Gazette of Chengdu municipal administration]. 1930–32.

Chengdu shi shizheng nianjian [Yearbook of Chengdu municipal administration]. 1927.

Chengdu wenshi ziliao xuanji [Selections on literature and historical materials of Chengdu]. 1960s–1990s. Chengdu.

Chengdu zhi tongxun [Newsletter of Chengdu history]. Ed. Chengdu shi difangzhi bianzhuan weiyuanhui, 1984–1988.

Chevalier, Louis. 1973. *Laboring Classes and Dangerous Classes in Paris During the First Half of the Nineteenth Century*. Trans. Frank Jellinek. New York: Howard Fertig.

Chizuka Reisui. 1926. *Shin nyū-Shoku ki* [Account of a recent trip to Sichuan]. Tokyo: Ōsaka yagō shoten.

Chongxiu Chengdu xianzhi [Revised Chengdu county gazetteer]. 1873. Collected in *Zhongguo difang zhi minsu ziliao huibian* [A collection of materials on folk customs in Chinese gazetteers]. Vol. Xi'nan (Southeast China), pt. 1. Beijing: Shumu wenxian chubanshe, 1988.

Cobb, R. C. 1970. *The Police and the People: French Popular Protest, 1789–1820.* Oxford: Clarendon Press.

Cohen, Myron L. 1990. "Lineage Organization in North China." *Journal of Asian Studies* 49.3: 509–34.

Coldham, Peter Wilson. 1992. *Emigrants in Chains: A Social History of Forced Emigration to the Americas of Felons, Destitute Children, Political and Religious Non-Conformists, Vagabonds, Beggars and Other Undesirables, 1607–1776.* Baltimore: Genealogical.

Combe, G. A. 1924. "Events in Chengdu: 1911." WCMN 5: 5–18.

Couvares, Francis G. 1983. "The Triumph of Commerce: Class Culture and Mass Culture in Pittsburgh," 123–52 in Michael H. Frisch and Daniel J. Walkowitz, eds., *Working-Class America: Essays on Labor, Community, and American Society.* Chicago: University of Illinois Press.

Cui Xianchang. 1982a. "Jiu Rongcheng de shisheng" [City voices in old Chengdu]. LMZ 4 (10): 86–92.

——. 1982b. "Jiu Chengdu chaguan sumiao" [A literary sketch of old Chengdu teahouses]. LMZ 6 (12): 92–102.

Culbert, Sheila Anne. 1986. "Sturdy Beggars and the Worthy Poor: Poverty in Massachusetts, 1750–1820." Unpublished dissertation. Indiana University.

Cunningham, Alfred. 1895. *History of the Szechuen Riots (May–June, 1895).* Shanghai: Shanghai Mercury Office.

Dai Wending. 1998. "Chenghuang miao zaji" [Miscellanies of temples of the City God], 380–87 in Chengdu qunzhong yishu guan, ed., *Chengdu zhanggu* [Anecdotes of Chengdu], vol. II. Chengdu: Sichuan daxue chubanshe.

Dai Zhili. 1959. *Sichuan baolu yundong shiliao* [Historical materials on the Sichuan Railroad Protection Movement]. Beijing: Kexue chubanshe.

Davidson, Robert J., and Isaac Mason. 1905. *Life in West China: Described By Two Residents in the Province of Szechwan.* London: Headley Brothers.

Davis, Susan G. 1988. *Parades and Power: Street Theatre in Nineteenth-Century Philadelphia.* Berkeley and Los Angeles: University of California Press.

DeGlopper, Donald R. 1977. "Social Structure in a Nineteenth-Century Taiwanese Port City," 633–50 in Skinner, ed., 1977.

Di Fan. 1966. "Chengdu zhi yangqin" [The dulcimer in Chengdu]. SWX 5 (45): 22–23.

Dingjinyan Qiaosou. 1805. *Chengdu zhuzhici* [Bamboo-branch poetry of Chengdu], 59–69 in Lin Kongyi, ed., 1986.

Dong, Madeleine Yue. 1999. "Juggling Bits: Tianqiao as Republican Beijing's Recycling Center." *Modern China* 25.3: 303–42.

Duara, Prasenjit. 1988a. *Culture, Power, and the State: Rural North China, 1900–1942.* Stanford: Stanford University Press.

——. 1988b. "Superscribing Symbols: The Myth of Guandi, Chinese God of War." *Journal of Asian Studies* 47.4: 778–95.

——. 1991. "Knowledge and Power in the Discourse of Modernity: The Campaigns against Popular Religion in Early Twentieth-Century China." *Journal of Asian Studies* 50.1: 67–83.

——. 1995. *Rescuing History from the Nation: Questioning Narratives of Modern China*. Chicago: University of Chicago Press.

Duis, Perry R. 1983. *The Saloon: Public Drinking in Chicago and Boston, 1880–1920*. Urbana: University of Illinois Press.

Dutton, Michael. 1998. *Streetlife China*. New York: Cambridge University Press.

Elliott, Mark. 1990. "Bannerman and Townsman: Ethnic Tension in Nineteenth-Century Jiangnan." *Late Imperial China* 11.1: 36–74.

Esherick, Joseph W. 1976. *Reform and Revolution in China: The 1911 Revolution in Hunan and Hubei*. Berkeley and Los Angeles: University of California Press.

——. 1987. *The Origins of the Boxer Uprising*. Berkeley and Los Angeles: University of California Press.

Esherick, Joseph W., and Mary B. Rankin, eds. 1990a. *Chinese Local Elites and Patterns of Dominance*. Berkeley and Los Angeles: University of California Press.

——. 1990b. "Introduction," 1–24 in Esherick and Rankin, 1990a.

Esherick, Joseph W., and Jeffrey N. Wasserstrom. 1990. "Acting Out Democracy: Political Theater in Modern China." *Journal of Asian Studies* 49.4: 835–65.

Evans, John C. 1992. *Tea in China: The History of China's National Drink*. New York: Greenwood Press.

Fang Chongshi and Shi Youshan. 1989. "'Mo Zhuangyuan' zhizhe Zhou Xiaohuai" [Number one scholar giving a lesson to Zhou Xiaohuai]. LMZ 1(49): 15–19.

Fang Xu. ca. 1900. "Huahui zhuzhici shiershou" [Twelve pieces of bamboo-branch poetry on the Flower Fair of Chengdu], 144–45 in Lin Kongyi, ed., 1986.

Faurot, Jeannette L. 1992. *Ancient Chengdu*. San Francisco: Chinese Material Center Publications.

Fei Zhu. n.d. (Yuan dynasty). *Suihua jilipu* [Record for festivals]. In *Mohai jinhu* [Golden kettle in a sea of ink], vol. 3.

Feng Jiaji. 1924. "Jincheng zhizhici baiyong" [One hundred pieces of bamboo-branch poetry on the Brocade City], 85–95 in Lin Kongyi, 1986.

Feng Yuxiang. 1890s. "Yaowang miao zhuzhici" [Bamboo-branch poetry on the Temple of Medicine King], 142–43 in Lin Kongyi, ed., 1986.

Fernández-Stembridge, Leila, and Richard P. Madsen. 2002. "Beggars in the Socialist Market Economy," 207–30 in Perry Link, Richard P. Madsen, and Paul G. Pickowicz, eds., *Popular China: Unofficial Culture in a Globalizing Society*. New York: Rowman & Littlefield Publishers, Inc.

Fleisher, Mark S. 1995. *Beggars and Thieves: Lives of Urban Street Criminals*. Madison: University of Wisconsin Press.

Fortune, Robert. 1853. *Two Visits to the Tea Countries of China*. 2 vols. London: John Murray.

Freedman, Maurice. 1966. *Chinese Lineage and Society: Fukien and Kwangtung*. London: Athlone.

Freeman, Michael. 1977. "Sung," 141–76 in K. C. Chang, ed., *Food in Chinese Culture: Anthropological and Historical Perspectives*. New Haven: Yale University Press.

Fu Chongju. 1987 [1909–10]. *Chengdu tonglan* [Investigation of Chengdu]. Originally eight volumes printed by Chengdu tongsu baoshe in 1909–10. Reprinted in two volumes by Bashu shushe, Chengdu, 1987. (The texts cited in this book are from the 1987 version, but illustrations are from the 1909–10 version.)

Gang Fu. 1995. *Chawenhua* [Tea culture]. Beijing: Zhongguo jingji chubanshe.

Gans, Herbert J. 1974. *Popular Culture and High Culture: An Analysis and Evaluation of Taste*. New York: Basic Books.

Gao Chengxiang. 1990. "Fu Qiaocun" [A biography of Fu Chongju], 483–86 in Ren Yimin, ed., *Sichuan jinxiandai renwu zhuan* [Biographies of modern Sichuan figures], vol. 6. Chengdu: Sichuan daxue chubanshe.

Gao Shunian and Wang Yongzhong. 1985. *Chengdu shichang daguan* [General information about Chengdu markets]. Beijing: Zhongguo zhanwang chubanshe.

Garrett, Shirley S. 1970. *Social Reformers in Urban China: The Chinese Y.M.C.A., 1895–1926*. New York: Cambridge University Press.

Gasster, Michael. 1978. "The Republican Revolutionary Movement," 465–534 in John K. Fairbank and Kwang-ching Liu, eds., *The Cambridge History of China*, vol. 11, pt. 2. Cambridge: Cambridge University Press.

Geertz, Clifford. 1973. *The Interpretation of Cultures*. New York: Basic Books.

Geil, William Edgar. 1911. *Eighteen Capitals of China*. Philadelphia & London: J. B. Lippincott Company.

Gernet, Jacques. 1968. *Daily Life in China on the Eve of the Mongol Invasion, 1250–1276*. Stanford: Stanford University Press.

Ginzburg, Carlo. 1982. *The Cheese and the Worms: The Cosmos of a Sixteenth-Century Miller*. Trans. John and Anne Tedeschi. New York: Penguin Books.

Goodman, Bryna. 1995. *Native Place, City, and Nation: Regional Networks and Identities in Shanghai, 1853–1937*. Berkeley and Los Angeles: University of California Press.

Graham, David C. 1927. "Religion in Szechuan Province." Ph.D. diss., University of Chicago.

Grainger, A. 1917a. "Chinese New Year Customs." WCMN 1: 5–11.

——. 1917b. "Chinese Festivals." WCMN 4: 5–12.

——. 1917c. "Various Superstitious." WCMN 9: 10–15; 11: 9–15.

——. 1918a. "Street Preaching, etc." WCMN 4: 5–13.

——. 1918b. "Popular Customs in West China." WCMN 6: 5–8.

Gramsci, Antonio. 1985. *Selections from Cultural Writings*. Ed. David Fogacs and Geoffrey Nowell-Smith. Trans. William Boelhower. Cambridge: Harvard University Press.

Grimes, Ronald L. 1982. "The Lifeblood of Public Ritual: Fiestas and Public Exploration Projects," 272–83 in Victor Turner, ed., *Celebration: Studies in Festivity and Ritual*. Washington, D.C.: Smithsonian Institution Press.

Guo Moruo. 1978 [1929]. *Fanzheng qianhou* [Before and after the 1911 Revolution]. Shanghai: Xiandai shuju. Reprinted by Sanlian shudian in *Moruo zizhuan* [Autobiography of Guo Moruo], vol. 1. Hong Kong, 1978.

Guomin gongbao [Citizens' daily]. 1912–49.

Gusfield, Joseph R. 1963. *Symbolic Crusade: Status Politics and the American Temperance Movement*. Urbana: University of Illinois Press.

Han Suyin. 1965. *The Crippled Tree: China, Biography, History, Autobiography*. New York: G. P. Putnam's Sons.

Hao Zhicheng. 1997. "Fuqin de gushi" [Stories about my father]. LMZ 1(97): 37–44.

Harrell, Stevan. 1982. *Ploughshare Village: Culture and Context in Taiwan*. Seattle: University of Washington Press.

Hartwell, G. E. 1921. "Reminiscences of Chengdu," WCMN 8 and 9: 5–27.

He Chengpu. 1986. *Chengdu yehua* [Night talks in Chengdu]. Chengdu: Sichuan renmin chubanshe.

He Manzi. 1994. *Wuzakan* [Five series of random talks]. Chengdu: Chengdu chubanshe.

Heller, Agnes. 1984. *Everyday Life*. Trans. G. L. Campbell. London: Routledge & Kegan Paul.

Hershatter, Gail. 1986. *The Workers of Tianjin*. Stanford: Stanford University Press.

——. 1991. "Prostitution and the Market in Women in Early Twentieth-Century Shanghai," 256–85 in Rubie S. Watson and Patricia Buckley Ebrey, eds., *Marriage and Inequality in Chinese Society*. Berkeley and Los Angeles: University of California Press.

——. 1992. "Regulating Sex in Shanghai: The Reform of Prostitution in 1920 and 1951," 145–85 in Frederic Wakeman Jr. and Wen-hsin Yeh, eds., *Shanghai Sojourners*. Berkeley and Los Angeles: Institute of East Asian Studies, University of California Press.

——. 1993. "The Subaltern Talks Back: Reflections on Subaltern Theory and Chinese History." *Positions* I. I: 103–30.

——. 1997. *Dangerous Pleasures: Prostitution and Modernity in Twentieth-Century Shanghai*. Berkeley and Los Angeles: University of California Press.

Honig, Emily. 1986. *Sisters and Strangers: Women in the Shanghai Cotton Mills*. Stanford: Stanford University Press.

——. 1992. *Creating Chinese Ethnicity: Subei People in Shanghai, 1850–1980*. New Haven: Yale University Press.

Hosie, Alexander. 1890. *Three Years in Western China*. London: George Philip & Son.

——. 1914. *On the Trail of the Opium Poppy: A Narrative of Travel in the Chief Opium-Producing Provinces of China*. London: George Philip & Son.

Hu Guofu. 1916. "Dao Cai hui zhuzhici" [Bamboo-branch poetry on memorial ceremony for Cai E], 160–61 in Lin Kongyi, ed., 1986.

Hu Tian. 1938. *Chengdu daoyou* [Guidebook of Chengdu]. Chengdu: Shuwen yinshuashe.

Huang, Philip C. C. 1985. *The Peasant Economy and Social Change in North China*. Stanford: Stanford University Press.

——. 1993. "'Public Sphere'/'Civil Society' in China? The Third Realm between State and Society." *Modern China* 19.2: 216–40.

——. 1996. *Civil Justice in China: Representation and Practice in the Qing*. Stanford: Stanford University Press.

Huayang xianzhi [Gazetteer of Huayang county]. 1816 (44 vols.) and 1934 (36 vols.). Chengdu. Reprinted by Taiwan xuesheng shuju.

Hubbard, George D. 1923. *The Geographic Setting of Chengdu.* Oberlin, Ohio: Oberlin College.

Hunt, Lynn A. 1978. *Revolution and Urban Politics in Provincial France: Troyes and Reims, 1786–1790.* Stanford: Stanford University Press.

——. 1984. *Politics, Culture, and Class in the French Revolution.* Berkeley and Los Angeles: University of California Press.

Inoue Kobai. 1921. *Shina fūzoku* [Chinese customs]. Shanghai: Nihondo shoten.

Jia Daquan and Chen Yishi. 1988. *Sichuan chaye shi* [A history of Sichuan tea]. Chengdu: Bashu shushe.

Jiang Yungang. 1943. "Qingmo Chengdu zhi shehui jianshe" [A social construction in late-Qing Chengdu]. *Lüxing zazhi* [Journal of travel] 17.10.

Jianqing. 1932. "Wuyue de Chengdu" [Chengdu in May]. *Shishi zhoubao* [Current affairs weekly] 7: 2–3.

Jinghuan and Zeng Ronghua. 1982. "Jincheng yiyuan hua Tianlai" [Tianlai's stories in the performing field of Chengdu]. CWZX 3: 133–41.

Johnson, David. 1985a. "Communication, Class, and Consciousness in Late Imperial China," 34–72 in Johnson, Nathan, and Rawski, eds., 1985.

——. 1985b. "City-God Cults in T'ang and Sung China." *Harvard Journal of Asiatic Studies* 45.2: 363–457.

——. 1989. "Actions Speak Louder than Words: The Cultural Significance of Chinese Ritual Opera," 1–45 in David Johnson, ed., *Ritual Opera, Operatic Ritual: "Mu-lien Rescues His Mother" in Chinese Popular Culture.* Berkeley and Los Angeles: Chinese Popular Cultural Project.

——. 1990. "Scripted Performances in Chinese Culture: An Approach to the Analysis of Popular Literature." *Hanxue yanjiu* [Chinese studies] 8.1 (15): 37–55.

——. 1994. "Temple Festivals in Southeastern Shansi: The *Sai* of Nan-she Village and Big West Gate." *Minsu quyi* [Folk customs and folk performances] 91: 641–734.

——. 1995. "Local Officials and 'Confucian' Values in the Great Temple Festivals (*Sai*) of Southeastern Shansi in Late Imperial Times." Paper presented to the Conference on State and Ritual in East Asia, Paris.

Johnson, David, A. J. Nathan, and E. S. Rawski, eds. 1985. *Popular Culture in Late Imperial China.* Berkeley and Los Angeles: University of California Press.

Kakehi Fumio. 1987. *Seito, Jūkei monogatari* [Stories of Chengdu and Chongqing]. Tokyo: Shūeisha.

Kanda Masao. 1905. *Seishin jijo* [Investigation of West China]. Tokyo: Noji zapposha.

——. 1936. *Shisen-sho soran* [Investigation of Sichuan]. Tokyo: Kaigaisha.

Kapp, Robert A. 1973. *Szechwan and the Chinese Republic: Provincial Militarism and Central Power, 1911–1938.* New Haven: Yale University Press.

Kasson, John F. 1978. *Amusing the Millions: Coney Island at the Turn of the Century.* New York: Hill & Wang.

Katz, Paul R. 1995. *Demon Hordes and Burning Boats: The Cult of Marshal Wen in Late Imperial Chekiang.* Albany: State University of New York Press.

Ko, Dorothy Y. 1994. *Teachers of the Inner Chambers: Women and Culture in China, 1573–1722.* Stanford: Stanford University Press.

Kuhn, Philip. 1990. *Soulstealers: The Chinese Sorcery Scare of 1768.* Cambridge: Harvard University Press.

K'ung, Shang-ren. 1976. *The Peach Blossom Fan.* Trans. Chen Shih-hsiang and Harold Acton. Berkeley and Los Angeles: University of California Press.

Lao She. 1978. "Chaguan" [The teahouse], 73–144 in *Lao She juzuo xuan* [A selection of Lao She's modern dramas]. Beijing: Renmin wenxue chubanshe.

Leclant, Jean. 1979. "Coffee and Cafes in Paris, 1644–1693," 86–97 in Robert Forster and Orest Ranum, eds., *Food and Drink in History: Selections from the Annales.* Baltimore: Johns Hopkins University Press.

Levy, Dore J. 1988. *Chinese Narrative Poetry: The Late Han through T'ang Dynasties.* Durham: Duke University Press.

Li Boxiong. 1988. "'Yangfangzi zoulu'—qiche chudao Chengdu de gushi" ["Foreign houses walking": Stories of early motor vehicles in Chengdu]. LMZ 6(48): 29–31.

Li Hsiao-t'i. 1998. *Qingmo de xiaceng shehui qimeng yundong, 1901–1911* [Lower class enlightenment in the late Qing period: 1901–1911]. Taipei: Institute of Modern History, Academia Sinica.

Li Jieren. 1947 [1926]. "Shimin de ziwei" [Residents' self-protection], 124–35 in Li Jieren, *Haoren jia* [The good family]. (This story was written in 1926.) Shanghai: Zhonghua shuju.

——. 1980 [1936]. *Baofeng yuqian* [Before the storm], 275–662 in *Li Jieren xuanji* [A selection of Li Jieren's works], vol. 1. Originally published in Shanghai by Zhonghua shuju in 1936. Chengdu: Sichuan renmin chubanshe.

——. 1980 [1937]. *Dabo* [The great wave], 3–1631 in *Li Jieren xuanji*, vol. 2, pts. I–III. Originally published in Shanghai by Zhonghua shuju in 1937. Chengdu: Sichuan renmin Chubanshe.

Li Qiao. 1990. "Jingxi zizhi de xisu" [The custom of respecting printed paper]. LMZ 1(55): 128–30.

Li Wenzhi. 1957. *Zhongguo jindai nongye shi ziliao* [Materials on the history of modern Chinese agriculture], vol. 1. Beijing: Sanlian shudian.

Liang Deman and Huang Shangjun. 1998. *Chengdu fangyan cidian* [A dictionary of Chengdu dialect]. Nanjing: Jiangsu jiaoyu chubanshe.

Liao T'ai-ch'u. 1947. "The Ko Lao Hui in Szechuan." *Pacific Affairs* 20 (June): 161–73.

Liao Yiwu (Laowei). 2001. *Zhongguo diche fangtan lu* [Interviews of people at the bottom of Chinese society]. Two vols. Wuhan: Changjiang wenyi chubanshe.

Lin Kongyi, ed. 1986. *Chengdu zhuzhici* [A collection of Chengdu bamboo-branch poems]. Chengdu: Sichuan renmin chubanshe.

Lin Wenxun. 1995. *Chengdu ren* [Chengdu people]. Hangzhou: Zhejiang renmin chubanshe.

Link, Perry. 1981. *Mandarin Ducks and Butterflies: Popular Fiction in Early Twentieth-Century Chinese Cities.* Berkeley and Los Angeles: University of California Press.

Link, Perry, Richard Madsen, and Paul G. Pickowicz, eds. 1989a. *Unofficial China: Popular Culture and Thought in the People's Republic.* Boulder: Westview Press.

——. 1989b. "Introduction," 1–13 in Link, Madsen, and Pickowicz, eds., 1989a.

Liu, Kwang-ching, ed. 1990. *Orthodoxy in Late Imperial China*. Berkeley and Los Angeles: University of California Press.

Liu Keji. 1996. "Jiuli sanfen de fan tanzi" [Food stalls in Chengdu]. LMZ 4 (94): 98–101.

Liu Shiliang. 1923. "Chengdu Qingyang gong huashi zhuzhici" [Bamboo-branch poems on the Flower Fair at the Green Goat Temple in Chengdu], 96–99 in Lin Kongyi, ed., 1986.

Liu Yuan. ca. 1790. "Shuzhong xinnian zhuzhici" [Bamboo-branch poetry on the Chinese New Year in Sichuan], 125–30 in Lin Kongyi, ed., 1986.

Lo, Irving Yucheng, and William Schultz. 1986. *Waiting for the Unicorn: Poems and Lyrics of China's Last Dynasty, 1644–1911*. Bloomington: Indiana University Press.

Longmenzhen [Folk tales]. 1981–97. Chengdu.

Lu, Hanchao. 1995. "Away from Nanking Road: Small Stores and Neighborhood Life in Modern Shanghai." *Journal of Asian Studies* 54.1: 93–123.

——. 1999a. *Beyond the Neon Lights: Everyday Shanghai in the Early Twentieth Century*. Berkeley and Los Angeles: University of California Press.

——. 1999b. "Becoming Urban: Mendicancy and Vagrants in Modern Shanghai." *Journal of Social History* 33.1: 7–36.

Lu Zhaoyue. 1988. "Shaanxi huiguan de xiezi" [Scorpions in the Shaanxi native place association hall]. LMZ 3(45): 83.

Luo Shang. 1965. "Chaguan fengqing" [Teahouse customs and practices]. SWX 1965.10 (38): 21–23.

Luo Ziqi and Jiang Shouwen. 1994. "Pingshu yiren Zhong Xiaofan quwen" [Interesting stories about the story-teller Zhong Xiaofan]. LMZ 4 (82): 58–61.

Mair, Victor H. 1985. "Language and Ideology in the Written Popularizations of the Sacred Edict," 325–59 in Johnson, Nathan, and Rawski, eds., 1985.

Maniai. 1898. "Maniai you Chengdu ji" [Maniai's notes on travel in Chengdu]. *Yubao* [Chongqing news] 9.

Mann, Susan. 1997. *Precious Records: Women in China's Long Eighteenth Century*. Stanford: Stanford University Press.

McDougall, Bonnie S. 1984a. "Writers and Performers: Their Works, and Their Audiences in the First Three Decades," 269–304 in McDougall, ed., 1984.

——, ed. 1984b. *Popular Chinese Literature and Performing Arts in the People's Republic of China, 1949–1979*. Berkeley and Los Angeles: University of California Press.

McEligott, Anthony. 1983. "Street Politics in Hamburg, 1932–33." *History Workshop* Autumn (16): 83–90.

Meserve, Walter J., and Ruth I. Meserve. 1979. "From Teahouse to Loudspeaker: The Popular Entertainer in the People's Republic of China." *Journal of Popular Culture* 8.1: 131–40.

Min Changquan. 1911. "Xinhai zhuzhici" [Bamboo-branch poetry in 1911], 156 in Lin Kongyi, ed., 1986.

Mote, F. W. 1977. "The Transformation of Nanking, 1350–1400," 101–53 in Skinner, ed., 1977.

Muchembled, Robert. 1985. *Popular Culture and Elite Culture in France, 1400–1750*. Trans. Lydia Cochrane. Baton Rouge: Louisiana State University Press.

Naitō Rishin. 1991. *Sunde mita Seito: Shoku no kuni ni miru Chūgoku no nichijo seikatsu* [Chengdu as I lived it: The Chinese today in the land of Shu]. Tokyo: Saimaru shuppankai.

Nakamura Sakujirō. 1899. *Shina man yū dan* [Travelogue of China]. Tokyo: Sesshikai.

Naquin, Susan. 1976. *Millenarian Rebellion in China: The Eight Trigrams Uprising of 1813*. New Haven: Yale University Press.

——. 2000. *Peking: Temples and City Life, 1400–1900*. Berkeley and Los Angeles: University of California Press.

Nasaw, David. 1993. *Going Out: The Rise and Fall of Public Amusements*. New York: Basic Books.

Ng, Mau-Sang. 1994. "Popular Fiction and the Culture of Everyday Life: A Cultural Analysis of Qin Shouou's Qiuhaitang." *Modern China* 20.2: 131–56.

Nichizawa Haruhiko. 1985. "Yamucha no hanashi" [Tales on drinking tea]. *GS-Tanoshii chisiki* vol. 3: 242–53.

——. 1988. "Gendai Chūgoku no chakan—Shisen shō Seito no jirei kara" [Teahouses in modern China: A case of Chengdu, Sichuan]. *Fū zoku* [Social customs] 26.4: 50–63.

Ozouf, Mona. 1988. *Festivals and the French Revolution*. Trans. Alan Sheridan. Cambridge: Harvard University Press.

Peiss, Kathy. 1986. *Cheap Amusements: Working Women and Leisure in Turn-of-the-Century New York*. Philadelphia: Temple University Press.

Peng Maoqi. ca. 1810. "Jincheng zhuzhici sishou" [Bamboo-branch poetry on the brocade city], 31 in Lin Kongyi, ed., 1986.

Peng Qinian. 1963. "Xinhai geming hou chuanju zai Chengdu de xin fazhan" [New developments in Sichuan opera in Chengdu after the 1911 Revolution]. SWZX 8: 159–72.

Perdue, Peter C. 1986. "Insiders and Outsiders: The Xiangtan Riot of 1819 and Collective Action in Hunan." *Modern China* 12.2: 166–201.

Perry, Elizabeth J. 1980. *Rebels and Revolutionaries in North China, 1845–1945*. Berkeley and Los Angeles: University of California Press.

——. 1993. *Shanghai on Strike: The Politics of Chinese Labor*. Stanford: Stanford University Press.

Pickett, Joseph P., et al., eds. 2000. *The American Heritage Dictionary of the English Language*. 4th edition. Boston: Houghton Mifflin Company.

Pittenger, Mark. 1997. "A World of Difference: Constructing the 'Underclass' in Progressive America." *American Quarterly* 49(1): 26–65.

Polo, Marco. 1961 [1271–95]. *The Travels of Marco Polo*. New York: New American Library.

Porter, Noah, ed. 1913. *Webster's Revised Unabridged Dictionary*. G & C Merriam Co.

Qian Liancheng. 1985 [1820s–50s]. *Chanjian zhiyi* [Drawings of street people]. Chengdu: Sichuan renmin chubanshe.

Qian Ren. 1928. "Xu Qingyanggong huashi zhizhici" [New bamboo-branch poems on the Flower Fair at Green Goat Temple], 99–107 in Lin Kongyi, ed., 1986.

Qiao Zengxi, Li Canhua, and Bai Zhaoyu. 1983. "Chengdu shizheng yange gaishu" [General information about the course of change and development of Chengdu municipal administration]. CWZX 5: 1–22.

Qimeng tongsu bao [Enlightenment colloquial news]. 1902. Chengdu.

Qin Nan. 1914. *Shu xin* [A Sichuan memoir], 365–75, 533–68 in SXGS 1.

Qing Yu. 1909. "Chengdu yueshi zhuzhici" [Bamboo-branch poetry on monthly fairs in Chengdu], 181–84 in Lin Kongyi, ed., 1986.

Qu Wenbin. 1999. *Zhongguo qigai shi* [A history of beggars in China]. Shanghai: Shanghai wenyi chubanshe.

Raeff, Marc. 1983. *The Well-Ordered Police State: Social and Institutional Change through Law in the Germanies and Russia, 1600–1800.* New Haven: Yale University Press.

Rankin, Mary B. 1986. *Elite Activism and Political Transformation in China: Zhejiang Province, 1865–1911.* Stanford: Stanford University Press.

——. 1990. "The Origins of a Chinese Public Sphere: Local Elites and Community Affairs in the Late Imperial Period." *Etudes Chinoises* 9.2: 14–60.

Reed, Bradly W. 2000. *Talons and Teeth: County Clerks and Runners in the Qing Dynasty.* Stanford: Stanford University Press.

Rhoads, Edward J. M. 2000. *Manchus and Han: Ethnic Relations and Political Power in Late Qing and Early Republican China, 1861–1928.* Seattle: University of Washington Press.

Riis, Jacob A. 1924 [1890]. *How the Other Half Lives: Studies Among the Tenements of New York.* New York: Charles Scribner's Sons.

Rosenzweig, Roy. 1983. *Eight Hours for What We Will: Workers and Leisure in an Industrial City, 1870–1920.* New York: Cambridge University Press.

Ross, Andrew. 1989. *No Respect: Intellectuals and Popular Culture.* New York: Routledge.

Rowe, William T. 1984. *Hankow: Commerce and Society in a Chinese City, 1796–1889.* Stanford: Stanford University Press.

——. 1989. *Hankow: Conflict and Community in a Chinese City, 1796–1895.* Stanford: Stanford University Press.

——. 1990. "The Public Sphere in Modern China." *Modern China* 16.3: 309–29.

Ryan, Mary P. 1990. *Women in Public: Between Banners and Ballots, 1825–1880.* Baltimore: Johns Hopkins University Press.

Schak, David C. 1988. *A Chinese Beggars' Den: Poverty and Mobility in an Under-Class Community.* Pittsburgh: University of Pittsburgh Press.

Schoppa, R. Keith. 1982. *Chinese Elites and Political Change: Zhejiang Province in the Early Twentieth Century.* Cambridge: Harvard University Press.

Scott, James C. 1985. *Weapons of the Weak: Everyday Forms of Peasant Resistance.* New Haven: Yale University Press.

Sennett, Richard. 1977. *The Fall of Public Man: On the Social Psychology of Capitalism.* New York: Vintage Books.

Service, John S., ed. 1989. *Golden Inches: The China Memoir of Grace Service.* Berkeley and Los Angeles: University of California Press.

Sewell, William G. 1971. *The People of Wheelbarrow Lane.* South Brunswick and New York: A. S. Barnes & Company.

——. 1986. *The Dragon's Backbone: Portraits of Chengdu People in the 1920's.* Drawings by Yu Zidan. York: William Sessions Limited.

Sha Ding. 1963. *Zufu de gushi* [My grandfather's story]. Shanghai: Shanghai wenyi chubanshe.

——. 1982 [1940]. "Zai Qixiangju chaguan li" [In the Fragrant Chamber Teahouse], 140–56 in *Sha Ding xuanji* [Selections from Sha Ding]. Chengdu: Sichuan renmin chubanshe.

Shao, Qin. 1997. "Space, Time, and Politics in Early Twentieth Century Nantong." *Modern China* 23.1: 99–129.

——. 1998. "Tempest over Teapots: The Vilification of Teahouse Culture in Early Republican China." *Journal of Asian Studies* 57.4: 1009–41.

Shao Yun. 1988. "Chengdu paoge shilue" [A short history of the Gowned Brothers in Chengdu]. *Chengdu zhi tongxun* [Newsletter of gazetteer of Chengdu] 1 (16): 55–65.

"Shengyuan jingqu zhangcheng" [Regulations of the Chengdu police]. In *Sichuan jingwu zhangcheng* [Regulations of the Sichuan police] vol. 2. No date, late Qing.

Shi Jufu. 1936. *Sichuan renkou shuzi yanjiu zhi xinziliao* [New materials on Sichuan population statistics]. Chengdu: Minjian yishi she.

Shi Tiyuan. 1962. "Yi Chengdu baolu yundong" [On the Railroad Protection Movement in Chengdu]. *Xinhai gengming huiyilu* [Memoirs of the 1911 Revolution], vol. 3: 42–67. Beijing: Wenshi ziliao chubanshe.

Shu Xincheng. 1934. *Shuyou xinying* [Reflections on a tour of Sichuan]. Shanghai: Zhonghua shuju.

Sichuan baolu tongzhihui baogao [Newsletter of the Sichuan Railroad Protection Association]. 1911. Chengdu.

Sichuan Chengdu diyici shangye quangonghui diaochabiao [Investigative report on the first commercial industrial fair in Chengdu, Sichuan]. 1906. Chengdu.

Sichuan guanbao [Sichuan official gazette]. 1904–11. Chengdu.

Sichuan jiaoyu guanbao [Sichuan educational official gazette]. 1907–11. Chengdu.

Sichuan sheng wenshi guan, ed. 1987. *Chengdu chengfang guji kao* [Materials on urban construction and historical sites in Chengdu]. Chengdu: Sichuan renmin chuban she.

Sichuan shengzhengfu shehuichu dang'an [Archives of the Social Department of the Sichuan Provincial Government]. 1912–49. In the Sichuan Provincial Archives, *guangzong* 186, *anjuan* 1431.

Sichuan tongsheng jingcha zhangcheng [Regulations of the Sichuan provincial police], 1903. From the Archives of the Police Ministry (1501), vol. 179, in the First Historical Archives (Beijing). Part I. Security: I-1, Regulations on Households; I-2, Regulations on Detention of Unemployed Vagrants, Expulsion of Violent Beggars, and Mendicants, Insane, and Drunken People; I-3, Regulations on Inspection for Gambling and Thieves' Dens and Heterodox Sects; I-4, Regulations on Inspection for Weapons; I-5, Regulations on Control of Public Gatherings; I-6, Regulations on Dangerous Objects and Maintenance of Roads; I-7, Regulations on Sedan Chairs, Horse Carts, and Pedestrians; I-8, Regulations on Markets; I-9, Regulations on Curfews; I-10, Regulations on Teahouses; I-11, Regulations on Opium Houses; I-12, Regulations on Saving Sick People on the

Street; I-13, Regulations on Helping People Who Are Lost; I-14, Regulations on Finding and Returning Lost Goods; I-15, Regulations on Appeals. Part II. Customs Reforms: II-1, Regulations on Inspection of Prostitutes; II-2, Regulations on Inspecting Local Opera Scripts and Purifying Theaters; II-3, Regulations Prohibiting Bizarre Speech, Bizarre Behavior, and Bizarre Clothing. Part III. Hygiene: III-1, Regulations on Rectifying Lavatories and Prohibiting Urinating on the Street; III-2, Regulations on Trash; III-3, Regulations on Inspection of Food.

Sichuan wenshi ziliao xuanji [Collected literary and historical materials of Sichuan]. 1960s–90s. Chengdu.

Sichuan wenxian [Documents on Sichuan]. 1960s–70s. Taipei.

Sichuan xuebao [Sichuan school news]. 1905–07. Chengdu.

Sichuan ziyiju diyici yishi lu [Record of the first meeting of the Sichuan Assembly]. 1910. Collected in SXGS 1.

Siu, Helen F. 1989. "Recycling Rituals: Politics and Popular Culture in Contemporary Rural China," 121–37 in Link, Madsen, and Pickowicz, eds., 1989.

Skinner, G. William. 1964–65. "Marketing and Social Structure in Rural China." *Journal of Asian Studies*. 24. 1: 3–43; 24.2: 195–228; 24.3: 363–99.

——. 1971. "Chinese Peasants and the Closed Community: An Open and Shut Case." *Comparative Studies in Society and History* 13.3: 270–81.

——, ed. 1977. *The City in Late Imperial China*. Stanford: Stanford University Press.

Smith, Richard J. 1991. *Fortune-tellers and Philosophers: Divination in Traditional Chinese Society*. Boulder: Westview Press.

——. 1994. *China's Cultural Heritage: The Qing Dynasty, 1644–1912*. Boulder: Westview Press.

Stanley, Amy Dru. 1992. "Beggars Can't Be Choosers: Compulsion and Contract in Postbellum America." *Journal of American History* 78.4: 1265–93.

Stansell, Christine. 1986. *City of Women: Sex and Class in New York, 1789–1860*. New York: Alfred A. Knopf.

Stapleton, Kristin. 1993. "Police Reform in a Late-Imperial Chinese City: Chengdu, 1902–1911." Ph.D. diss., Harvard University.

——. 1996. "Urban Politics in an Age of 'Secret Societies': The Cases of Shanghai and Chengdu." *Republican China* 22.1: 23–64.

——. 1997a. "County Administration in Late-Qing Sichuan: Conflicting Models of Rural Policing." *Late Imperial China* 18.1: 100–132.

——. 1997b. "Interpreting Humor in History: Two Cases from Republican China." Draft prepared for presentation at Johns Hopkins University on February 4, 1997.

——. 2000. *Civilizing Chengdu: Chinese Urban Reform, 1875–1937*. Cambridge: Harvard University Asia Center.

Storch, Robert D., ed. 1982a. *Popular Culture and Custom in Nineteenth-Century England*. New York: St. Martin's Press.

——. 1982b. "Introduction: Persistence and Change in Nineteenth-Century Popular Culture," 1–19 in Storch, ed., 1982a.

Strand, David. 1989. *Rickshaw Beijing: City People and Politics in the 1920s*. Berkeley and Los Angeles: University of California Press.

Strauch, Judith. 1983. "Community and Kinship in Southeastern China: The View from the Multilineage Villages of Hong Kong." *Journal of Asian Studies* 43.1: 21–50.

Sun Bin, Zhang Youlin, Li Wanchun, Liu Shifu, Xiong Xiaoxiong, Pan Peide, and Xie Kexin. 2000. *Lao Chengdu* [Old Chengdu]. Original scroll painting.

Suzuki Tōmō. 1982. "Shinmatsu Kō-Seku no chakan ni tsuite" [Teahouses in late Qing Jiangsu and Zhejiang], 529–40 in *Rekishi ni okeru minshū to bunka: Sakai Tadao sensei koki shūgaku kinen ronshū* [People and culture in history: An essay collection in honor of Sakai Tadao]. Tokyo: Kokusho kankōkai.

Takeuchi Minoru. 1974. *Chakan: Chūgoku no fudo to sekaizo* [Teahouses: A general picture of Chinese social customs]. Tokyo: Taishukan shoten.

Tan Shaohua. 1984. "Sanqing hui" [Three celebrities society]. LMZ 4 (22): 118–21.

Tanaka Issei. 1985. "The Social and Historical Context of Ming-Ch'ing Local Drama," 143–60 in Johnson, Nathan, and Rawski, eds., 1985.

Thompson, E. P. 1974. "Patrician Society, Plebeian Culture." *Journal of Social History* 7.4: 382–405.

Thompson, Roger R. 1995. *China's Local Councils in the Age of Constitutional Reform, 1898–1911*. Cambridge: Council on East Asian Studies, Harvard University.

Tōa Dōbunkai. 1917. *Shina shōbetsu zenshi* [Investigations of China's provinces], vol. 5, Shisen-sho [Sichuan province] Tokyo: Tōa Dōbunkai.

——. 1941. *Shinshu shina shōbetsu zenshi* [New investigations of China's provinces], vols. 1 and 2, Shisen-sho [Sichuan province]. Tokyo: Tōa Dōbunkai.

Tongsu huabao [Popular pictorial]. 1909 and 1912. Chengdu.

Tongsu ribao [Popular daily]. 1909–11. Chengdu.

Torrance, (The Rev.) T. 1916. "The History of the Chengtu Wall." WCMN 10: 14–19.

Turner, Victor. 1984. "Liminality and the Performative Genres," 19–41 in John J. MacAloon, ed., *Rite, Drama, Festival, Spectacle: Rehearsals Toward a Theory of Cultural Performance*. Philadelphia: Institute for the Study of Human Issues.

Vale, J. 1904. "Sz-Chuan Police Force." WCMN 3: 56–59; 4: 82–86; 5: 106–11; 6: 125–27.

——. 1906. "The Small Trader of Szchuan." WCMN 10: 237–38; 11: 255–62.

——. 1907. "Beggar Life in Chentu." WCMN 4: 8–11; 7: 7–10: 9: 6–7; 10: 7–11.

——. 1914. "The Art of the Startler." WCMN 2: 28–30; 3: 28–30; 8: 12–14.

Vincent, David. 1982. "The Decline of the Oral Tradition in Popular Culture," 20–47 in Storch, ed., 1982a.

Von Glahn, Richard. 1991. "The Enchantment of Wealth: The God Wutong in the Social History of Jiangnan." *Harvard Journal of Asiatic Studies* 51.2: 651–714.

Wakeman, Frederic, Jr. 1995a. *Policing Shanghai, 1927–1937*. Berkeley and Los Angeles: University of California Press.

——. 1995b. "Licensing Leisure: The Chinese Nationalists' Attempt to Regulate Shanghai, 1927–1949." *Journal of Asian Studies* 54.1: 19–42.

Wallace, Edward W. 1903 and 1907. *The Heart of Sz-Chuan*. Toronto: Methodist Mission Rooms. Two editions.

Walmsley, Lewis. 1974. "Szechuan—That Green and Pleasant Land," 1–8 in Brace, ed., 1974a.

Walters, Ronald G. 1978. *American Reformers, 1815–1860*. New York: Hill & Wang.

Wang Chunwu. 1993. *Paoge tanmi* [Exploring the secrets of the Gowned Brothers]. Chengdu: Bashu shushe.

Wang Dayu. 1993. "Sichuan paoge" [Secret societies of Sichuan]. SWZX 41: 139–63.

Wang Di (Wang, Di). 1984. "Qingmo xinzheng yu wanhui liquan" [New Policies and recovering economic rights in the Late Qing]. *Sichuan daxue xuebao* [Journal of Sichuan University] 2: 91–101.

———. 1985. "Qingmo xinzheng yu Sichuan jindai jiaoyu de xingqi" [New policies and the rise of modern education in late-Qing Sichuan]. *Sichuan daxue xuebao* [Journal of Sichuan University] 2: 95–111.

———. 1986. "Wanqing Sichuan nongye gailiang" [Agricultural reforms in late-Qing Sichuan." *Zhongguo nongshi* [Journal of Chinese agricultural history] 2: 38–51.

———. 1987a. "Zhou Shanpei" [A biography of Zhou Shanpei], 122–29 in Ren Yimin, ed., *Sichuan jinxiandai renwuzhuan* [Biographies of modern Sichuan figures], vol. 4. Chengdu: Sichuan daxue chubanshe.

———. 1987b. "Qingmo xinzheng yu jindai xuetang de xingqi" [The New Policies and the rise of modern schools in the late Qing]. *Jindaishi yanjiu* [Journal of modern history] 3: 245–70.

———. 1987c. "Lun qingmo shanghui de sheli yu guanshang guanxi" [A discussion of the establishment of chambers of commerce and the relationship between merchants and officials during the late Qing]. *Shixue yuekan* [Historiography monthly] 4: 39–44.

———. 1987d. "Qingmo sheli shangbu shulun" [A discussion on the establishment of the Ministry of Commerce during the late Qing]. *Qingshi yanjiu* [Journal of Qing history] 1: 23–27.

———. 1988. "Qingmo shiye zhengce yu jingji fazhan" [Industrial-commercial policies and economic development in the late Qing]. *Sichuan daxue xuebao* [Journal of Sichuan University] special issue 37: 148–61.

———. 1989a. "Wanqing zhongshang zhuyi yu jingji biange" [Mercantilism and economic reform during the late Qing]. *Shanghai shehuikexueyuan xueshu jikan* [Journal of the Shanghai Academy of Social Sciences] 4: 63–70.

———. 1989b. "Qingdai Chongqing yimin, yimin shehui yu chengshi fazhan" [Migrants in Chongqing: Their social organization and urban development]. *Chengshishi yanjiu* [Journal of urban history] 1: 58–79.

———. 1989c. "Qingdai Chongqing renkou yu shehui zuzhi" [Studies in population and social organization in Chongqing during the Qing dynasty], 310–78 in Wei Yingtao, ed., *Chongqing chengshi yanjiu* [A study of Chongqing city]. Chengdu: Sichuan daxue chubanshe.

———. 1992. "Educational Reform and Social Changes in Sichuan, 1902–1911." Paper presented at the annual meeting of the Association for Asian Studies, Washington, D.C., April 5, 1992.

———. 1993. *Kuachu fengbi de shijie: Changjiang shangyou quyu shehui yanjiu, 1644–1911* [Striding out of a closed world: A study of society in the upper Yangzi region, 1644–1911]. Beijing: Zhonghua shuju.

——. 1994. "Wanqing jingzheng yu shehui gaizao" [Late-Qing police forces and social reform], 193–209 in *Xinhai geming yu jindai Zhongguo* [The 1911 Revolution and modern China], vol. 1. Beijing: Zhonghua shuju.

——. 1998a. "Street Culture: Public Space and Urban Commoners in Late-Qing
Chengdu." *Modern China* 24.1: 34–72.

——. 1998b. "Street Culture: Public Space, Urban Commoners, and Local Politics in
Chengdu, 1875–1928." Ph.D. diss., Johns Hopkins University.

——. 1999. "The Rhythm of the City: Bamboo-Branch Poetry and Public Life in
Late-Qing Chengdu." Paper presented at the annual meeting of the Association
for Asian Studies, Boston, March 14, 1999.

——. 2000a. "The Struggle for Drink and Entertainment: Men, Women, and the Police in Early Twentieth-Century Chengdu." Paper presented at the annual meeting of the American Historical Association, Chicago, January 9, 2000.

——. 2000b. "The Idle and the Busy: Teahouses and Public Life in Early Twentieth-
Century Chengdu." *Journal of Urban History* 26.4: 411–37.

——. 2001. "'Doctor Tea': Teahouse Workers in Republican Chengdu." Paper presented at the annual meeting of the Association for Asian Studies, March 23,
2001.

Wang, Mingming. 1995. "Place, Administration, and Territorial Cults in Late Imperial China: A Case Study from South Fujian." *Late Imperial China* 16.1: 33–78.

——. 1997. *Shanjie de jiyi: Yige Taiwan shequ de xinyang yu rensheng* [Memories of
a mountain road: Belief and life in a Taiwan community]. Shanghai: Shanghai
wenyi chubanshe.

Wang Qingyuan. 1944. "Chengdu pingyuan xiangcun chaguan" [Rural teahouses
on the Chengdu plain]. *Fengtu shi* [Folkways] 1.4: 29–38.

Wang Tianshou. "Jiu Chengdu xingchang jianwen" [What I saw and heard on the
execution ground in old Chengdu]. LMZ 2 (62): 50–53.

Wang Qingyu, ed. 1992. *Sichuan fengsu chuanshuo xuan* [A selection of tales about
Sichuan social customs]. Chengdu: Sichuan minzu chubanshe.

Wang Zaixian. ca. 1850. "Chengdu zhuzhici" [Bamboo-branch poetry of Chengdu],
133–34 in Lin Kongyi, ed., 1986.

Wang Zhihang. 1987. "Zizhong muou xi jinxi" [Puppet shows in Zizhong: Past
and present]. SWZX 36: 66–75.

Ward, Barbara E. 1985. "Regional Operas and Their Audiences: Evidence from
Hong Kong," 161–87 in Johnson, Nathan, and Rawski, eds., 1985.

Wasserstrom, Jeffrey N. 1991. *Student Protests in Twentieth-Century China: The
View from Shanghai*. Stanford: Stanford University Press.

Watson, James L. 1985. "Standardizing the Gods: The Promotion of T'ien Hou
("Empress of Heaven") Along the South China Coast, 960–1960," 292–324 in
Johnson, Nathan, and Rawski, eds., 1985.

Watson, Rubie S. 1985. *Inequality Among Brothers: Class and Kinship in South
China*. New York: Cambridge University Press.

Weber, Max. 1958. *The City*. Trans. Don Martindale and Gertrud Neuwirth. New
York: Free Press.

Wei Yingtao. 1981. *Sichuan baolu yundong shi* [A history of the Sichuan Railroad
Protection Movement]. Chengdu: Sichuan renmin chubanshe.

——, ed. 1990. *Sichuan jindai shigao* [A history of modern Sichuan]. Chengdu: Sichuan renmin chubanshe.

Wei Yingtao and He Yimin. 1983. "Lun Tongmenghui yu Sichuan huidang" [A study of the Alliance League and Sworn Brotherhood] in *Jinian Xinhai Geming qishi zhounian xueshu taolunhui lunwenji* [An essay collection of the conference on the 70th anniversary of the 1911 Revolution]. Beijing: Zhonghua shuju.

Wei Yingtao and Zhao Qin, eds. 1981. *Sichuan xinhai geming shilian* [Historical materials on the 1911 Revolution in Sichuan]. Vols. 1 and 2. Chengdu: Sichuan renmin chubanshe.

Wen Shu, Wu Jianzhou, and Cui Xianchang . 1984. "Jiu Chengdu de renshi" [The labor market in old Chengdu]. LMZ 2 (20): 15–27.

Wen Wenzi, ed. 1990. *Sichuan fengwu zhi* [Customs in Sichuan]. Chengdu: Sichuan renmin chubanshe.

West China Missionary News. 1899–1943. Chongqing and Chengdu.

Whyte, William F. 1981 [1943]. *Street Corner Society: The Social Structure of an Italian Slum*. 3rd edition. Chicago: University of Chicago Press.

Wilentz, Sean. 1983. "Artisan Republican Festivals and the Rise of Class Conflict in New York City, 1788–1837," 37–77 in Michael H. Frisch and Daniel J. Walkowitz, eds., *Working-Class America: Essays on Labor, Community, and American Society*. Chicago: University of Illinois Press.

Wilson, Ernest H. 1929. *China: Mother of Gardens*. Boston: Stratford Company.

Wolf, Arthur P. 1974. "Gods, Ghosts, and Ancestors," 131–82 in A. P. Wolf, ed., *Religion and Ritual in Chinese Society*. Stanford: Stanford University Press.

Wu Haoshan. 1855. *Benzhuo liyan* [A collection of clumsy slang], 69–77 in Lin Kongyi, ed., 1986.

Wu Jianzhou and Wu Shaobo. 1989. "Zher ye youge qiji wangchao buyi—buji jiu Rongcheng de qikai gushi" [An addendum to "There is a miracle kingdom"—Stories of beggars in old Chengdu]. LMZ 6.54: 26–31.

Wu Xiaofei. 1994. "Maishuiren yu jiqishui" [Water carriers and running water]. LMZ 3 (81): 9–14.

Wu Yu. 1984. *Wuyu riji* [Wu Yu's diary]. Two vols. Chengdu: Sichuan renmin chubanshe.

Wyman, Judith. 1997. "The Ambiguities of Chinese Antiforeignism: Chongqing, 1870–1900." *Late Imperial China* 18.2: 86–122.

Xiandai hanying cidian [A modern Chinese-English dictionary]. 1988. Beijing: Hanyu jiaoxue yu yanjiu chubanshe.

Xiandai hanyu cidian [A modern Chinese language dictionary]. 1998. Beijing: Shangwu yinshuguan.

Xiao Han. 1986. "Chengdu shangye chang de xingshuai" [Rise and fall of the Commercial Center in Chengdu]. LMZ 6 (36): 36–48.

Xiliang. 1905. "Shenming jingzheng baihua gaoshi" [An official public notice of police force in the vernacular]. Chengdu.

——. 1959. *Xiliang yigao* [The papers of Xiliang]. Vol. 1. Beijing: Zhonghua shuju.

Xing Jinsheng. 1902–32. "Jincheng zhuzhici chao" [A collection of bamboo-branch poetry of the brocade city], 164–66 in Lin Kongyi, ed., 1986.

Xinhua zidian [A new Chinese dictionary]. Beijing: Shangwu yinshuguan.

Xiuqing, Hou Shaoxuan, Xiong Zhuoyun, and Mi Qingyun. 1988. "Jiefangqian Chengdu de Yangzhou jinü" [Yangzhou prostitutes in Chengdu before liberation]. LMZ 5(47): 56–65.

Xu, Xiaoqun. 2001. *Chinese Professionals and the Republican State: The Rise of Professional Associations in Shanghai, 1912–1937.* New York: Cambridge University Press.

Xu, Yinong. 2000. *The Chinese City in Space and Time: The Development of Urban Form in Suzhou.* Honolulu: University of Hawaii Press.

Xu Shiwen. 1983. "Qingyanggong wai pian shenxian" [A swindler outside the Green Goat Temple]. LMZ 4 (16): 95–99.

Xu Xinyu. 1985. *Shuyou wenjian lu* [Travel notes on Sichuan]. Chengdu: Sichuan renmin chubanshe.

Xue Shaoming. 1986 [1936]. *Qian Dian Chuan lüxing ji* [Travel notes on Guizhou, Yunnan, and Sichuan]. Chongqing: Chongqing chubanshe.

Xue Xuan. ca. 1420. "Xiao zhuzhige" [Songs of bamboo branch], 120 in Lin Kongyi, ed., 1986.

Yamakawa Hayamizu. 1909. *Hashoku* [Sichuan]. Tokyo: Seibunkan.

Yang, C. K. 1961. *Religion in Chinese Society.* Berkeley and Los Angeles: University of California Press.

Yang Huai. 1982. "Shentongzi yu Mantianfei" [A magical boy and a wandering man]. LMZ 1 (7): 65–70.

Yang Wuneng and Qiu Peihuang. 1995. *Chengdu da cidian* [Dictionary of Chengdu]. Chengdu: Sichuan cishu chubanshe.

Yang Xie (Liudui Shanren). 1804. *Jincheng zhuzhici baishou* [One hundred bamboo-branch poems of the brocade city], 42–59 in Lin Kongyi, ed., 1986.

Yao Zhengmin. 1971. "Chengdu fengqing" [Folk traditions in Chengdu]. SWX 5 (105): 17–21.

Ye Chunkai. 1996. "Jiefangqian Chengdu guancaipu yitiaojie" [The coffin street in pre-liberation Chengdu]. LMZ 1 (91): 96–101.

Yeh, Wen-hsin. 1992. "Progressive Journalism and Shanghai's Petty Urbanities: Zou Taofen and the *Shenghuo Weekly,* 1926–1945," 186–238 in Frederic Wakeman Jr. and Wen-hsin Yeh, eds. *Shanghai Sojourners.* Berkeley and Los Angeles: Institute of East Asian Studies, University of California.

——. 1995. "Corporate Space, Communal Time: Everyday Life in Shanghai's Bank of China." *American Historical Review* 100.1: 97–116.

Yerkovich, Sally. 1977. "Gossiping as a Way of Speaking." *Journal of Communication* 27.1: 192–96.

Yi Junzuo. 1943. "Jincheng qiri ji" [Seven days in Chengdu], 177–210 in *Chuankang youzong* [Travel notes on Sichuan and Xikang]. Zhongguo lüxingshe, n.p.

Yokoyama Tsuneo. 1940. *Unnan Shisen tōsaki* [Account of a survey of Yunnan and Sichuan]. Tokyo: Kaizōsha.

Young, Ernest P. 1977. *The Presidency of Yuan Shih-k'ai: Liberalism and Dictatorship in Early Republican China.* Ann Arbor: University of Michigan Press.

Yu Xiu. 1999. *Zhongguo qigai diaocha* [An investigation of Chinese beggars]. Beijing: Zhonghua gongshang lianhe chubanshe.

Yuan Han. 1992. "Shisheng suoji" [Records of city voices]. LMZ 4 (70): 108–11.

Yubao [Chongqing news]. 1898.

Yun Tao. 1933. "Sichuan gelaohui de neirong dagang" [Substantive outline of Sichuan Brotherhood Society]. *Shishi zhoubao* [Current affairs weekly] 4.15: 15–16; 4.17: 15.

Zelin, Madeleine. 1990. "The Rise and Fall of the Fu-Rong Salt-Yard Elite: Merchant Dominance in Late Qing China," 82–109 in Esherick and Rankin, eds., 1990.

Zhang Dafu. 1981. "Gao Baxi" [Magician Gao]. *Chengdu fengwu*, vol. 1: 109–12.

Zhang Fang. 1995. "Chuantu suibi" [Informal essays on Sichuan customs]. LMZ 3 (87): 95–98.

Zhang Jiqing. 1981 [1820s–60s]. *Daoxian huanhai jianwenlu* [Notes on the Daoguang and Xianfeng periods]. Beijing: Zhonghua shuju.

Zhang Kaiyuan and Lin Zengping, eds. 1981. *Xinhai geming shi* [A history of the 1911 Revolution]. Vol. 2. Beijing: Renmin chubanshe.

Zhang Xiushu. 1979 [1959]. "Wusi yundong zai Sichuan de huiyi" [A memoir of the May Fourth Movement in Sichuan] 868–87 in *Wusi yundong huiyilu* [Memoirs of the May Fourth Movement]. Vol. 2. Beijing: Zhongguo shehui kexue chubanshe.

Zhang Xuejun and Zhang Lihong. 1993. *Chengdu chengshi shi* [A general history of Chengdu]. Chengdu: Chengdu chubanshe.

Zhao Erxun dang'an [Zhao Erxun Archives] in the First Historical Archives (Beijing). 1909. Vol. 507.

Zheng Yun. 1981. "Yifu duilian de miaoyong" [A smart use for a matched couplet]. *Chengdu fengwu* vol. 1: 82–83.

Zheng Yunxia and Jiashu. 1989. "Jiushi jianghu" [River and lake runners in the past]. LMZ 3 (51): 1–11; 4 (52): 25–37; 5 (53): 69–79.

Zhong Maoxuan. 1984. *Liu Shiliang waizhuan* [An informal biography of Liu Shiliang]. Chengdu: Sichuan renmin chubanshe.

Zhong Shixiu. 1911. "Du *Tongzhihui Ribao* yougan zhuzhici" [Bamboo-branch poems on reading the Railroad Protection Association Daily]. SBTB, no. 25.

Zhou Chuanru. 1926. *Sichuan sheng* [Sichuan province]. Shanghai: Shangwu yinshuguan.

Zhou Shanpei. 1957. *Xinhai Sichuan zhenglu qinliji* [My experiences in the Sichuan Railroad Protection Movement]. Chongqing: Chongqing renmin chubanshe.

Zhou Xun. 1987 [1936]. *Furong huajiu lu* [Talking about Chengdu's past]. Chengdu: Sichuan renmin chubanshe.

Zhou Zhiying. 1943. *Xin Chengdu* [New Chengdu]. Chengdu: Fuxing shuju.

Zhou Zhiying and Gao Sibo. 1987. "Chengdu de zaoqi huaju huodong" [Early modern drama activities in Chengdu]. SWZX 36: 53–65.

Zumthor, Paul. 1990. *Oral Poetry: An Introduction.* Trans. Kathryn Murphy-Judy. Minneapolis: University of Minnesota Press.

Index